THE COMPLETE BOOK OF
BUILDING & FLYING YOUR OWN PLANE

Patrick Stephens Limited, a member of the Haynes Publishing Group, has published authoritative, quality books for enthusiasts for a quarter of a century. During that time the company has established a reputation as one of the world's leading publishers of books on aviation, maritime, military, model-making, motor cycling, motoring, motor racing, railway and railway modelling subjects. Readers or authors with suggestions for books they would like to see published are invited to write to: The Editorial Director, Patrick Stephens Limited, Sparkford, Nr Yeovil, Somerset, BA22 7JJ.

THE COMPLETE BOOK OF
BUILDING & FLYING YOUR OWN PLANE

Geoff Jones

Patrick Stephens Limited

To Angela, Simon and Siân

While every effort is taken to ensure the accuracy of the information given in this book, building and flying your own plane without previous experience could be dangerous. No liability can be accepted by the author or publishers for any loss, damage or injury caused by errors in, or omissions from, the information given.

With homebuilding and kitplanes there is a continual change taking place in many of the facets, legislation, regulations, data etc. The reader is advised to check all information, including the Appendices, with the appropriate authority before making any critical decisions.

First published in 1992

British Library Cataloguing-in-Publication Data:
A catalogue record for this book is available
from the British Library.

ISBN 1 85260 334 8

Patrick Stephens Limited is a member of the
Haynes Publishing Group P.L.C.,
Sparkford, Nr Yeovil, Somerset, BA22 7JJ.

Printed in Great Britain by J.H. Haynes & Co. Ltd.

Contents

Acknowledgements

AS IN ANY book of this nature, I am indebted to a host of individuals, organisations and friends from around the world who have willingly and unselfishly contributed facts, figures, anecdotes and photographs. Without their help this book would not have been possible.

It has been a cause of never-ending amazement as to how willingly the world's homebuilders have provided me with information. As the 20th century draws to its conclusion, impersonality, brashness and money-orientated self-motivation have become by-words for personal attitudes. It is therefore encouraging to find that in the majority the world's homebuilders have not succumbed to some of these baser elements of existance. A world-wide brotherhood where traditional values still seem to exist has been my experience in the preparation of this book.

Of particular note, for his continuing help and advice in getting this book from the 'drawing-board' stage to the 'Permit to Fly', is Ken Ellis. Personnel from several renowned organisations have helped considerably, particularly Ray Delves, Ken Craigie, Francis Donaldson, Dave Wise and Stuart MacConnacher from the Popular Flying Association (PFA) in Britain; Bonnie Higbie, Billy Henderson, Susan A. Hibben, Ben Owen, Paul and Tom Poberezney from the Experimental Aircraft Association (EAA) in the USA; and Louis Cariou and Jacques Avril from the Reseau du Sport de l'Air (RSA) in France.

Individuals/organisations who more than deserve honorable mentions include J. Bell from the BMAA, Nigel Beale from Cyclone Hovercraft, Border Aviation, David Cook (CFM MetalFax), Ken Fern, Peter Harvey, John Isaacs, Neville Langrick, Peter R. March, Mark Parr, John Penney, Richard Riding, Ivan Shaw, John W. R. Taylor and Peter Underhill from the Jodel Club, all from Great Britain. From the USA the staff and management of *Kitplanes*, particularly Dave Martin and Chuck Stewart, Mark Brown (Aero Designs), Robert Chambers (Robrucha), Don Downie, Bob Herendeen, Dick Kurzenberger, Jim Metzger (Avid Aircraft), NASM (Smithsonian Institute), Ladislao Pazmany, Burt Rutan, Alf Scott (Sequoia Aircraft) and Ted Setzer from Stoddard-Hamilton.

Others from Europe include Marcel Morrien and Henk Wadman from Holland; Richard G. Robinson from Ireland; Jan Waldahl from Norway; Kai Christensen and Magnus Pedersen from the KZ and Veteranfly Klubben, Denmark; Philippe Balligand from Belgium; Pierre Gaillard, Roger and Jean-Claude Junqua, Marcel Jurca and Jean Pottier from France; Max Brandli from Switzerland; Sig Alfredo Alemani from Italy; Jan Simunek from Czechoslovakia; and Eva Simo-Avarosy and Mr Baliko from Hungary.

Other thanks go to Ildefonso D. Durana from Argentina; Clive Canning and Jane Canaway from the SAAA in Australia; Chris Heintz, Peter Cowan and Roy Charlton (RAA Canada) in Canada; Luciene Saucede from New Caledonia; Bruce Small from the AACA in New Zealand; and Bob Ewing and Peter Hengst from the EAA in South Africa.

Finally, a big and almighty 'thank you' to my wife Val and daughter Siân who have both encouraged and supported work on this book over several years.

Preface

HOMEBUILT AEROPLANES HAVE been the source of ridicule and misunderstanding for many, many years. This misunderstanding has stemmed from ignorance or the apparent aim of the popular media to gain cheap gratification from what they consider to be the eccentric, scandalous or unusual. This media 'hype' will inevitably continue, but those who know, those who think and those who have any inkling about light aviation in the 1990s will need little reminding that the world of homebuilts and kitplanes has all but cast off its mantle of incredulity and unreliability, to be at the very forefront of light aviation developments.

As the years and decades have passed, homebuilding has always appeared on 'the edge' of aviation, from the amazement and disbelief exhibited by the few witnesses to Sir George Cayley's coachman careering through the air, to the sceptics who ridiculed the Wrights and the officials who first promoted and encouraged Henri Mignet and then washed their hands of him.

Even more recently there have been rogues and

misguided homebuilt philanthropists; Jim Bede has almost assumed a similar infamy to that of Mignet 40 years before him. There have been and still are so-called homebuilt plan and kit purveyors who are frankly misguided imposters. To design a homebuilt and fly a prototype is one thing—then to develop the design through a comprehensive flight test programme, to prepare detailed and accurate drawings backed up by stress and performance calculations, to produce a comprehensive construction manual and then to provide the customer support that many builders require, demands considerable commercial, personal and financial resources on the part of the purveyor. Many have fallen by the wayside over the years, with many potential builders disillusioned, disappointed and financially worse off.

Of those builders who choose a proven design with adequate 'back-up' there are probably more than 50 per cent who give up or abandon their projects as the initial aspirations of building and flying their own plane turn to the reality of the many hundreds of hours cooped up in a workshop with the first-flight day getting farther and farther away as more and more insurmountable constructional problems rear their heads. But the '80s and '90s have seen the arrival of the true kitplane, and the advent of such affordable aircraft has helped to lessen the attrition rate of incomplete and abandoned projects; sales of over 1,000 kits each of the KitFox and Avid Flyer bear witness to this. At the other end of the kitplane market the use of composites has revolutionised homebuilding. Four- and five-place kitplanes that outperform more conventional production light aircraft are a fact of life in the USA—with over 330 Stoddard-Hamilton Glasair kitplanes now completed and flying around the world, they combine with the other prolific kitplane manufacturers to far exceed the worldwide production of more conventional light aircraft and to form the basis of a multi-million-pound/dollar international industry.

But amidst all the euphoria about new materials, sleek new designs and affordable kitplanes we must not forget the ancestors of the modern-day homebuilt and kitplane. For this we do need to go back even as far as the 1930s and Henri Mignet, important as he was, but only to the modern-day pioneers in the USA, France and Britain during the 1940s, '50s and '60s, many of whom are still alive today. Their designs and their negotiations with national and governmental bodies in many cases provided the basis on which homebuilders and their representative organisations today enjoy the respect and esteem that they do.

Flying can be one of the most pleasurable and rewarding pastimes imaginable, and that pleasure is heightened still further if the plane being flown is a homebuilt. But, like all flying, it does not suffer fools gladly. The worldwide homebuilt aeroplane movement is growing phenomenally at present—its reputation is high and must stay that way. I hope that this book will help to swell further the interest in homebuilt aeroplanes—including rotorcraft such as kitbuilt helicopters, autogyros and gyrocopters, which are not included in this book—and that this growth will continue safely and enjoyably on a worldwide scale.

Geoffrey P. Jones
Guernsey
Channel Islands
March 1992

Foreword

by Ray Delves, ARICS
Chairman, Popular Flying Association (PFA)

FOR CENTURIES, Man was mystified by the marvel of flight. It confounded great artists and scientists. Yet, when the dream was finally realised, it was in a homebuilt plane flown by an amateur pilot.

This had to be so. In 1903 there were no professionals. Wilbur and Orville Wright designed and built their machine in their own bicycle workshop. They had an all-consuming desire to fly.

The same fanaticism drove the Rutans, Yeager and their team to accomplish their unrefuelled global flight with *Voyager.* The same dedication now moves thousands of men and women, all around the world, to build and fly their own planes.

This book tells you about those people. From Sir George Cayley's unhappy coachman, who was sent aloft in the first manned glider, to Clive Canning, a grandfather who flew from Australia to England and back in an aircraft he had built himself, the book chronicles enthusiasts' hopes, achievements, and failures.

It details the choice of designs and kits now available for the prospective homebuilder, shows how various countries facilitate their construction, and describes those events at which homebuilt aircraft and their builders gather to exchange views and information.

But, more than that, Geoffrey P. Jones has imbued his book with the spirit – the enthusiasm and dedication – of homebuilders worldwide. Like the two Frenchmen who flew their homebuilts to the North Pole, he has striven to portray the homebuilt movement 'because it is there!'

And there it most definitely is. Homebuilding has now really come of age. The sad withdrawal of the American manufacturers Cessna and Piper from the light aircraft market has meant that more and more pilots have come to recognise the advantages of the greater choice, lower cost and innovative design offered by a homebuilt aircraft.

Indeed, homebuilt aircraft now encompass the entire aviation spectrum, from crop spraying behind what used to be the Iron Curtain, to executive transport. But, in the middle, there remains that hardcore of enthusiasts who build simply because they want to fly.

I commend this book to you. It will not tell how to build or how to fly, but it may well persuade you to join that band of enthusiasts. Nearly 500 years ago, Leonardo da Vinci said: 'There shall be wings'. Now, there are wings, thousands of them. Let this book help you get yours!

Hove, Sussex, England
March 1992

CHAPTER 1

Before the beginning

'The art of flying, or aerial navigation as I have chosen to term it . . . is a subject rather bordering upon the ludicrous in the public's estimation.'

Sir George Cayley, 1809

POPULAR HEARSAY ON the subject of a person building his or her own aeroplane has always treated the subject with some disbelief. The popular press and even some more learned journals have run stories over the years with dramatic headlines such as 'Man Builds Aeroplane in Loft' or 'Garage Aircraft Factory'!

From the days of the very first homebuilt aeroplanes—Sir George Cayley in the 18th and 19th centuries being one of the pioneers—an air of disbelief has surrounded that mystical handyman, the homebuilt aeroplane enthusiast. Only perhaps now, in the last decade of the 20th century, as leisure pursuits grow ever more diverse and unusual, has the homebuilder or experimental aircraft constructor gained an air of acceptance. Notwithstanding, the homebuilder himself (or herself, as there are growing numbers of the fairer sex joining the ranks) usually shuns publicity anyway, content to beaver away at their all-consuming passion, the homebuilt aeroplane.

But what is a homebuilt aeroplane, and when did this pastime or hobby start? A homebuilt aeroplane is one that is not commercially available in fly-away form and which involves its owner in varying degrees of construction work in order to produce a flyable aeroplane. From this must be distinguished refurbishment/rebuild projects on aeroplanes that at one time were commercially manufactured. And the beginning? That is more difficult.

Before the Industrial Revolution in Europe, virtually nothing was commercially manufactured in the sense that we recognise today. Trading between countries and nations went on, but tended to be in high-value produce such as gold, silver, spices and cloth. Manufactured goods were the province of 'cottage industry', with local tradesmen, blacksmiths, coopers, carpenters and weavers satisfying a very local demand. The fight for survival by the majority of people precluded the availability of time or wealth to lavish on anything other than absolute basics.

The ruling classes were the possible exception. Wealth both inherited and fought for gave them the ability to employ and control vast numbers of people, and to manufacture the luxuries of that particular era. Yet these luxuries did not of course encompass the aeroplane. Horse-drawn carriages were such a luxury, though, and much as the car is regarded as an outward status symbol today, so was the carriage in pre-internal combustion engine days.

Limitation of aeroplane development has always been governed by the availability of a power source. Yet before the invention of the internal combustion engine the principles of flight were being extensively studied.

Man dreamed of flying like the birds. Aristotle in the 4th century BC likened flying to swimming, believing that birds flapped their wings downwards and backwards, pressing themselves up and along against the air which lay behind. The ill-starred exploits of that other Greek, Icarus, are well known.

Of more practical use in the understanding of building and flying home-made aerial devices were the kite-builders of history. As in so many cases, the Chinese are popularly credited with the invention of kites at least several centuries before Christ, and kites also have the distinction of being amongst the earliest of discreet technological objects to have a continuous history to this day. Developed initially for adult amusement, they were of two main types. First there was a simple, rectangular design consisting of a framework of crossed sticks covered by fabric or paper and using a multi-leg bridle attached to various points on the ground; as well as performing at kite festivals, they were also used by the Chinese to lift heavy objects, and even men. *Circa* 196 BC General Han Hsin used such kites to measure the distance between his troops and an enemy stronghold, while other examples, the inventions of Mo Tsu and Kungshu Phan—contemporaries of Confucious—probably pre-dated those of Han Hsin. The second type of kite was usually smaller and more ornamental, representing insects, animals, men and dragons, and was entirely recreational in usage.

These kites can be defined as *aerodynes*—flying machines that are heavier than air. They maintain flight at a positive angle to the horizon by means of lift resulting from airspeed in a horizontal wind, or by the operator running with a line attached to the kite to induce artificially the effect of wind. The kite's aerofoil surfaces produce both lift and drag—the higher the lift : drag ratio, the greater the angle of flight. The Chinese must therefore have understood the basic concepts of flight, and kites rapidly came into use for religious, recreational and military purposes throughout most of Asia and Oceania.

Two important concepts have already cropped up in these descriptions of early kite aviating—'recreation' and 'sticks covered with fabric'. These could be regarded as the fundamentals of the homebuilt aeroplane, at least in its original forms.

European kites post-date the Chinese by many centuries. A book completed in 1327, *De nobilitatibus sapientiis et pridentiis regum* by Walter de Milemete, shows clear evidence of the existence of kites. Three soldiers are shown holding a kite, using it to drop a bomb over the wall of an enemy castle. A similar kite is shown in a German manuscript of 1430. With the opening of trade routes between Europe and Asia in the 17th century, the use of Asian-type kites and technology became common throughout Europe, but this seemed to herald the demise of the kite as a piece of military equipment and its use more as a plaything for children.

Some of the early kite-flyers, as well as being 'homebuilders', were also recreational aviators, and all were practical aviators. They must have known their creations intimately, having 'hands-on' experience in both building and flying them.

Leonardo da Vinci (1452–1519), the Italian painter and inventor, was one of many people at around that time who engaged in theories of flight and flying machines based on flapping and gliding experiments. Despite meticulous and sophisticated observation of bird flight, da Vinci could not support his creations by rational theory. However, his skill as a great painter and illustrator has left mankind an unrivalled legacy, the very first homebuilt aircraft plans. Although pushing ingenuity far beyond practicality, da Vinci's attention to detail—on a par with that in his famous anatomical drawings—could teach several contemporary homebuilt aeroplane plan purveyors a thing or two. Had da Vinci, from his resultant analyses, concentrated more on gliders than on his obsession with flight by flapping, he might well have made advances far ahead of his time. But then that is the gift of hindsight. As far as is known da Vinci did not actually translate his plans into reality. But aviation's loss was certainly art's gain.

'The Father of Aerial Navigation' is one of the many accolades bestowed upon the scholarly Yorkshire baronet Sir George Cayley (1773–1857). That this accolade was given by another 19th-century aeronautical pioneer, William Samuel Henson, in 1846 is indeed remarkable. Cayley's 'firsts' were numerous and he came to typify the many aeronautical experimenters that were to proliferate during the 19th century and beyond the watershed of the Wright brothers' historic flight in 1903. It is significant perhaps that the name 'experimenters' was coined for homebuilders, particularly in the USA during the second half of the 20th century, and they grouped together under the name 'Experimental Aircraft Association'.

Cayley was comparatively unknown to historians of technology until as recently as the 1960s. At the age of 23 he produced his first aeronautical device and exemplified the maxim—followed by many experimenters before him and nearly every successful one after him—of making models to prove principles. Cayley's model was of the successful Launoy and Bienvenu helicopter of 1784, which had two contra-rotating rotors operated by a bow string. He didn't know the origin of this 'toy' but, having read a description of it, he substituted four feathers stuck into a cork for each rotor instead of the Frenchmen's twin-bladed silk-covered frames. He was encouraged by its performance, and the significance of being able to build a 'machine' which could 'rise in the air by mechanical means'. By 1799 Cayley had set himself apart from other flight thinkers and experimenters, having worked out the difference between thrust and lift, an essential in moving away from the ornithopter or bird-flight philosophy traditional for many centuries.

Cayley's first plans for a homebuilt aeroplane, a fixed-wing example with cruciform tail-unit and paddle propulsion, were engraved on a silver disc (preserved in the Science Museum, London) but were complemented by voluminous manuscripts including a highly professional plan view of this machine. By 1804, despite diversions from lighter-than-air machines (balloons), Cayley had produced plans, drawings and a model of what ranks as the first modern configuration aeroplane in history. It was a kite (the wings) fixed on top of a pole (the fuselage) at a 6° angle of incidence, and a cruciform tail-unit (the tailplane) attached by a universal joint and lowered to a positive angle of incidence of 11.5°; a moveable weight on the underside of the pole was used to adjust the centre of gravity. Cayley described the flight of this homebuilt model: 'It was very pretty to see it sail down a steep hill . . . the least inclination of the tail towards right or left made it shape its course like a ship by the rudder'.

Cayley's aeronautical experiments are now well documented in considerable detail in historical aviation literature, but they culminated in 1849 in the construction and flight of his 'boy-carrying glider'. A tri-plane with a wing area of 338 square feet and an empty weight of 130 lbs, it was a highly sophisticated machine, having a wheeled 'car' for the pilot to lie in and a pilot-operated elevator-cum-rudder as well as propulsive flappers. 'A boy of about ten years of age was floated off the ground for several yards on descending a hill and also for about the same space by some persons pulling the apparatus against a very slight breeze by a rope,' wrote Cayley. An improved model, with the rudder now riding on the elevator, and thus independently adjustable, soon followed; the wing was covered in fabric, deriving its curvature from air pressure rather than a built-in camber, like a modern Rogallo hang glider wing.

Cayley called his machines 'parachutes' and in 1853 his ultimate achievement in homebuilt aeroplanes was his 'coachman carrier'; a modified version, the 'new flyer', made the world's first man-carrying (but not piloted) glider flight across the dale at Brompton. The unwilling but now famous passenger was the Baronet's coachman. To this historic event Mrs Thompson, Cayley's grand-daughter, was an eye-witness and she left a poignant description of the flight for future generations:

> 'Of course, everyone was out on the high east side and saw the start from close to. The coachman went in the machine and landed on the west side at about the same level. I think it came down rather a shorter distance than expected. The coachman got himself clear, and when the watchers had got across, he shouted, "Please, Sir George I wish to give notice. I was hired to drive, and not to fly" . . . That's all I recollect. The machine was put high away in the barn, and I used to sit and hide in it (from Governess) when so inspired.'

Cayley had not only founded the science of aerodynamics and invented the modern fixed-wing-

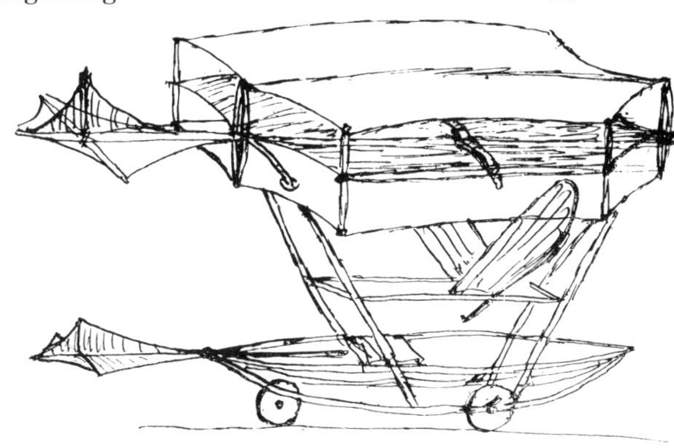

Cayley's 1853 sketch of his 1849 boy-carrying machine, showing the triplane wing structure, tail-unit and wheeled car, with pilot-operated elevator-cum-rudder, and propulsive flappers. (Science Museum)

aeroplane concept, he had in building and flying models and full-sized machines also become the world's first true builder of homebuilt aeroplanes. The significance of Sir George Cayley is no better evoked than by Wilbur Wright (one of the Wright brothers) in 1909 when he wrote: 'About 100 years ago an Englishman, Sir George Cayley, carried the science of flying to a point which it had never reached before and which it scarcely reached again during the last century'.

Several other pioneer aviators of the 19th century embodied the spirit of the modern homebuilder in their researches and experiments with gliders, albeit that with hindsight their efforts were crude and without the relative sophistication now available. Otto Lilienthal (1848–1896), a German, was the first to combine a mature theoretical insight with a high degree of practical aeronautical skill, even though he believed that successful flight by man could be achieved by a close imitation of the flapping flight of birds. Despite this, however, most of his experimenting was done with fixed-wing hang gliders. In a frenzied five-year spell between 1891 and his untimely fatal crash in 1896, Lilienthal designed, built and flew 18 different types, 12 of them monoplanes, the others biplanes. They were all strongly constructed and braced, plenty of attention being given to stress and loading. He generally flew/glided from high ground. His death resulted not from any structural weakness of his aircraft but from the inadequacy of his control system to cope with sudden changes of attitude in a gusting wind.

Scotland's Percy Pilcher (1866–1899) was contemporaneous with Lilienthal, although only in a practical sense from 1895 onwards. Structural failure in Pilcher's fourth glider design, the Hawk, was to bring a premature end to his life in 1899. A bamboo rod snapped in the tail-plane as he was

A replica of Octave Chanute's biplane glider with its cruciform tail-unit. (Alan Curry/Ken Ellis Collection)

flying at about 33 ft (10 m) in poor weather conditions, and the aircraft fell out of control—Pilcher died three days later from injuries sustained. Structural integrity of a design combined with structural integrity of the materials from which it was constructed were to be two of the most important factors governing the future development of homebuilt aircraft. Pilcher was making up for lost time in his aviation work prior to his death and was well advanced with the development of a powered glider, and the design, construction and testing of the lightweight motor with which he intended to power it.

Also a late starter was the French-born American Octave Chanute (1832–1910) who was to encourage and support the Wright brothers in their work. In 1896 Chanute's first multiplane glider was built and flown by a younger colleague, A. M. Herring; the design crystallised into a biplane glider with a cruciform tail-unit. Chanute was a 'stability man', showing little interest in controllable aerofoil surfaces as a solution to the problem of flight control, although like the main pioneers of this time he was adamant that success in the design and construction of flying machines was best achieved through experience gained in the air. The necessity and benefits of the flight test, another important element in the development of the true homebuilt aeroplane design in future decades, was in its formative years.

There were many claimants prior to the Wright brothers to the title of making the world's first powered, sustained and controlled flight in an aeroplane, although none truly merited it. In New South Wales, Australia, well away from the mainstream of experimental homebuilding of aeronautical devices, Lawrence Hargrave (1850–1915) conducted experiments with kites which helped this skilful draughtsman and first class mechanic with the design of his man-carrying box-kite aeroplane of 1896. Whilst his box-kites were successful, his aeroplane was not, but his legacy in the 1900s was that many European-built aeroplanes were powered derivatives of the Hargrave kite.

In France Alphonse Pénaud went on from model aeroplane design to the real thing—in 1876 he patented a twin-propeller monoplane design with retractable undercarriage, extremely sophisticated for the time but never to leave the drawing-board. Also in France, at Armainvilliers in October 1890, Clément Ader became the first human to rise from level ground in a self-propelled flying machine. His *Eole* had a brilliant engine for its time, but with great bat-like wings spanning 49 ft (14.49 m) there was no way of controlling the areoplane other than by moving the steam throttle. He made a 'tentative' flight on 9 October and was airborne for an estimated (164 ft) 50 m.

Ader had worked extensively on the power-plant for his aeroplane, realising its importance—it weighed only about 2.5 lbs (1.13 kg) per horsepower, whereas most contemporary engines weighed from 12 to 150 lbs (5.5 to 68 kg). In partially solving his element of the aeroplane building and flying equation, Ader led the way in the problem the solution of which was to be make or break for light aeroplane and homebuilt aeroplane designers and builders for the next 90 years—a suitable engine and an optimum power-to-weight ratio from that engine.

* * *

Wilbur and Orville Wright, the Wright brothers, in their success achieved at the Kill Devil Hills, North Carolina, USA, on 17 December 1903, became the first successful homebuilders. Aviation was their hobby, a respite—albeit a rapidly growing and all-consuming fanaticism—from their work of selling and manufacturing bicycles. Sons of a United Brethren Church bishop, they lived in Dayton, Ohio, where first the sale and then the manufacture of bicycles provided a comfortable living for them and helped with funds for their aeronautical experiments.

The 59-second, half-mile flight on that famous day was not a chance or isolated event, but the culmination of studies and experiments by the brothers that had emanated from the focus of attention generated by the tragic death of Otto Lilienthal in 1896. They also absorbed an extensive knowledge of the history and current state of the art, despite discarding much of it to start afresh with their own ideas. They possessed characters, qualities and temperaments that many a 1990s homebuilder would do well to emulate—modesty, pertinacity and an inventive talent combined with the ability to train themselves as meticulous aircraft engineers and knowledgeable pilots.

A biplane kite with a 5 ft (1.5 m) span was the Wrights' first aircraft, designed to test their theories of wing warping for control, with the added benefit of a fixed horizontal tail-plane and the innovation of moveable wings; these could be shifted forward or backward in relation to each other to control the centre of pressure, the tail-plane then acting as an automatic elevator. The experiments were successful, so a full-scale glider with a 17 ft (5.2 m) wingspan was planned as soon as they could spare sufficient time from their business commitments to build it.

It was similar but not identical to their model prototype. They had decided that the horizontal surface should be in front of the main wings to act as an elevator—wing warping was also incorporated, but the position of the wings was fixed relative to each other. Because of the changes they flew this No 1 glider as an unmanned kite for the majority of the time, but did make a few manned and pilot-controlled flights as well as a few piloted free glides. Their choice of test site was also pertinent to the science of test flying, an essential part of any successful homebuilt aeroplane project, for the same thought and reasoning went into the choice of the site as into every other aspect of the Wright brothers' work. They wanted an isolated location with steady winds, and the added advantage of

The first man-carrying flying machine on its first flight by the Wright brothers on 17 December 1903. (Science Museum)

plenty of soft, sandy ground to make the results from any crashes less painful. This is why the desolate and unlikely Atlantic coastal dunes at Kitty Hawk, North Carolina, were destined for universal eminence.

After flights with the No 1 glider in October 1900, the No 2 was constructed the following year with a larger span and wing area, a wing camber and an anhedral 'droop', with the pilot laying prone at the centre. Free glides of up to 389 ft (118 m) were achieved. The brothers now began to doubt some of Lilienthal's theories which they had incorporated into their design, so decided to abandon them and use their own knowledge, theories and intuition for their No 3 glider, built during August and September 1902 and taken to the Kill Devil Hills during September and October. For the first time they added a double fixed fin at the rear. Although there were further flight problems, by means of experiments they finalised the design by incorporating a single moveable rudder which moved with the wing-warp as a result of cables fastened to the warp cradle—this counteracted the warp drag prevalent before. This was still a hand-launched glider, but one in which they made hundreds of perfectly controlled glides, the longest being 622½ ft (190 m) and lasting 26 seconds.

Superb pictorial records of these experiments, with the Wrights flying their homebuilt gliders and aeroplanes, provide a lasting tribute to these bicycle manufacturers, because as well as their hobby of building and flying aeroplanes they were also pioneers in the science of photography.

The addition of an engine to the glider was not the sequence of events. The Wrights were determined to achieve flight in a powered aeroplane but lacked a suitable lightweight engine and a propeller. What does the homebuilder do if he can't buy a part or component off the shelf? Yes, he fabricates it himself. And although the average homebuilder today rarely has to build his own engine, he frequently uses an automotive engine and converts it for aerial use. The carving of propellers by homebuilders is still a common practice (see Chapter 8), although the Wrights had the added difficulty of first having to develop the theories and technology.

During 1903 they designed and built their 12 hp engine, which was fitted to the biplane Wright Flyer in a pusher configuration and drove two geared-down propellers through a cycle-chain transmission in tubes. With a wing span of 40 ft 4 in (12.3 m), a wing area of 510 sq ft (47 sq m) and an empty weight of 605 lbs, the Wright Flyer had a skid undercarriage which rested on a small wheeled yoke running on a rail. Tethered whilst the engine was run up, it ran along the rail under its own power then lifted clear of the yoke when speed produced sufficient lift—it was not catapult launched for these early first flights.

Orville Wright went into the history books as the

The Wright brothers' workshop in Dayton, Ohio, with a selection of tools and machines used in the construction of some of the world's first homebuilt aeroplanes. (Smithsonian Institution, Washington DC)

A replica Wright Flyer seen from behind, showing the single engine driving two geared-down propellers. (Ken Ellis Collection)

first pilot of a successful powered aircraft when, at the Kill Devil Hills at 10.35 on Thursday 17 December 1903, he successfully lifted the Wright Flyer into the air and flew for 12 seconds covering 152 m (500 ft) air distance. Four flights were made that day with Wilbur taking the honours for the longest, lasting 59 seconds and covering over half a mile of air distance, achieving a speed of about 30 mph.

It was not until November 1907 that a flight of a full minute's duration would be achieved by an aeroplane designed and built in Europe. The significance therefore of the Wrights' achievement was all the more remarkable.

The brothers did not rest on their laurels, however, but sought to develop their ideas further. May 1904 saw the Wright Flyer II flown from much closer to their home at Huffman Prairie, east of Dayton. They made over 80 short flights that year and completed the first 360° circuit.

And, like many contemporary homebuilders, the Wrights could not get building and flying out of their blood. They pressed on and in 1905 their Flyer III achieved a 38-minute flight which covered over 24 miles. From here onward, though, the Wrights went commercial. Having developed their product, they now went into the marketplace to sell this innovative world-leader and, unlike some modern homebuilt aircraft 'designers' who have launched into sales with less-than-adequate plans for their aircraft shortly after completion of the test flying on their prototype, the Wrights took a two-year break between the 1905 flights of the Flyer III before sales of their design were achieved. In the USA they built seven examples between 1907 and 1909, and in Europe licences were granted for construction of the aeroplane (basically the Wright Flyer III, now commonly known as the Wright type A) in France, Britain and Germany.

Although not usually accepted as homebuilders in the modern sense of the term, that is exactly what the Wright brothers were. The many analogies seen in their and their predecessors' pioneering experimentation culminated in the 1909 watershed which marked the year in which the powered aeroplane was established as a new and practical vehicle. To this day homebuilt aeroplane designers and builders lead the world in technology and achievements, often ignored by commercial aerospace manufacturers. Rutan and Yeager's non-stop unrefuelled global circumnavigation in December 1986 is one of the more recent such achievements (see Chapter 17).

From the inspiration and technological achievements of the Wrights, new names entered the aviation vocabulary—Voisin, Santos-Dumont, Henry Farman, Glenn Curtiss and, in 1908 in the USA, the Aerial Experiment Association, 45 years before the Experimental Aircraft Association (EAA) was founded. Aviation as we know it had begun—and so had the history of homebuilt aeroplanes.

CHAPTER 2

The first true homebuilts: 1919–39

TEN YEARS ON from the Wrights' 'watershed' in 1909, the concepts and development of the aeroplane had changed to a previously unimaginable extent. The First World War had seen to this, so that in 1919 there were relatively sophisticated and reliable aeroplanes commercially available from a variety of manufacturers and an abundance of pilots available to fly them. An almost bottomless pit of surplus Avro 504Ks was available in Britain for civil flying, while in the USA the Curtiss Jenny fitted the bill nicely. These were both large, relatively high-powered machines, though.

Times were hard after the Great War and there was only a handful of private civil aircraft owners flying regularly. None the less in 1921 one of the first true British homebuilts materialised at Heaton, Newcastle-upon-Tyne, 20-year-old F. Harold Lowe's HL(M).9 Marlburian. Not unlike the pre-war Morane-Saulniers, his wood/fabric, side-by-side two-seat monoplane was powered by a 60 hp Gnome engine and flew for the first time early in 1921. It was built from locally available raw materials, in true homebuilt tradition, but incorporated engine, wheels, propeller and instruments from other aircraft, taking five months of spare-time work to design, and then 840 hours to construct. The size of the Marlburian was dictated by the small dimensions of the shed Lowe had available for construction—an ever-present problem for home-builders. After many successful flights and civil registration as G-EBEX to the Northern Aerial Transport Company, the Marlburian crashed on 25 November 1922.

In August 1922 the *Daily Mail* offered a prize of £1,000 to anyone who between 16 and 21 October could glide the furthest distance in a flight exceeding half an hour's duration at a competition site at Firle Beacon, Itford Hill, in Sussex. Thirty-five entries were received, but this number dwindled to about 12 actual participants. There were entries from commercial companies, including de Havilland's DH.52 and the Handysyde glider built by the Air Navigation Company of Addleston. There was also the homebuilt Sayers S-C-V designed by Captain W.H. Sayers, light aeroplane correspondent of *The Aeroplane*. The British Brokker glider was a home-built if ever there was one; a Bristol Fighter fuselage married to the upper wing of a Fokker D.VII but with many other modifications, it flew well for more than an hour, despite its mongrel heritage.

The winner at Itford was to be Frenchman Maneyrol flying a tandem-winged Peyret glider. He stayed in the air for well over 3 hours.

Itford had sowed the seeds in many minds of the possibility of adding small engines to gliders, an activity that was already widespread in both France and Germany. The DH.53 was born from this concept, but this was the product of a commercial company rather than a homebuilt design. Other commercial companies such as Avro, Vickers, Shorts, English Electric and the Air Navigation and Engineering Co (ANEC) went on to produce such developments, but they cannot be considered as homebuilts.

Ones that can, though, came from a group of enthusiastic employees at the Royal Aircraft Establishment (RAE) at Farnborough. In October 1922, under the chairmanship of Flt Lt P.W.S. 'George' Bulman, a club was formed to design, build and fly light aircraft and gliders. Designed by S. Child, the first aircraft was completed in August 1923, the RAE Zephyr. It was a single-seat pusher biplane resembling the First World War FE.8 fighter with its twin-boom tail. Power was from a 500 cc Douglas motor-cycle engine rated at onely 3½ hp, although at its full 4,000 rpm it generated more like 17 hp. Bulman made the maiden flight with the Zephyr on 6 September 1923 at Farnborough, lifting off in calm conditions in only 80 yards and flying

The RAE Hurricane built for the 1923 Lympne light aeroplane trials. (Ken Ellis Collection)

successfully for 15 minutes before a perfect landing. It was registered G-EBGV.

The RAE club had a second aeroplane well advanced by this time, the RAE Hurricane. The Spur for this design was the 1923 Lympne light aeroplane trials conducted under the auspicies of the Royal Aero Club. There were three main prizes: £1,000 donated by the *Daily Mail* for the machine accomplishing the longest flight of more than 50 miles with one gallon of fuel, open to any nationality; £500 from the Duke of Sutherland under the same criteria, but for British entrants; and the £500 Abdulla prize for the machine covering two circuits of a 25-mile course in the fastest time.

It was the Abdulla prize that attracted the RAE club and their Hurricane. The aeroplane had a triangular-section fuselage with a flattish top, shoulder-level wings, motor-cycle rims with heavy-gauge spokes, and another Douglas motor-cycle engine, this time of 600 cc. Unfortunately the Hurricane G-EBHS did not meet the date deadline for the fly-off for the Abdulla prize, and when it did get into the air it averaged only 58.5 mph against a fastest opposition of 76.1 mph. It was none the less a valiant attempt by this homebuilt amongst aeroplanes bearing auspicious and famous names.

The 1923 *Daily Mail* light plane trials spawned another aeroplane that can only be categorised as a homebuilt. Less auspicious than most was Percy Salmon's unorthodox Tandem. Salmon was chief draughtsman at the RAE drawing office at Farnborough, but worked independantly of the other RAE group, first designing and then building in his bedroom at the Senior Officer's Staff Quarters of the RAE Mess this wood/fabric tandem-winged aeroplane. However a 3½ hp Bradshaw engine could do nothing to achieve flight for the Tandem, and although many attempts were made, Salmon never achieved a speed of much more than 15 mph. Although it was completed in September 1923 and registered G-EBHQ, the Tandem never appeared at Lympne, never flew and was later burned.

Another important stipulation of the Lympne trials was the 'gate test'. This was a far-sighted requirement with which many modern homebuilt designs would do well to comply. It demonstrated to the panel of judges at Lympne the manoeuvrability of an aeroplane on the ground by requiring the participating aircraft to be man-handled through a 10-foot (3.05 m) gap—it also meant that thought had to be given to the easy detachment and subsequent re-attachment of the wings and control cables. Very few subsequent homebuilt designs would have had success laid at their doors here, particularly those utilising their own undercarriage rather than a trailer or detachable bogie. Eric Clutton's British-designed and built Flying Runabout Experimental Design, FRED, which first flew in November 1963, was one such homebuilt (see Chapter 3).

One of the conclusions drawn from the 1923 Lympne trials was the general inadequacy of using 'heavy' off-the-shelf motor-cycle engines to power light aircraft. Another was more attention to weight saving in construction, and although this applied to those light aeroplanes designed and built by commercial companies, these consideration also became the two most important factors influencing the world of the homebuilt aeroplane throughout its history.

Trials were again held at Lympne in 1924, this time for a two-seater. Only half of the 16 original entrants qualified, competing for the increased prize money. Companies such as Bristol, Westland, Hawker and Parnall designed and built light planes for these trials, as well as the lesser-known Scottish company, William Beardmore & Co Ltd. Distinguished from these was one entrant, the Cranwell CLA.2, designed and built by the staff and apprentices of the RAF College Cranwell's Cranwell Light Aeroplane Club. The lecturer in charge of the engineering lab at Cranwell was the club's designer,

The Cranwell CLA.2, designed by Flt Lt Nicholas Comper. (Ken Ellis Collection)

Flt Lt Nicholas Comper.

This Club's entry was, like the RAE's Zephyr before it in 1922, a homebuilt, with Comper having the foresight to see that a market might exist for such an aeroplane, designed as a robust, low-cost and low-powered trainer. He further felt that the design could be built by amateurs of limited means and facilities in their spare time, the first tangible evidence that there was considered to be a potential market for a homebuilt aeroplane design in Britain.

As it happened, the CLA.2 was a rather crude biplane design, but with its 32 hp Bristol Cherub engine (only 55 per cent efficient) it was seriously underpowered, though reliable. It flew slowly but safely for 10 hours during the trials, covering a distance of 762.5 miles and winning the £300 SMMT reliability prize. An historical 'first' for a homebuilt?

During an Air Ministry evaluation, the CLA.2 was crashed and written off. However, the Ministry paid compensation to the Cranwell club and this, together with their prize money, helped to finance the CLA. 3, their bid for the 1925 Lympne event.

Like many subsequent homebuilt designs, the CLA. 3's construction was preceded by a proof-of-concept scale model. It was an extremely small parasol-winged monoplane built of wood and fabric with considerable attention to streamlining. Powered by a 32 hp Bristol Cherub engine, Nick Comper first flew the CLA 3 (G-EBMC) in July 1925 just before the Lympne trials, and it was the only new aircraft at that year's event. Its performance was a little slower than the 100 mph (165 kmph) predicted, but at 87 mph (140 kmph) it was still quite a nippy little machine and quite manoeuvrable once Comper had learned to fly it. The CLA. 3 was scrapped in 1929.

For 1926's Lympne trials, Comper designed the CLA. 4, a two-seater biplane with the upper wing shorter in span than the lower (an inverted sesquiplane layout). Two were built by the Club, later G-EBPB and 'PC, powered by a standard Bristol Cherub III, although the second was to be powered by a revolutionary new seven-cylinder radial engine designed by another Cranwell officer, Captain Douglas Rudolph Pobjoy.

Service groups were also building 'homebuilts' during the 1920s. At the Halton Aero Club, made up of members from the RAF School of Technical Training at RAF Halton, the Education Officer was C.H. Latimer-Needham, and he planned, together with a group from Halton, to compete in the Lympne trials. A two-seater biplane, the Halton HAC.1 Mayfly, with a spruce fuselage frame covered with plywood, took to the air on 31 January 1927 at RAF Bicester powered by a 32 hp Bristol Cherub III engine, being registered the following month as G-EBOO. It was too late for the Lympne trials series but successfully competed in various air races until, later in 1927, it was decided to try to make it faster by removing the lower wing to convert it to a monoplane—this became the Halton HAC.2 Minus which was to be a regular attendee at air events throughout Britain in the late 1920s.

Far away in Iraq during the 1920s British imperialism was still very much in evidence. Flt Lieut Crawford was based at Hinaidi and, helped by Corporal Howden and LAC Farmer, designed and built during 1924 the all-wood single-seater Crawford Monoplane. Initially it was to be fitted with a 500 cc ABC engine and was completed by 11 December 1924. However, it was not flown, the engine being thought to have insufficient power. So they set about building a new power-plant incorporating two 500 cc ABCs in one. Unmarked except for RAF roundels, the Crawford Monoplane first flew in February 1925 before it was shipped to Britain in 1926; it was kept at Lee-on-Solent but never flew there before being scrapped.

Another unregistered homebuilt project at this time was the Bircham Beetle, built by two RAF officers at RAF Bircham Newton in 1924. The

Beetle was a hybrid comprising an original forward fuselage, the rear fuselage of a Bristol F.2b, the lower wing of a Fokker D VII and the rudder from an Avro 504, powered by a small two-cylinder Douglas engine. Whether it flew is not certain—in concept, though, its philosophy of utilising easily obtainable parts from other aircraft is one which has been followed by several homebuilt designers subsequently, the French Leglaive-Gautier LG.150 and Canadian Ceckady (see Chapter 7) being two such examples built during the 1980s.

1929 saw another cannibalisation of other aircraft in the design and building of Flying Officer John Clarke's Clarke Cheetah. The Cheetah's fuselage was an original design but the rest came from other aircraft—the parasol upper wing was from a DH.53, the smaller lower wing was the discarded lower wing from the Halton HAC.1 Mayfly, and other DH.53 parts were utilised including the tail; it was powered by a 35 hp Blackburn Thrush engine. It first flew at Brough, Yorkshire, in 1929 and was registered G-AAJK.

Clarke was killed later in 1929 and the Cheetah passed through several owners until in 1936 Flying Officer Richard Hopkinson bought it and sent it to Luton Aircraft at Gerrards Cross for redesign and reconstruction work financed by his uncle, Martin Hopkinson. The Cheetah became the Martin Monoplane, now with a 32 hp Bristol Cherub III engine and looking very much like a DH.53. It was first flown, now as G-AEYY, on 6 July 1937 and the remains of it exist to this day, part incorporated in Mike Russell's DH.53 Humming Bird rebuild at Bishops Stortford, and part as Messrs Lake, Raby and Brabham's Martin Monoplane restoration at Henham.

The inter-war period proved prolific in terms of homebuilding although it was virtually all done on an ad hoc basis without any formal controls. Then 'Flea-fever' swept Britain as a result of Henri Mignet's HM.14 Pou du Ciel/Flying Flea homebuilt design (see below), which precipitated the authorities into setting up an 'Authorisation (or Permit) to Fly', the first being issued to Stephen Appleby for his Flea G-ADMH and dated 24 July 1935. There was still no organisation such as the PFA to look after the general interests of homebuilders, although the Air League took on the mantle of promoting the construction of Fleas in Britain. So with poorer communications than in the 1990s, individuals could proceed with homebuilt projects virtually unhindered by officialdom—many such projects were Fleas.

In the case of the Flea in Britain there were other anomalies as well. The basic HM.14 Flea had a design fault, a 'slot effect' between the two wings which made the aircraft unstable in certain attitudes. In a shallow nose-down attitude the two wings effectively became one larger one, and the 'slot' was lost. The amount of pivot available on the forward wing was not able to counteract this, so the aircraft would continue in an ever-increasing dive. Pushing the stick forward to recover only made the matter worse. The design flaw and the fatal crashes that resulted prompted official Ministry tests at the RAE, undertaken in association with the Air League, which had promoted the Flea and homebuilding for the man in the street. These tests

The Mignet HM.14 Flying Flea G-AEBB built by K. W. Owen at Southampton, which received its 'Authorisation to Fly' in March 1936 and is now preserved by the Shuttleworth Trust at Old Warden, Bedfordshire. (Air Portraits)

complemented those undertaken in France. On being given the test results, the British Ministry sought to ban the Flea in the autumn of 1936, their control taking the form of stopping the issue of new 'Authorisations' and the renewal of existing ones. However, Fleas were still completed and, paradoxically, a few 'Authorisations' were still issued, the Flea living on beyond the 'ban' until the outbreak of the Second World War.

British homebuilt aircraft not mentioned elsewhere in chapter 2 and completed in the inter-war years between 1918 and 1939 (in alphabetical order by type)

Type	Date of First flight	Regn	Notes
Addyman Ultra-Light	1936	–	
Angus Aquila	1930/31	G-ABIK	
Barnwell BSW.1	1938	G-AFID	
Blake Bluetit	1930s	unregd	
Brown Monoplane	1930s	–	
Burgoyne-Stirling Dicer	1939	G-AECN	
Crossley Tom Thumb	1937	–	
DeHavilland Tech'l College TK.1	1934	G-ACTK	
TK.2	1935	G-ADNO	Extensively modified in 1938
TK.4	1937	G-AETK	
TK.5	1939	G-AFTK	
Dudley Watt DW.2	1933	G-AAWK	
Durham Ultra Lights	1931/2	–	
Fenton Cheel	1931	G-ABHZ	Unfinished and not flown
Gibb Biplane	1930s	–	
Gordon Dove	1937	G-AETU	Production type but aimed at being sold in kit form
Granger Pink Emu	1924	–	
Granger Linnet	1926	–	
Granger Archaeopteryx	1930	G-ABXL	Preserved at Old Warden
Gunton Special (Pietenpol Aircamper)	1939	G-AFRW	See Pivot Monoplane below
Gurney Grice Mosquito	1930s	–	
Heath Parasol (US homebuilt design)	1936	–	Started in '36 but not completed until 1949 as G-AFZE
Hill Pterodactyl	1925	–	Glider—became J8067 at RAE
Hinkler Ibis	1930	G-AAIS	
Howitt Monoplane	1937	G-AEXS	
McClure ?	1938	G-AFJY	Never completed
Mosscraft No 1 & No 2	1937/9	G-AEST/G-AFMS	
Navarro	1918	–	Built aircraft in 1910 and '30s
Noel WeeMite	1933	G-ACRL	Built and flown in Guernsey
Person-Pickering KP.2	1933	G-ACMR	
Pivot Monoplane	1945	G-AGOO	Used parts from the Gunton Special G-AFRW (see above)
Shapley Kittiwake I & II	1937/8	G-AEZN/G-AFRP	(2-seat version)
Surrey Flying Services AL.1	1929	G-AALP	
Taylor-Watkinson Dingbat	1938	G-AFJA	
Taylor Ultralights A.101/2/3	1930s	–	
Taylor Experimental	1937	G-AEPX	Crashed on maiden flight killing designer, R. Taylor
Wheeler Slymph	1931	G-ABOI	Built in Iraq before being shipped to England

With grateful thanks to Ken Ellis's *British Homebuilt Aircraft Since 1920*

Several other significant homebuilts appeared in Britain in these inter-war years. The Granger brothers' three designs were archetypal homebuilts in the true pioneering spirit of the hobby, and other designs that had their gestation before the war helped to provide the platform for homebuilders in Britain after the hostilities, such as the Luton LA-4 Minor and the Currie Wot, of which more in a moment.

In almost Wright brothers and Mignet style, the Granger brothers, Nottinghamshire lace manufacturers, experimented in the early 1920s with their own gliders. The third glider was started late in 1924 and, when it was nearing completion, an

The Taylor Experimental, built during 1936, was of all-metal construction – it crashed on its first flight on 7 January 1937, killing its designer R. Taylor. (Ken Ellis Collection)

ex-RAF pilot, C. Newham, joined the group and suggested the installation of an engine. An old 400 cc ABC was used and the all-wood biplane was completed in July 1926. Named the Linnet, the Granger brothers' second true homebuilt (the Pink Emu glider in 1924 had been their first) made many 'high-speed' runs at Hucknall aerodrome, Notts, but would only 'hop', the longest hop being about 300 feet (91 m) and up to a height of 20 feet (6 m) under its own power. They had to content themselves with learning to fly and test flying the Linnet while being towed behind a car, with the aircraft in its gliding mode.

In 1926, after a Mr B. Howard had joined the group, they formed the Experimental Light 'Plane Club, a significant event in the history of British homebuilding. They decided to build an autogyro, but after abortive tests with a 6-foot model decided to be slightly less ambitious and studied the design of a tail-less aircraft based on the Pterodactyl concept of Captain G.T.R. Hill (see the accompanying table). C.H. Latimer-Needham, who had helped with the Halton Mayfly design, joined the Club and helped them perfect their design which was finalised as the Archaeopteryx, a swept-back, parasol strut-mounted wing monoplane powered by a 32 hp Bristol Cherub I engine.

Although they started construction of the Archaeopteryx in 1926, it was not completed and ready for flight until October 1930 when it made its

The Granger Archaeopteryx G-ABXL, now preserved in flying condition by the Shuttleworth Trust at Old Warden. (Author)

maiden flight at Hucknall. It had wing-tip mounted ailerons which could be used as elevators if needed, and at the tail there was just the rudder. There were few problems during the first flights, which were all apparently conducted within the airfield boundary, so the Granger brothers and the other Club members flew the Archaeopteryx without any Certificate of Airworthiness until 1932, when a tightening of the regulations forced them to register the aircraft. G-ABXL was its marks, and by the end of 1934, now able to travel away from home (Nottingham's Tollerton airport), it had flown 50 hours, with flying visits to Castle Bromwich and Sywell recorded. In June 1935 it made an epic flight south to the RAF Flying Club Display at Hatfield. The following year it was put into storage at Chilwell, Notts, until in 1968 it was rescued and restored. In June 1971 it was flown again by its new custodians, the Shuttleworth Trust at Old Warden, Bedfordshire, where it is still preserved and regularly flown.

The 1935 Air Ministry 'Authorisation to Fly', which pioneered the formal adoption of homebuilt aircraft in Britain, gave permission for homebuilts to be flown with the following conditions:

1. Flights only permitted within Great Britain and Northern Ireland
2. No flights permitted over populous areas or a concourse of people
3. No passengers, goods or mail to be carried for hire or reward
4. No aerobatics in the aircraft
5. No flights to be undertaken unless the aircraft is in an adequate state of repair and good working order
6. A valid and current third-party persons and property insurance to be in force for the aircraft
7. The aircraft not to be flown so that its insurance is invalidated
8. The permission, valid for a year, may be withdrawn at any time

This Authorisation system did not, however, stop the Granger brothers and their Experimental Club, and it did not stop Flying Fleas from being built and flown. One of the many 'developments' of the Flying Flea during the late 1930s was the Luton LA-4 Minor. The name C.H. Latimer-Needham crops up again in this context, as the designer of the tandem-winged Luton LA-2. A wood and fabric design, the LA-2 had ailerons and a conventional tail unit, and was also constructed differently from the Flea. It was powered by a 34 hp Anzani inverted-V air-cooled engine and flew in late 1936, although not with any degrees of success, at Barton-le-Clay, Bedfordshire.

The LA-2 was to be called the 'Minor', but its successor, the LA-3, was in fact the first to carry this name. The LA-3 was a design which evolved from the LA-2 but which had a conventional but re-designed parasol high wing mounted above the single-seat open cockpit and fuselage taken from the LA-2. The Luton Aircraft Company built these aircraft, their motive being to sell plans of their small ultralight aircraft for home construction after designing and proving their concept.

The LA-3 Minor prototype was completed in February 1937, and received its 'Authorisation' on 3 March, the day it was flown for the first time, registered G-AEPD, at Heston. The prototype Luton LA-4 Minor was built at the Luton company's new works at Gerrards Cross, differing in only small design details from the LA-3 but having a 40 hp ABC Scorpion instead of the Anzani engine; the prototype, G-AFBP, also first flew in 1937. Two Luton Minors were completed by homebuilders from plans in Britain before the war, both of them previously Flea builders, and one of the aircraft, G-AFIR built by J. S. Squires of Leicestershire, is still in existence today. Two others were started but not completed.

This small pre-war 'production' of Luton Minors by homebuilders and the availability of plans helped to form the basis of the post-war homebuilt aircraft movement in Britain, as the Minor was one of the few indigenous designs available for Ultra Light Aircraft Association (ULAA) members and subsequently Popular Flying Association (PFA) members to build. One of the first post-war Minors was Jim Coates's version, the Swalesong SA-1 G-AMAW, which first flew at RAF Waterbeach in 1948.

In March 1958 C.H. Latimer-Needham and Arthur Ord-Hume founded Phoenix Aircraft Ltd and acquired the Luton design rights, not only for the LA-4 Minor but also for the two-seater cabin homebuilt, the LA-5 Major. They modernised the Minor's design and re-stressed it to meet the latest airworthiness standards and sold plans of the Minor—as well as of the Major and several other homebuilt designs—to hundreds of homebuilders in Britain and around the world. Subsequently the PFA took over the rights for the sale of Luton Minor drawings, and they are still available to homebuilders today. Estimates of the numbers of Minors completed and flown by homebuilders vary, but it must certainly be in excess of 100, around 40 of them in Britain and with a variety of different engines.

From the same pre-war era came the Currie Wot single-seat biplane of 1937. John Robert Currie was its designer, his requirement being for a simple, safe and cheap-to-run single-seater with no frills and suitable for operation by flying clubs. Two prototypes were built at the Cinque Ports Flying Club at Lympne in Kent where Currie worked, G-AFCG and G-AFDS, each powered by a 40 hp Aeronca JAP engine. Ostensibly they were not homebuilts, and both examples were destroyed in a bombing raid during the war. It was not until John Isaacs (see Chapter 7) acquired the original Wot drawings in 1957 and persuaded Vivian Bellamy to construct two post-war examples at the Hampshire Aeroplane Club that the possibility of the Wot as a homebuilt design became a reality. The 'new' prototype G-APNT first flew on 11 September 1958 at Southampton's Eastleigh airport, and sets of plans for the Currie Wot were then sold at £12 10s (£12.50) to homebuilders. During the 1960s and '70s it became a popular type, particularly for British homebuilders. Plans are still available for the Wot from the PFA, with 19 examples now flying in Britain.

The French experience

French homebuilding was dominated in the inter-war years by one man, Henri Mignet. The first flight of his prototype Mignet HM. 14 at the Bois de Bouleaux on 10 September 1933 was but the culmination of a succession of developments that had started at his family home at Saintes in western France in 1912 when, following correspondence with the German glider pioneer Gustav Lilienthal, he built a glider from bamboo canes and brown wrapping paper reinforced with strings. A primitive start for this innovative 19-year-old Frenchman, but one that was to reap much satisfaction—and sorrow—in the decades that followed.

Mignet's was a self-taught man and his development work of designing and flying his own planes continued after the First World War through a succession of designs, the HM.1 through to the HM.7, none of which could be described as successful. He did achieve some success with his HM.5 hang glider in 1923, winning a prize at the Congress of Motorless Flight at Vauville on the Cherbourg peninsula.

It was Mignet's HM.8, though, that hit the French headlines in a modest way in 1928. Using an Anzani engine and other bits and pieces from earlier designs, in Charente on the beach at Royon he was able to fly himself in his own aircraft design for the first time. The HM.8 was a conventional aircraft constructed of wood and fabric with a parasol wing which had a pronounced dihedral and was mounted on struts above the open single-seat cockpit—the tail-plane was of the all-flying kind and had conventional fin and rudder.

One of many experimenters, Mignet differed from many of the others in that he wanted to share his design, building and flying experiences on the HM.8 with a wider audience. In the 22 March 1928 edition of the French magazine *Les Ailes*, Mignet wrote his first article, *L'Aviation de l'Amateur est-elle une Possibilité?*. Mignet felt that commercial

Top *Jim Coates's version of the pre-war Luton Minor, one of the first homebuilts to fly in Britain after the Second World War.* (Author)

Above *The first post-war example of the Currie Wot.* (Author)

Below *Henri Mignet, the early 'Patron Saint of Homebuilders' at least in Europe.* (Author)

manufacturers had completely neglected the needs of the man in the street when it came to producing aircraft, and his article stirred up a wealth of discussion and argument on the subject in France. Regardless, the word 'amateur' had now been introduced into the French avaition vocabulary. In the three years following the publication of his article he dealt with mounds of correspondence and guided several of his colleagues in the construction of their HM.8s.

In October 1931, confident of his product and of his market, he published a book, the first edition of *Le Sport de l'Air* in which he described how to build a ultralight HM.8 for a cost of £50 plus an engine.

How much this crusade was innovative thought on Mignet's part, or whether he had been influenced by the US developments published in magazines there such as *Modern Mechanix* and *Popular Science* during the 1920s, and aircraft such as the Heath Parasol, Irwin Meteorplane and Pietenpol Aircamper, may never be known. Certainly the HM.8 bore more than a passing resemblance to the Heath Parasol.

None the less, Mignet achieved an objective of getting hundreds of Frenchmen thinking in terms of aviation, and into their workshops building and then flying their own homebuilt aeroplanes. An estimated 200 HM.8s were completed in France, although with no formal 'Permit' or registration system in

Above *A Mignet HM.8 wing under construction by Emanuel Lerin in France in the early 1930s.* (Author's Collection)

Below *Emanuel Lerin's HM.8, completed in 1936.* (Author's Collection)

force at the time it is impossible to assess numbers accurately. The HM.8 movement provided the springboard for Mignet and his 'disciples' to move on to his subsequent design, the HM.14 Pou-du-Ciel or Flying Flea. The Flying Flea story is quite well know and is told in detail in the excellent book *Henri Mignet and his Flying Fleas* by Ellis and Jones, published by G.T. Foulis (Haynes). This covers all the pre-HM.14 designs and the extensive and world-wide Flea phenomenon that continues apace into the 1990s.

Mignet became known as the 'Patron Saint of Homebuilders'. Like him or hate him, his major contribution to sport aviation and the homebuilt aircraft movement, not only in Europe but throughout the world, is unquestionable. The title 'Patron Saint' is the least that can be bestowed on this free-thinking, innovative and often mis-understood pioneer of homebuilts.

The USA

Fleas were built in some numbers in the USA almost as soon as the Air League's English translation of Mignet's book *Le Sport de l'Air* was published, but the euphoria with which the Flea was greeted and built in Britain and France was not repeated to the same extent in America because it was rather late on the scene and also rather primitive compared with some of the homebuilt designs that had started to appear there in the 1920s.

Such a vast country as the USA was ripe for homebuilt aeroplanes and experimentation. Individuals and small groups pottered away independently in most parts of the country in the years following the end of the Great War. Surplus aircraft parts were freely available and although the big heavy ex-military engines such as the OX-5 that powered the Curtiss JN-4 'Jenny' were not really suitable for lightweight or ultralight homebuilt types, in true American pioneering fashion the first US homebuilders achieved moderate, if largely unpublicised, success. In any event, if a man wanted his own light plane in the early 1920s he had little choice but to go out and build it himself.

An early and little known pioneer homebuilder was John Fulton 'Jack' Irwin from Alameda, California. It was balloons that first fascinated him until in 1912 he bought plans from Glenn Curtiss—yes, even before the Great War, the homebuilt aeroplane business was taking shape—and built a 'modified' Curtiss-type pusher. Later that year he built another plane to his own design, using the modified Mitchell car engine used in the Curtiss, but now mounting it in front.

By 1919, after a period in the Services during which he continued to study aircraft and engine design he had realised the importance of a lightweight and reliable engine for homebuilts and sports planes. He considered the Harley Davidson motorcycle engines too rough at low speeds and with too high an rpm. Ed Heath, another light plane pioneer in the USA, had already converted a Henderson motor-cycle engine, and although it was quite heavy it was the best then available. Irwin eventually plumped for a 19 hp V-twin with overhead valves, the Flying Merkel, produced by the Merkel-Light Motor Company, for his 1919 homebuilt, the Irwin Meteorplane, which flew remarkably well according to reports.

However, Irwin was dissatisfied with the engines available, so designed and built his own, a four-cylinder, two-stroke, radial air-cooled type with a 79 cu in displacement and aluminium alloy cylinders with steel linings; its finished weight with carburettor, Bosch magneto and propeller hub was only 64 lbs (29 kg), extremely favourable when compared to the weight of some of the modern Rotax-type engines (see Chapter 8). It produced 20 hp at 1,400 rpm and 25 hp at 1,750 rpm, and ran very smoothly.

Interviewed about his early exploits for the EAA's magazine *Sport Aviation* in February 1977, Irwin said, 'I offered my plane [the Meteorplane] in kit form at first and the components could be bought in instalments. The easiest way to get started was to buy the kit for the fin and rudder for $3.50. The empenage kit cost $12.00, the fuselage $75.00 and the wings were $12.50 each. The young men and boys were eager and bought a lot of kits. My biggest resistance came from mothers of the young men who were afraid of what might happen to them. As the sales of plans and kits increased I was able to turn my attention to tooling up for the manufacture of my engine . . .'

This was a major insight into homebuilding and kitplanes as early as 1920 in the USA, and Irwin went on to manufacture complete Meteorplanes. His engine was also quite successful, priced at $650.00 outright but only $400.00 for anyone who bought a complete set of parts to build their own Meteorplane. About 75 to 80 engines were produced as well as 'hundreds' of kits and over a thousand sets of plans for the M-T-2 Meteorplane from which he thinks about 100 aircraft were actually built and completed.

Irwin stayed in business until the early 1930s, with his factory at Sacramento, California, producing aircraft, kits and engines. He competed in air races and events during the 1920s, but a road accident in 1930 and the US Department of Commerce's clamp-down on aviation, particularly on those in the business of selling kits and plans, sounded the death knell for Irwin's business, although he did produce a few more Meteorplanes

One of the first practical kitplanes for home construction, Jack Irwin's Meteorplane M-T-1 with its 20 hp Irwin radial engine and available in the USA from 1924 onwards. (Ritch Rundstrom Collection)

at Watsonville, California, during the '30s. An Irwin F-A-1 Meteorplane, NC10685, is preserved today in the Oakland Museum, Oakland, California.

Another early US homebuilt pioneer was Harvey C. Mummert. He was a project engineer with the Curtiss company and this obviously provided him with essential experience and back-up in the design and construction of his trio of designs. Monocoque fuselages, tapered cantilever wings, metal propellers and, in two of his aircraft, retractable undercarriages were some of the unlikely and advanced features for homebuilts that Mummert pioneered in the 1920s and '30s.

One of his first successful designs in 1921 was the Cootie biplane. Its fuselage was of wood monocoque construction, consisting of three layers of veneer strips set at 45° to each other wrapped around a wooden mould. The strips were glued together and when stuck were removed from the mould and fuselage bulkheads inserted. A war-surplus 28 hp Lawrence engine was used which, although unreliable and running rough for much of the time, still enabled Mummert to fly frequently from Curtiss Field, Long Island. The Cootie had a wing span of 18 ft (5.5 m), a length of 12 ft (3.7 m), stood only 5 ft (1.5 m) high and had an empty weight of 352 lbs (160 kgs).

1923's offering from Mummert was a cantilever monoplane using the same fuselage construction method as the Cootie but powered by an 18 hp Harley-Davidson V-twin motor-cycle engine, making it rather underpowered. It flew on several occasions but crashed into telephone wires, so that was the end of that machine.

The 1924 Dayton Air Meet at Wright Field saw the first light plane races in the USA, not dissimilar from the trials held at Lympne in Britain in the 1920s, sponsored by the *Daily Mail*. This US event

Harvey Mummert's 1923 monoplane, another early homebuilt in the USA. (Smithsonian Institution, Washington DC)

attracted six entrants, and the chance to meet and compete against designers and pilots of a like mind had an immediate appeal to Mummert. His Sportplane No 3 was designed and built for the Dayton Air Meet; a conventional low-wing cantilever monoplane of all-wood construction, the fuselage was a plywood box with spruce longerons and cross members, rather ordinary looking compared with his first biplane, the Cootie. However, the Sportplane No 3 did include considerable innovation. The fuselage terminated in a horizontal knife-edge on which was mounted a single-piece elevator, no stabilizer being required because of the shape of the fuselage. From the side, the fuselage looked a bit like that of the modern Sorrell Hiperbipe. The wing span was 26 ft (7.9 m) and was a thick cantilever structure using a Curtiss 35B airfoil with a maximum chord of 6 ft (1.83 m) at the root and 4 ft (1.22 m) at the wing-tip. Mummert used the same Harley-Davidson V-twin engine from his Sportplane No 2 and, with a weight similar to its predecessor, the No 3 flew at a maximum speed of 65 mph (107 kmph).

Mummert was successful in winning the 50-mile 'speed and efficiency' race at Dayton in 1924 at an average of 38 mph (63 kmph). A Driggs-Johnson DJ-1 homebuilt, which had two forced landings, came second, and these were the only two to finish out of the six competitors.

In 1925 Mummert used his No 3 to compete in the 1925 air races at Mitchell Field, Long Island, but was out-classed by the Powell Racer fitted with the newly available Bristol Cherub engine.

Mummert's last designs were both racers built for the All American Air Derby and National Air Races in 1931 and '32 respectively. The former involved a 554-mile (914 km) cross-country event for planes powered by Cirrus engines. Both these last two designs were low-wing monoplanes and both were revolutionary for their time, having retractable undercarriages.

Contemporary with both Irwin and Mummert in the USA in the 1920s was the better-known Ed Heath who popularised the kitplane concept and the principal of homebuilt aeroplanes more than any other. He and the designers he enlisted were responsible for seven different aircraft in all, but it was his single-seat parasol-wing Heath Parasol that achieved the greatest acclaim and popularity amongst US builders of the time. In fact, the original Parasol was suggested to Heath and designer Clare Linsted by Weston Farmer, Editor of Fawcett Publications magazine *Modern Mechanix*. Farmer contributed the Thomas-Morse wings and 20 hp Henderson Motor-cycle engine for the prototype Parasol which first flew in 1926. *Modern Mechanix* published plans for the Parasol and Heath subsequently sold nearly a thousand kits on an instalment plan similar to that devised by Irwin—about 50 Parasols were factory built as well.

The Heath LN Parasol followed in 1931 and became the only kit aeroplane to be fully approved by the US Government. However, far fewer kits were sold than of the Parasol; a few LN Parasols were also factory built.

A variation of the LN Parasol was the CNA-40 Midwing designed by Jim Church. It made its debut at the Chicago World's Fair in 1933, an ideal aeroplane for amateur construction, cheap and easy

Ray Disesa's Heath Parasol based at Madeira Beach, Florida, was flown to the EAA's Sun'n'Fun Fly-In in April 1988, 57 years after the design first appeared in the USA. (Author)

The two-seater Pietenpol Aircamper is still being built and flown by homebuilders in the 1990s. (Author)

to build and easy to fly. But by now the Depression had set in and although several kits for the Midwing were sold and several were factory-built, it was the end for Heath's aspirations in the homebuilt aeroplane world.

Bernie Pietenpol flew his first homebuilt biplane, powered by a Ford Model T engine rated at 35 hp, in the 1920s at Spring Valley, Minnesota, in the USA. This was a homebuilt in the true sense of the word, and Pietenpol later said, 'Everything in this aircraft was either bolted or riveted together as I didn't own a drill or welding torch. I had to test fly it and learn to fly simultaneously.' After experiments with other engines, Pietenpol deduced that his original choice of the Ford engine was best, that is until they produced their Model A engine.

A homebuilt aircraft design that has become a classic and as enduring as any other resulted in 1928, the two-seat parasol-winged Pietenpol Aircamper. It was an attempt to produce an easy-to-build, lightweight, cheap, strong and easy-to-fly light aircraft that would be within the reach of the average man in the street who wished to take up flying as a hobby. Many examples of the Aircamper are still being built around the world in the 1990s.

Peitenpol used the pages of *Modern Mechanix* to share his aeronautical experiences with the would-be aviators of America in 1930 and had the same effect there as Mignet did in France several years later. As well as sets of plans at $7.50 each, Pietenpol sold kits of basic wooden parts needed in the construction of Aircampers for $70.00 each. He went on to design the complementary single-seat Pietenpol SkyScout and publicised this through the pages of *Modern Mechanix*—the Depression was looming, though, and very few SkyScouts were built.

Bernie Pietenpol died at Cherry Grove in 1984, but plans of his Aircamper are still available today, in a form updated in 1957 by John Grega of Bedford, Ohio.

Another contemporary of Pietenpol who took homebuilding in the USA away from the more traditional wood/fabric aircraft to steel tube/fabric-covered fuselage construction was 'Ace' Corben from Madison, Wisconsin. He also refined the kitplane concept. He designed his Corben Baby Ace for homebuilders in the 1920s, using a Henderson motor-cycle engine for power. When Ford's Model A engine became available, the Super Ace followed, able to cruise at 85 mph (140 kmph), 10 mph (16 kmph) faster than the Baby Ace. These were publicised in the now well-used way, through the pages of magazines, this time *Mechanix Illustrated*. A side-by-side two-seater, the Corben Junior Ace, followed in the early 1930s with an open cockpit and parasol wing—an enclosed cockpit was also offered for builders who wanted to fly in the northern States throughout the year. As well as plans-built and kitplane versions of these three Corben designs, they were also available complete, a Junior Ace selling for $1,265.00.

Whilst in Europe the 1930s saw light avaition and homebuilding burgeoning, Corben, Pietenpol,

A Corben Baby Ace homebuilt designed by 'Ace' Corben in the 1920s, one of the first popular homebuilts to feature a steel-tube fuselage. This example, pictured in 1988 at Ashville, North Carolina, has a Continental A.65 engine. (Author)

The Thorpe/Paulic T.3 on its initial flight in 1939—note the 'NX' series registration. (Allen Hess)

Heath and the like were in for hard times in the USA. The Depression started the rot for homebuilts and kitplanes, and what that did not stop, many of the State governments did. Regulations were introduced across the USA banning the private construction of aircraft so that by 1936 there were few places left where an individual could build and fly his own plane. Even factory-built versions of homebuilt designs were outlawed because they did not have full certification. In 1938 the US Federal Government banned non-certificated aircraft and pilots completely, so homebuilding was officially 'dead'. It was only in the State of Oregon that some freedom of the skies was preserved, and not surprisingly it was from this corner of the USA that the first post-war rumblings of activity from the nation's homebuilders came (see Chapter 3).

However, there were corners of activity in the USA during the 1930s despite this official line. John Thorpe and Rudy Paulic started work on the design of their T.3 all-metal homebuilt in 1933. It flew for the first time at Western Avenue airport, Los Angeles, in 1939. This large OX-5-powered low-wing cabin monoplane was the third that Paulic had worked on. Thorpe was to become famous in homebuilding and light aviation after the war (see Chapter 12). The T.3, though, was the exception at this time.

The Second World War officially put paid to any latent homebuilding opportunities when, in the early 1940s, all recreational flying in the USA was banned. What had followed the First World War as a 'heady' and fast-growing hobby with an active but small industry to supply it during the 1920s, faltered in the early 1930s. It took more than 20 years to pick up the momentum again, first in Oregon and the establishment of the 'Experimental' category, and then with the formation of the Experimental Aircraft Association (EAA) (see Chapter 9) in January 1953.

CHAPTER 3

Picking up the pieces: the '40s and '50s

VERY MUCH LIKE the post-First World War situation, the period after the Second World War saw a glut of both war-surplus aeroplanes and pilots in Britain. It was a period for tightening the belt in the world of aviation after the frantic advances and production between 1939 and 1945. The Ministry was disposing of aircraft, particularly the plentiful supply of surplus trainers such as the Tiger Moth and Miles Magister, and those instrumental in re-establishing civil aviation and private flying would hardly set out on the laborious task of designing and building their own aircraft when one of these surplus machines was available off the shelf for as little as £100 each!

Notwithstanding, there were those ardent avaitors in Britain—and in France, the United States and elsewhere—who wanted nothing of this war-surplus and wished to continue the movement that had started in the 1930s of designing and building one's own aircraft. However, the Pou-du-Ciel or Flying Flea debacle from pre-war was still very much in the mind of British officialdom, and in 1946 only the repair and reconstruction of aircraft was allowed by amateurs. One such aircraft to be re-built in 1946 was the Luton Minor G-AFIR, which Arthur Ord-Hume virtually reconstructed, with the exception of the registration letters! On 26 October 1946, thanks to the work of Yorkshireman Ronald Clegg who had written a letter to the magazine *Flight*, a meeting was convened of nine interested persons who agreed to form the Ultra Light Aircraft Association (ULAA).

Clegg's inspiration for the ULAA arose after he was demobbed from the Royal Navy in 1946. Whilst based with the Merchant Navy in Boston, Mass, for 12 months in 1930–31 he learned about the Heath Parasol, which was (as mentioned in Chapter 2) probably the first widely available homebuilt and kitbuilt aircraft in the world. He embarked on a private study of light aircraft design and conceived the idea of some sort of co-operative group effort directed at building and operating ultralight aircraft. He also completed the design of his own ultralight, the single-seater Salmson AD9 radial-engined biplane called the Sparrowhawk. His efforts to build the prototype in North London, after he returned permanently to England, were not only thwarted by the adverse publicity towards amateur-built aircraft in 1935 and '36 as a result of the Flying Flea crashes that had occurred, but also because the Government's Civil Air Guard scheme was now providing a way for enthusiasts to learn to fly for 5s (25p) per hour.

Following the 1946 meeting the aims of the ULAA were formulated, and after lengthy discussions with the Air Registration Board (ARB) in August 1947, the ULAA was given approval on behalf of the ARB to cover the design and construction of ultralight aircraft by their members in a Special Category Certificate of Airworthiness. This was similar to the pre-War 'Authorisation to Fly' introduced as a result of the Flying Flea (see Chapter 2). The ULAA was tasked with vetting designs and arranging for projects to be inspected, and it was on its recommendation that the Certificate for an aircraft was then issued. The system has changed very little by the 1990s, with the Popular Flying Association (PFA), the ULAA's successor, doing exactly the same thing with homebuilts.

Another aim of the ULAA, in fact a priority in its early years, was to provide cheap flying for the man in the street. The idea of group construction and group operation of ultralight and homebuilt aircraft was also born. Aircraft types available to ULAA members wanting to build or operate were few—the Heath Parasol and the similar Luton Minor were both pre-war designs, as was the Currie Wot. There were also aircraft such as the Fairey Junior and the Tipsy Junior, Belgian designs, the BAC Drone, the American Aeronca C.3, the

The Slingsby T.29B Motor Tutor of 1948, one of Britain's first post-war homebuilts. (Ken Ellis Collection)

highly specialist Zaukoenig, the Slingsby Motor Tutor, the one-off Britten Norman BN-1F—and that was about it. It was an uninspiring selection when the possible alternatives were Tiger Moths, Austers and Hawk Trainers (civilianised Miles Magisters).

Despite this dearth of suitable aircraft, at least the British organisation was formed, became operational and established at a very early stage the important formal precedent of being able to control and vet the construction of homebuilt aircraft on behalf of officialdom. To put the ULAA in context, it is interesting to note that in the USA at this time the Experimental Aircraft Association (EAA) was nearly six years away from formation.

France

Europe's major homebuilt aircraft proponents are the French. They had been at the forefront of the movement in the inter-war years and, as we have already seen, Henri Mignet with first his HM.8 and then his HM.14 Pou-du-Ciel or Flying Flea had rightly become known as the 'Patron Saint of Homebuilders'. Even before the cessation of hostilities the latent enthusiasm of French amateur aviators was once more evident. Mignet himself was working on his development of the HM.210, the HM.280 'Pou-Maquis', for use by the French Resistance until the Armistice rendered it unnecessary. Even before this, though, it is known that in September 1944 Jean Blanchet secretly flew his JB.1 Chantecler, a personalised version of Mignet's HM.8 with a modified wing and fitted with a 17 hp Aubier-Dunne V2D engine. In addition French aircraft manufacturers were waiting in the wings with design projects started during the war, hoping to

Henri Mignet prepares the HM.280 'Pou-Maquis' for flight. The undercarriage leg was more complex because it featured steerable mainwheels. (RSA, via Jacques Avril)

capitalise and make their mark upon France's decimated aircraft industry as soon as peace had returned.

Adolphe Lachassagne was another homebuilder in France who could not wait to get going again. Before the war he had built a series of homebuilt designs, the AL.1 as far back as 1912, then in 1922 the AL.2, until in August 1939 he completed the AL.7 with its unusual wing arrangement and 19 hp Aubier-Dunne engine. After the war it was registered F-WBBN and flew in 1945—it is now preserved at the Musee du RSA at Brienne-le-Chateau in France.

Claude Piel, working during the war for the French company CAPRA, had read Henri Mignet's book *Le Sport de l'Air* and using his aeronautical and woodworking experience designed and started the construction of his CP.10 which was basically a Flea but with less wing dihedral, a simpler NACA 23010 wing profile, a fixed rather than pivoting wing, conventional controls and a rudder. The CP.10 first flew at Moiselles airfield in September 1948, the start of a famous lineage of homebuilt—and factory-produced—Piel designs which would influence not just France's but the whole world's homebuilt aircraft movement for the rest of the century.

Many HM.14s survived the war and a whole string of amateurs got their aircraft back into airworthy condition again as soon as they could. The first flight after the Liberation is credited to Maurice Guerimet from Auxerre flying his HM.14, No 147, originally built in 1936 and now registered F-WFAQ. There were also many others, mainly flying HM.14s.

France was to follow the lead given by the British authorities in terms of homebuilt aircraft legislation. Realising the widespread enthusiasm for homebuilding that Mignet had stirred, and embarrased by so many Fleas flying 'unofficially', France had decided to regularise the situation in 1938. Mignet had been instrumental in the formation of the Réseau des Amateurs de l'Air (RAA) in 1935, basically a club for Flea-builders and pilots but, as might be expected, a flourishing and active organisation for amateur builders generally. When on 28 July 1938 the French Air Ministry introduced the *Certificat de Navigabilité Restreinte d'Aeronef* (CNRA), or Restricted Certificate of Airworthiness (See Appendix 4), they were adopting a system similar to the 'Authorisation to Fly' or 'permit' system adopted earlier in Britain, which as we have seen had sprung from 'Flea fever' in 1935–36.

November 1946 was a major watershed for French homebuilders. In view of the amateur activity already described, the Secretary General of Civil and Commercial Aviation reintroduced the CNRA system, aimed at reducing the tendency towards recklessness with which the amateur movement had become associated.

Later that month a meeting was held sponsored jointly by the Valenciennes Pou Club, whose President was Robert Guidon who had orginally thought of forming a Pou-du-Ciel Club of France, and the *Amicale d'Aviation Légère de Lyon* (Friends of Light Aviation in Lyon), with a view to forming a national group to support the interests of amateur aircraft builders. From this regional meeting came arrangements for a national meeting to be held in Paris, and in 1947 the Réseau du Sport de l'Air (RSA) was founded with Pierre Lacour as its first President;

The Lachassagne AL.7 F-WBBN was an unusual tandem-wing design, completed in 1939 and then flown after the war in 1945. (Author)

A Starck AS.70 derivative, the AS.71, with a Walter Mikron engine and similar to André Starck's prototype, which was one of the first post-war French homebuilts. (Author)

although in contention, Henri Mignet was not even voted to one of the seven other council seats—but that's another story!

The RSA administered the construction of homebuilts by its members under the CNRA system on behalf of officialdom, with a revised CNRA being introduced in August 1951 in the light of the first four years' experience.

Mignet's HM.290—drawing on the best points of the HM.210 and HM.280—became one of the first new homebuilt designs to be available to the French amateur after the war. It was publicised for the first time in the French magazine *Les Ailes* in April 1946, and two months later in Belgium. Literally hundreds of amateur aviators bought HM.290 plans, not only in France and Belgium but also in England, Canada, the USA and many other countries—and, more importantly, started building the aircraft.

André Starck was another of the first post-war French homebuilt aircraft pioneers with his single-seater, low-wing cabin monoplane, the Starck AS.70 Jac. It first flew on 23 May 1945 and was honoured as the first aircraft to receive a CNRA after the war. Then in 1946 came Roger Adam with his high-wing, two-seater cabin monoplane, the Adam RA.14 Loisirs, followed by the RA.15 Major. Plans for both types were still available to would-be builders until quite recently. A flood of new homebuilts continued to appear in France during 1946—even a modified version of the American Piper Cub, transformed by Jean Poullin as the Poullin J.5A. Another prolific French homebuilder, Jean Van Lith, revealed his Van Lith IV which he had been building in a cave in the South of France during the occupation, and registered it as F-WBGX.

The prolific number and variety of these first French homebuilts illustrates the latent enthusiasm that existed in France together with the more enlightened attitude to all aspects of sport aviation

The start of it all—the prototype Jodel D.9, originally F-WEPF but now F-PEPF, which first flew in January 1948, and is now displayed in the Musée de l'Air at Le Bourget. (Author)

First flown at Barton in 1971, acquired by Jodel Club founder Peter Underhill and rebuilt 'from the ground up' at Gransden by him, this is Jodel D.9 G-AXOI. The engine has a new backplate, Bendix magnetos, a Stromberg C150 carb and new inlet manifold, amongst other 'improvements'. The final item of 'new' equipment is the shoe-horn to assist 'ample' Peter's entry to and exit from the small cockpit! (Author)

in the re-building of the country's aviation industry after the war. Brief details of these homebuilts are given in the table overleaf.

The most significant new homebuilt of this era was the result of the association of Edouard Joly and his son-in-law, Jean Delemontez, the Jodel D.9 which first flew from a field near Beaune on 20 January 1948. Joly was another pre-war Flea builder and was founder of the Aero Club de Beaune; Delemontez, who married Joly's daughter, trained as an aeronautical engineer. After the war the two men formed a business partnership as Avions Jodel repairing German gliders, but also consolidating their ideas on a simple recreational aeroplane to be built of wood and fabric and powered by a 25 hp Poinsard engine, one that Joly had managed to keep hidden during the occupation.

For their prototype D.9, the Bébé (Baby), they drew the outline design directly on to the wood and fabric, capitalising on their considerable depth of knowledge and skill in design and construction. The Bébé, as its designation indicates, was their ninth design. After two years' work, including introducing the unusual wing with 'bent-up' wing-tips that has become the trademark of thousands of Jodels in following years and combines light weight and strength with aerodynamic efficiency, they successfully flew the prototype, but really only as a personal experiment with no intention of selling plans or embarking on commercial production of the design. It was not until a Dr Barret de Nazaris visited Beaune and flew the little Jodel D.9 that word got out about this remarkable little aeroplane. Barret wrote several articles for French magazines after his flight and obviously conveyed his enthusiasm for the design, as Joly and Delemontez were inundated with enquiries for plans from potential homebuilders throughout the French-speaking world.

The Jodel's significance in the history of homebuilding and light aviation is its wings, already mentioned. The aerodynamic efficiency they give is partly as a result of the NACA 23012-profile centre section which supports the aircraft during normal cruise with the outer 'bent' tips being at a zero angle of attack. At slower speeds, on landing and take-off, the centre section is at a higher angle of attack, so that the wing-tips become positive and start to contribute to lift, stability and excellent handling. The angle of the outer section dihedral, its washout and the change of airfoil section from the outer rib of the centre section to the wing-tip, all help to produce this low induced drag.

The table overleaf shows the absolute plethora of other homebuilts that were appearing in France at this time—in total contrast to Britain. That the Jodel should succeed in capturing builders' imaginations whereas most of the others listed did not is a further credit to the design, particularly its unique wing; it also explains why homebuilders around the world are still building and flying the type in profusion in the 1990s.

Plans were drawn up for the D.9 and builders were able to start constructing their own examples, albeit with a variety of different engines and modifications, a hallmark of any homebuilt design when submitted to the idiosyncrasies of the individual homebuilders. However, Joly and Delemontez, trading now as Avions Jodel, took another unique step which has since become the norm in the homebuilt world, and this was the sale along with the plans of a licence to authorise the individual to build a Jodel.

Post-war French homebuilts, 1945–52

First flight date	Designer	Type	Regn	Engine and notes
23/5/45	André Starck	Stark AS.70 Jac		45 hp Salmson
?	Henri Mignet	Mignet HM.280	F-PFKE	One of two built for ALAT
1/8/45	Adolphe Lachassagne	Lachassagne AL.7	F-WBBN	19 hp Aubier Dunne (preserved at Brienne-le-Chateau)
16/3/46	Roger Adam	Adam RA.14 Loisirs	F-PFBB	40 hp Train
13/4/47	Roger Adam	RA.15 Major	F-PCZL	75 hp Continental
? /46	Jean Blanchet	Blanchet JB.60	F-PCDL	60 hp Salmson
? /46	Pierre Carmier	Carmier T.10	F-WBBG	40 hp Train
? /46	Jean Chapeau	Chapeau JC.1 Levrier	F-WCDQ	40 hp Salmson 9
? /46	Jean Chapeau	JC.2	F-PANO	70 hp Minie
? /46	Jean Chapeau	CB.10	F-WDVL	70 hp Minie
? /46	René Gasne	Gasne RG. 3	F-WBGN	25 hp Poinsard
			later F-PEVC	
? /46	Pierre Lavoisier	Lavoisier Monoplane	?	20 hp Gnome et Rhone
23/4/48	Pierre Lavoisier	Lavoisier LP.24	F-WEPZ	27 hp Ava
? /46	M. Delassale	Delassale LD-45	F-WBBU	40 hp Train
? /46	M. Delassale	MDG LD.261 Midgy	F-BCAM	40 hp Train
			also F-PCAN	
16/11/47	M. Delassale	MDG LD.261	F-WEAM	75 hp Mathis G4F
? /47	Robert Planchais	Planchais LD-45-IV	F-PHQN	60 hp Walter
? /46	Robert Poullin	Poullin J.5A/J.5B	F-PDVD	65 hp Continental (other modified Cubs also)
? /7/46	Jean Van Lith	Van Lith IV	F-WBGX	34 hp ABC Scorpion (preserved at Brienne-le-Chateau)
? /47	Andre Brodeau	Brodeau 7	F-WCDN	45 hp Mengin 2BI
? 5/47	Maurice Brochet	Brochet MB.50	F-PEAD	40 hp Salmson
? /47	Remy Gaucher	Gaucher RG.45 Club	F-WCDI	40 hp Train
13/6/47	Rene Leduc	Leduc RL.16	F-WCDT	50 hp Zundapp
? /6/47	M. Mulot	Mulot AM.220 Sport	F-WCZS	(ex OO-AFS) One of two examples built in Belgium
? /47	Pierre Servais	Servais PS.01		25 hp Poinsard
1950		PS.10	F-WFRI	32 hp Sarolea, then 35 hp Anzani
? /47	M. Lagrevol	SETCA Milan	F-WCZZ	90 hp Regnier 4EO
? /47	Max Williams	Williams 28X	F-PEAT+F-PFOC	40 hp Salmson
? /48		Motorfly	F-WEAZ	Volkswagen (preserved at Brienne-le-Chateau)
15/7/51	Lucien Miettaux	Miettaux Ortolan	F-WFUR	Version of Motorfly
29/7/48	Aero Club de Suresnes	A.C. de S. Abeille	F-WBGU	60hp Salmson 9Adr, also 65 hp Continental
? /48	M. Allard	Allard D.40 (HM.280)	F-WFKA	
? /48	Antoine Bassou	Bassou Sport	F-WCZO	Salmson
? /48	M. Coulaud	Coulaud-Meo HM.8		40 hp Train
? /48	Emilien Croses	Croses EC.1	F-WCZP	50 hp Boitel
? 9/48	Robert Fleury	Fleury RF.10 Vedette	F-PEPR	30 hp Poinsard
? /48	M. Geffroy	Geffroy O1		30 hp Mengin
? /48	E. Grenet	Grenet G.47 Twin	F-PDVQ	2x40 hp Salmson
? /48	Alfred Huc/André Raynaud/Charles Guiraud	H/R/G/ Lou Riatou	F-WFKR	35 hp Poinsard

21/1/48	Edouard Joly/Jean Delemontez	Jodel D.9	F-PEPF	25 hp Poinsard (preserved at Musée de l'Air)
5/8/48	Leon Lacroix/Barret de Nazaris/Raymond Bourdin	L.N.B.-11	F/WFKQ	40 hp Volkswagen
? /49	M. Dumolard	Dumolard 01(2LB-7)	F-WFOQ	Poinsard
15/1/50	Leon Lacroix	Lacroix-Bourdin 2LB-9	F-WFAO	35 hp Cherub
1/11/51	Lacroix/Nazaris/Bourdin	L.N.B.-11	F-WGGX	65 hp Continental
? /48	G. Ligreau	Ligreau GL.4		30 hp Volkswagen
25/9/48	Claude Piel	Piel CP.10 Pinocchio	F-WFDA	25 hp Poinsard
? /49	Aero Club de Pithiviers (Badez/Giraud/Mercier)	B.G.M. Bagimer	F-PFAR	75 hp Minie 4C2 (Cub derivative)
	Aero Club de Pithiviers (Badez/Giraud/Mercier)	B.G.M. Bagimer II	F-WFOK	
17/2/49	Georges Briffaud	Briffaud GB.4	F-WCZB	25 hp AVa
	Georges Briffaud	Briffaud GB.5	F-WCZB	40 hp Mathis
3/1/49	Jean Dabos	Dabos Roitelet	F-WFAC	25 hp Poinsard
6/8/49	Maurice Brochet	Brochet MB.40	F-WFOH	65 hp Continental
24/6/49	Maurice Brochet	MB.60	F-WFKT	83 hp Salmson
1/2/49	Yves Gardan	CAB GY.20 Minicab	F-BFDT	65 hp Continental
2/4/49	Roger Druine	Druine Aigle 777	F-PFKG	40 hp Train
? /49	Rene Leger	Leger RL.1	F-PBNR	24 hp Volkswagen
? /49	Pierre Meunier	Meunier PM301 Dauphin	F-WFOX	105 hp Hirth 504A2
18/6/49	Roland Payen	Payen PA. 47 PleinAir	F-WFKY	65 hp Continental
17/11/49	Andre Starck	Starck AS.80 Holiday	F-WFRE	75 hp Regnier
? /50	Felix Bassou	SCAL Bassou FB.31	F-WFOL	40 hp Salmson
16/7/50	Lucien Tieles	Boisavia B80 Chablis	F-WBGO	65 hp Continental
? /50	Henri Saissac	Cabanes-Saissac CS-01	F-WFUO	60 hp Salmson
16/12/50	Amateurs Mazamet in Tunisia	Coutou Cri-Cri	F-WFKH	70 hp Minie Horus
? /9/50	Roger Druine	Druine D.3 Turbulent	F-PFUJ	Ava 4-00
5/5/50	Societe des Avions Jodel	Jodel D.11	F-PBBF	45 hp Salmson 9ADB
29/5/50	E. Krueger	Krueger EK.51 Welcom	F-WFOG	27 hp Ava
? /50	A. Soigneux	Soigneux Monocoupe	F-PMVX	105 hp Hirth
11/6/50	Andre Starck	Starck AS.90 NewLook	F-PGGB	18 hp Aubier-Dunne
20/12/51	Roger Druine	Druine D.5 Turbi	F-WFUU	45 hp Beaussier (2-seat Turbulent)
? /51	Albert Gatard	Gatard AG01 Alouette	F-PFDA	32 hp Poinsard
14/5/51	Wilfred Giraud and Gilbert Castex	Giraud Elytroplan	F-WDVG	35 hp Mengin
? //9/51	Guy Mangin	Mangin MRC.1		45 hp Persy
4/7/51	Pierre Morin	Morin PM.1	F-WGGF	25 hp Volkswagen
30/11/51	Louis Notteghem	Notteghem LN.01		60 hp Walter Mikron
1/7/51	Claude Piel	Piel CP.20 Pinocchio	F-WGGI	25 hp Volkswagen
? /51	Paul Rigault	Rigault RP.01R	F-PABO	35 hp Mengin
? /52	Claude Durand	Durand Beauregard	F-PGYM	30 hp Volkswagen
? /52	Humbert Guelton	Guelton HG.2	F-PEAV	105 hp Hirth 504
23/6/52	Rene Leduc	Leduc RL.19	F-PAGT	Hirth HM.60-R (preserved at Brienne-le-Chateau)
5/6/52	Max Plan	Plan PF.204	F-PBGE	75 hp Minie 4DC32
?/6/52	Jean Poullin	Poullin JP.20	F-WFUX	65 hp Continental (modified PA-15 Vagabond)
15/8/52		JP.30	F-WGIR	90 hp Franklin
?/10/52	Maurice Verrue and M. Deswarte	Verrue Mighty Midget	F-WDUI	25 hp Volkswagen

Tabulation prepared from data provided by Pierre Gaillard.

A Jodel D.119, a two-seater derivative of the single-seater D.9, at Granville, France, in 1990. (Author)

A three-seater Jodel D.10 was conceived but it was the French Government's design competition for a two-seater club trainer that caused Avions Jodel to abandon the D.10 and move quickly to the D.11, which was designed as an enlarged side-by-side, two-seater cabin version of the D.9, and first flew on 5 May 1950. It was competing against aircraft such as the Gardan Minicab, SIPA 903 and Piel Emeraude, and after two prototypes had been built Avions Jodel were contracted to build another ten. Homebuilders also demanded plans, so these were sold and are still available to homebuilders today.

Commercial production of the D.11 in various forms followed in France, the start of an epoch of French light aircraft production with the characteristic 'bent-up' wing-tips that still continues. As far as homebuilders are concerned, Delemontez has again been responsible for a resurgence of interest—if it ever died, that is—in the 1980s with his re-vamped two-seater, the Jodel D.18, a classic wood/fabric homebuilt being constructed in vast numbers by homebuilders throughout France and the world (see Chapter 11).

Claude Piel's CP.10 has already been mentioned and he appears again in the accompanying table with his CP.20 Pinocchio which first flew in July 1951. It was a single-seater which featured for the first time the semi-elliptical wing that became a common feature of subsequent Piel designs.

In an exact mirror of the Jodel D.9 story, Piel developed the CP.20 into the side-by-side two-seater CP.30, to be called the Emeraude. It was in 1951 that he started modifying the CP.20 design by enlarging the fuselage, increasing the wing area and re-stressing and strengthening the airframe for a larger engine and greater payload. He started cutting wood for the new CP.30 in July 1953, helped considerably by Yves Chasle and Robert Denize. Assembled at Mitry-Mory airfield, the prototype was painted a combination of sea green and dark green and, by a ballot of those involved with the project, the name Emeraude was chosen. Denize took the left-hand seat and Piel the right for the Emeraude's first flight on 19 June 1954 powered by a 65 hp Continental.

Commercial production ensued in several countries, as well as the sale of plans to homebuilders, and Piel went on to design a multitude of homebuilt designs before his untimely death in August 1982. Plans are still available from his son and wife in France and from the authorised distributor of plans for Piel designs, M. E. Litner of Repentigny, Quebec, Canada. The many variants of his CP.30 design remain the most popular, and in 1990 a CP.328 Super Emeraude built by Nigel Reddish from Kirkby-in-Ashfield, Nottinghamshire, was awarded the prestigious Air Squadron Trophy by the PFA for the 'Best Homebuilt' at its large annual international air rally at Cranfield, England.

Many of these early post-war French homebuilders were to follow similar paths to Joly/Delemontez and Piel and play an active and influential part in the French and worldwide homebuilt movement for the remainder of the 20th century. Roger Druine is typical with his D.3 Turbulent and D.5 Turbi, the former being part of the backbone of Britain's slowly blossoming homebuilt aircraft movement in the '50s and '60s—had Druine not died at the tragically young age of 37 in 1958, the inventory of his designs would doubtless have rivalled Piel and Jodel. André Starck is another name that crops up frequently throughout the whole of the post-war era in French homebuilding, his AS.70 Jac and its derivatives providing the design on which many of the early French homebuilders cut their teeth in the 1940s and '50s. In the 1970s he was still producing innovative prototypes: his biplane/linked-wing AS.37 (F-WYBQ) had twin pusher props driven by a single centrally-mounted

Above *The cockpit of a British example of the Druine D.31 Turbulent, flown by Eddie Clapham in Britain.* (Author)

Below *Albert Gatard's AG.01 Alouette, completed in 1951.* (Author's Collection)

engine, while the AS.27 Starky (F-PURC) had a similar wing with ailerons at 45° in the boxed-in wing-tip, counteracting the need for wing dihedral and making the structure exceptionally rigid. These are typical examples of the innovative experimental designs that continue to spring from a succession of French homebuilders.

Albert Gatard built his first homebuilt, the AG.01 Alouette (F-PFDA) in 1951. Better known is his low-wing single-seater AG.02 Poussin of 1960–61, which like his subsequent designs had a unique control system involving the use of a variable-incidence lifting tail-plane of large area. Instead of altering the wing angle of attack to increase lift, the pilot lowers full-span slotted aileron/flaps and adjusts the tail-plane to maintain pitching equilibrium so that the aircraft climbs at no more than 4° to the horizontal. His AG.04 Pigeon was the same, but was a two-seater high-wing design.

Unusual wing and control systems have been the hallmarks of all Pou-du-Ciel or Flying Flea derivatives. Emilien Croses, one of Mignet's most ardent 'disciples', produced his first Flea design, the Croses EC.1, in 1948, and it was just the start of a prolific design career that embodied Mignet's principles; in the long run he was to prove even more popular in terms of the numbers of successful examples of his designs that homebuilders have built and successfully flown. Croses's EC.3 Pouplume was perhaps the first true microlight or ultralight (ULM in France) homebuilt as far back as June 1961 when his prototype first flew with a tiny 10 hp Monet Goyon engine. When his EC-6 Criquet

prototype first flew in July 1965 it was again a wood and fabric variant of Mignet's tandem-wing concept, but a side-by-side two-seater that looked stylish and was to become the most widely built example of the Flea, excepting of course the original HM.14s. Croses also became a pioneer of the use of composite construction with his Croses Mini Criquet (see Chapter 4) and more recently, in association with his sons Yves and Alain, has reverted to ULMs with the two-seater Rotax-powered Airplume.

Other names and personalities include Roger Adam, whose RA.14 and 15 are still available to homebuilders in plan form 45 years after their maiden flights; Jean Van Lith, who continues to make homebuilts; Max Plan, whose PF.204 was the forerunner of the Bussard (F-PTXT), a classic Formula One air-racing aircraft; and Maurice Brochet and Yves Gardan, who both designed and built aircraft that have been adopted for commercial use as well as home production in moderate quantities. France's wartime Occupation may have been harsh reality at the time, but with the latent enthusiasm engendered by Mignet's Flea revolution before the war, combined with a healthy Government attitude, France became and still retains its place as probably the world's number one nation for homebuilts and the homebuilder.

The United States

Rivalling France's status must be the United States of America, homeland of the famous Experimental Aircraft Association (EAA) which has done so much to promote homebuilding and air education, not just in the USA and Canada but also, through its many 'Chapters' or Branches, throughout the world. It was not always this way, however.

The USA, as has been demonstrated in Chapter 2, was where homebuilding as a serious and accepted pastime first became a reality with the Heath Parasol. After the war, however, this vast nation was rather like Great Britain, with thousands of war-surplus aircraft of all shapes and sizes and an aircraft industry that had to adapt from the bounties of large-scale wartime production to meet the rigorous needs of a much smaller civil market.

For instance, after the war at Piper's Lock Haven plant, Pennsylvania, the airfield was packed with unsold and surplus Cubs and Super Cruisers as well as bulging stores of materials and components. William Shriver was bought in by Piper's in an attempt to prevent what would have been almost certain extinction. His solution in 1947 was a cheap and economical side-by-side production two-seater, the PA-15 Vagabond. Twelve weeks from conception to its first flight on 29 October, it incorporated many components from the earlier Piper models and a 65 hp Continental engine. When production started in January 1948 it sold for a mere $1,900, giving the potential recreational pilot—of whom there were many—a far easier option than to expend thousands of hours on designing and building his own aeroplane.

And as well as Pipers there were Cessnas, Taylorcrafts and Aeroncas, some at even cheaper prices than the PA-15. And for any potential homebuilders the source and availability of almost any component they needed, and particularly the excellent small horizontally-opposed Continental and Lycoming engines developed to perfection during the war, meant that the US homebuilder was in a most enviable position should he want to start a project.

All private aircraft were officially grounded upon the USA's entry into the war. After the hostilities the Civil Aeronautics Administration (CAA), the forerunner of the Federal Aviation Administration (FAA), which had been formed in 1938 by the Civil Aeronautics Act, was responsible for all aspects of civil aviation and the national airspace. Whilst there was 'general aviation' in profusion, the CAA did not recognise that there was such a thing as the homebuilt aeroplane or the homebuilder.

The true homebuilder has to be a pastmaster at scrounging components for his project. It keeps the cost down, accelerates progress and can be a diversionary enjoyment from the mainstream construction. Post-war America was a scroungers' paradise, and the few cells of homebuilding around the States could put together an aircraft for under $1,000 with little trouble. These cells did have some early co-ordination by George Bogardus from Troutdale, Oregon, under the banner of the American Airman's Association. The AAA financed Bogardus for a visit to the CAA in Washington, DC, to plead the case for the recognition of homebuilding and fun flying. His visit proved successful, and the CAA cautiously agreed that his type of aviation was possible, and with certain restrictions, acceptable to them.

In August 1947 Bogardus flew his Little Gee Bee

George Bogardus in 1947, one of the main protagonists of post-war US homebuilts. (Owen Billman)

George Bogardus at Deer Park airport, Long Island, in his Little Gee Bee on the way to lobby the CAA in Washington, DC, in 1947. (Owen Billman)

(NX 31250) legally for the first time, including a transcontinental flight to Washington, this time to push for specific amendments to the regulations relating to amateur-built planes. The result was the issue by the CAA of a formal statement, 'Safety Regulation Release Number 236', permitting certification of homebuilts (see Chapter 17).

Initially, therefore, a homebuilt aircraft project in the USA now had to be inspected by a local CAA safety agent. As there were no guidelines for the agent to follow it was purely a subjective assessment on his part, but the door had been opened and the various nationwide small groups of builders could come out into the open, including those in Oregon, the only State not to stymie the pre-war homebuilt movement.

One of the most active cells of early post-war homebuilding in the USA was in the Milwaukee area of Wisconsin. A young pilot on full-time duty with the Wisconsin Air National Guard named Paul Poberezny and a small group of other interested builders got together there in 1950–51 to help each other with their aircraft. As Chapter 9 will reveal, Poberezny was to become one of the most singularly significant personalities in the world of homebuilding and sport aviation through his founding and long-term Presidency of the EAA.

Those early post-war American homebuilts, like

The 1948 Goodyear Air Races at Cleveland, showing an impressive array of homebuilts.

those in Europe, were basic unsophisticated aircraft for fair-weather fun flying. An aspect of the American scene at this time that indirectly pushed the barriers of homebuilding forward started with the 1947 National Air Races at Cleveland, Ohio. Thanks to a three-year sponsorship deal with the Goodyear Tire & Rubber Co the first 'formula-type' race was flown, limited to single-seater aircraft with stock engines of 190 cu in displacement or less. The rules further encouraged safe designs and sound construction techniques and enabled the 'small guys' to compete in the popular and exciting world of air-racing.

These first 1947 'homebuilt' racers were all powered by Continental 85 engines, and in the first Goodyear Trophy Race were achieving speeds of 160 mph-plus. Most designs were mid-wing, tail-dragger monoplanes. Steve Wittman's 'Buster' won that first Goodyear in 1947, with Art Chester's V-tail 'Swee' Pea' coming second. In third and fourth place were a couple of aircraft designed by Tony LeVier, Cosmic Winds. A subsequent Cosmic Wind, 'Ballerina', was built for the 1949 Goodyear and flown into fourth place by Vince Ast. The aircraft came to Britain in 1961, was registered G-ARUL, was a regular part of the Tiger Club inventory at Redhill, participated in many Formula One air races in Britain, and is still flying today.

Some of the names from these air-racing days have become part of homebuilding folklore subsequently: Steve Wittman, already mentioned, who went on to design the Tailwind side-by-side two-seater, the dominant two-seat homebuilt in the USA for many years after the prototype first flew in 1953; Curtiss Pitts, who designed and built his Pitts 'Li'l Monster' for the 1951 Detroit races but had already designed and flown his S-1D Special biplane in 1944, an aircraft that soon became a classic in its own time; and Tom Cassutt, who built his Cassutt Special for the 1953 air races. And as the popularity of these Formula-type air races continued through the 1950s, the pilots and designers quickly became the heros that the burgeoning American homebuilt movement looked up to.

In 1948 David Long, then the Chief Engineer with Piper's, completed the prototype of another all-metal construction, low-wing, tail-dragger monoplane, the Midget Mustang. He flew it in the National Air Races in that year, and the following year took it to fourth place in the Continental Trophy Race at Miami. Again it was a one-off, equivalent to a homebuilt but not intended for other builders. However, in the 1950s Robert Bushby, a research engineer with Sinclair Oil Co, built the first true homebuilt Midget Mustang, which was to become another extremely popular design amongst American homebuilders. He used drawings, jigs and certain components from the aircraft's designer, David Long, who had since died. Bushby's prototype, the MM-1-85 Mustang with a 85 hp Continental, first flew on 9 September 1959, followed in July 1963 by the MM-1-125 with a 125 hp Lycoming engine; Bushby then began producing Mustangs in partial kit form as well as selling plans of the design—over 900 are estimated to have been built subsequently throughout the world.

Ray Stits ranks amongst these early pioneers and probably also started on the 'homebuilt road' thanks to an infatuation with flying and these post-war midget racers. As a boy he had hung round the airport near his home at Phoenix, Arizona, and 'bummed' his first flight in a J-3 Cub in 1936. He did

Cosmic Wind, a design of 1947. This particular example, 'Ballerina', was imported into Britain in 1961. (Author)

Top *A Bushby Midget Mustang built by Jim Spear at Reno, Nevada, on finals at Merced, California, in June 1990. The original Mustang first flew in 1948, and Robert Bushby's re-worked homebuilt version first flew in September 1959.* (Author)

Above *Ray Stits's Sky Baby with its 7 ft 2 in wing-span, which still holds the accolade it won in 1952 of the 'World's Smallest'.* (Author)

not start to learn to fly until 1942, and during the war he went into the USAAF as a ground crewman. While working at Battle Creek, Michigan, he helped build one of the Goodyear racers for Marge Hurlbert. Whilst working on this, apparently someone pointed out that Steve Wittman had built the then smallest plane in the world, his 'Chief Oshkosh', with a 12-foot wingspan. Stits, with little thought, said, 'I'll bet I can design and build one smaller than that', and set to work on the original Stits Junior with its 8 ft 10 ins wing-span and powered initially by the Aeronca E113C two-cylinder engine, though later fitted with an 85 hp Continental C-85.

Martin Young flew the prototype, N1293, for Stits in 1948 and knocked the undercarriage off during what must have been a hairy first flight. Stits then recruited a much lighter—160 lbs—Bob Starr to fly the repaired Junior and things went much better. Stits and his family first moved from Michigan to Phoenix, which is where he started design work on his Stits Playboy. But soon the Stits family, Starr and the Junior settled at Flabob/Riverside airport in Southern California in 1951 and it was there, whilst being demonstrated to Arnold Cole, then vice-president of the Pacific Air Races, that the Junior hit a fence and turned over whilst landing; happily Starr was uninjured.

Stits and Starr then heard that someone else was building a smaller aircraft than the Junior, so they decided to try to retain their accolade of designing and flying the 'World's Smallest'. In 1952 they completed their biplane tail-dragger Stits Sky Baby, N5K, which had a tuned 112 hp Continental engine, a Cessna-type spring landing gear and a wing-span of only 7 ft 2 ins (2.22 m). A long-armed pilot could sit in the cockpit and almost touch each wing-tip with his arms outstretched! First flights were made on the longer 6,000-foot hard runway at nearby Chino airport with Starr flying and Roy Outcen as the official CAA observer. An 'official' first flight was then made for the press and public at Palm Springs. The Sky Baby had a landing speed of 80 mph (129 kmph) and was extremely tricky to fly. Only one was built, but it still retains the title of the 'World's Smallest Aircraft' which it proudly wears on display in the EAA Museum at Oshkosh, Wisconsin, (see Chapter 9) where it is on loan from the Smithsonian in Washington, DC.

Following these successful experiments, Stits went back to work on the aircraft he had started whilst in Phoenix, the Stits SA-3 Playboy. He built the prototype in three months, a low-wing single-seater with a fixed landing gear and 22 ft 2 ins (6.76 m) strut-braced wings; for its first flight it was powered by a 65 hp engine, soon to be substituted with an 85 hp Continental. The prototype, N8K, first flew in 1953 and performed well, so the following year Stits started advertising blueprints for sale to other amateur builders. His brochure described the Playboy as 'a high-performance, aerobatic sportplane, easy to build, easy to fly, economical and designed especially for the homebuilder'. The blueprints cost between $15 and $25 and over the subsequent years a flood of over 1,500 potential builders bought them. The Playboy's appearance coincided with the resurgence of interest in amateur-built light aircraft in the US and it was this design, along with the Wittman Tailwind, the Corben Baby Ace and several others such as Barney Oldfield's Baby Great Lakes, the Pitts Special, Smith Miniplane, the Stolp-Adams SA-100 Starduster and the Meyer's Little Toot, that were the mainstay of the US movement well into the 1960s.

Stits himself sold one of his first sets of Playboy blueprints to Lou Stolp and George Adams, who traded a set of wheel-spats with Stits as payment. That was the inspiration for Stolp and Adams to design and build their bi-plane SA-100 Starduster, the first of a long line of Stolp homebuilt designs.

Stits went on to design other homebuilts such as the SA-3B Playboy in 1955, a two-seater variant of the plane with the same name, selling over 900 sets of plans for it in due course. He then had the revolutionary idea—at least for an American with an enviable source of cheap Continental engines available—to design a single-seater homebuilt suitable to be powered by a converted Volkswagen car engine. This was the Stits SA-5A Flut-R-Bug tri-geared monoplane with a welded steel-tube fuselage covered with fabric and wood/fabric wings. He subsequently produced five assorted variants of the Flut-R-Bug but was ahead of his time and could not easily obtain VW engines, so he settled instead for the trusty 65 hp Continental for the single-seater and the 90 hp Continental for the two-seater SA-6A and 'B versions. Stits also broke new ground by

G-BGLZ, a Stits SA-3 Playboy; this example was imported into Britain in 1979. (Author)

Ray Stits with the prototype Flut-R-Bug at Flabob, California. (Don Downie)

selling 25 complete kits of the SA-6B as well as over 800 sets of plans, plus pre-fabricated parts for those builders who wanted them.

Stits's prolific output continued with the SA-7 Sky Coupe, the first true American microlight/ultralight, the SA-8A Skeeto, and the SA-11A Playmate, all for the homebuilder. His business, Stits Poly-Fiber Aircraft Coatings, selling Stits Poly cloth and paints together with general provisions for the home-builder, is still going from strength to strength, based at Riverside, California. Stits is a legend in his own time and very much responsible for the foundation of the prolific and enthusiastic homebuilt movement in the USA. The EAA took up the 'banner', but Stits was one of the pioneers that provided the 'pole' which enabled early members to build and fly their own planes.

Great Britain

We have seen how the formation of the ULAA in Britain preceded its American 'cousin' by six years. However, the prolific design and operation of sport and homebuilt aircraft in the USA—and France—completely overshadowed the homebuilt movement in Britain during the 1950s in terms of indigenous new designs, project completions and general activity.

It was pre-war and French designs on which the early British homebuilders had to rely. Then, as now, Britain was almost completely devoid of successful native homebuilt aircraft designs, and the few homebuilders in existence were working on Luton Minors and Majors, Roger Druine's Turbulent and Turbi and the biplane Currie Wot. A notable exception was John Taylor, whose Taylor JT.1 Monoplane, a single-seater, wood/fabric tail-dragger powered initially by a JAP J-99 engine, was conceived and built in an upstairs flat in Ilford, Essex, between 1958 and '59. On 4 July 1959, with Wing/Cmdr O.V. 'Titch' Holmes at the controls, the prototype Taylor Monoplane G-APRT took to the

The Taylor Titch prototype in which John Taylor was killed in 1967. (K. Woolcott)

skies for the first time at White Waltham. It was the start of a remarkable history for the Monoplane and the subsequent derivative, the Titch, one of Britain's few internationally successful homebuilt designs.

Tragically, John Taylor was killed in 1967 whilst flying his prototype Titch. His wife Eve and now his son Terry continue to sell plans for the Monoplane and Titch; nearly 1,000 sets of Monoplane plans have been despatched to over 35 different countries, and at least 100 are known to have flown. Speaking in 1959, before the first flight of the Monoplane, John Taylor described the aeroplane's evolution:

'My desire to build a small ultra-light plane dates back to my school days in the 1930s. It seemed to be just a natural urge thwarted by two constant companions, lack of money and lack of facilities for building. Although I didn't realise it, I had no design knowledge either! The alternative was building models and then designing both the aircraft and their engines . . . these yielded a great deal of amusement and information, but the urge for a full-sized effort persisted.

'After years of hesitation, and many discussions with my wife, I decided it was now or never. My initial ideas for a two-seater began to look expensive so I shelved the lot and started the design of a single-seat, low-wing job to the following specifications:
1) Money—£100
2) Dimensions—to suit our upstairs dining room
I also had the faint hope that this machine might be suitable and adaptable for amateur construction like the Turbulent.

'To obtain my layout the first considerations were that the aircraft would be for sport flying and the requirements narrowed to small in size, low initial cost, easy to maintain, cheap to operate and safe to handle [NB Henri Mignet's criteria for his Flying Flea were not dissimilar to these!] A 35 bhp engine was my proposed power. Then sketches were made until I had something which looked about right, even though a bit short. The final small sketch was then scaled up and the various items shown in their respective positions to ensure the design would progress, without finding later that the rear spar was passing through the pilot's body, or that an aileron cable was required to pass through the top of one's trousers. From here onwards it appeared to be a question of advanced planning.

'Due to the aircraft being built in one room, separate wing panels became essential, with the accompanying joints, etc. Also the fuselage was to be of limited length, though I did not regard this as of too much importance, as a "safe" aerofoil section, together with adequate tail

The prototype of Eric Clutton's FRED homebuilt, one of Britain's few indigenous and successful post war homebuilt designs. (Ken Ellis Collection)

areas and some adjustment of the ratios in the control system, can, to a large extent, combat the disadvantage of a short fuselage. The moderate aspect ratio quickly decided the size of the wing panels for a given area, the room decided the overall length and the finance determined the engine, a 36 bhp JAP. Whilst a reliable engine, I have redesigned the exhaust system and heated air intake to improve appearance.

'On completion of the general layout the window of the flat was measured to ensure that the components would go through. I then started the stressing calculations, which together with drawings took seven months. With design work completed, construction was started, the facilities consisting of one ordinary dining table, an assortment of wood-working tools loaned by a good friend, several clamps, a small lathe and bags of enthusiasm—the latter being of some importance. I estimated the construction would take about 18 months of evenings and weekends. Having worked some 11 months of that time, I now estimate about 14 months. Then my neighbours will enjoy the sight of my little aeroplane being loaded on to a lorry from the window of my upstairs flat, and shortly afterwards I hope to enjoy the pleasure of realising my life's ambition by flying an aircraft built by "yours truly". I must add that during construction I gained much advice from our genial friend Doug Binachi— on more than one occasion his ever present enthusiasm lifted me from the depths on those few occasions when one wonders—"Is it worth it?"' (*Reprinted from an article written for* Popular Flying, *February 1959*).

Taylor's story in its quaint frankness is as relevant now as it was in the 1950s. Cutting your cloth according to your means, the availability of a suitable and practical engine, and the availability of a mentor for advice and encouragement, are still three of the most important factors contributing to the successful completion of a homebuilt aircraft project.

Britain's other successful homebuilt designs, the FRED and Isaacs Fury (See Chapter 7), were still several years away. It was a start, though, as Britain began, albeit more slowly than neighbouring France or the USA, to pick up the pieces after the war. Construction materials used were largely the traditional wood/fabric in Britain and France, but in the USA more extensive use was made of welded steel-tube/fabric and metal construction. These methods of construction were to serve the homebuilder well through the 1960s and early 1970s as the worldwide movement changed rapidly into third gear.

Post-war British homebuilts, 1945–52

Date of first flight	Designer/Builder	Type	Regn	Notes
Did not fly	R. G. Bracewell	Pivot Monoplane	G-AGOO	Used parts of the Gunton Special G-AFRW; broken up in Dec '46
Did not fly	R. S. Finch	Luton Minor	G-AHMO	Started in 1946 but never finished
? /47	R. E. Carr	Wren Goldcrest	G-AICX	Scott Squirrel. Certification problems; broken up later in 1947
?/12/47	Slingsby's	T.29 Motor Tutor	G-AKEY G-AKJD later	Scott A.2S. Conversion of glider, re-engined with JAP J-99 in 6/48
? /51	S Hants Ultra Light Aero Club	Heath Parasol	G-AJCK	ABC Scorpion. Built in 1948 but sold to Airways Aero Assoc who re-engined it with a JAP J-99 for first flight
Did not fly	J. N. D. Heenan	Planet Satellite	G-ALOI	Gipsy Queen 32. First flight attempted at Blackbushe in 1949 but abandoned
? /4/45	Brunswick Tech High School, Germany	Zaukoenig V.2	G-ALUA	Zundapp Z9-92 imported by RAE Farnborough in 1945
Did not fly	D. E. Felce	Luton Minor	G-ALUZ	Scott Squirrel. Built in 1949 at Hinckley, Leics
? /48	E. O. Tips, Avions Fairey, Belgium	Tipsy Junior	G-AMVP	Aeronca JAP J-99. Imported as OO-ULA in '48
? /50	J. R. Coates	Luton Minor/Swalesong SA.1	G-AMAW	Bristol Cherub III, but later re-designated SA.1. Built at Hitchin, Herts
26/5/61	John Britten/Desmond Norman	BN-1F Finibee	G-ALZE	JAP J-99. Built in 1951 at Bembridge, IOW, but not completed and flown until '61
? /49	Abbots-Baynes	Scud III	G-ALJR	2½ hp Villiers. Built in 1935 and flown at Woodley; registered in 1949

NB This tabulation is not as 'thoroughbred' as the French homebuilt table, containing several imports to Britain as well as a high proportion of projects that never flew. In the French table every aircraft listed is believed to have flown.

CHAPTER 4

The materials/shape revolution: the '60s and '70s

'Oddly enough, the decision to use all-composite glass-foam/glass-sandwich structure for the VariEze prototype was mainly an expedient rather than an attempt to develop improved technology—it was not known if this method of construction would be light enough or durable enough for anything beyond the prototype.'

Burt Rutan, 1974

WOOD AND FABRIC had been the traditional materials for homebuilt aircraft construction, with the use of metal for important structural fittings. Although complete metal structures or combinations of metal and fabric, or metal and wood and fabric, had all been utilised in the design and construction of homebuilts, there was a materials and shape revolution on its way which could be summed up in one word—composites.

Probably more than any other homebuilt, the Rutan VariEze, and the LongEz and Defiant that it spawned, will be synonymous with the first use of composites in the construction of homebuilt aeroplanes. And one has to concede that through their work not only in materials usage but also in the design shapes they were able to create, the application of this 'first' accolade to Burt Rutan and his brother Dick is partly justified. However, their successful use of composite materials was really the culmination of research and experience from around the world.

California's surfers had long known about the lightweight, durable qualities of composites in the construction of their surfboards. Before them, though, the world's defence and commercial aerospace industry had pushed the gates open on the use of composites for an expanding number of airframe application, but, in the 1960s and early 1970s, never to the extent of using it for a complete airframe or major structural components.

The exception to this was the West German glider and sailplane industry which had perfected the use of composites in its quest for improved design, strength and performance parameters. It was the

G-LASS, the first Rutan VariEze built in Britain. (Nigel Scoines)

Dick Rutan with the prototype LongEz over the Colorado River at Bullhead, Arizona. (Don Downie)

Akafleig Stuttgart FS-24 Phönix which was the first sailplane to be built of glassfibre. It was originally developed in 1951 under the direction of R. Eppler and H. Nägele at the Stuttgart Academic Flying Group, and their attempts to reduce weight without increasing wing area led them to try a balsa-wood core stiffened on its exterior by layers of paper and glue. Project work had to be suspended but later, with an injection of a financial subsidy to enable further research to proceed, combined with the availability of the first glassfibre strengthened polyester resins, they were able to retain balsa as a core and as a filling material for the sandwich skin and use glassfibre as an outer skin.

The monocoque fuselage was constructed in the classic two-piece 'kit model' manner with a sandwich skin of glassfibre and balsa wood. The two fuselage halves were then glued together and the join strengthened by layering with an overlap of further glassfibre. The wings were constructed in exactly the same way with the upper and lower surfaces being stuck together and the 'apertures' for the ailerons, flaps and rudder simply cut out. Plywood was also used to strengthen certain parts. The first flight took place on 27 November 1957, when the era of true aviation composite construction technology can be said to have officially got off the ground.

Eight Phönixes were subsequently built and all were known to be still flying over 20 years later, the first and simplest testament to the design life and durability of composite structures. Many other West German glider designers followed the lead of the Phönix during the 1960s; a direct development was the all-glassfibre Bolkow Phoebus that first flew in April 1964 and of which 253 examples were built in the following six years. Glasflügel took over construction of the all-composite BS.1 which had first flown in 1962 and quickly came to be regarded as having one of the highest performances of its time. They also built the H.301 Libelle which first flew in March 1964, the first of thousands of composite gliders to be built by this famous German company. Schleicher flew their all-composite AS-W.12 in December 1965 and Schempp-Hirth their Cirrus in January 1967. By 1970 composite airframe technology was not only 'old hat' to the German sailplane manufacturers, but was also a way of life essential to a company's survival in this highly competitive and specialist field.

France was also close behind West Germany, and Breguet's B.905 Fauvette single-seater that first flew in 1958 also utilised a plywood/foam sandwich—6 mm plywood with 8 mm Klégécel (an expanded plastic)—for its rear fuselage and wing construction. The Fauvette also had a moulded plastic foam nose section, although it was not a true 100 per cent composite because the centre fuselage had a steel-tube construction, albeit covered with moulded polystyrene. The futuristic Siren Edelweiss designed by Dr J. Cayla which first flew in September 1962 was used by French pilots competing in the 1963 World Gliding Championships in Argentina and was constructed using a mostly composite structure—the cantilever wings had a single-spar foam-filled wooden structure with only eight ribs, covered with a ply/Klégécel sandwich. Similarly the fuselage was also constructed from this ply/Klégécel combination.

Britain's sole glider and sailplane manufacturer, Slingsby's, tried to keep abreast of the competition in the 1960s with a change from traditional wooden to metal construction. They decided to embark on the licence manufacture of a German Glasflügel glassfibre design, the Kestrel, commencing production in 1970. The Vega, which first flew in 1977, was Slingsby's first wholly designed glassfibre sailplane. In the USA, Schweizer was the main glider and sailplane manufacturer and they stuck with metal construction as did several other companies. It was not until Arthur Zimmermann and Wolfgang Schaer flew their Concept 70 Standard-Class sailplane in 1970 that the USA had its first indigenous all-glassfibre sailplane. This had shoulder-set cantilever wings consisting of a glassfibre/PVC foam sandwich—the fuselage was a glassfibre monocoque structure reinforced with a steel-tube frame.

The marriage of glassfibre and composite construction with special laminar-flow wing sections revolutionised gliding as a sport in the 1960s. Glassfibre confers great strength without the penalty of weight and has the added advantage of being extremely smooth, reducing drag to a minimum. It was also to prove much easier to work and in due course made the high-performance, amateur-built/homebuilt sailplane a reality.

Various terms and trade names have already been used, all loosely grouped under the name 'composites'. Aviation composites are generally a combination of glass or carbon fibres in a resin matrix (glassfibre) and/or some of the numerous different foam products such as urethane, polyurethane, styrofoam and PVC foam. Basically, composites are a 'plastic' plywood made up from layers of material to give strength and form. There can be no hard and fast rules in this changing and idiosyncratic field, but generally there are a minimum of three layers, with hard outer shells of glassfibre sandwiching an inner layer of a foam-type material. As a result the homebuilt designs that utilised this composite construction technology fall roughly into two categories: the mouldless types such as the famous Rutan VariEze; and the pre-moulded kitplane types that correspond to life-size plastic model kits, components for which are simply stuck together.

Whilst the VariEze of Burt and Dick Rutan in the USA is usually quoted as the first all-composite homebuilt, it can only carry this accolade if popularity and widespread acceptance are then added to the claim. France is probably the holder of the true 'first' title, if it really matters, the specific aircraft type concerned being the Piel CP.80 Zef, a single-seat low-wing monoplane powered by a 90 hp Continental C90. Frenchman Claude Piel became interested in the sport of Formula One air-racing in the early 1970s, and with such classic wood/fabric homebuilt designs to his credit as the CP.30 Emeraude and CP.60 Diamant already well known and respected in homebuilt circles, he decided to add a Formula One racer design. This was the CP.80.

Michel Calvel of L'Hospitalet du Larzac in France took an interest in the design and through discussions with Piel and his studies of composite materials and structures, chose to construct his Zef,

Michel Calvel's CP.80 Zef was built in France in the early 1970s and was arguably the first homebuilt to make extensive use of composite construction. (Pierre Gaillard)

The first British Pereira Osprey amphibian homebuilt, G-BEPB, was completed at Sandy, Beds, by John Zwetsloot and was shown for the first time at Cranfield in 1984. Extensive use of composites was made in the construction of the hull. (Author)

which turned out to be the first to fly, from laminated plastics—composites. This was in the summer of 1973, two years before Rutan first flew his prototype VariEze.

Also in France at the same time a derivative of Henri Mignet's infamous tandem-wing Pou-du-Ciel or Flying Flea was again pioneering the world of homebuilding with a high percentage of its airframe built from composites. Emilien Croses from Macon had already designed several tandem-wing homebuilts immediately popular with French homebuilders, particularly his side-by-side two-seat Croses EC-6 Criquet which had first flown in 1965. Around 1970 he designed a single-seater variant, the Croses Mini-Criquet, and enlisted the help of George Flicot and M. Millet to construct the prototype. The fuselage, engine cowling, fin, wing spars, upper wing support struts and main landing gear legs were fabricated from a polyester resin and glassfibre sandwich, with the wing ribs and other components made from Klégécel. The Mini-Criquet first flew at Abbeville in 1975, another composite homebuilt that pipped the VariEze to the post!

Back in the United States homebuilders were starting to seek alternatives to the conventional wood/fabric and metal construction options. Difficult and streamlined shapes are always the bane of the homebuilder whose often limited facilities, finances and skill make fabrication of these items from conventional materials to the high standards demanded an impossible dream. George Pereira from Sacramento, California, had designed and flown his single-seater Osprey 1 flying-boat in 1971. His two-seater development, the Osprey 2, was begun in January 1972, and whilst the basic all-wood fuselage structure was conventional in construction, the hull or lower fuselage shape was given a deep coating of polyurethane foam. This was then 'sculpted' to give the all-important hull shape of a flying-boat before being covered with layers of protective glassfibre cloth bonded to the foam with resin. The hull of a flying-boat experiences considerable forces and shocks during water operations as it is struck by small waves and therefore needs to be extremely strong. The foam and glassfibre—composite—finish to the Osprey 2 had excellent shock-resistant properties and is extremely light. The wing-tip floats were constructed in the same way. The Osprey 2's first flight took place in April 1973, and it was very much a leader in the homebuilt field in the USA in its use of composites.

There were also several other early pioneering designs that owed their existence almost entirely to the more extensive use of composites and were pre-VariEze. First of these was Ken Rand and Stuart Robinson's Rand Robinson KR-1, a single-seater low-wing tail-dragger monoplane. Rand and Robinson were flight test engineers at Douglas Avionics in California. Rand had graduated from the University of Illinois and had had a preoccupation with radio-controlled models since before high school, so his numerous sketches of aeroplane designs soon began to resemble the eventual KR-1, and his ideas for a radio-controlled model developed into a real aeroplane. Work on the KR-1 design and construction got seriously under way in 1968 and it was completed four years later in time to be displayed at the Experimental Aircraft Association's famous fly-In at Oshkosh, Wisconsin, USA. Rand and Robinson had built this prototype for a mere $536.00 and a year of the building time had been devoted to their research and testing of the type of cloth, resin and foam combination they would use in its construction. Their aim was to design a low-cost, quick-build aeroplane with better than average performance. They saw pioneering use of foam and plastics as the only reasonable way to achieve this, and their efforts were rewarded after the KR-1's first flight in February 1972 when, after trailering their aircraft to Oshkosh, it was awarded the 'Outstanding Achievement Award' by the EAA for best application of new materials.

KR-1 construction was also eased by the use of composites, although initially Rand and Robinson had no intention of selling plans or kits of their progeny. The wing had a conventional spruce front spar and lighter plywood rear spar but most of the wing ribs were formed from styrofoam plastics with the interstices filled with a styrofoam slab. The whole structure was then covered with Dynel epoxy to seal and strengthen it. Similarly with the fuselage, which had a basic spruce and plywood framework but the curved upper part of which was carved from styrofoam then covered with Dynel. The tail was roughly the same as the wings.

With a 1,700 cc Volkswagen engine for power, the KR-1's maximum speed was noted at 200 mph (322 kmph) and achieved Rand and Robinson's initial design criteria admirably. Plans were made available to other homebuilders by popular demand, and 20 years later, although Robinson parted company with Rand in 1979 and Rand himself was killed later that year, Rand's wife Jeannette currently quotes sales of well over 6,000 sets of KR-1 plans and over 8,000 for the two-seater KR-2. Lance Neibauer, who is now a prominent figure on the kitplane scene (see Chapter 5) with his Lancair two-seat and four-seat composite kitplanes, cut his teeth in homebuilding by constructing one of the first KR-2s to fly.

Another pioneering composite homebuilt design to come out of California in the early 1970s, and which owed its existence and success entirely to the use of composites, was the War Aircraft Replicas half-scale Focke-Wulf 190. Peter Nieber developed the design at Santa Paula, California, as the first of what was proposed as a complete range of scaled-down replica Second World War aircraft for the amateur builder. Design work on the first of these, the FW-190, started in July 1973, construction started in February of the following year and by 21 August 1974 the prototype had flown.

One of the difficulties homebuilders had found in trying to create scale replicas of fighters such as the FW-190 was achieving the shape. Curved and streamlined shapes of the originals were achieved in mass-production factories with every facility available at the time, but scale the shape down and take away the factory engineering facilities, and bending conventional ply or sheet metal to the stringent curves required becomes an almost impossible task. Enter composites and their ability to be carved into

The cockpit of an Irish-built example of the Rand KR-2. (Peter Underhill, Ken Ellis Collection)

shape. We have already seen how the hull of the Osprey 2 was carved, and that is exactly how Nieber achieved the accurate curves and shape of his 190 replica. As British homebuilder Mark Parr from Guernsey in the Channel Islands (see Chapter 13), who completed a WAR FW-190 in 1984, said, 'It's not really homebuilding in the conventional sense of the word, it's more like art and sculpture forming the aircraft's shape. Endless hours have to be spent carving, sanding down, then filling and re-sanding the polyurethane foam before the final shape is achieved and ready to be coated with the glassfibre cloth and resin outer skin'.

A typical WAR replica from the range which as well as the FW-190 grew to include a Vought F.4U Corsair, Republic P.47 Thunderbolt, Hawker Sea Fury, Zero and, most recently, a North American P.51 Mustang, is constructed very much like the Rand-Robinson KR-1. There is a primary wooden structure for the wings of front and rear spars, and a mix of plywood and polyurethane foam wing ribs the aerofoil contours of which are built up with the foam and then carved and sanded to the exact shape. The finished surface is a high-strength laminated fabric with a glassfibre epoxy resin covering. The basic fuselage is a wooden laminated spruce box structure covered with plywood on to which the polyurethane foam is bonded and the final contours built up with the now familiar carving, sanding, filling, sanding, filling, etc routine and a fabric/epoxy covering. Again, not a 100 per cent composite structure, but involving the builder in the use of previously untried materials and enabling him to achieve goals simply, cheaply and effectively that a few years before had been unattainable.

Against this background the most famous, pioneering and widely-built composite homebuilt of its time, the Rutan VariEze, was still in gestation out in the Mojave Desert east of Los Angeles, California.

A comprehensive library of books has already been written and published on the history of the pioneering work of the Rutan family in the world of homebuilding and aviation in general (Chapter 17 charts Rutan and Yeager's epic non-stop unrefuelled round-the-world flight in the composite Voyager). Dick Rutan was an ex-USAF fighter pilot and Vietnam veteran, and his brother Burt, five years his junior, was an early aircraft modeller who soloed in an Aeronca 7AC Champ after only 5 hours 15 minutes of flying and later worked for seven years as a Flight Test Project Engineer at the famous Edwards Air Force Base in the Mojave Desert. The brothers were part of a tight-knit family and their parents reckoned they had 'avgas in their veins'! They were responsible not only for giving the homebuilt world the first 100 per cent composite aircraft but at the same time a reincarnation of the strange 'canard' shape—the reverse of conventional aircraft layouts with the elevator at the nose and a pusher engine behind—which went back to those very first truly successful homebuilders, the Wright brothers.

Burt Rutan was the 'designer' of the pair, if labels

Construction detail of the War Aircraft Replicas half-scale Focke-Wulf 190.

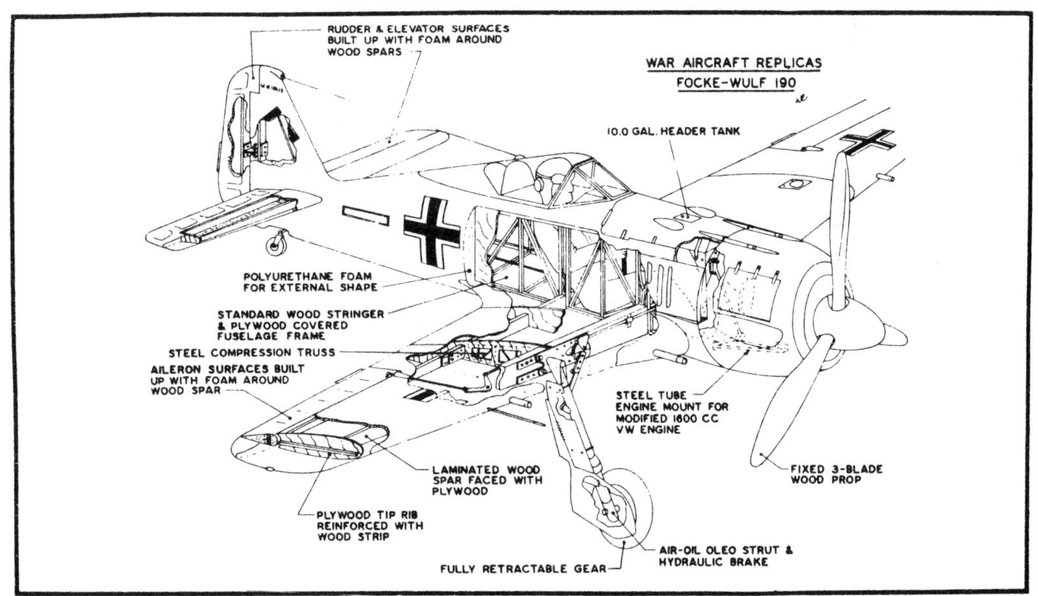

have to be given. He built his first radio-controlled model 'canard' design in 1964 whilst at California Polytechnic University (Cal Poly) at San Luis Obispo. By 1966 he was testing a one-fifth scale canard model, pole-mounted on the roof of his car because Cal Poly's wind-tunnel wasn't big enough. Driving the car at 80 mph at night over 10 to 20-mile runs he collected what he described as 'beautiful data' from the tests. Rutan's inspiration for a canard design had come from the Swedish company Saab, whose canard fighter, the Viggen, with its double-delta, short take-off and landing (STOL) and Mach 2 performance, impressed him. He started to design and build something smaller—as a homebuilt project—whilst working at Edwards AFB in 1968, before he moved east to Kansas City to take up a new job there with another homebuilt pioneer, Jim Bede. He shipped the wooden airframe, christened the VariViggen, to Kansas with him so that he could complete its construction, as this had been part of the deal he had struck with Bede as a condition of moving East.

Rutan's VariViggen was an amalgam of conventional homebuilt constructional materials—the wings had spruce spars, plywood ribs and skins covered with Ceconite, all except the outboard aft wing panels which were of flush-riveted metal construction. The whole fuselage was a wooden structure, seating two in tandem with a tail-mounted pusher engine, and whilst a few components such as the engine cowlings were glassfibre, there was no evidence of composites in its construction.

It was the VariViggen's shape that was unconventional, at least for a homebuilt, and that above all else was probably the main reason why the design was soon attracting US homebuilders' attention even before its first flight at Newton, Kansas, in May 1972. Nine weeks later the interest turned to fanatacism when Rutan flew the prototype into the 1972 EAA Oshkosh Fly-In. Most of the teething problems with the design centred around the nose gear—it had a retractable tri-gear—but Rutan confessed that its performance was really best at low speeds showing no conventional stall and being able to climb, cruise, glide, turn and land with continuous full aft stick at a stable speed of only 52 mph (84 kmph). Little wonder that Rutan won every spot-landing contest he ever entered when flying the VariViggen.

Burt Rutan's VariViggen had not of course been the first home-built 'canard' aircraft, and certainly was not the first canard, as the Wright brothers' work gives early testimony. In wartime Britain George Miles pondered the possibility of a true tandem-wing layout in which both horizontal surfaces were true lifting surfaces with the centre of gravity somewhere between the two. His deliberations were an attempt to provide a neat solution to a shipborne fighter so that the pilot could be located in

An early photo of Burt Rutan at about the time that the LongEz was being developed. A model of the VariViggen is in front of him on his desk. (Don Dwiggins)

Rutan's historic VariViggen prototype at the Rutan Aircraft Factory at Mojave, California, before it was donated to the EAA Museum at Oshkosh—with hindsight, a very significant aeroplane. (Author)

the nose with an unobstructed view, the engine at the rear and armament and fuel in between. Also the wing-span could be kept minimal without the expensive, weighty, time-consuming and often problematical wing-folding mechanisms from which carrier-based aircraft suffered.

Under Miles's direction Ray Bournon designed the Miles M.35 Libellula as an unofficial private venture. 'Libellula' is the generic name of the dragonfly species, which the M.35's tandem wings were thought to resemble. The M.35 first flew in May 1942, but it was terribly unstable, and the reaction of the Ministry and Admiralty was negative. It had been designed and built in six weeks, but the unenthusiastic official response meant that this particular project died.

Miles, however, was fascinated by the 'canard' concept and applied the principle to the role of heavy bomber—a six-engined and later an eight-engined design were proposed but never built. Later came the smaller M.39 Libellula proposal for a high-altitude, lightly armed, high-speed bomber which developed into the M.39B. This was actually built and flown for the first time in July 1943, powered by two 140 hp de Havilland Gipsy Major engines fitted to the rear wing. However, after extensive RAE trials it was handed back to Miles, although the extensive design and test data accumulated was forwarded to the US Army and thence to several American aircraft firms. Miles's M.63 Mailplane project in 1944 was the last of his attempts to gain acceptance for his Libellula or 'canard' ideas; it was to be jet-powered but never got further than the drawing board and wind-tunnel model stage.

Other historically significant 'canard' designs prior to Rutan include the canard glider designs of Wolfgang Klemperer in the 1920s. His idea was that the canard configuration would be able to sense rising air and pull up into them to gain altitude! Another Second World War canard project was the Curtiss-Wright Ascender, an interceptor fighter with a pusher Allison engine.

This canard wing arrangement became the Rutan hallmark and its principles need to be appreciated as it has come to play such a significant role in the history and development of homebuilt aircraft. The VariViggen and subsequently the Ezes have a loaded canard wing which is designed to provide aerodynamic angle-of-attack limitation and thus to be stall-proof. The Rutans maintained all along the simplicity of this arrangement, as Miles had many years before in Britain; the canard is basically a tandem wing with one pair in front of the other (not overlapping or one above the other as in Henri Mignet's Flying Flea designs), with the front wing always smaller than the rear. The front wing provides pitch control, with only flaps (not elevators) on the rear wing; both wings are lifting rather than one being like the tail of a conventional aircraft layout with a down load that causes drag. As Rutan says, 'Nothing on the canard design is *lifting down*'.

With hundreds of hours on the prototype VariViggen, ideas for an improved, lighter, faster homebuilt with the same canard configuration had been mulling around in Rutan's mind and on his drawing board for quite a while. Design work on a successor, the VariEze, is officially quoted as commencing in early 1974, although this was initially a high-wing/low-canard configuration built of metal. However, structural complexity and excessive weight along with instability problems gleaned during flight tests with one of the models caused the VariEze Mk1 to be abandoned. Persevering, Rutan tested further models and by late 1974 had achieved a design very similar to the VariEze. This has since become part of homebuilding history, for it was at this stage that a decision was made to use an all-composite structure for the prototype.

As the quote at the start of this chapter reveals, it was 'an expedient rather than an attempt to develop technology'. The composite structure enabled quick construction of the prototype, but what Rutan did not know was whether it would be light or strong enough for anything other than the prototype—the VariEze was a research aircraft to investigate canard aerodynamics with little or no thought to its potential as a homebuilt. Rutan knew very little at this stage about quality control when working with composites to ensure uniform strength of the airframe or maximum life expectancy. The aircraft's skins were deliberately 'beefed up' to compensate for these unknowns and, as it happened, had excellent surface durability, a 12 g ultimate load factor and a realistic low weight even including the 62 hp Volkswagen engine fitted to the prototype.

From fabricating the first component to the first flight of the VariEze took four months, the historic debut occurring at Mojave on 21 May 1975. Inclusion of new futuristic-looking NASA-developed winglets not only helped reduce induced drag, improving the climb and cruise efficiency but also helped to set the design radically apart from anything seen before. One of Rutan's ideas for the prototype N7EZ, was a series of long-distance record attempts. In the end only one world distance record was achieved, of 1,638 miles in August 1975.

With 100 hours of test flying achieved and the many teething troubles of the new aircraft in the process of being tamed, consideration turned during the summer of 1975 to the possibility of selling plans of the design to other homebuilders. Still to be sorted out was a suitable and reliable engine, a reduction in stall speed, an improved roll control at low speeds, and the nose undercarriage leg kneeling mechanism. The main problem with the low-speed handling was the poor lift from the chosen airfoil. A new canard wing airfoil using the results of research conducted in Britain at the University of Glasgow was built and Rutan designed ailerons to be installed on the rear wing. These were the main solutions and when N7EZ was flown again the stall was lowered by 8 mph and roll rates at low speeds improved.

Construction of a second prototype was started in the winter of 1975 incorporating these developments and with a larger 100 hp Continental 0-200 fitted. Registered N4EZ, it first flew in March 1976 and eventually in July of that year, after many more hours of test flying and minor modifications, Rutan decided that the time was right to go public with the VariEze and started to sell plans to homebuilders.

By early the following year, a few enthusiastic homebuilders had already completed their VariEzes. There were, however, many further problems with the design that came to light, serving as a warning to any over-zealous homebuilder that 'all that glitters is not gold' and that 'discretion is the better part of valour', to use two well-known

Open house at the 'RAF', Mojave, during one of Burt Rutan's birthdays in the early 1980s, before the Voyager flight. (Don Downie)

Another Mojave homebuilt—two QAC Quickie IIs over the desert in the early 1980s. (Don Downie)

proverbs. Nonetheless, the Rutan design certainly changed the world of homebuilding, not only in its innovative design but also in its use of composite materials. The business Rutan established at Mojave, California, to develop and market his homebuilts, the Rutan Aircraft Factory, bought a new significance to the initials RAF! Thanks to the Rutans, Mojave was to become as famous in home-built aeroplane circles as Indianapolis in motor-racing and Ascot in horse-racing. The materials and shape revolutions in homebuilding had come together almost simultaneously, and although all those earlier exponents of the use of composites had helped to pave the way, none did it more significantly than Rutan.

The significance of Rutan's VariEze and the subsequent homebuilt designs that it spawned warrant a closer look at how the basic VariEze composite airframe is constructed, although anyone considering such a project is reminded that this is only the briefest resumé of a complex and multi-faceted science.

A VariEze's structure is glass and foam without a mould. The wings and canard foreplane are built of unidirectional glassfibre with a rigid urethane foam core, while the fuselage comprises large sheets of rigid urethane foam with wood strips as corner fillers and an internal and external covering of the same unidirectional glassfibre as used for the wings. Light alloy extrusions are fixed to the composite structure for engine and undercarriage mounts.

Glass cloth is the basic airframe raw material with multiple layers laminated together. As well as the unidirectional glassfibre, with most of the glass volume woven parallel to one edge of the cloth, there is also bidirectional cloth available. The latter is used in tight corners, whereas the unidirectional is used in areas where the primary loads are in one direction, such as on the wing skins. Laminating and strengthening the basic glassfibre is epoxy, a 'system' made up of resin and hardener, the composition of which can be varied to produce a variety of physical and working properties.

A further warning is pertinent at this stage, because not everyone can work with such materials—being basically chemicals, they have to be used with care and in the correct, almost clinical way. Some builders have experienced allergies, rashes and more serious complaints as a result of constructing with composites. It by no means effects everyone, but it is worth checking first and using barrier cream or protective gloves when working with composites.

The epoxy 'systems' have to possess workability and strength but at the same time protect the foam core from heat damage and solvent attack. Different 'systems' are used in the construction of a composite airframe such as the VariEze dependant on the type and area of work and the speed of curing that is most appropriate for that particular location. Heat is generated by the curing and as it hardens even more heat can be generated. It thus has to be used in small quantities and extremely carefully.

The filler is the next important material in composite construction. It is used to fill uneven voids, to glue foam blocks together and as a bond between foam and glass skins. Then there are the cotton fibre/epoxy mixtures for structural joints or durability, general polyester body-fillers for temporary fixtures, and the foams, which come in three main varieties.

The building techniques in composite construction are also different: hot wire cutting, which is as it sounds; foam shaping, which is basically sculpture; glass lay-up; and, overriding all these, quality control, which in glass-foam-glass composite construction such as that of the VariEze is visual because of the transparency of the finished product.

After the VariEze came the LongEze, the Defiant, and various research and experimental aircraft, and the rest, as they say, is history, culminating in the Voyager (see Chapter 17) and, in commercial aerospace, the Beechcraft Starship.

Mojave spawned another unusually-shaped homebuilt during the 1970s when Gene Sheehan and Tom Jewett approached Burt Rutan to design and develop an airframe around the small 18 hp Onan engine that they saw as the way ahead in optimum power-to-weight engines for small homebuilts. The result was the unusual Quickie, the prototype, N77Q, first flying late in 1977 in a tractor tail-less canard 'biplane' configuration. Sheenhan and Jewett formed the Quickie Aircraft Corporation (QAC) at Mojave to market this innovative single-seater composite homebuilt (soon to be developed as a side-by-side two-seater, the Q.II), but with the addition of another major innovation, that they would sell kits of the Quickie to builders. This may not have been a new phenomenon in homebuilding but was certainly a first for a composite design, as the Rutan VariEze was a plans-only aircraft.

Rubbing shoulders at Mojave there was some rivalry and cross-fertilisation between the RAF and QAC, with both organisations starting to plan ambitious project from their meagre beginnings, a non-stop unrefuelled circumnavigation of the world being the ultimate goal. Jewett was subsequently to be killed in his quest to achieve this, but the Rutans were to triumph, adding another achievement to the composite aircraft and shape revolution that they started at Mojave, California, and from which the whole world of homebuilding and aerospace in general was to reap benefits.

CHAPTER 5

The '80s and the kitplane

COMPLETE KITS FOR a full-size aeroplane have been the homebuilder's dream since the birth of the movement. In Chapter 2 we saw how the first kits were made available to those wanting to build the Heath Parasol and Irwin Meteorplane during the late 1920s in the USA. Later, in the 1930s, for $70 builders of the Pietenpol Aircamper could buy a 'kit' of wooden parts needed to construct an aircraft. Much, however, was left to the individual builder's own discretion. More recently (see Chapter 3) Ray Stits sold kits in the mid-1950s of his SA-6B Flut-R-Bug.

At one time or another many purveyors of plans and blueprints for homebuilt aircraft have dabbled either themselves or through sub-contractors in the sale of kit components to ease the task of the homebuilder. This was invariably on a small scale and of minimal benefit to the frustrated builder. However, the introduction and widespread availability of plastic model kits manufactured by companies such as Airfix and Revell during the 1950s begged the question in every homebuilder's mind: 'Why not a full-scale model kit?'.

The first 'modern' exponent to provide the answer to this was Frank L. Christensen from Afton, Wyoming, with his Christen Eagle I single-seater sport biplane which he developed into a tandem two-seater, the Eagle II. Design of the Eagle II started in June 1974, construction commenced in August 1975 and the prototype flew for the first time in February 1977. The Eagle II was designed both for commercial production and also for homebuilt construction—the aeroplane is broken down into 25 sub-assemblies or parts-kits, each kit making up a separate portion of the aircraft with everything the builder need including the all-important and very detailed construction manual. Each of these subkits is dispatched to the builder in a hermetically sealed poly-wrap, even to the extent of having a small blade stuck to the outside of the

A Christen Eagle II at Merced, California, in June 1990; this was one of the first 'modern' kitplanes. (Author)

packaging to enable the builder to cut it open upon receipt.

The beauty of this 25-kit breakdown for the Eagle II is that it enables the builder to spread the cost of construction over a period of time, to suit his particular rate of progress and perhaps more importantly, his bank balance. Christensen designed the kits for the maximum ease of construction, a builder requiring only common hand-tools and little prior knowledge and experience of aircraft construction. This is where one of homebuilding's most essential ingredients is so important—a good and comprehensive construction manual. With this and all the kits, Christensen estimates a build-time of 1,400 to 1,600 man-hours. However, although this estimate may be reasonably accurate for the Eagle II, it is the type of statistic that the experienced homebuilder will recommend to be taken with a large pinch of salt. Many purveyors of homebuilt kits will woo the unsuspecting homebuilder with promises of completion in a small number of man-hours, but invariably a first-time builder will end up taking three or four times as long as the statistic quoted in the glossy brochure that first attracted him!

Manufacture of Eagle II kits started in October 1977 and by 1990 nearly 700 complete aircraft kits had been dispatched, with about half of them known to have been completed and flown. Such comprehensive attention to detail has a price, though—in early 1991 a complete Eagle II kit was selling the $64,000, beyond the pockets of many grass-roots homebuilders, but filling a much-needed niche for those requiring a two-seater aerobatic biplane. All rights to the Eagle were sold by Christensen in 1991 to Englishman Malcolm White who continues to manufacture Eagles at Afton, Wyoming, as Aviat Inc.

The Eagle II has a conventional welded steel-tube fuselage structure which is covered by removable light alloy panels in the cockpit and engine area, then with fabric for the rear fuselage. The wings are an amalgam of wood and metal, the former for the spars and ribs and the latter for the leading and trailing edges and the I-type interplane struts. This structure is then covered in polyester fabric, and the kit even includes the well-known patented colour scheme for the finished aircraft. Power comes from a brand new 200 hp Avco Lycoming AEIO-360 flat-four engine which gives the aircraft a tremendous rate of climb (645 m or 2,120 ft/min) at sea level, and an economical cruise speed of 254 kmph/158 mph.

Nonetheless, the Eagle's skeletal airframe is totally conventional, and is in fact no different in concept from those early pre-war and post-war homebuilts. But it is its comprehensive kit status that set the standards in the 1970s and '80s by which others were to be judged.

The last chapter charted the arrival and acceptance of the use of composite construction for homebuilts, and this development also saw the introduction of a new word into the homebuilder's vocabulary – the 'Kitplane'. Whilst the Eagle II is most definitely a kitplane, it seems that it was these composite designs that made the name acceptable. Perhaps these 'plastics' equated more closely to the Airfix model kit concept of forming a fuselage by sticking two halves together. One of the first of these modern kitplanes on the market has at the same time also been one of the most successful, most sophisticated and most popular. This aircraft is the Glasair.

The name Glasair is generic, with several different models available to the homebuilder during the last decade, all the products of the Washington State-based company Stoddard-Hamilton. Unlike the Eagle II, the Glasair kits are not 100 per cent comprehensive. When the crate of parts arrives at the builder's workshop, he will still have to source and accquire an engine, instruments, avionics, upholstery and many other components. However, the airframe, undercarriage, engine-bearers, cowlings, etc, are all included in the kit and in very little building time a Glasair constructor will have a lot to show.

Whilst in his final year at the University of Washington, Tom Hamilton, who was still in his early twenties at the time, designed his own two-place tandem-seat light aeroplane, the stubby-shaped low-wing Lycoming 0-235-powered SH-1, which Tom's younger brother, Bruce, nick-named the 'Pocket Rocket' because of its small size and fast speed. Difficult to fly, it created some 'very exciting moments' during its short flying career but, despite these drawbacks, from a constructional point of view it was a very ambitious first project which established a trend that was to become the basis of Stoddard-Hamilton kitplane designs in subsequent years. Hamilton produced a full set of 'female' moulds with which to form the basic elements of the airframe and it became one of the very early composite homebuilts in the 1970s, from the same era as Burt Rutan's first mouldless VariEze.

In 1976, with the experiences of the SH-1 still fresh in his memory, Tom Hamilton started work on a new design, loosely based on the SH-1 but with his aim of achieving considerably improved performance and handling. He was assisted by his older brother Steve, a design engineer with Boeing at nearby Seattle, and with invaluable assistance from Boeing's computer design facilities and several of Tom and Steve's aeronautical engineering friends, the first aircraft design to be called Glasair crystallised.

At what was once the biggest pig farm west of the

The prototype Glasair TD, N88TH, first flew in 1979 and was the forerunner of the modern composite kitplane. It was flown to Oshkosh in July 1987 for display in the EAA Museum. (Stoddard-Hamilton)

Mississippi, but which had since been converted into an airfield, construction work on the first S-H Glasair TD (tail-dragger) started in 1978. Claimed as the world's first pre-moulded composite kitplane, the Glasair TD prototype N88TH first flew from the 'pig farm' in 1979, powered by the same 115 hp Avco Lycoming 0-235 flat-four engine that had been used in the SH-1. This prototype's significance was demonstrated when it was flown to Oshkosh, Wisconsin, in July 1987 for display in the EAA's Museum.

Stoddard-Hamilton's facilities were somewhat basic in 1979–80 but their overheads were low and with plenty of youthful enthusiasm and an aircraft that was living up to its creators' expectations, people began to take notice. A second prototype was built, N89SH, this time fitted with a larger 150 hp Avco Lycoming 0-320 engine and a higher canopy. Completed in late 1980, the two Glasair prototypes were extensively tested over the next two years. In July 1981 the Glasair TD was flown to the EAA's Oshkosh Fly-In where it was awarded the 'Outstanding New Design' accolade, and the homebuilt aircraft world, until then embroiled in the hype of the Rutan 'canard' designs, began to look towards Washington State and the sleek but more conventional Glasair kits as another avenue down which to travel in pursuit of new homebuilt ideals.

The top-of-the-range Glasair, the Glasair III, first flew in July 1986, and this model provides the classic kitplane photograph reproduced here with the finished product behind and its component parts laid out in front. The basic configuration and structure of this and all the preceding Glasair TD and RG models is side-by-side seating for two, a tapered cantilever low one-piece wing built of glassfibre and foam composite with a continuous main spar of moulded glassfibre, four ribs per wing, and skins of glassfibre coated with gelcoat. Options are available with wing-tip winglets, wing-tip extensions and larger fuel tankage.

The fuselage construction is very much like that of the wings, comprising the two main composite half-shells and a belly panel, with only the firewall and two bulkheads. These apparently minimal structures give amazing strength, now being cleared for g limits at 1,600 lbs (726 kg) AUW and for +6/−4. Aerobatics, particularly in the more powerful Glasair III, are part of its appeal, and ex-US Aerobatics Champion Bob Herendeen is frequently to be seen aerobating the G.III prototype at US airshows and fly-ins (see page 89).

The tail is a conventional cantilever unit constructed, like the wings, of composites, with an integeral fin swept back from the rear fuselage and a fixed tab on the rudder. Many options exist within this basic framework and, as with any homebuilt,

A completed Glasair III together with a set of typical kit components. (Author)

The Glasair III prototype which first flew in July 1986.

the individual builder's own idyosyncracies will make every Glasair that little bit different.

The first five TD kits were fabricated at the 'pig farm', followed by another five during which a move to bigger premises took place; the offices and R & D remained at the 'pig farm' close to Boeing's Renton facility until 1984. As interest and sales of the Glasair product grew rapidly, the entire operation was then moved 50 miles north to Stoddard-Hamilton's present headquarters at Arlington Airfield, Washington; they now have 50 employees, 20,000 sq ft of manufacturing space and 14,000 sq ft of office and hangar space.

Tom Hamilton met Ted Setzer at the University of Washington whilst they were studying dentistry, and after Setzer had completed a period of commercial fishing in Alaska he returned to Washington to join Hamilton in his aeronautical endeavours. Tom's brother Bruce managed the tooling and manufacturing and was instrumental in developing the new processes involved in manufacturing the Glasair airframe. The fourth member of the Glasair 'team' was aero engineer and test pilot Bob Gavinsky, an integral part of the design team and also invaluable for ironing out some of the problems once the prototypes were flying. Commenting on this last member of the team, Setzer says, 'Wouldn't it be great if all engineers had to do their own test flying—it sure forces them to be accurate in their work!'

In July 1982 Stoddard-Hamilton flew their Glasair RG for the first time, a tri-gear retractable version of the established kitplane, just in time to make that year's Oshkosh Fly-In. The RG was designed, like the TD before it, to be powered by engines such as the 160 and 180 hp Avco Lycoming flat-fours, which the builder had to accquire separately from the kit. The next model addition was the Glasair FT (fixed tricycle) which first flew in February 1985 and was a cheaper-to-build model; it was basically an RG but with the retractable tri-gear replaced by a stylish, faired and spatted non-retractable tricycle undercarriage. In 1986 all of these basic Glasair models were superseded by refined and updated models, the Glasair IIs, and in a relatively short history the company had delivered 700 kits worldwide, with at least 120 examples known to have flown by then.

A completed Glasair II would cruise at 200 mph on 55 per cent power and when the 'IIs' were first introduced a kit cost about $15,000 plus freighting charges. To help builders with the relatively expensive task of buying and building their aircraft, Stoddard-Hamilton introduced their 'System 4 Ownership' deal. Each Glasair type is divided into four separate kits that make project financing easier, reduce the amount of storage and workshop space required and enable the construction rate to be tailored more precisely to a builder's individual requirements—Stoddard-Hamilton will even prepare sub-kits of the four major kits to aid particular builders.

With the demise of the US light aircraft industry, more and more light aircraft owners are turning to kitplanes in the 1980s and '90s to fulfil their aircraft requirements. A goodly proportion of these, having the finance but not the time to construct these kits themselves, have employed local fixed-base operators to construct their aircraft for them. Howie Keefe, former air-race pilot and holder of the 6 hr 21 min record for a flight between Los Angeles and Washington, DC, in his P-51 Mustang, is one such person. His Glasair RG II was built for him by Dick

Loading tests on a wing of a Glasair at Stoddart-Hamilton's factory at Washington, DC.

Dobson, and although not quite a Mustang it is the nearest practical aircraft to it, being able to cruise at 240 mph at 8,000 feet over a range of 1,100 statute miles behind its 180 hp Lycoming IO-360 at a fuel burn of 9.5 gph (25 mpg). Keefe's comprehensively equipped Glasair is conservatively valued at $149,000 and was an Oshkosh 'Outstanding Workmanship' award winner several years ago.

In 1991 the cheapest Glasair kit is the Glasair II-S TD at $16,900—the top-of-the-range Glasair III is $33,500. The II-S models were introduced in 1990 and incorporated features including a stretched fuselage length, hence the 'S' designation. These kits contain all the glassfibre parts and fabrication materials, the windshield and canopies, extruded control hinges and innumerable parts unique to the designs including the spar and wing attachment fittings, the canopy latching system, control springs and specially machined control fittings. It is still claimed to be one of the most comprehensive composite kitplane kits available, and when the Glasair II models appeared Stoddard-Hamilton also introduced a considerably simplified construction process, lopping an estimated 40 per cent off the build-time from their original kits.

No mention of Glasairs would be complete without a look at the Glasair III, the veritable Spitfire of the homebuilt world. Conceived as long ago as

The Glasair II-S RG introduced in 1991 by Stoddard-Hamilton.

Dave Morgan and his Glasair III kitplane, the first to be completed by a customer in the USA.

1984–85, the prototype N54ORG was first flown just before Oshkosh 1986. Bob Gavinsky describes the III's 6 hr 20 min, 1,800-mile flight from Seattle to Oshkosh that year: 'The aeroplane flew really well. At 2,250 rpm on its 300 hp Lycoming IO-540 engine, the cruise was between 250 and 290 mph ground speed depending on altitude which was generally between 11,500 and 17,500 feet. It's a bit like flying a little fighter—I've never flown a P.51 Mustang but would like to think that the Glasair III is comparable on a slightly lesser scale.'

A steady trickle of Glasair IIIs have been completed in the USA, and in Britain one has been built at the College of Aeronautics, Cranfield. Whilst the restrictions on US builders of aircraft such as the Glasair III are few and they can be flown in IFR conditions, the guardians of homebuilding in Britain, the Popular Flying Association (PFA), will not at the time of writing sanction 'amateur' construction of kitplanes or homebuilts such as the Glasair III (see Chapter 9, page 119). Their limitations include a maximum engine capacity of 180 hp and they restrict aircraft built under their 'Permit' system to VFR/non-airways operations. The British Glasair III was built under direct jurisdiction of the CAA, but despite this is still a homebuilt, albeit the ultimate in sophistication and speed.

Many world class records have been broken by the Glasair III. Over 1,150 kits had been delivered by 1991 and Stoddard-Hamilton have bought new standards of excellence to the world of the homebuilt and kit aeroplane. They have shown what a committed, soundly run, properly financed and dynamic company with a good product can do. They have upheld the ideals of the US light aircraft industry whilst Cessna and their compatriots have all but deserted it in their class. Using the Glasair III airframe, Stoddard-Hamilton even tried to move out of the amateur market into military trainers—their turbo-powered development, the AT-9 Stalker, had a 420 shp Allison 250-B.17D turboprop engine which gave the aircraft a normal cruise speed of 366 mph (589 kmph) and a never-exceed speed of 403 mph (649 kmph). The prototype, N253LC, first flew in July 1988 and, like several other homebuilt and kitplane designs, was seen as a contender in a growing military market for aircraft of this type in training and utility work (see Chapter 6).

Another composite, two-seater kitplane from the USA that is also proving very popular with builders throughout the world is at the other end of the spectrum from the Glasairs. This is the side-by-side two-seater Aero Designs Pulsar and more recent Pulsar XP. Emanating from the San Antonio area of Texas, Aero Designs Inc is the 'baby' of graduate aerospace engineer Mark Brown. The Pulsar kit differs from the Glasairs in three main respects:

1. It is a less sophisticated and easier-to-build kitplane
2. This simplicity results in a cheaper aircraft to build and fly
3. The kit which Aero Designs supply is virtually complete including the engine

Mark Brown summarises the Pulsar thus: 'We've broken the build-time barrier with a top quality, pre-moulded kit; and we've controlled the cost by keeping it simple. It doesn't have a six-cylinder Lycoming or a disappearing landing gear, lots of bells and whistles! But if you fly for fun then you've found the way—the Pulsar'.

This, you may say, is typical of the overly optimistic sales hype that many homebuilt and

An AT-9 Stalker flying over Washington State having just set a new world STOL speed record.

kitplane purveyors have spouted over the last 20 years, many of them American and many of them failing to live up to expectations. True—but putting my head firmly on the block I honestly believe that Mark Brown has got it right with the Pulsar. I saw and flew the prototype in 1989 and thought that then—three years later I still believe it and hope that you will come to understand why by looking at the history and development of the design and at the aircraft itself both in construction and in the air.

Mark Brown obtained an Aerospace engineering degree and went on to do post-graudate studies in finite element analysis and composites (finite element analysis is a detailed computer method of analysing loads and stresses). He then started an eight-year period involved with commercial aircraft manufacturers, first Aero Commander, where he designed a new wing for their 690-series twin; then on to LTV-Dallas, working on the manoeuvring flap system for their A-7 jet; followed by four years at

Aero Designs Inc's beautifully streamlined, economic yet efficient two-seater Pulsar composite kitplane.

Fairchild where he processed the specifications for FAA certification of aircraft composites. This work, as well as other structural analysis within the aircraft industry, eventually helped him to qualify as a fully approved and registered professional aeronautical engineer and in turn assisted in his appointment as a FAA Designated Engineering Representative, a highly respected and responsible position.

It was while Brown was working on composite structures at Fairchild that he saw their full possibilities for homebuilt aircraft applications, such as the use of pre-pregnated glassfibre and foam sandwich structure for fuselage and empenage—this was during the late 1970s when the composite revolution was already well under way (see Chapter 4). He set himself the objective of designing a very simple, economical and efficient single-seater recreational aircraft—simplicity and economy were to be based on the use of a two-cycle, ultralight, high power-to-weight ratio engine, and the efficiency of the design would be based on aerodynamic cleanliness and light weight through the use of advanced composite structures. This aircraft was the Star-Lite, the prototype of which first flew on 17 May 1983. It was also built with the specific intention of participating in the 1983 ARV (air recreation vehicle) competition organised by *The Western Flyer Magazine* and sponsored by DuPont's Kevlar Division , the EAA and AOPA. The Star-Lite won the ARV contest as well as being selected as the 'Outstanding New Design' by the EAA at their Oshkosh '83 Convention.

It is all very well designing and building a one-off prototype, but many dreamers in the world of homebuilts and kitplanes fail when it comes to translating their initial ideas into efficient and practical production. This is nowhere more evident than with composite aircraft, as the high-temperature moulds and other tooling necessary to ensure a high-standard, quality controlled component product each time around is very expensive. The 'finance gap', the gap between producing the initial aircraft product, the extensive test and development work and the start of substantial cash-flow into the business to counteract the vast capital outlays, is a real test of resolve. It is a daunting time, particularly for those impoverished, undercapitalised aviators who really should have been content with leaving well alone after the flight of their prototype.

It took Mark Brown over a year to complete tooling so as to be in a position to offer customers their first Star-Lite kits, production starting in August 1984. With a production rate of one kit per week and the Star-Lite being offered in both tail-dragger and tri-gear configuration, it was the start of a 120-kit production run that was to continue for five years. Part of the Star-Lite's success was its use of the 40 hp two-cylinder Rotax 447 engine, a very light yet punchy performer that had been proved by the American microlight (ultralight) fraternity in a variety of designs. It gave the Star-Lite a cruise speed on 75 per cent power of 120 mph and a range at 65 per cent power of 400 miles, albeit quite noisy—a VW or Continental 'jockey' also had to get used to the rpm gauge reading of 3,000 in the taxi and 6,000 whilst cruising—cylinder-head temperatures of 350° F and exhaust gas temperatures of 1,220° F also take some getting used to. The high rpm, though, is the engine speed, the propeller turning at slightly less than half that speed.

A sobering reminder of the responsibilities and tragedies of the world of homebuilding came in late 1986 when a Star-Lite crashed in the USA, killing its pilot. Brown immediately called all Star-Lite owners and told them to ground their aircraft. After meetings with the FAA investigators, Brown determined that the probable cause of the accident had been aileron flutter caused by an unauthorised modification to part of the right aileron linkage; the right wing separated from the fuselage before it hit the ground. Brown was understandably shocked but immediately set about devising an inspection procedure to ensure that no other Star-Lites could have excessive play in their aileron system.

The Star-Lite design attracted the attention of several British builders and two of the first were Southampton-based Paul Clifton and Alan Clarke. In the garage of Paul's house, their Star-Lite (tail-dragger version) quickly took shape in 1988—a visitor to the workshop at this time was Martin Faro, who tried the 80 per cent complete Star-Lite for size, declared his liking for the aircraft and promptly ordered a kit. Both the British Star-Lite's first flew in 1990 and Martin's G-FARO (tri-gear version) went on to win the PFA's Don Foreman Trophy for the 'Best Composite Aircraft' at the Cranfield '90 rally. During the building process, the PFA in Britain carried out their 'vetting' of the design, a standard procedure prior to their granting type approval for any homebuilt design in Britain (see Chapter 9 for further details), an approval that the Star-Lite design subsequently aspired to. (A detailed résumé of building a Star-Lite kit is given in Chapter 15).

The Star-Lite proved to be a victim of its own success and Mark Brown soon realised that the market for the aircraft was becoming saturated— in any case he felt a more sociable two-seater version was what was now required, and started design work on the side-by-side two-seater Pulsar, already mentioned. As with the Star-Lite he considered that above all else it had to be simple to build and fly, and as a complementary goal it should also be economical to operate and aerodynamically efficient. As

The tail-dragger version of the single-seater Star-Lite during construction by Paul Clifton and Alan Clarke at Southampton in March 1988—it was completed as G-SOLA. (Author)

Brown told me, 'The technical approach to these goals was high tech, state-of-the-art construction materials—oven-cured pre-pregnated composites—and a super-simple lightweight engine that turned out to be the Rotax 582 dual ignition engine. As with all other modern homebuilts, the Pulsar achieves excellent performance on low power through its relatively small size—resulting in low wetted area and low drag—and its low weight.

'Pulsar tooling started in January 1987 and again the time and tooling cost was my biggest problem. The Pulsar prototype (N500SS) first flew in April 1988 and a few days later I roaded it from Texas to the EAA's Sun'n'Fun Fly-In at Lakeland, Florida, because I hadn't flown off sufficient hours for my permit yet wanted to debut it at this major show. Response was fantastic—a major encouragement that you've got the correct formula—and delivery and production kits began to appear in July that year. The production rate built up to one kit per week and by May 1990 we'd delivered 75 Pulsar kits. One of the biggest challenges with any kit or

Martin Faro won the award for the 'Best Composite Aircraft' with his Star-Lite at Cranfield in 1990. (Author)

Above left *The basic Marco J-5 kit which in Europe includes the KFM engine.* (Author)

Left *The Marco J-5 in flight.* (Author)

Above *The super-efficient Flash III composite two/three-seater from Luxembourg.* (Author)

Below *Developed in Canada is this sleek four-seater amphibian homebuilt, the Seawind 2000. This one was built in Florida by Dick Moore and was the first of the type to fly.* (Author)

homebuilt is to provide the builder with an easy-to-read yet totally comprehendable and comprehensive manual and then to keep it up to date with all the short cuts and amendments that builders come up with—even many years after the first flight of a homebuilt design, that design evolves, like any manufactured product. I like to think that the Pulsar builders manual is one of the best around, a fact I think you'll find any Pulsar builder will verify.'

A detailed breakdown of the philosophy behind and practical detail of the Pulsar's design and construction is given in Chapter 15. A comparison is also made with a two-seat Cessna 150.

The plethora of kitplanes available to the prospective homebuilder in the 1980s and '90s is daunting. Continuing with some of the composite kitplanes, there are two European designs that represent opposite ends of the spectrum. Designed in Poland, built in Germany and marketed from France, the single-seater Marco J-5 is a truly international kitplane. Developed by Jaroslaw Janowski in Poland as the wood/fabric high-wing pusher-engined J-1 Don Kichot (Don Quixote) which first flew in 1970, the Marco J-5 was developed from this by the Marko Electronic Company who manufactured some component glassfibre and epoxy parts. Marco then exported them to Hewa Technics in Germany who completed the kits and also manufactured complete aircraft. Aviasud Engineering in Frejus, France, have been the main distributors in Europe. The Marco J-5 is almost a sailplane-like design with a single mainwheel and wing-tip outrider undercarriage wheels, v-tail and 30 hp KFM 107ER pusher engine.

In contrast, but also constructed like the Marco—and the Pulsar and Glasairs—is one of the few indigenous designs to come from Luxembourg—the Wolff Sky-Wolff. Starting as a three-seater low-wing tri-gear long-range cabin tourer, Paul Wolff first built his proof-of-concept Wolff Flash III in 1984 and '85. It had tip-tanks and a standard range with two persons and baggage of 2,045 miles (3,291 kms). Wolff considered that the production kits should be full four-seaters and set about a major modification of the design, unveiling the new Sky-Wolff at Florida's EAA Sun'n'Fun Fly-In in April 1989, having shipped and roaded the as yet unflown prototype (LX-LPW) across the Atlantic. Wolff Aircraft Engineering Inc was set up in California with the intention of manufacturing and marketing Sky-Wolff kits in the USA. Sadly, though, the future of the Sky-Wolff project is now uncertain as Paul Wolff was killed in 1990 whilst test flying the aircraft.

Another ambitious kitplane project is the Canadian-designed Seawind 2000, a four-seat amphibian design with the single tractor engine mounted high on the tail as on a Trislander. In 1973 Len and Roger Creelman wanted an amphibian for business and pleasure and considered commercially produced types too expensive and homebuilt types inadequate in seating and performance. They consequently built two prototypes from wood and aluminium to test the hull design on water, but had to wait until 1978 for the Canadian Department of Transportation to relax its ban on the construction of composite homebuilts. In August 1982 they flew a third example, the composite production prototype. The Seawind is constructed of glassfibre, vinylester and PVC foam composites, materials which enable the easy manufacture and construction of its beautiful streamlined shape. It took the next six years to perfect the design and to tool up for the manufacture and sale of kits, now the responsibility of Seawind International Inc at Haliburton in Ontario. Power is preferably supplied by a 200 hp Lycoming IO-360 and provides a true four-seater amphibian capable of a cruise speed of 165 mph (266 kmph) and a 1,200-mile (1,931 km) range—but it is likely to set a builder back anything up to US$100,000.

Completing the 'big-boys' in the kitplane world, and in the same sort of price range, is the Cirrus VK-30, another US design that first flew in February 1988 at Baraboo, Wisconsin. This stylish four/five-seater has a tail-mounted propeller powered by an engine mounted within the fuselage—a 290 hp Lycoming IO-540 is suggested, although Don Brose's California-built example has a 250 hp Allison turbine installed. By 1991 several US examples had flown, but none have yet appeared in Europe.

Details of other composite kitplanes currently available are given in Appendix 6. Some of the more popular types, mostly of US origin, are the Aero-Composite Sea Hawker, a two-seater amphibian; the Aero Mirage TC-2 two-seater; and another amphibian, the four-seater Freedom Master Air Shark. Probably worth a book on its own is Neico Aviation's extremely popular Lancair series of two-seater designs, complemented in 1990 by the appearance of the beautiful Lancair IV four-seater. Lancairs are now available in Europe via the exclusive European distributors in Lugano, Switzerland, Aerotech SA, who took the bold step of displaying a Lancair at 1990's SBAC Farnborough Air Show.

Rights to a former US composite kitplane, the motor-glider Silhouette, were purchased in 1989 by Lunds Tekniske in Norway, bringing yet another European country into the kitplane forum. Nat Puffer's three-seat version of the Rutan LongEz, his side-by-side-seat Cozy, is another composite kitplane design that has deserted its US origins to be taken up by European interests—Uli and Linda Wolters in Germany now market mainly plans for the type, although some kit components are available. The four-seater Cozy IV can be built from

The debut of the first British-built example of the Cozy at Cranfield in 1989. (Author)

plans available in the USA. Similar is the four-seat 'canard', the Velocity, Dan Maher's brainchild from his headquarters at Sebastian in Florida. A development of the kitplane, the Velocity 173 was announced by Maher in 1991 and is intended to fill the gap that non-availability of new production Cessna 172 has left.

From Glasair country in Washington State, Ken Wheeler introduced his four-seater Wheeler Express in 1987, but in 1990 went through a very rough patch with a couple of crashes and possible liquidation of his company. Despite these problems the Express is very much alive and kits are available. Finally comes another four-seater, Nick Jones's White Lightning, another hot-rod with a 250 mph cruise speed behind a 210 hp Continental IO-360.

These are some of the main designs, although

N141NH was the second Maher Velocity to be flown. A four-seater composite 'canard', it is typical of high-performance kitplanes. (Author)

Despite a forced landing on the central reservation of US Route 40 at Wilmington, Delaware, in September 1986, Nick Jones's White Lightning was soon back in the air and the problematical fuel management error sorted out. N100WL is a four-seater composite kitplane. (Author)

British readers should be warned that few of them are approved or even eligible under the PFA's Approved Aircraft Designs listing. There is nothing to say, though, that you couldn't be the first, either dealing through the PFA or directly with the CAA!

The Pulsar is close to the ideal of the plane for the man in the street. Although looking considerably more sophisticated and expensive than in fact it is, real grass-roots homebuilt and kitplane aviators might prefer something more rugged, particularly if they have to operate from grass or dirt strips. The 1980s, as well as seeing the acceptance and proliferation of composite kitplanes, also heralded the start of the 'Cub-a-like revolution'.

Piper's commercially manufactured Piper Cub and similar types such as the Taylorcraft and Aeronca were built in large numbers during the Second World War, and became available as surplus in vast numbers not only in the late 1940s but on through the following decades as air forces around the world finally disposed of these basic liaison and army observation types. Particularly in the USA, many of them were also built after the war in various marques for the civil market, and during the resurgence of civil pilot training in the 1950s and early '60s it is a fair bet that more than two-thirds of student pilots did their first flying in either a Cub or an Aeronca.

The microlight and ultralight revolution started in the late 1970s and early '80s when sport aviators started to attach small domestic and industrial-use engines to conventional hang gliders. Developments were rapid, both in the design of airframes and also of engines. In particular it was the high power-to-weight ratio Rotax engines, built by the Bombardier company and first utilised for powering snow-mobiles in Austria and Canada, that helped to change the face of this aspect of aviation. Rotax is now probably the world's largest producer of light piston engines (see Chapter 8).

It seemed that everyone in the 1980s was designing and building microlight/ultralight aircraft that roughly resembled the ubiquitous Piper Cub. Two-seater and single-seater versions were available for the homebuilder and kitplane builder, some made of wood and fabric and some, like the original Cub (fuselage anyway), from metal tube with fabric covering. There was the Wag-Aero Cubby, Jesse Anglin's J-3 Kitten, Mike Fisher's Koala and Super Koala, Light Miniature's single-seat Cub and Aeronca 'replicas', the Protech PT-2, etc.

Another such design was the work of Dan Denney at Boise, Idaho, his Kitfox design very quickly gaining in popularity and assuming a generic name like the Cub. Denney was a medical administrator in the US Air Force and learned to fly in a military aero club whilst based in Spain. During the late '70s and early '80s he started building a Smyth Sidewinder homebuilt, completing about 25 per cent of the work but estimating that he needed at least another 1,500 hours work to put it in the air. This did not encourage him, so he set to work on designing his own quick-build homebuilt, a side-by-side two-seater high-wing tail-dragger, the Avid Flyer. Denney subsequently wanted to make many alterations and amendments to this design to meet his own fast-evolving specifications of the ideal kitplane in this category, so he parted company with his partners in the Avid Flyer and started building his much modified version. This was the Kitfox, which he first flew in 1984 and in which during the next two years he accumulated 450 hours' flight time, representing 65 per cent of his total logged piloting time. His prototype (N84DD) was fitted with the 52 hp Rotax 503 which gave good performance, but later he added the Mk II version with the 65 hp Rotax 532 engine. This second prototype (N85DD) converted good performance into the 'spectacular' category as far as climb, take-off run and handling were concerned. During the first nine months of 1986 Denney sold 55 Kitfox kits, a high percentage of which were completed and flown—a common problem with homebuilts is that a builder's initial enthusiasm soon wanes, as in the case of Denney's own Sidewinder. This high completion figure was proof that Denney had got the formula right.

Five years later, in 1991, Denney was passing an historic landmark with the Kitfox, notching up his 1,000th sale and establishing the Denney Aerocraft Company as the world's biggest aircraft producer by numbers, and also the fastest-growing aircraft company in the world. He is now building aircraft kits at the rate of 50 per month and shipping them all around the world. A complete kit (including engine and basic instruments) in early 1991 was selling for $19,000—British agents, Junipa Sales (Aviation) Ltd at Wisbech in Cambridgeshire, were selling the kits at this time for customers to pick up from their works at £10,800. Brian Davies, Junipa's Managing Director, told me, 'There are now 83 Kitfoxes in Britain, 62 of which we've sold in the last couple of years. It's a record we're proud of as it represents nearly ten percent of worldwide sales of the kit'. Asked about the Kitfox itself, he said, 'Denney has continually modified, improved and updated the design since Day 1. He has just introduced the Mk III version with a gross weight increased from 950 to 1,050 lbs, a lengthened fuselage, an enlarged and re-designed fin and rudder, and now suitable for the larger 79 hp Rotax 912 four-cylinder four-stroke engine, the first that Rotax has designed and built specifically for the aircraft industry. This Mk III Kitfox can transport two fairly large people plus fuel and some baggage and is ideal for anyone considering fitting the Denney add-on option kits of skis or floats? (Newer, more recent Mk IV and Speedster versions are also now available.)

The worldwide sales of the Kitfox have included a deal with the Philippine Aircraft Company who have a licence to build and sell assembled aircraft there. A large sale has also been concluded to government agencies in Mexico. For British builders considering the Kitfox, the good news is that the design is fully approved by the PFA for amateur construction and operation under a 'Permit to Fly'. They recommended several small modifications to Denney's basic kit, but Junipa and Britain's other Kitfox agents, Border Aviation, sell all their kits in Britain with this modification package included. Once a customer's kit arrives he requires few specialised tools, the 4130 steel tubing fuselage frame being already completely welded—around 500 hours construction-time is probably a realistic figure for an average builder, and at 1991 prices a builder can have one of the cheapest and most practical new aeroplanes around, including a radio and instrumentation, for about £14,000 plus his building time. This is another example of a modern kitplane bringing aviation in a practical form to the proverbial man in the street.

Fortunately Britain also has a contender in the kitplane marketplace. David Cook pioneered many facets of microlighting in Britain, inspired partly by the far-sighted American homebuilder Volmer Jensen. In 1983 Cook flew the prototype of his Shadow two-seater microlight, a tandem-seat high-wing, tri-geared aircraft with a pusher engine (again a

Dan Denney alongside his Kitfox Mk II at Sun'n'Fun in 1989. (Author)

Kitfoxes can easily be fitted with floats to broaden still further a homebuilder's flying experience. (Author)

Rotax) mounted at the back of the fuselage and the tail supported on a tubular boom that protrudes out of the trailing edge of the wing. Looking like a cross between a microlight and a conventional aeroplane, the CFM (Cook Flying Machines) Shadow is available as a complete aircraft as well as in kit form.

A top-of-the range Shadow kit in 1991 with a 64 hp engine retails at just under £12,000—again this is a complete kit, like the Kitfox and Pulsar, and is also an approved PFA design in Britain. Further details of building a Shadow are given in Chapter 16.

Dreams of flying an aircraft he has built himself will always haunt the aviator. For those who give up dreaming and take that extra step, the homebuilt aeroplane will either make or break them—but helping to reduce those in the latter category are the kitplanes. The 1980s saw the kitplane develop and mature from uncertain and doubtful beginnings to professional and practical aeroplanes. With the commercial light aircraft production demise in the USA in the 1980s, it is the kitplane that is taking light aviation into the 21st century, a major achievement for the world's homebuilt aircraft movement.

CHAPTER 6

Kit-cubs, crop-dusters and battledress

HOMEBUILTS AND KITPLANES have now established themselves as the strongest force in light aviation. From a position where homebuilders and their products were scoffed at and ridiculed by the ill-informed, the history of light aviation in the last three decades has seen the industry—for it now has a very significant annual turnover and workforce throughout the world—come full circle.

This is no better illustrated than with the Piper Cub, which was introduced in 1937 as the Piper J-3 Cub, a modified version of the Taylor J-2. In the next ten years nearly 22,000 examples were built; 5,673 were used for Army liaison duties (the L-4 series), while variants in subsequent years included the PA-18 Super Cub, which itself was a development of the PA-11 with enlarged tail, flaps, twin wing tanks and a variety of engines from 95 up to 150 hp. Military versions of the PA-18 were also built in large numbers—the L-18 had a 95 hp and the L-21 a 125 hp engine.

FAA Type Approval of the Super Cub was achieved on 18 November 1949. Production of the type was continuous until the early 1980s, a minor record in itself, after which although you could still buy a new Super Cub, it was to special order only. Christen Industries (see Chapter 5) of Afton, Wyoming, took up the design in 1985 as their A-1 Husky and, although externally similar to the Super Cub, it was a completely new design. There was, however, still a strong but specialised market for the Super Cub-type aircraft, well illustrated by the abundance of Cub-alike homebuilt/kitplane designs that appeared on the market during the 1980s (see page 74).

At the EAA's Sun'n'Fun Fly-In at Lakeland, Florida, in April 1988, Piper's new owner, Stuart Millar, made the announcement that the PA-18 Super Cub would soon be back in production—at the same time he announced a new version of the PA-28 Cherokee, the Cadet, all part of his plan to help stimulate light aircraft production in the USA and, of course, the famous Piper Aircraft Corporation itself.

The announcement about the Super Cub was doubly interesting to homebuilders because it was to be available in kit form as well as a finished aircraft. A new precedent was also established with the FAA in the USA, which agreed to allow Super Cub kits to be licensed with a standard airworthiness certificate instead of the usual experimental designation. This meant that 'amateur'-built Super Cubs could be used for hire or reward, crop-dusting, banner towing, flight instruction or glider towing.

Pre-fabricated kits of several Piper designs had previously been manufactured, but for assembly in several South American countries.

The orders came flooding in to Piper's Vero Beach factory in Florida where Cub production had taken place before its cessation and was now resuscitated. All-new tooling and jigs were provided at Vero Beach and the first Super Cub kit left the factory late in 1988 with production of kit and factory-built examples sold out until mid-1989. Exactly who the purchasers of these kits were is not clear because they were not cheap. Without an engine, $24,195 was the early-'89 asking price, and $35,395 with a Lycoming 0-320-A2B engine included.

The PA-18 kit arrives at the builder's workshop in nine boxes, with the parts required first being packed at the top of the box. A comprehensive and extremely detailed builder's manual is also provided. The kit is 99 per cent comprehensive except for tools, paint and radio, and in the USA and Canada builders can arrange with Piper for their licensed representatives to make the two mandatory visits to inspect the aircraft during construction that will then qualify the finished product for a standard FAA airworthiness certificate. The first

The famous Super Cub was re-introduced by the Piper Aircraft Corporation in 1988 – as a kitplane! (Piper Aircraft Corporation)

inspection is pre-cover and the second a final inspection that includes a first flight test to ensure that the inspector is happy with all he has checked and that no mods have been made! An additional charge is made for these checks.

Piper's welders put in about 300 hours of TIG welding in manufacturing the tubular metal Super Cub airframe before the kits leave the factory. They also paint the rear fuselage frame white for easier identification of cracks that might subsequently occur. The main structure of the wings has changed from the older, commercially produced versions. The wooden spars and ribs had disappeared to be replaced by aluminium parts, although some wooden components are still used, including the hard-wood wing-tip bows, still made by the original supplier. All the smaller parts arrive in the kit marked and packed in vacuum-sealed plastic bags and, where appropriate, primed and painted. Pre-sewn covers made of Ceconite 7600 cloth are

Moulins, France, 1989, and amongst a posse of Avid aircraft was this tri-gear version of the Avid Flyer in a semi-military colour scheme. (Author)

included. Wheels, tyres, control stick, wiring, propeller, etc, are all included in the kit.

Piper's efforts were well-intentioned but suffered during 1990 from a cash-flow problem, despite a very healthy order-book. 1991 started with take-over discussions; French aerospace manufacturer Aerospatiale's Socata subsidiary was at one time cited as being a possible buyer. Most recently, production in Canada has emerged as Piper's most likely saviour – whether the Cub in kit form will be part of the new inventory remains to be seen. The prospect for Piper's survival were not good, though. Whether the Super Cub will survive as a kitplane/homebuilt option in the future is not yet clear—the continuing interest in Cub-alikes such as the Kitfox and Avid Flyer and the re-entry of the 50-year-old Taylorcraft design to production are clear indications that the homebuilt, kitplane and light aircraft industry has gone full circle.

Battledress

Israel's use of microlights for counter-insurgency attacks, and a variety of other commercial or military applications such as crop-dusting, illustrates a viable role for the cheap, easy-to-build flying machine. Economies in many air forces are precluding the expenditure of hundreds of thousands of pounds for each aircraft. Finland, for instance, has spent US$365,000 per unit for 30 Valmet Leko trainers with 200 hp engines, fixed gear and moderate performance.

Alfred Scott, President of the Sequoia Aircraft Corporation, which markets plans and kits for the Italian-designed all-wood Falco, says on the subject, 'I'm always astonished at the amount of money some countries spend on indigenously-produced aircraft—Finland is a recent example. So much money is needed for design and tooling for often limited production. For a while I had an International Military Sales Representative in Washington DC. He knew the military market well and tried hard to break into it with Falco plans and kits but inevitably pointed out that all the foreign purchasing officers had many inducements and fringe benefits bestowed upon them by the 'big' companies they were dealing with. We soon realised that to play in this arena we had to play the same game as everyone else. It's not my scene and company economies precluded it anyway.

'I'm obviously biased but I think that building the Falco as a military trainer in a Third World country, where there's cheap labour, is a sensible proposition particularly when you consider the popularity of the similar, also Stelio Frati-designed, SF.260 in such countries. From my point of view breaking into these kind of countries is essentially a marketing problem—we do hear from governments around the world from time to time but you can't push on a string.'

Alfred Scott and Sequoia Aircraft Corporation's one breakthrough has been with the Chilean Air Force in South America. Like many countries, Chile was seeking to establish its own aircraft industry, following Embraer's example in Brazil. They got going initially as IndAir, set up in 1980 by the Chilean Air Force (CAF), in a deal with Piper Aircraft receiving and building kits of 27 Piper PA-28 Dakotas. In 1984 ENAER was formed by a decision of the Chilean Government, which although a separate company is entirely a military organisation composed of officers and enlisted men. Englishman Graham Gates was in charge of the new Piper project at ENAER, designing and building the Pillan,

Making its debut at the 1987 RSA rally at Brienne was this crop-dusting version of the Croses Airplume kitplane. (Author)

a tandem two-seater fully aerobatic trainer developed from many components found in the PA-28 Dakota and the PA-32 Saratoga. But this was a different type of kitplane, outside the scope of this book.

General Maté, second in command of the CAF, was the man behind the decision to embark on a Falco 'homebuilt' project. Chile is somewhat Prussian with a strong European population, many of them of German origin. Sequoia's Alfred Scott explains the rest of the story: 'The General said, "Why don't we build a Falco?", and everyone clicked their heels and said "Aye-aye-, sir"—that was the end of the decision process. I was contacted by the CAF Mission in Washington DC and all my contacts were with them, a very nice bunch of people who had a large office on Connecticut Avenue overlooking the Hilton Hotel. We shipped them the Falco kits and plans that were available around 1982 and then followed several years of construction during which time I had lots of contact with the Chileans. At that time our kits and construction manual were still in their very early stages [see Chapter 11 for full details of building a Sequoia Falco] and I was struggling to keep up with their demand. There was also a problem because some of the kits we shipped to them couldn't be found. After a year and a half of interminable phone calls, they eventually turned up in one of their warehouses in Washington! This didn't help with the speed of the Falcos' construction, which was further complicated by poor communications with the crew building the plane in Chile. They spoke only Spanish and if they had a question about some aspect of its construction, it would be relayed to a Colonel who spoke poor English and little familiarity with technical translation and the details of the construction. Sometimes his questions would be direct from Chile, but most were relayed through their Washington office. I would frequently have to guess at the *real* question because often it didn't make sense—we would then translate the answer into Spanish, back down the chain of communications to the actual Falco building crew. I kept begging them to establish a more direct link with me but I was never successful. If only Fax machines had been available then!

'They eventually flew their Falco (CC-PZE/F-8) around about 1985, ran into a few minor teething problems including a cracking exhaust system and voltage drop problem with the landing gear system, but these were soon sorted and as far as I know the aircraft is still flying well. ENAER's efforts were concentrated on the Pillan, and although their Falco project was seen as the first of a production run which they would sell to wealthy Chileans, I'm afraid that nothing came of that. ENAER have gone on to

A Chilean Air Force Falco built from Sequoia Aircraft Corporation plans and kits, which first flew in about 1985. (Sequoia Aircraft Corporation)

Pazmany PL-IBs built by the Chinese Nationalist Air Force. (Pazmany Aircraft Corporation)

sell the Pillan in several countries including Spain and have more recently designed and produced their first wholly indigenous light aircraft, the side-by side, two-seater, all-composite 115 hp Lycoming-powered Namcu.'

The Namcu was displayed in the West for the first time at 1990's Farnborough Air Show.

The Falco is the epitome of a wooden homebuilt. But by contrast, using all-metal construction, but again with a similar side-by-side two-seater low-wing tri-gear undercarriage configuration, are several other designs that have been built in quantity for the military trainer market, having started life as homebuilt projects.

Ladislao Pazmany from San Diego, California, is the man behind the all-metal Pazmany designs. Pazmany designed his PL-1 Laminar in the early 1960s, taking an estimated 5,000 hours of work. He then got colleagues John Green and Keith Fowler to build the prototype, a task that took about 4,000 hours before if was first flown on 23 March 1962 with Cdr Paul Hayek, USN, and Lieut Richard Gordon—a NASA Gemini/Apollo astronaut—as the test pilots. By January 1976 the prototype PL-1 had logged more than 1,500 hours' flight time. It had a 95 hp Continental C-90-12F engine and its all-metal structure and laminar-flow wing contributed to a fairly complex design by homebuilt standards. None the less, Pazmany sold 375 sets of plans and construction manuals for the PL-1, including one set to the Aeronautical Research Laboratory of the Chinese Nationalist Air Force at Taichung, Taiwan.

Students and instructors at the ARL, under the supervision of General Ku and Colonel Leeat Taichung, took 100 days to built their first PL-1, its first flight taking place on 26 October 1968. Four days later it was formally demonstrated to Generalissimo Chiang Kai-Shek and then, after extensive flight testing and evaluation, the decision was made to establish a production line of the type to be used as basic trainers for CAF cadets. The aircraft would be powered by 150 hp Lycoming 0-320 engines and re-designated the PL-1B, but were locally known as the AIDC PL-1B Chienshous. Fifty-eight examples were built in Taiwan between 1970 and '74.

In 1982, with improvements in relations between Taiwan and the USA, a batch of about five of these PL-1Bs found their way back to the USA. Surplus to requirements, and with the addition of some entrepreneurial skill, the intention was to sell them as cheap ready-made trainers. Stored at Mojave, California, in 1982 awaiting buyers, more interest seemed to be generated by the teak packing cases that they had arrived in than the aircraft themselves! In 1991 45 AIDC PL-1Bs were still reported operational at Kang Shan Air Base alongside Beech T-34 Mentors.

Pazmany's homebuilt designs for military applications did not stop here. An improved version of the PL-1 with a wider cockpit and simplified construction to speed build-time and cut down weight was designed by Pazmany in 1967–8. The prototype was built by Mr H. Rio at Ramona, California, and first flew on 4 April 1969 with a 125 hp Lycoming 0-290-G engine. It also featured the laminar-flow wing of the PL-1, but the wing was also easily detachable for ease of construction, storage and maintenance/repair. The all-metal airframe was stressed to +6g and had no compound curvatures, simplifying construction by eliminating the need for sheet-metal-forming machinery.

Plans for the PL-2 were marketed by Pazmany like the PL-1: one of the first to buy the aircraft and adopt it was the South Vietnamese Air Force which

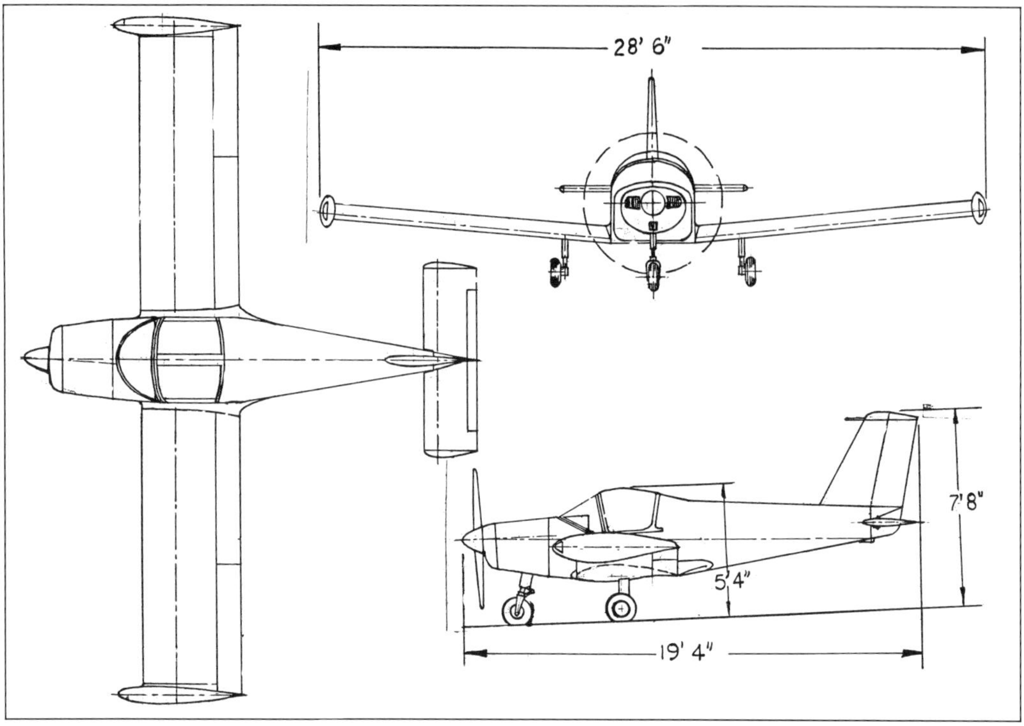

Three-view drawing of the Pazmany PL-2.

was looking for a cheap and practical all-metal trainer. Using resources pooled from several bases, their PL-2 first flew on 1 July 1971, and although production of ten more examples was planned, the Vietnamese War overtook events and it is thought that only the one aircraft (TP.001) was built and flown.

The PL-2 has proved popular with civilian home-builders and military/government builders alike, with an estimated 50 examples having been completed and flown around the world. The Royal Thai Air Force, and those of the Republic of Korea, the Republic of Singapore and Sri Lanka all built single examples to evaluate the type as a trainer for indigenous construction in the early 1970s. The Miyauchi Manufacturing Co of Japan also bought plans from Pazmany and built and flew one example. Potentially the largest production run for the PL-2 was in Indonesia, where construction of their version started in September 1973 at Linpur Aircraft Industries at Bandung for evaluation as a military trainer. It was called the LT-200 and the first aircraft (IN-201) flew on 9 November 1974; it was soon followed in December by construction of another three modified and improved examples, the first of a proposed production run of 30 LT-200s.

A South Vietnamese Air Force Pazmany PL-2. (Pazmany Aircraft Corporation)

The LT-200 had the characteristic Pazmany all-metal fuselage of semi-monocoque construction, constant chord wing, tricycle fixed gear undercarriage, and stressed to +6 and −3g to meet the US aerobatic requirements of FAR Part 23. Glassfibre wing-tip fuel tanks supplemented the 21-gallon (95-litre) main tank, feeding the 150 hp Lycoming 0-320 engine.

Again the LT-200 was seen as way of establishing an aircraft industry in Indonesia and the LT-200

An Indonesian Air Force Pazmany PL-2 built during 1974 at Linpur alongside Polish Wilgas (known as Gelatiks). Two PL-2s are believed to have been built between 1974 and '76 by Linpur Aircraft Industries at Bandung. (Col Ir Yuwono)

prototype was the country's first indigenously-produced aircraft. The prototype and the other three started were built at Linpur between 1974 and '76 alongside examples of the Polish Wilga utility aircraft (known locally as the Gelatik). Despite the production plans for the LT-200, Linpur were absorbed into the new Nurtanio Aircraft Industries group and the series production of the LT-200 was shelved so that the organisation could devote its efforts to the Bolkow Bo 105 and CASA C-212 programmes.

The most recent quasi-military application of the Pazmany PL-2 has been in Argentina where students at the Escuela Nacional de Educacion

A PL-2 built by students of No 1 Trade School of the Argentine Air Force in December 1987.

A Pazmany PL-4 built by students of ENET in Argentina stops in front of a crowd of officials and press after its first flight on 19 December 1986. The test pilot is Lt Gustavo Graciani of the Argentine Air Force. (Pazmany Aircraft Corporation)

Technica (ENET) No 1 Trade School of the Argentinian Air Force completed an example and flew it the first time in December 1987. It is civil registered as LV-X88.

Pazmany's other homebuilt design, the single-seater all-metal PL-4, first flew in July 1972. An example of this aircraft, with a T-tail, tail-dragger fixed undercarriage and powered by a converted Volkswagen car engine (approximately 50 hp), was built from plans in Argentina by ENET and preceded their PL-2. Students at the No 1 Trade School at El Palomar Air Base under the directorship of Hector Laguarde first flew their PL-4 on 19 December 1986—the test pilot for this flight was Lieut Gustavo Graciani.

In November 1973 Lt Col Roy Windover, Director of the Air Cadets Programme at the Canadian Ministry of Defence, evaluated the PL-4 prototype

The Glasair II-S during the USAF's evaluation in 1990 for its Cessna T-41 (C.172) replacement programme. (Stoddart-Hamilton)

and proposed that 200 of the type should be built for the Cadets. Two pre-production PL-4As were built to evaluate different engine options. Prison inmates were supposed to construct the basic components, the rest of the aircraft being built by the Cadets themselves, but the programme seemed to founder in the late 1970s.

Wood and metal homebuilt designs have featured so far in this evaluation of military/governmental applications of homebuilts. One of the more recent examples was in late 1990 when both the Stoddard-Hamilton Glasair II-S and the Glasair III composite kitplanes were flown by the United States Air Force as part of its evaluation of types for its Cessna T-41 (C.172) replacement programme. Stoddard-Hamilton teamed up with Arocet Inc of Tulsa, Oklahoma, to demonstrate these examples of state-of-the-art composite kitplanes in competition with the British Slingsby T.67 Firefly, the Piper Swift-Fury, the Mooney AT/EFS (militarised version of the standard Mooney 252 TSR), the Aerospatiale TB-20 Trinidad and the SF.260. The USAF operate Enhanced Flight Screening Programs at their Air Force Academy in Colorado Springs and at Reese AFB, Hondo, Texas, and want to replace the ageing Cessnas with an aircraft that more effectively challenges pilot candidates. During August 1990 the two Glasairs demonstrated take-offs, landings, stalls, spins and other aerobatic manoeuvres, as well as maintenance procedures and damage tolerance and repair techniques on the aircraft's composite structures.

Stoddard-Hamilton's other 'baby' with eyes on the military trainer market was their AT-9 Stalker, a turbo-powered beefed-up version of the Glasair III. The prototype, N253LC, first flew on 24 July 1989 with a 420 hp Allison model 250 turboshaft engine. In about 1986 the Allison Gas Turbine Engine Division of General Motors was seeking low-cost Asian suppliers of this engine, and they forecast pricing of such an unit at $55,000 to $75,000, a considerably more attractive price tag than the (then) $160,000 or 1991 price of $200,000-plus.

Stoddard-Hamilton were seeking the market niche for a low-cost military turboprop trainer at about half the cost quoted by other turboprop manufacturers. As most military programmes are considered 'public use' and do not therefore require such stringent certification standards, Stoddard-Hamilton felt that their forecast price tag of $300,000 for an Asian-built Allison turbo version of the Glasair III (AT-9 Stalker) would be attractive enough to overshadow the fact that the Glasair was not certified. Allison provided an engine on consignment for the prototype proof-of-concept AT-9 while Stoddard-Hamilton located an ex-Air Force Glasair III customer and did not have to twist his arm very much to persuade him to construct his Glasair with the Allison engine.

The performance was 'thrilling', according the Stoddard-Hamilton's President, Ted Setzer: 'The new owner flew over 150 hours on flight tests in the first couple of months and everything looked good

The AT-9 Stalker is Stoddart-Hamilton's development of their Glasair III kitplane with a turboprop engine for military applications. (Author)

so we ran an advertisment in February 1989 in a Special Training Programs supplement published by *Aviation Week & Space Technology* and were swamped with worldwide enquiries.'

Unfortunately two major problems cropped up and effectively grounded the AT-9 programme. Allison was not satisfied with the quality of the castings and manufacturing processes of its Asian sub-contractor, so scrapped the Asian engine programme. As a result the AT-9 price tag with a standard US-built Allison was not nearly as attractive to those who had enquired, and many of these were also not satisfied with the aircraft not being certified. Far more devastating, though, was the loss of the prototype AT-9 with its owner in a fatal accident in May 1989 during what appeared to be a minimum demonstrated take-off roll when the aircraft experienced a Vmc departure stall, crashed and was destroyed.

Stoddard-Hamilton is a relatively small but highly professional employee-owned company and the cost and effort of duplicating another example of the AT-9 were beyond its means. In any case they felt that the market niche for such a trainer had disappeared with the demise of the Asian engine source. There is now, however, considerable interest from potential military customers in their Glasair II-S FT, the stretched (14 inches/356 mm longer) version of the Glasair II TD, FT and RG models introduced in 1990, which have improved aesthetic appeal and better longitudinal stability. A new turbocharged version of the Glasair III has also been introduced in 1991.

Setzer explained to me how he regards the development of the military market for Glasairs: 'Over the past few years we have discussed the Glasair FT and RG for use as trainers with several foreign countries and government representatives and also dealt with "requests for quotation" for both complete aircraft and complete kits for proposed in-country assembly training programmes. Our price for a complete Glasair II-S FT with dual throttles, engine, avionics, instruments and propeller included, as well as other military flight training specifications, is $98,000—a complete kit for in-country assembly taking advantage of their lower labour rates would cost them about $58,000 and be a far more attractive alternative. Firm orders from any military user have yet to be finalised, though.'

Stoddard-Hamilton are happy to trade on their excellent reputation, with their aircraft having accumulated over 100,000 flying hours to date and with orders for new Glasair kits continuing to arrive at their Arlington headquarters at a comfortable rate. They have also been instrumental in forming the Sport Aircraft Manufacturers Association (SAMA) in 1990 which is actively lobbying the FAA for differentiation between the 'Experimental' homebuilt category and a new 'Primary' category for small single-engined personal-use aircraft.

Homebuilt and kitplane applications as military trainers, whilst thus commercially unsuccessful to date, have a new aspirant to the cause, a development of the Swearingen SX-300 two-seater all-metal homebuilt. At Sun'n'Fun in 1988 an SX-300 was demonstrated by Forrest Molberg on behalf of the Jaffe Aircraft Corporation of San Antonio, Texas. There were then high hopes of sales of its military derivative to the Turkish Air Force, and a mock-up of this derivative, the SA-32 Turbo-Trainer, was also displayed at Farnborough that year. Demonstrations to the USAF were also reported but not confirmed until the tragic news broke that Molberg had been killed on 9 January 1989 flying Jaffe's SX-300 N6Y near Wright-Patterson AFB, Ohio, when the starboard wing detached (the wing structure was different from that planned for the SA-32T). A few days later, in the same edition of the *Aviation Week & Space Technology* supplement as that in which Stoddard-Hamilton took their AT-9 advert, details were given of Douglas Jaffe's SA-32T Turbo-Trainer. It was claimed to benefit from four years' flight experience with several SX-300s, one of which had set a new world speed record of 314 mph (518 kmph) in its class. The SA-32T is a heavy wing-loaded aircraft that simulates the type of plane that students will fly later in their military training. An Allison 250-B17D turboprop is planned for the SA-32T and the projected climb rate is 3,700 fpm (1,128 mpmin).

Completions of homebuilt SX-300s have been steady, but Swearingen deliberately restricted the issue of 'Build Licences' to 50 so that he could wind up the homebuilt side of the business, sell the rights to Jaffe and concentrate on his new SA-30 executive jet project. Whether the SA-32T becomes the first successful commercial development of a homebuilt design is still speculative.

One of the more interesting uses of a homebuilt by the military is in Iran, mainly because of that country's 'off-limits' political situation during the Iran-Iraq war. The Islamic Revolutionary Guards Corps (Air Industries Division) announced in Tehran on 22 February 1988 that the first flight of their IRGC Fajr (Dawn) had taken place, that it could be used for military purposes, and that it was to be put into full-scale production soon afterwards. Although claimed to be of Iranian design, photos seen in the West show the Fajr to have a striking resemblance to the Neico Lancair two-seater composite kitplane. Local modifications are possible but it is almost certainly a Lancair although Neico Aviation Inc of Redmond, Oregon will not be drawn on the subject. In any event, they may not necessarily know because a kit bought by any customer could then be passed on to a third party such as the Iranians. It

The modified version of the Swearingen SX-300, the SA-32T Turbo Trainer, is now being marketed to air forces around the world, including one member of NATO. (Author)

appears from photographs to have a wooden laminated propeller and a smart, almost civilian-type colour scheme. It could be in use in the training or aerial reconnaissance role.

The Iraq CMI organisation is also reported to have completed two examples of the CFM Shadow in 1989 for oil pipeline and real-time video monitoring. The 1991 Gulf War has not brought forward any new information, and construction of further examples is highly unlikely.

Much nearer to home, a British homebuilt has operated until quite recently in a military colour scheme and with the military serial XW784 (having been also civil registered at one time as G-BBRN).

The Kittiwake all-metal homebuilt constructed by apprentices at RNAS Lee-on-Solent between 1969 and '71, and subsequently commissioned as a Navy aircraft, XW784. (Peter R. March)

This is a single-seater Mitchell-Proctor Kittiwake I, an all-metal tri-geared homebuilt used at RNAS Yeovilton as a glider tug. It was as long ago as 1968 that the Royal Navy Air Engineering School, after refurbishing a Walrus aircraft, decided that construction of a 'real' aeroplane might be the next logical step for the apprentices. A metal homebuilt was chosen, as being of practical use in training, and the Kittiwake fitted the bill nicely; it was simple to construct with standard materials, yet involved a number of engineering processes to give the right sort of challenge. In addition, the Training Schools glider towing aircraft were getting tired, and when the Kittiwake was complete it could perform that valuable duty.

The Ministry of Defence would not approve any money for the project, but with limited funds it was decided to start work anyway in January 1969 and, like most builders, the Apprentices, under the guidance of Lt Cmdr M. Cudmore RN, started work on a control surface to get the feel of homebuilding in metal, although the 26 swg skin was very much thinner than anything the trainees were used to and therefore simpler to handle.

Roy and Ann Proctor's plans were considered excellent and by July 1969 most of the individual components were complete. Finding the 'T' extrusions for the main spares took some time, but in the end some of larger section was found and cut down to length. (Drawings were subsequently modified for an alternative spar construction without extrusions.) The mainplanes were the largest components in terms of sheet metalwork—the ribs were attached to the main and rear spars and then the rib pitches marked on the skin for it to be pre-drilled. It was then a simple job to lay the skins on the ribs, sight the rib line through the holes and mark out the rib positions. It was possible to cover the mainplanes with large wrap-round skins, thereby avoiding longitudinal joins.

In December 1969 the first financial injection came through in the form of a grant from the Nuffield Trust so that special parts and components, and the new Rolls-Royce 0-200 Continental engine, could be purchased. Datum on the Kittiwake is the top fuselage longeron, so the rear fuselage was constructed with it in the inverted position, then turned and married to the centre section. This section, known as the torque box, had previously been fitted with the mainplanes to ensure correct alignment. By November 1970 the main airframe was complete with engine and undercarriage fitted—it looked like a real aeroplane at last.

Unfortunately Lt Cmdr Cudmore had to leave HMS *Daedalus* (Lee-on-Solent) and the project at this stage, but he was soon replaced by Bill Daysh and John Shears for what could be described as the most difficult phase of the whole project, the fitting out. This took nearly a year but, very appropriately for this homebuilt constructed by the Royal Navy, it was on Trafalgar Day, 21 October 1971, that the Kittiwake first took to the air.

It served as an immensely valuable exercise for the 200-plus trainees and instructors who had been involved in the construction over the three years of the project. This happened over 20 years ago, and one wonders why nothing similar—at least so successful—has ever happened since. In the USA, the EAA actively encourages and supports air education through the construction of homebuilts in schools and colleges, and in Australia Howard Hughes has started his School-Flight Programme with his Light Wing kitplane design.

In 1970 Craft Apprentices in the Royal Navy were not allowed to work on operational aircraft. Although the Kittiwake wears a service serial number, all the paperwork leading to its final inspection and certification was handled by PFA Engineering just like any other civilian homebuilt project. However, a duplicate and more highly-detailed record of the project books was kept by the builders for the Admiralty.

It was soon necessary for the Navy Kittiwake (only the second to be built) to qualify for a Special Category Certificate of Airworthiness on the recommendation of the PFA, and the aircraft was insured on the London civil aviation market. Then when it qualified it was commissioned into the Royal Navy as a service aircraft. Its strength and durability have been proven because despite several mishaps it has been operating as a glider tug at RNAS Yeovilton until very recently. Perhaps the Royal Navy should build and fly more homebuilts—they would certainly be cheaper than Sea Kings or Sea Harriers!

At about the same time as the Kittiwake's construction at Lee-on-Solent, a design by Roy Proctor (who was partly responsible for the Kittiwake), the two-seater all-metal Proctor Petrel, was being built by apprentices at the British Aircraft Corporation's works at Preston, Lancashire, as a similar training exercise. Fitted with a Continental 0-240A engine and appropriately registered G-BACA, it flew at Warton for the first time in 1978, another small example of the albeit limited role played by homebuilt aeroplanes in the commerical world.

This commercial use has also seen several types employed for airshow aerobatics. The Pitts Special biplanes flown by innumerable pilots are one example, and in 1979 the Eagles Aerobatic Team was formed with Charlie Hillard, Tom Poberezney and Gene Soucy flying a formation aerobatic act in three Christen Eagle IIs. Continuing this tradition more recently, the veteran aerobatic performer whose name became synonymous with the Pitts and who was a member of the US Aerobatic Team between

Bob Herendeen alongside the Glasair III that he uses for his popular air show act in the USA.

1965 and '71, Bob Herendeen, started flying his own newly-completed and highly-modified Glasair III (N111BH) during the 1991 airshow season in the USA. This Glasair is enhanced with 79 per cent larger ailerons and 'spades', which produce a dazzling roll rate, and has an enlarged rudder to perform precision manoeuvres that match a Pitts. This new Glasair III reaches speeds of 335 mph (553 kmph) during his performance. Herendeen was well known for his aerobatic demonstrations in the Glasair III prototype (N54ORG) prior to this.

None of these examples around the world have been epoch-making events, but each in its own small way demonstrates, if it be needed, how homebuilt designs can quite adequately take their place amongst the 'big boys' to great effect. This sphere of the homebuilt and kitplane aircraft history is almost certainly set to grow during the coming decades.

CHAPTER 7

Esoterics, odd-balls and replicas

WHETHER HOMEBUILDING HAS had more than its fair share of rogues and rip-off merchants is doubtful, but as in any walk of life the undesirable and unscrupulous will crop up somewhere to catch the unsuspecting public. Certainly homebuilding history has had its 'characters', although often their motives have been well-meaning. Such a pastime has also attracted the inevitable 'dreamers' who believe that they have found the 'promised land', and inevitably these, either through their designs or ideas, are considered eccentric by the majority.

One only has to look at the 'Patron Saint' in France, Henri Mignet. His well-meaning endeavours to get the man in the street into the air, cheaply and for fun, in his case in the homebuilt HM.14 Pou-du-Ciel (Flying Flea), was a quest that many have tried to emulate since. Mignet's design flaw was soon corrected, but not before fatalities, and in many quarters his name became a subject of derision. None the less he was a genius and a free-thinking designer of a whole string of light/homebuilt aircraft who has now hopefully achieved his deserved status in the history of aviation.

Regulatory bodies have always been the bane of the free-thinker and experimenter. Even the bodies that control homebuilt aircraft construction themselves come in for considerable amounts of criticism, not least Britain's own PFA, which has been unreservedly slated in many quarters for its conservatism, lack of imagination and restrictions, stifling innovative and free-thinking design and construction techniques. Notwithstanding, homebuilding, particularly in France and America, is littered with those 'salt of the earth' characters whose designs and ideals have helped to raise the homebuilt and light aviation world to its present status.

Mention homebuilding in the USA and the name James (Jim) Bede will soon crop up. Like Mignet before him he was a free-thinking innovative aeronautical designer beset by bad luck, and his Bede BD-5, which bought him his bad reputation was, like Mignet's HM.14 just one of a string of aircraft designs, many of them successful.

Bede's efforts to introduce one of the first mass-produced kitplanes without doubt detrimentally affected people's views of them, although his intentions were generally assumed to be honourable. Design work on the BD-5 started in February 1967 and it was first announced in early 1970, a sleek, fast bullet-like single-seater with a tail-mounted pusher engine and a short wing-span (14 ft 4 in/4.37 m). Construction of the prototype started in December of that year, and the maiden flight took place on 12 September 1971.

Few aircraft kits were available in the early 1970s, the Pitts Special being one of them. Bede had cut his teeth on the BD-1, which became the American Aviation AA-1A Yankee when Bede lost control of the company set up to manufacture the design. This went on to be a successful production light aircraft, later as the Grumman American AA-1B, spawning the AA-5 four-seater, the design pioneering the use of metal-bonded construction in light aircraft. Bede's 'Love One' (an acronym for Low Orbit Very Efficient Number One), or BD-2, was a bold attempt at an aircraft design for a round-the-world flight. It had a much-modified Schweizer 2-32 sail-plane fitted with a nose-mounted Continental 10-360 engine that could produce 225 hp at take-off and be throttled back to 30 hp for low-fuel-consumption cruising; it also boasted a jettisonable tricycle-dolly undercarriage, outrider wheels at the wing-tips, total fuel tankage of 471 gallons (2,139 litres) and a liquid-oxygen system for high-altitude breathing. It first flew on 11 March 1967 and Bede expected to be able to fly around the world in 150-170 hours' (one week) flight time, with several stops but for a fuel cost of only $230. An attempt to fly non-stop from the USA to Paris did not start because of unfavourable weather,

Jim Bede's BD-4 cabin homebuilt. (Ken Ellis Collection)

and Bede then went on to set a closed-course record of 8,973.38 miles (14,441.22 km) between 7 and 10 November 1969, staying aloft for 70 hrs 9 mins.

Bede's next project was his BD-4 kit, for which he set up Bede Aircraft Inc to sell plans and kits of parts to homebuilders. Like other Bede designs, the BD-4 used a tubular wing spar which also served as a fuel tank. Variants of the BD-4 made it either a two-seater or four-seater, its high strutless wing, boxy fuselage and tricycle gear being its distinguishing features. Thousands of sets of plans have been sold over the years and both tri-gear and tail-dragger versions regularly appear at homebuilt aircraft fly-ins in the USA. A British example (G-BEKL) was completed and flown at Shobdon, Herefordshire, in October 1977 with a 150 hp Lycoming engine.

Spurred by the success and acceptance of the BD-4 and seeing that there was a considerable market for homebuilt aircraft, Bede next conceived the infamous BD-5, an all-metal design with a retractable landing gear. Burt Rutan was part of the design team, with chief test pilot Les Bervin, and, as pilots who eventually completed and flew their BD-5s will testify, they got it just about correct. There were five main versions of what Bede conceived as a low-cost, high-performance kitplane:

1 BD-5B:basic kitplane version with 70 hp engine
2 BD-5D:factory-produced version of the basic 5B
3 BD-5G:improved version with new wing-section; aerobatic
4 BD-5J:jet-powered (Microturbo TRS18 turbojet)
5 BD-5S:engineless sail-plane version soon deleted from the range

More than 6,200 people ordered the certificated '5D' model, paying their $400 deposits. Over 3,000 other customers also paid their $400 deposits for the '5B' kitplane version and many of them paid up in full; although receiving some of their kit, these were never fully delivered. With kit prices ranging from $2,000 to $3,600, there were considerable sums of money at stake.

Bad management is partly to blame for the failure of the BD-5 project. Money problems were exacerbated by engine supply problems when the German firm of Hirth, which was to have supplied power plants for the aircraft, went out of business after Bede had invested about $1 million of his money in engine tooling for them. These engine upsets and difficulties with other suppliers of parts created cash-flow problems for Bede, resulting in numerous schemes to try to keep the project afloat and to keep one step ahead of the creditors. The 5D programme is thought by some observers to have been created to help solve cash-flow problems with the 5B work. The lack of a suitable power plant also led to the 5S and, even before the prototype had flown, Bede was advertising this aircraft to flying schools as an inexpensive glider option. His package for setting up such a gliding school included three

Many examples of the BD-5 are now flying in the USA. (Author)

BD-5Ss and a Bede BD-6 (a smaller single-seater version of the BD-4, which would be the tug aircraft).

He tried with the Bede Discount Club to improve the company's financial standing, customers being encouraged to order instruments and avionics from the Club for Bede to fit 'free' into their factory-produced 5D versions. But he was already well down the slippery slope, and in 1979 the Bede bubble finally burst, a Sheriff's sale of remaining assets recouping very little for the ten-thousand-odd anxious and disillusioned customers. This left those who had received partial kits, minus engines, landing gear parts, propeller drives, the engine and other essentials and, of course Bede himself, who lost a large family fortune.

Had his financial problems been overcome, his aircraft could well have been the success of which he dreamed. Dave Martin, editor of the US magazine *Kitplanes* and an ex-US Navy F-4 Phantom radar intercept officer, flew a completed BD-5 fitted with a turbo-Honda engine in 1985 and reported: 'It was fast and highly manoeuvrable yet surprisingly stable—light and extremely responsive without being overly sensitive. That is a difficult balance to achieve. I liked the handling a lot.' This aircraft was the work of Keith Hinshaw, who in 1971 as a 'hobby' became one of Bede's first and largest dealers. Despite all the difficulties he has remained a BD-5 partisan and has helped many of the 50 or so BD-5 builders in the USA who have persevered to complete and fly their aircraft, including several jet-powered versions. The US airshow circuit also boasts a BD-5J 'act' sponsored by the Budweiser Beer Company—now that's a recommendation!

Bede's effect on the homebuilding and the kitplane world was devastating—it helped to instil caution in over-enthusiastic customers but probably lost thousands to the homebuilding cause altogether around the world, a deficit from which it took many years to recover, but recover it did, as Chapters 5 and 6 clearly show.

Jim Bede hit the aviation headlines again in 1991 when he showed his two-seater BD-10 supersonic homebuilt jet prototype at Oshkosh. There are many sceptics of Bede's latest £150,000-apiece project, and only time will now tell if its future is to redeem his name.

A dilemma in the world of homebuilding is the actual definition of a homebuilt. Not built on a commercial production line, or not built by a full-time professional aero-engineer and not sold commercially—these are some criteria that may define a homebuilt aeroplane. Research projects—often seen as trail-blazing or eccentric depending on your point of view—have appeared in many forms throughout the history of aviation, and many of these fall into the homebuilt category by virtue of

Cockpit detail of the BD-5. The permanently mounted radio is an STS AV7600 Navcom. There are no IFR instruments except the turn coordinator, and the builder has not even added lights. Note the gear and flap handles in the middle of the cockpit coming up from the floor; note also the right-side stick. (Don Downie)

some of the above criteria, and the USA, where the authorities are far less restrictive, has nurtured more than its fair share.

Long before Bede conceived his 'pusher' BD-5 and the Rutan designs gained acceptance, two North American aviation engineers, Walt Fellers and Ron Beattie, together with Roger Keeney, had designed and built their 'Sierra Sue' pusher at Torrance, California. Between 1945 and 1953 an estimated 11,400 hours of engineering time and 5,600 hours of building went into the 'Sierra Sue' project, which had been conceived as a single-seater aircraft built to Goodyear Trophy racing specifications, and as a test bed to investigate the effects of a wing flying through undisturbed air, compared to the disturbed air in conventional configurations.

It accumulated about 200 almost trouble-free flying hours, was flown by North American test pilots, was leased to Northrop Aircraft, and was studied by the USAF at Wright-Patterson AFB and Dulles in Washington, DC. In 1985 'Sierra Sue' was moved to the California Museum at Exposition Park, Los Angeles, for preservation, but not before engineers on the futuristic but ill-fated Lear Fan executive/business aircraft project had studied and flown the aircraft. It was no coincidence that the Lear Fan was a pusher.

The Professor of Aerospace Engineering at the University of Michigan in the late 1950s was one Edgar J. ('Ed') Lesher. An inveterate aviation enthusiast in Ohio since his teens, he graduated with a mathematics degree and later a Master's degree in aero engineering. He worked for the Douglas, Convair and Stinson aircraft companies as well as teaching and researching at various universi-

Roger Keeney, who helped build 'Sierra Sue', at the controls of this early Lear Fan look-alike. (Author's Collection)

ties between 1938 and 1962. In 1958 he visited one of the first small annual fly-ins organised by the EAA at Curtis-Wright Field in Milwaukee (before it moved to Rockford, Illinois, then Oshkosh, Wisconsin), and after studying the 20 or so homebuilt aircraft in attendance decided that he could design and build his own plane—something slightly more racy and unconventional. This was his first attempt at home-building, but he quickly decided on an all-metal two-seater tail-pusher configuration and, between his teaching work at the University, spent many hundreds of hours at his drawing board working on preliminary plans, building clay models and moulding in each slight design change that he came up with. He eventually started construction of the aircraft in the workshops of the University in February 1959.

A conventional semi-monocoque around aluminium extrusion was the basis for the construction of Lesher's first project, which he named the Nomad. A NACA 23015 wing airfoil provided low drag, good lift and a fairly thick section to provide strength. Scoops under the wing provided induction air for the carburettor and ram air for cooling the 100 hp Continental 0-200E engine, which was located behind the cockpit. One of his major problems was getting the power back to the propeller mounted at the rear tip of the fuselage. A Dodge Flexidyne coupling was installed following severe shaft vibrations from his first installation, and the tortional vibration was then kept much lower.

By October 1961 Lesher moved his Nomad from the workshop to Willow Run airport, Detroit, and he soon had it assembled and on the runway performing high-speed taxi runs. Centring the ailerons rectified the Nomad's tendency to roll, and after 20 short hops Lesher took his aircraft into the air for the first time. It behaved much like a jet and he found no significantly undesirable characteristics in the aircraft that had taken 5,000 hours and $4,000 to build. In 1962 he flew the Nomad to the EAA's annual fly-in convention, then at Rockford, Illinois, and won the Association's 'Most original design' award.

A friend of Lesher's, Leon Davis (designer of the Davis DA-2 and DA-5 all-metal homebuilts), discussing the public reception and performance of the Nomad at Rockford, suggested to Lesher that there were many world records waiting to be broken. He sought information on the Federation Aéreonautique Internationale (FAI) Class C-1a Group for light aircraft weighing less than 500 kg (1,102 lbs) and began to consider the type of aircraft that might be most suitable for such record attempts. A 50 hp engine was his optimum choice, but none were available so he plumped for the 100 hp from the Nomad which would reduce range performance at low speeds but increase high-speed and altitude performance. The somewhat heavy Lesher even had to lose weight himself if he was to pilot the new aircraft—2 stones or 28 lbs was his target, and in doing this he also increased his personal fitness, an essential for anyone undertaking endurance record flights.

By October 1962 Lesher had completed preliminary design work on his all-metal aircraft with its retractable tricycle undercarriage, which he had now named Teal. By February 1963 the wings, with integral fuel tanks extending from root to tips, had been completed, but it was to take until April 1965 for the Teal to be fully completed and ready for its first flight. Again at Willow Run airport, taxi runs

Ed Lesher's Teal in the workshop at the University of Michigan. (Author's Collection)

Aero System's Dynamic Trick at Moulins in 1988 was basically a powered hang glider attached to a rubber dinghy for marine operations. (Author)

and high-speed runs followed by short hops culminated in the first flight proper on 28 April, a take-off requiring 3,000 feet of runway. August 1965 saw Lesher at Rockford again, this time with his Teal; he received an Achievement Award from the EAA for the design of the new aircraft.

It was not until May 1967 that he was ready to have a crack at some of the FAI records. He went on to set closed-circuit speed records around 500, 1,000 and 2,000 km courses (311, 621 and 1,242 miles respectively) at average speeds of 291, 272 and 262 kmph (181, 169 and 163 mph respectively) in the Teal, and quickly became the aviation celebrity of the era. An unfortunate crash occurred in May 1968 and soon after, as an invited guest at the Las Vegas Air Show, he was asked if he was going to re-design and re-build the Teal. 'The Teal will do everything I want it to—some parts can be used again and I have the patterns for the rest.' It took Lesher 14 months to reconstruct the Teal, when N4291C once more became a familiar sight at homebuilt aircraft fly-ins, a remarkable aeroplane built and flown by a remarkable man.

Europe has seen far fewer odd-balls and esoterics than the USA. France, though, is a good hunting ground for such aircraft, and each year's big international homebuilders' fly-in organised by the Reseau du Sport de l'Air (RSA), which looks after the interests of homebuilders in France (see Chapter 10), is always host to several. A couple of very basic flying machines that hardly fit into the homebuilt category typified 1988's RSA, held that year for the first time at Moulins in central France. Using a mix of hang-glider and seafaring 'technology', the Aero System's Dynamic Trick was a basic Rogallo-winged hang glider with an alloy tubular 'airframe' beneath it to which was attached a small Rotax two-stroke engine in 'pusher' configuration. It could operate off land, but the example displayed at Moulins was much more ambitious as the base of the framework was attached to a conventional rubber dinghy for waterborne operations. How effectively it worked on water is questionable as the drag and 'stick' between dinghy and water must have had the Rotax engine working overtime. Aero System was advertising kits of the complete craft for sale, but the queues were not very long!

A flying machine that packed away into the boot of your car was also on display at the 1988 Moulins. The Jet-Packet (similar to the Freedom Fliers Ascender manufactured in Texas, USA) had lift from a ram-air parachute attached to the aviator's back to which was also harnessed a small engine and shrouded pusher prop. The intrepid aviator starts by pulling the engine chord, holding the throttle in his hand—with the chute spread out behind, the pilot runs forward as fast as possible until the backwash from the engine catches in the parachute and gives the whole device, including the pilot with his legs now tucked up in front of him, lift-off. Once airborne the pilot's legs can be rested and the machine can manoeuvre about the skies, turning to the right by a pull down on the right-hand side group of parachute chords and vice versa to go left. Climbing is achieved by application of throttle, and descent simply by controlled reduction of throttle. The question soon arises concerning heavy landings—in a conventional aircraft, tyres, undercar-

Moulins 1988—knees tucked up and the ram-air parachute providing lift, the Jet-Packet pilot gets airborne. (Author)

riage and springs take the shock—in the Jet-Packet, broken femurs could be a costly reminder of this way of joining the birds!

It should be stressed in deference to the RSA that neither of these last two 'homebuilts' were registered, and whilst they were being flown at the RSA fly-in, they appeared to be operating entirely unofficially.

Moulins '88 saw two other more conventional but contrasting homebuilts in the 'odd-ball' category. A real 'Heinz 57 varieties' homebuilt was the Leglaive-Gautier LG.150, described as a practical and easy-to-build two-seater touring aeroplane, although in my opinion it was lacking somewhat in style. It is, however, an economical and practical aircraft that first flew in November 1986, and part of Fernand Leglaive and Roger Gautier's philosophy in designing the LG.150 was to use parts from commonly

Incorporating pieces from other light aircraft including an Emeraude and Cessna 150, the prototype LG.150 F-PYTG, seen here at Moulins in 1988, has an original-designed metal fuselage. (Author)

available production types, so that the homebuilder could pick up complete and more difficult assemblies from scrapped, crashed or retired aircraft. The wings are wood and fabric and, with a few modifications, the same as those used on the Piel Emeraude. The wing roots are modified to incorporate the fuel tanks which come from a Gardan GY-80 Horizon, and the non-retractable tricycle undercarriage consists of the nosewheel from a Socata Rallye and mainwheels/disc brakes from a Cessna 150. Finally the cowlings, which conceal the 150 hp Lycoming 0-320 engine, are from a Robin HR.200. All these types are common in France, but British and US builders embarking on a LG.150 might have some difficulty.

Very similar in concept to the LG.150 is the Canadian Ceckady, the work of Peter Cowan from Ontario. His ideas were the same, but using various Cessna parts attached to a welded steel-tube fuselage to produce a tail-dragger aircraft that has been flown extensively on floats and skis.

Back at Moulins, the last of 1988's crop of odd-balls was the Farner SC.430 Colibri single-seater motorglider. It was also flown to the PFA's Cranfield rally in July 1989 by Ernst Ruppert from its home base at Schanis in Switzerland. With a 70-foot (21.3 m) narrow-chord wingspan in a 'canard' configuration, the wings have a slight dihedral from the roots, and approximately two-thirds out convert to anhedral with large winglets at the tips. The whole airframe is of composite construction; the small cockpit pod sits low beneath the long-span rear wing on an almost hidden and retractable tricycle undercarriage, and a small pusher KFM engine is completely enclosed in the rear of the fuselage pod. A shaft runs over the top of the large rudder to the prop, which has folding blades for soaring flight. Exotic sculpturing is one way of describing the foreward fuselage with its curved nose extending upward and the forward canard control surface perched delicately at its tip. As the SC.430 (registered HB-2036) landed and took off at both Moulins and Cranfield, one could see the enormous wings flew upward for flight and, as the speed lowered, flew downward. It first flew in 1985 and before these two appearances had also debuted at the Swiss homebuilt fly-in at Colombier in 1985.

The British conservatism and restrictions that have stifled much innovative thinking amongst well intentioned and would-be homebuilt experimenters have all but eliminated the odd-ball. Only marginally in this category, but a fine example of how with determination and perseverance officialdom can be overcome, is Yorkshireman Ivan Shaw. His TwinEze, albeit a modification to Rutan's basic VariEze design, is a fine example of design and construction by an amateur to enhance an already superb American design and at the same time participate in revolutionary development work on two pairs of entirely new light aero engines.

Shaw was one of the first to complete a VariEze

This beautifully sculptured motorglider, the 'canard' SC.430, still has its enormous span wings flexed upwards as it ends its landing run at Moulins in 1988. The tiny pusher KFM motor has folding prop blades for soaring flight. (Author)

Ivan Shaw's TwinEze. (Author)

in Britain (G-IVAN) and spent three happy years successfully flying it. However, he realised as he accumulated hours in the VariEze that there were many shortfalls with the design, and his first thoughts were to modify his aircraft to LongEz standard. He started building spars and wings for the composite LongEz, but even this he felt could be improved.

Beechcraft's commercial Starship project was already running at this time and provided considerable inspiration, but what concerned Shaw was the inconsistency of this high-technology airframe married to a low-technology engine. His first ideas were to fit a retractable undercarriage to the hybrid Vari/LongEz and in 1984 G-IVAN was retired to Shaw's workshop to be set upon with saws and screwdrivers. Wings were removed and newly designed spars and strakes were built and fitted on to the original VariEze fuselage. Inspiration from the Starship and discussions over a pint in the local helped the new aircraft's concept to gel into what became the TwinEze; no larger than a VariEze, it had even better performance and lift statistics than a LongEz and the added benefits of twin-engined safety.

The question of which engines to use led Shaw first to Lotus who were planning to build their 50 hp 4-45s four-cylinder air-cooled engine for light aircraft; however 18 months passed with no sign of Lotus coming up with the engines, so he approached Hewland Engineering Ltd. They have been well-known as builders of gearboxes for racing cars for 20 years, and had recently been the designers and builders of a new three-cylinder water-cooled in-line engine for Richard Noble's ambitious but fated ARV Super 2 commercial light aircraft programme. With help from Mike Hewland, Shaw decided in January 1986 to adopt these engines for the project.

On a reflective note, when I talked to Shaw in the summer of 1988 he commented on the difference between building a homebuilt from plans or a kit and designing and building a completely new aircraft, which is what the TwinEze was. 'With the former the builder should only have to do the work once—barring small mistakes low on the learning curve—but in aircraft design and development its a whole new ball-game, at least ten times more time-consuming. There's considerable research and re-design of items and it all boils down to how cheaply you can put things in the scrap bin!'

Very few twin-engined homebuilts have been built, particularly in Britain (the diminutive French Cri-Cri is one). Shaw was breaking much new ground in terms of engine type, numbers and aircraft design—the PFA's Engineering Committee, renowned in the 1980s and before as a very conservative bunch, were far from keen and must have thrown the proverbial 'wobbler' upon seeing Shaw's TwinEze proposals—they told him in no uncertain terms to 'go away—this project cannot be built as it hasn't been done before'. Their attitude was unfortunate, particularly as Shaw was a skilled and respected composite aircraft builder. There was the option of achieving certification of the aircraft through the CAA, as Shaw's colleague Don Foreman did with his larger twin-engined Rutan Defiant, and as several Rotorway Exec kit-helicopter builders have done. But Shaw was determined to complete the TwinEze through the established PFA permit system, a course of action that required almost as much effort and perseverance as the design and construction of the aircraft itself.

The Hewland AE-75 engines, weighing 135 lbs with radiator, special 2:1 reduction gear (these engines are normally 3:1) and propeller, were fitted into the TwinEze. The gear-retract system was designed, built and fitted, and proved one of the project's greatest challenges. It fits on to existing fuselage hard points and works rather like that of a Cessna 210, the main gear legs coming together then rotating backwards through 115° into the tail cone. This gear has 6 inches (150 mm) less track than on the original VariEze. The aircraft was virtually complete by early 1987, and by the end of April, Shaw had completed 25 hours of ground running, taxiing trials, high-speed take-off runs and the occasional short hop. Much of his time during 1987 was devoted to dealing with the bureaucracy thrown up against him; it took six months for the necessary paperwork to be released to authorise a test flight, and in the meantime Shaw had to road his TwinEze to the PFA's big Cranfield fly-in in July 1987. At long last Shaw was able to make the first flight in the aircraft at Gamston, Lincolnshire, in October of that year, and whilst there were several problems that had to be sorted out such as fuel vapour locking and engine cooling, the aircraft was remarkably vice-free with a climb of 2,000 fpm and a speed of 182 mph (300 kmph) recorded. He was even able to assess the single-engined capability when he shut down one of the engines and reported very little yaw.

By the time Cranfield 1989 had arrived, the next chapter of the TwinEze story was revealed by Shaw. Gone were the two Hewland engines and in their place were two Norton NR642 rotary engines, rated at 91 hp and weighing 134 lbs each with coolant and exhaust systems. Shaw emphasised that the replacement of the Hewlands had nothing to do with any shortfalls, but he considered that as the new Norton engines had become available with a much higher power-to-weight ratio and he was anxious to continue development work on the aircraft, it was an obvious step. The TwinEze was first flown with these new engines in July 1989 and Shaw was ecstatic about the amount of power available—a very fast cruise speed was indicated in excess of 200 mph (330 kmph) and with its two 48-gallon (218-litre) fuel tanks fitted, a range of 1,450 miles (2,390 kms) was possible carrying a 500 lb useful load.

Shaw received some compensation at Cranfield '89 for his earlier hassle when his TwinEze was awarded not only the Benjamin Tiger Trophy for the 'Best original design' but also the Don Foreman Award for the 'Most innovative use of composites in an amateur-built aircraft' by the PFA's judging committee. The Norton rotary engines were displayed for the first time at the EAA's Oshkosh fly-in a few weeks after Cranfield, where a packed forum tent listened enthusiastically to the news that Norton would soon have both certified and uncertified versions of their NR642 on sale in the USA. As for the TwinEze, Shaw is still undecided as to whether to offer plans to other homebuilders wishing to build one. But what is certain is that in a US-dominated industry it is a pleasure to report that Ivan Shaw with his TwinEze has done something to redress this balance.

Replicas

Of all the many types of homebuilt aircraft around, the category which contains more examples of the 'odd-ball' and 'esoteric' than any other is the warbird replica. *Real* warbirds are a rich man's game, but the homebuilder can dabble and fantasise with his own more economic and often smaller-scale versions of anything from a Spad to a Stuka. Some full-size replicas have also appeared, many constructed professionally for film purposes, while others are like Dan McCue's North American NA-50 (P.64) at New Hampshire in the USA, created from an AT-6 Texan airframe to become the only airworthy example of the type in existence.

Northern Aeroplane Workshops from Yorkshire have added another interesting concept to the world of replicas, the 'late production version'. Started in 1973 and completed and flown in 1991, their almost exact replica of a Sopwith Triplane has been built from original plans and is fitted with an original 130 hp Clerget rotary engine. When NAW's founder, John Langham, first conceived the project, Sir Thomas Sopwith was still alive, as was the Triplane's designer Herbert Smith and several First World War RNAS pilots. The idea was to get them to sign out the aircraft on completion, but as so often happens with homebuilt projects, and particularly something as daunting as a Triplane replica, initial estimates of five or six years to completion stretched to the 18 years which in fact it took.

From the outset, the Shuttleworth Trust at Old Warden, Bedfordshire, was closely involved in the Triplane project the deal being for them to supply materials and two original Clerget engines from which one good one would be made; then upon completion the aircraft would become part of their collection of flying vintage aeroplanes. Using the original plans as closely as possible, the Triplane (registered G-BOCK and in the colours of N6290 of No 8 (Naval) Squadron) is as authentic as it could be with the exception of some materials; wood and metal, for example, are now supplied in metric dimensions as opposed to the Imperial units used in 1916. Such a valuable replica (homebuilt) also needed to be protected against the ravages of time, and timber and metal treatments were also applied to ensure this.

Inspired by the NAW Triplane, John Penny from Eckington, Sheffield, who built and flew Britain's first Evans VP-1 homebuilt, decided to build his own

A replica North American P.64, flown to Sun'n'Fun by Daniel McCue from New Hampshire. (Author)

Triplane replica in parallel with NAW's only to speed up the process by utilising the simpler construction techniques learned from the VP-1 and making it more sociable by fitting side-by-side seating. A modern Lycoming 0-320 engine was fitted to G-PENY and it flew for the first time in November 1988 with British Aerospace's chief test pilot John Lewis at the controls. The construction techniques may have been simpler but it still took 16 often frustrating years for Penny to complete it.

The multitude of replicas built by homebuilders is diverse and quite daunting. Some of the most popular have been the half-scale fighters designed by War Aircraft Replicas at Santa Paula, California. Using a mix of wood and composite construction (see Chapter 13), the construction of a replica Focke-Wulf 190, Hawker Sea Fury, Vought Corsair, Mustang or even a Japanese Zero is possible. Fred Sindlinger in Washington State, USA, designed and flew a 5/8ths scale version of a Hawker Hurricane and is still selling plans to prospective builders. In Canada, Replica Plans do the same as Sindlinger, but their aircraft is a First World War SE-5A biplane; the prototype first flew in 1970 fitted with a Continental engine, and six have been completed in Britain. Equally popular, particularly on the air show circuit, are full-size Fokker Triplane replicas.

An extremely popular replica subject for homebuilders is one of Britain's few indigenous homebuilt designs, the Isaacs Fury. John Isaacs started construction of his 7/10ths scale wood/fabric replica of the famous 1930s fighter biplane at his Hampshire home in 1961. It was loosely based on that other British homebuilt stalwart, the Currie Wot (see Chapter 2). The prototype Isaacs Fury (G-ASCM) first flew on 30 August 1963 with a 65 hp Walter Mikron engine, but was later modified to a Mk.11 standard with re-design and re-stressing of the airframe and the fitting of a 125 hp Lycoming 0-290 flat-four engine. There are about 10 examples

Cranfield '89 saw the debut of John Penny's Triplane replica. (Author)

John Isaacs's extensively modified Currie Wot is now a 7/10ths scale Hawker Fury. (Author)

currently flying in Britain and several worldwide, including three in New Zealand. A good friend and mentor of John Isaacs is Vivian Bellamy and, between 1980 and '85, the two of them, with help from many other quarters, constructed a full-size Hawker Fury replica at Lands End, fitting an original Kestrel V engine acquired from New Zealand for the late Hon Patrick Lindsay. The replica first flew on 11 December 1985.

Probably the world's most evocative warplane and fighter is the Vickers-Supermarine Spitfire. Virtually any aviator would jump at the chance of flying a real Spitfire given the opportunity, but actually to own a Spitfire, though is an even more unobtainable goal—unless you build your own replica!

For this reason there have been more attempts to re-create the Spitfire in scaled down (and full-size) form for the homebuilder than any other single type with the possible exception of the North American P.51 Mustang. The name John Isaacs immediately crops up again in the context of the homebuilt Spitfire, for having designed, flown and sold plans for replica Hawker Furys, he set to work

Graham Jones (left), builder of Isaacs's Fury G-BKFK, with John Isaacs, its designer, at Cranfield in July 1988. (Author)

in 1969 on a 6/10ths scale Spitfire replica, the reproduction of the type's exotically curved shape posing an immediate and daunting challenge. As he describes in his excellent autobiography, *Aeroplane Affair*, the problem of scale replicas is that the pilot cannot be scaled down as well! A median has to be chosen between making the scale replica too big and re-positioning the centre of gravity with disastrous consequences. By a process of careful calculation, compromise and cunning, Isaacs's Spitfire replica came out at its 6/10ths scale with a 'manageable' wing-span of 22 ft 1½ ins and suitable for the 90–100 hp engine he had in mind. Wood and fabric were the materials chosen and construction started at Easter 1969, with small amounts of spruce left over from the Fury project being used to construct the Spitfire's tail surfaces. The wings followed, together with diversions to help with Viv Bellamy's Avro 504 full-size replica (G-ATXL, which was exported to the USA in 1970), and the construction of a suitably large workshop at his house in Southampton to accommodate the 22-foot long one-piece wing.

This problem of a suitably large workshop is one commonly experienced by most homebuilders, particularly for projects with one-piece wings. There are many homebuilt designs, however, that have taken this problem into account and although some of the claims of purveyors of plans and kits are accurate, that their aircraft can be built in a standard garage, many are not. This 'standard garage' may in fact be a 'standard American double garage'!

By the summer of 1970 Isaacs began to think about cutting wood for the construction of the Spitfire's fuselage. This is 19 ft 3 ins long, and although he had lengthened the workshop, it was only 10 feet wide. The wing was to be built integral with the fuselage, so to ensure that the two would match each other exactly, his solution was to build the forward fuselage, from the engine firewall to the back of the cockpit, on to the wing. Then, having drilled the four wing attachment holes in the fuselage frame, and satisfied himself that the two blended together precisely, he unbolted the fuselage section from the wings, put the wings to one side and continued construction of the rear fuselage, scarfing extensions to the longerons on this front section which had been deliberately left protruding aft for this later exercise.

After many long months of construction, a trial assembly of semi-complete airframe parts in Isaacs's back garden assured him that everything fitted accurately and was symmetrical. But this was just the end of the beginning, as with a home-designed homebuilt everything has to be worked out from scratch. The undercarriage, canopy, engine, propeller, fuel tank, instruments, control cables and pulleys, engine bearers, wheels, brakes, etc, all had to be bought, built or 'borrowed'. A 100 hp Continental 0–200 engine from a condemned Jodel became available and this was stored in an upstairs bedroom at Isaacs's house awaiting its time.

Four years' work had produced many part-complete components, but there was still a mass of work to do. By May 1974 Isaacs optimistically thought completion was in sight for that summer. How wrong! It was not until Easter 1975 that the largely complete Spitfire airframe was ready to be moved from Southampton for final assembly at Thruxton airfrield. More than two weeks of furious and continuous work on assembly and fitting out were made more urgent by a sudden announcement that all aircraft were to be evicted from the hangar at Thruxton—and this wooden aeroplane would need safe hangarage. The pressure was growing to complete all ground tests, obtain the necessary 'Permit to Fly' from the PFA, then fly the aircraft and get it away from Thruxton. It was the evening of 5 May 1975 when Viv Bellamy took the prototype Isaacs Spitfire (G-BBJI) into the air on its maiden flight. After 25 minutes aloft, including several practice landing passes, he completed the test flight and reported back to a very excited, jubilant yet anxious Isaacs: 'OK—there's nothing wrong with it though it is a little bit nose heavy.' Then he added, 'Your aeroplane does 150 mph'.

Another replica Spitfire designer/builder is the Romanian, now naturalised Frenchman, Marcel Jurca. Jurca ranks high as one of the most prolific producers of homebuilt aircraft designs. His MJ.2 Tempete and MJ.5 Sirocco date from the Tempete's first flight in June 1956 and have been respected and highly regarded wood/fabric designs amongst homebuilders worldwide ever since. More recently his replica designs have included the following:

1. Jurca MJ.7: two-thirds-scale replica of P.51 Mustang
2. Jurca MJ.77 'Gnatsum' (Mustang backwards): three-quarters-scale P.51
3. Jurca MJ.8: three-quarters-scale replica of a Focke-Wulf FW.190
4. Jurca MJ.80 'One-Nine-O': full-size replica of a FW.190
5. Jurca MJ.9 'One-O-Nine': three-quarters-scale replica of a Messerschmitt Bf.109
6. Jurca MJ.90: full-size replica of a Bf.109
7. Jurca MJ.10'Spit': three-quarters-scale replica of a Spitfire
8. Jurca MJ.100: full-size replica of a Spitfire
9. Jurca MJ.12 'Pee-40': three-quarters-scale replica of a Curtis P.40

All these replicas can be built from Jurca-supplied plans (or from his agent Ken Heit in Flint, Michigan,

John Isaacs's Spitfire replica unfortunately suffers from several features that detract from a 100 per cent similarity to the original Spitfire. (Author)

USA) using wood and fabric, including the MJ.10 and MJ.100 Spitfire replicas. Jurca estimates that there is at least 4,000 hours of work involved in building an MJ.100, so to be realistic that probably means at least 6,000.

Jurca's interest in flying started early and his big disappointment, which may have led to his infatuation with replicas, was that because of his 6 ft 1 in height he was too tall to fly Bf.109s during the Second World War. His plans for the Spitfire replicas were drawn not only from reference book three-view drawings but also, more significantly, from close and detailed inspection of a preserved Spitfire Mk, IX in the Musée de l'Air collection in Paris. Jurca and Heit were permitted to study this aircraft and spent many hundreds of hours tracing contours taken from this and the three-views on to 1/16 inch plywood, producing the drawings for the full-size MJ.100 first before considering the scaled-down MJ.10.

The full-size Spitfire (and the Bf.109) is designed to be powered by a 650 hp Ford all-aluminium 602 cu in engine to a specific modification designed by Fred Greschwender in Texas. However, one builder, Simon Richards, a Briton living in France, has acquired a 400 hp Gypsy Queen engine from a DH.104 Dove and may well have flown his Spitfire replica by the time this is published. Also in France, Jean-Claude Beaudet is steadily working towards completion of his MJ.100 replica using Jurca plans.

Heit sounds a note of caution to over-ambitious potential amateur fighter pilots: 'Jurca takes as much as 18 months to complete a set of plans for some of his replicas—even the plans I sell for him are expensive at US$800 a set. That's just the start of the expense in time and money, and we do not enjoy selling drawings that will strain anyone's budget. We want a builder to be able to afford to build and to finish the project. Even our information packs are strictly amateurish, telling prospective purchasers the aircraft's size and brief construction details.' That's a refreshingly candid approach.

Another Spitfire replica from France is a modified version of the Jurca MJ.10, known as the MB.10. Registered F-PEMB, it is the work of Montpellier-based builder Michel Boudeau and was completed and flown for the first time in 1985. Built of wood and fabric and powered by a 105 hp Continental engine, it can cruise at 130 mph and certainly looks authentic in the air. Head-on it is not quite so convincing, as the cowled cylinders of the Continental engine detract from the smooth lines of the Merlin-powered original.

Yet another Spitfire replica with Gallic origins is the work of A.D. Laurence. This is the Pfalzkuku, another three-quarters-scale replica, built largely of wood and fabric and powered by a small Lycoming flat-four engine the cylinder heads of which protrude on each side of the cowling. Although based in France, at Avranches in Normandy, the Pfalzkuku is registered in Britain as G-KUKU and was constructed whilst Laurence was working in Berlin. Its hand-cranked retractable undercarriage requires considerable concentration and effort after take-off, each main leg being individually cranked up, an operation that takes a couple of minutes.

Discourses on replicas could warrant a whole book in themselves, but a final, almost random, choice illustrates what a dedicated homebuilder with the right skills, equipment, temperament and motivation can produce. Call him esoteric or odd-ball, but Dick Kurzenberger has designed and built an all-metal seven-tenths-scale replica of the famous Junkers Ju-87A Stuka dive-bomber at Horseheads, upper New York State, USA. A skilled metalworker and ex-wartime pilot approaching retirement, he was looking for a homebuilt aircraft to build in his spare time, preferably something unique and fun to fly. With only three original Stukas preserved of the 5,000 built, he felt that a Ju-87 homebuilt would be

A. D. Laurence's Avranche-based three-quarters-scale Spitfire replica G-KUKU. (Author)

nothing if not unique.

With no plans available, Kurzenberger had to start from scratch. One of his most important criteria was similar to that of John Isaacs with his Spitfire; the Stuka replica had to fit into his relatively small hangar, so the wing-span could not be more than 40 feet. Also he would be building it in his garage at home, so the wing centre section had to fit through the garage door. He used photos, model plans and wartime drawings of original Stukas to draw his plans, and with a lathe, milling machine and sheet metal saw amongst his inventory of tools he started construction in 1981. He had already acquired a 260 hp Lycoming GO-435 engine to use as a power-plant so the drawings were prepared around this. All the metal wing-ribs were individually hammered out, and the cowling and front fuselage that he had first thought of forming in composites ended up being metal. He acquired the landing gear from a scrapped Fairchild PT-19 and the three-bladed prop from a crashed Aero Commander. The work-load was phenomenal, and it took seven years of almost full-time work, and over 10,000 hours of building-time, to complete.

In the air it seems that the replica has acquired some of the quirks attributed to the original, made more interesting by the affect of the concentrated scale. 'Ideally this Stuka should be another 18 inches longer,' says Kurzenberger. 'As it is, the centre of gravity is very sensitive and it flies completely differently depending on whether it's being flown solo or with a passenger. It's also very noisy due to the all-metal airframe and big engine.' Asked if he intended to sell plans or kits of his design, the reply summed up those odd-ball and esoteric homebuilders: 'Who else would want an aeroplane that was so difficult to build and fly anyway?'

The gull-shaped wings and trailing edge differential ailerons were just two of the problems Kurzenberger overcame in the construction of his Stuka replica. (Author)

Peter Sturgeon's VW 1834 conversion on bench test in June 1983 before being fitted to his Viking Dragonfly. (Ken Ellis Collection)

The Lycoming 0-320 fitted to John Penny's Sopwith Triplane replica. (Ken Ellis Collection)

the Anzanil from France and the Douglas and Scott in Britain were some of the most widely used, converted as necessary for aeronautical use.

Power-to-weight was generally poor. A two-cylinder in-line air-cooled, two-stroke Scott engine, as used to power many Flying Fleas, had a capacity of 652 cc and was rated at 34 hp—it weighed 85 lbs (38.5 kg). The smaller two-cylinder horizontally opposed air-cooled Douglas engine had a capacity of 500 cc, was rated at 17 hp and weighed 58 lbs (26.3 kgs). By comparison, today's converted two-cylinder two-stroke Kawasaki motor-cycle engine, the TC-440A, for use in many microlights will push out 72 hp yet weighs less than the Scott engine from the mid-1930s.

One of the best lightweight aero engines to be built in Britain in the 1920s was Roy Fedden's Bristol Cherub series of flat-twin horizontally opposed air-cooled engines. Bristol took over the assets of the failed Cosmos Engineering Co in January 1920, and the Cherub was the first small engine to pass the Air Ministry's new 'type test' introduced in 1924. The Cherub I, rated at 24 hp at normal engine speed of 2,500 rpm, could be bought in either direct-drive or geared form. The more powerful Cherub III followed, rated at 33 hp at 2,900 rpm. The Cherub was used by the Granger brothers in their Archaeopteryx and in several other early homebuilts in Britain and the USA, including the Cranwell Light Aeroplane Club's CLA.2 and CLA.3 and the Powell Racer (see Chapter 2).

Other early British manufacturers whose engines were used for homebuilts included the All British Engine Company (the ABC Scorpion), the Douglas motor-cycle company, who built a special flat-twin engine for aircraft use, and, probably the most significant of all, Pobjoy Airmotors, founded by ex-RAF Cranwell Education Officer Capt D.R. Pobjoy. His very light seven-cylinder air-cooled radial engines first appeared in 1926, fitted to the CLA.4, and through the 1920s, '30s and well into the post-war homebuilding period the Pobjoy P.1 (67 hp), the 'R' (85 hp) and the Niagara (90 hp) were used extensively. The Currie Wot G-AVEY completed by Keith Sedgewick in 1967 at Halfpenny Green was one of many post-war homebuilts to be fitted with a Pobjoy.

France had several specialist light aircraft engine manufacturers in the 1920s and '30s, including Société de Moteurs Salmson. In 1930 British Salmson Aero Engines of Raynes Park, London, took out a licence to build the AD9 radial engine, although as far as homebuilts were concerned this engine was used much more extensively in its native France.

Two Czechoslovakian companies also provided a source of specialist aero-engines for homebuilts: one was Praga (the Ceskomoravska-Kolben-Danek Company of Prague) with their Praga B, a two-cylinder air-cooled twin-cylinder horizontally opposed flat 46 hp engine; the other more significantly, was Walter Motor Cars and Aero-Engines of Prague. This company was founded in 1920, and in 1929 introduced its air-cooled in-line engines including the Walter Minor and Mikron. Like the Pobjoy these were extensively used in homebuilts both before and after the war. John Urmston's Currie Wot, G-ARZW, described in his delightful book *Only Birds and Fools Fly*, was fitted with a Walter Mikron III for its first flight in April 1963, an engine it still uses.

Production of small lightweight aero engines in the USA was not as extensive as might be imagined. The Depression and the Federal clamp-down on the operation of amateur-built aircraft in the 1930s meant that the market was limited. However, Continental Motors Corporation of Michigan diversified from its main car engine production and in 1928 produced its own seven-cylinder A-70 radial engine. In 1931 a simple, lightweight and low-priced flat-four horizontally-opposed engine, the A40, was introduced, followed in 1938 by the improved A50; this in turn led to the A65, which became one of the most successful light and homebuilt aeroplane engines of all time.

Lycoming and Franklin also entered the fray for

A Pobjoy Niagara engine fitted to a Cowper Swift. (Author)

An unidentified Swiss HM.293 with a 45 hp Salmson in around 1950. (Author)

the same market as the A65, and their engines, both new and cannibalised from crashed or scrapped production aircraft, have proved an invaluable source for the homebuilder, as have the similar Continentals.

It has been Europe's answer to this American trio which has been the scenario ever since Day 1 of homebuilding. Companies around the world build hundreds of thousands of auto engines before ever considering the aero engine; they pump vast resources into car engine development and production, and these are therefore a far superior product to their aeronautical counterpart. Conversion of auto engines for aviation use, particularly for the more impoverished homebuilder, therefore seemed the sensible path to tread.

Germany gave the world the 'people's car', the Volkswagen, powered by its four-cylinder air-cooled horizontally-opposed engine, and this engine, suitably converted for aeronautical use, was homebuilding's saviour in the post-war period. It is still being extensively used, both in its converted-from-car-engine form and its specialist commercially produced form. The Jodel D.18 and D.19 (see Chapter 11), 1980s homebuilt aircraft, are specifically designed for the VW engine and its derivatives.

There are numerous VW conversion plans and kits available on both sides of the Atlantic. The engine is reliable and parts are readily available—it is even rumoured that the original VW engine was designed for an aircraft anyway! Normal car use for a 36 hp-rated VW produces 4,000 rpm or more, but fit a propeller of adequate size and pitch and this rpm just can not be attained—and if it could the propeller would not be able to stand that kind of speed anyway. A conversion is therefore necessary to maintain the full rated power output but to reduce the rpm. Many of these conversions are approved by organisations such as the PFA, but beware of any that are not! One of the most popular and well-proven VW conversions is that of Don Peacock from Fairford in Gloucestershire—suitable for any air-cooled VW up to 1,600cc, he will supply all the necessary plans and explanatory instruction manual together with 'a lifetime of free advice' for £24.00. He has also designed a 'Type 4' engine conversion (1,700-2,400cc or 60-80 hp) especially for homebuilts, but this is not yet fully approved on a general basis.

It is prudent at this point to record the PFA's views on engines for homebuilts because, like the aircraft designs themselves, there are engines that are approved for use and those that are not:

'Obviously it is desirable that CAA approved engines be used for your homebuilt whenever possible. In practice the home constructor will find such engines hard to come by or beyond his pocket and will therefore perhaps wish to convert some other engine for the purpose.

Single ignition will not be accepted on aircraft other than powered gliders. A powered glider is defined as an aircraft having a power-off glide ratio of at least 20:1.

If the engine to be converted has seen previous service—for example in a car—then a work-sheet for the engine will be required to show the amount of wear on moving components. In addition, crack-testing of rotating components will be required. Should crack-testing facilities not be available then the crankshaft, etc, should be replaced with new

CHAPTER 8

Engines and propellers

'Every significant aircraft and homebuilt aircraft improvement has been preceded by an important power-plant improvement. It has always been that way. The power-plant has to come first. Then you design to get the maximum performance out of that power-plant.'
John Thorpe, California, 1980 (Thorpe is the designer of the T-18 homebuilt and many commercial aircraft including the Piper PA-28 Cherokee)

THERE HAVE BEEN several discernible eras in light aviation and homebuilding, all of them determined by the type of power-plant available:

* The early years—the 1920s and '30s—when there were Moths and Travalairs, the original practical light aircraft. Homebuilts were either relegated to being fitted with cast-off-war-surplus engines or converted motor-cycle engines (with a few exceptions).
* The Second World War, which bought tremendous developments including, in the USA, the Cub and Taylorcraft. Small flat-four engines such as the Lycoming Continental and Franklin were built in large numbers and became surplus around the world for homebuilt use. The Volkswagen car engine was also widely available and convertible for aviation use.
* The hang gliding era, which spawned microlighting/ultralighting and the demand for small, high power-to-weight ratio alloy engines in sufficient quantities to make them commercially viable for manufacture.

Engines

Choosing the engine to power the homebuilt or kitplane of your dreams is almost more important than the choice of aircraft itself. It is a hard fact of life that in spite of the rapid technological development of airframes and designs for homebuilt and kitplane aircraft, the development of factory-produced aircraft engines has fallen sadly behind. Aircraft engine technology has also fallen behind the equivalent technology in the car and motorcycle industry.

Of those early engines used in the 1920s to power the first practical homebuilts (see Chapter 2), the aluminium alloy four-cylinder two-stroke air-cooled radial engine designed and built by Jack Irwin in California was probably the most advanced and practical for the small ultralight or homebuilt. Motor-cycle engines such as the Harley-Davidson,

A pre-war Harley-Davidson engine. (Author)

A Rolls-Royce Continental 0-200A engine installed in a WAR FW.190 replica homebuilt. (Mark Parr)

items. A sketch of the proposed conversion should be submitted to the PFA for checking. This should indicate all modifications sufficiently clearly for an evaluation to be made. Particular attention should be paid to the following:

1 Thrust bearing details
2 Magneto drive
3 Propeller hub
4 Oil-cooling
5 Carburettor heat

Details should also be given of the maximum take-off revs, power expected from the engine and also the maximum power at which the engine will be operated. Evidence of satisfactory ground running of the installation will also be required.'

Even a good factory-produced Lycoming or Continental taken from a production-type aircraft may require considerable work for your particular chosen homebuilt. The sales literature from a plans manufacturer may simply specify such an engine, but that is only the start of the story.

Take the War Aircraft Replicas from the USA such as the half-scale FW.190, a PFA Approved homebuilt design. The one built by Mark Parr in Guernsey (see Chapter 13) was fitted with a 100 hp Rolls-Royce Continental 0-200 taken from a French Aerospatiale Rallye. To fit this beneath—or inside—the tightly fitting, rounded cowlings of the Focke Wulf, several major modifications had to be carried out, including some to the oil sump and the carburettor. Parr also decided on electric starting for his aircraft, so had to wire up a starter motor and incorporate a small battery. Such a decision is an important one, particularly if you are going to fly your homebuilt to far-away locations where the services of an experienced person to hand-swing the propeller may not be available.

Many builders will have decided that once complete they will be running their engine on standard car petrol, commonly known as Mogas, an alternative to the 100LL Avgas sold at most airport fuelling facilities. If this is your decision then it is important to read the CAA Airworthiness Notice 98A; this complements the previous Notice 98 which listed those aircraft which may use Mogas, though previously from a 'dedicated source', Notice 98A now states that 'Aircraft which do not satisfy these conditions may be eligible for using Mogas in accordance with Airworthiness Notice 98A or as a result of Modification action approved by the CAA'. Other important points from 98A are:

- Unleaded Mogas is not approved for aircraft use
- Mogas must be purchased from a retail outlet with a high turnover, should be used as soon as possible and not left in the aircraft tank, for long periods
- Its important to note the limitations on height and fuel tank temperature and to keep an accurate record of Mogas used
- When operating with Mogas it is important to be vigilant, particularly in the regular use of carburettor heat, and these limitations should be placarded in the cockpit

Fortunately for those builders disinclined to venture into engine conversions, there are now several commercially available version of the ubiquitous VW engine available. In the USA HAPI had been delivering 40 to 82 hp VW engine conversions from about 1980, and in this time they sold over 1,000 of these National Association of Sport Aircraft Designers (NASAD) approved conversions. Mosler Motors Inc of Hendersonville, North Carolina, have

A HAPI engine in a Dragonfly built in the USA. The engine is topped with an oil-cooler. (Don Downie)

now taken over from HAPI. They also sell a small 'half-VW' engine, the two-cylinder Hornet, which produced 40 hp at 3,400 rpm, and the powerful Magnum 72-82 hp VW modification. The Magnum overcomes the VW's basic weakness, the valve train, by using individual heads and self-adjusting hydraulic valve lifters so that any resemblance to the original VW is small.

Nearer to home, Limbach in Germany, and Ateliers JPX and Rectimo Aviation SA in France manufacture VW variants, supplying them to both commercial aircraft manufacturers and homebuilders. Limbach started with the basic VW engine over 25 years ago and have improved it so much that its heritage has been almost lost. The Limbach engines are so reliable that they are fully certified under Joint Airworthiness Regulations (JAR) for use in motorgliders—for this reason the French Four-

An 80 hp Limbach 2000 installation in the Nicollier HN.700 Menestrel II. (Author)

nier series of motorgliders use them, and in Germany so do both Hoffmann and Scheibe. One potential disadvantage is that the Limbach engines are relatively expensive, but then Peter Limbach uses the finest quality materials and such reliability and peace of mind may be worth the extra expense.

JPX are more recent arrivals on the VW conversion scene, but their JPX4T60/A four-stroke is rated at 65 hp at 3,200 rpm and received full French certification in January 1985. These engines are popular with French homebuilders and have been used commercially to power the Robin ATL two-seater light aircraft since its first flight in 1983. JPX also manufacture two smaller engines, the PUL 425, an opposed two-cylinder 22 hp engine, and the smaller PUL 212, a single-cylinder 15 hp two-stroke, both of which are intended for microlight/ultralight aircraft use. Rectimo VW derivatives have been used in the Sportavia RF-4D motorglider.

John Thorpe's axiom concerning engine development preceding aircraft development has at no time been better illustrated than during the 1980s. Preceding this the sport of hang gliding had 'taken off' and resulted in allegorical comparisons with the Wright brothers, Henri Mignet and so on; then the hang gliding world ventured into the powered aeroplane sphere with the attachment of small two-stroke engines to their machines, and the first true modern-day microlights, ultralights and ULMs were born.

These aluminium two-stroke engines were mainly light in weight and cheaper than any comparable four-stroke. They were derived from industrial/commercial-use engines such as those built to power chain saws, small pumps, portable generators and so on. They came in two versions, liquid-cooled and air-cooled, of which the liquid-cooled was the more efficient and quieter.

Bombardier-Rotax GmbH Motorenfabrik of Gunskirchen, Austria, were one of the early suppliers of these engines, their normal use being initially to power small snowmobiles. Several of the hundreds of early microlight manufacturers used Rotax engines in their aircraft, including the Rotec, Teratorn and Eipper, and they quickly established the standard by which others are compared. Many other engines also became available, such as the Cuyuna, Fuji-Robin, Hirth, KFM, Kawasaki, Konig and Zenoah, all of which are still in use today for microlights and in some homebuilts.

A typical and popular Rotax engine in use in the early 1980s was the Rotax 503. This two-stroke engine weighed 82 lbs (37 kgs) with carburettor and exhaust, had a 496 cc capacity and produced 51 hp at 6,600 rpm. The 503 is still in production in 1991 and is one of the most popular and reliable lightweight two-stroke dual ignition engines around. Versions of all of Rotax's engines can be supplied

JPX's French-built small two-stroke engine, the PUL 425. (Author)

either for upright or inverted mounting, with the drive offset either towards or away from the cylinder head, and many Rotax gear reduction engines can be supplied with a noise reduction package

A new lightweight four-cylinder opposed two-stroke engine for homebuilts, the Hirth F.30 has a 1,042 cc cylinder capacity and was displayed at Wroughton in July 1991 by the ADD Aero Co from Petersfield, Hants. (Author)

The Rotax 503—dual ignition, twin-carb, fan-cooled version. (Cyclone Hovercraft Ltd)

consisting of air intake silencer and filter, and an exhaust after-muffler which is additional to the matched exhaust and silencer. Such an engine, with fuel pump, carburettors and exhaust system, cost about £1,500 in 1991, with reduction gearboxes and special silencers extra.

Another of Rotax's popular engines for home-builts and kitplanes is their Rotax 582 which comes in a variety of models. A twin-cylinder 581 cc 63 hp engine developed from the water-cooled 532 by the increase of its cylinder bore from 72 mm to 76 mm (2.83 in to 2.99 in), it has improved dual capacitor ignition for greater security and can be supplied with an oil pump which means that the engine can be used with 'pure' fuel (not oil/fuel mixture as in the two-strokes) and fresh oil from a separate oil tank. The 582 weighs 78.3 lbs (35.5 kgs) and will cost just over £2,000. This is the type of engine fitted to

The Rotax 582 dual ignition engine, shown with 'B'-type gearbox, electric starter and oil injection. (Cyclone Hovercraft Ltd)

The Rotax 912 80 hp engine, the first viable alternative to traditional light aircraft power-plants. (Cyclone Hovercraft Ltd)

many of the Denney Kitfox kitplanes, although with the introduction of the Kitfox III and IV the newer Rotax 912 four-stroke 80 hp engine with dual ignition is substituted for the 582.

The introduction by Rotax in 1988 of their 912 four-cylinder four-stroke engine provided the first genuine alternative for many years to the more traditional Continental/Lycoming/Franklin options for engines for homebuilts, and is Rotax's first engine designed specifically for aircraft use. Although it produces 80 hp it weighs only 138 lbs (62.6 kgs) and is very smooth and quiet, burning about 3.7 gph (17 lph) cruising at 75 per cent power. The popular Canadian-designed Murphy Renegade

Applications for the new larger Rotax 912 four-cylinder four-stroke engine increase almost daily. It takes the Murphy Renegade Spirit kitplane out of the microlight category and into the conventional homebuilt class. (Author)

Displayed at Cranfield in July 1989 for the first time, Ivan Shaw's TwinEze with its new Norton rotary engines. (Author)

Swiss engine designer Ernest Grünig (in dark glasses) demonstrates his Mazda rotary aero engine. (Author)

Spirit (PFA approved) two-seater biplane kitplane is now sold with the Rotax 912 engine as an optional fit.

Also approved for the Spirit is the new British-made Norton 90 hp P.64 rotary engine. This famous motor-cycle manufacturer is working with Teledyne-Continental in the USA to develop and expand its range of robust, lightweight liquid-cooled Wankel rotary engines for the light aircraft market. In parallel with their light aircraft engines they have built a series of rotary engines for use in remotely piloted vehicles (RPVs) and target drones.

One of the first British homebuilt aircraft to be fitted with the Norton 642 engines is Ivan Shaw's TwinEze (see Chapter 7). Shaw replaced a pair of British Hewland engines, with which his TwinEze had first flown, with the Nortons in 1989 because they represented an even higher power-to-weight ratio and improved the already good performance still further. They provide a smoother, quieter and more economic ride and are claimed to considerably reduce the maintenance requirement over more conventional engines. Each 90 hp engine weighs 130 lbs (60 kgs), and their success for Norton, Britain and homebuilt aviation is keenly anticipated.

Engine developments are always welcome, and a steady trickle of designers around the world continue to build new light aero engines and convert auto engines for aviation use. Ernest Grünig in Switzerland has converted a Mazda rotary auto engine: rated at between 150 and 200 hp, it has been fitted to a LongEze for evaluation. It weighs a relatively heavy 286 lbs (130 kgs) but he claims it will consume as little as 4.5 gph (20 lph) whilst running at 55-60 per cent power, and in the LongEze gives an endurance of 10 to 12 hours and a range of over 2,000 miles (3,300 kms).

In the USA there are several accredited auto engine conversions available, and here they do not suffer from the upper limit restriction of 180 hp imposed on British homebuilts by the PFA. Both Rover and Oldsmobile V8 engines and the Chevrolet 350 lightweight Rodec-block engines are popular conversions. These are rated at 200-250 hp and 300 hp respectively and have been fitted to George Morse's Prowler and to Steen Skybolts.

To wave the British flag again, Ron Webster from Kirby Muxloe, Leicestershire, should be mentioned. For the last 15 years he has been working on a private crusade, a new light aircraft engine. He initially built a 1,625 cc five-cylinder prototype with a dry weight of 124 lbs (56 kgs) and producing 45 hp at 2,000 rpm. The cylinders had a 77 mm (3.03 in) bore that was soon found to be too small. His Webster Whirlwind 5, developed from this, has an 85.5 mm (3.37 in) bore, a dry weight of 155 lbs (70 kgs), and is 1,865 cc with 55 hp at 2,100 rpm. It is hoped that this engine will find applications in specific homebuild types where a radial engine format is desirable.

Ron Webster's latest five-cylinder engine, the Webster Whirlwind 5, at Cranfield in 1987. (Author)

Propellers

Arguments about which is the most important part of an aeroplane will provide interminable discussion amongst pilots. High in the stakes of 'most important' must be the propeller, although in reality the aeroplane is like a cocktail that only succeeds if all the optimum component parts are present.

Propellers for homebuilts can, like the rest of the aircraft, be homebuilt as well, although there are an increasingly large number of commercial suppliers who will sell you either wooden, metal or composite props. They are usually fixed pitch, although there is a growing tendancy inherited from the microlight world of ground-adjustable props. A few elite homebuilts in the USA have variable-pitch props, but these are the exception. Basically the pitch will determine the performance of your homebuilt.

One of Britain's leading homebuilt propeller proponents is Ken Fern from Stoke on Trent, Staffordshire. He has been involved in the design and construction of propellers for many years and has published an excellent booklet 'The Simple Guide to Propeller Making' (available from Ken at 311 Congleton Road, Scholar Green, Stoke on Trent, Staffs ST7 3JQ, price £11.00 inc P & P). He admits that despite all his ten years' experience there is no special formula for the design of a propeller for a particular useage because there are so many variables involved. His trick in choosing a particular prop is to match the diameter/pitch and blade area to the engine size and type. It is often assumed that airspeed is directly related to the pitch, but this is not always true.

In all discussions of propellers the diameter is quoted first, followed by the pitch. Another quirk that lingers from the days of Imperial units is that diameter and pitch are still invariably quoted in inches, although metric conversions are simple. To prove the point about airspeed not necessarily being related to pitch, Fern has shown that a 70 × 50 (i.e. 70-inch diameter to 50-inch pitch) prop fitted to a Rolls-Royce Continental 0-200 engine in a Jodel gives a cruise speed of between 80 and 90 knots, and a 52 × 48 on a 1,834 cc VW conversion fitted to a Rand KR.2 gives a cruise of about 140 knots. Both of these propellers have a similar pitch (within 2 inches of each other) yet one results in a far greater cruise speed than the other.

Most common homebuilt designs have recommended engine fits and therefore there is considerable expertise available for advice on the best diameter/pitch combination for your particular needs; many plans and construction manuals will make this recommendation. It is then up to the builder, having built and flown his aircraft, to evaluate the performance obtained and decide whether a finer or courser pitch is required, or whether what he has is what he needs.

An example of the diameter/pitch evaluation for a particular homebuilt type was recently identified during the early stages of the flight testing of a new US-designed two-seater composite kitplane, the KIS (Keep It Simple), designed and flown in Oxnard, California, by Rich Trickel. (Trickel's company, High-Tech Composites Inc, is a subcontractor to Neico Aviation, manufacturing major vacuum-bag moulded composite parts for the Lancair 235 and Lancair IV kitplanes.) The prototype KIS, which first flew in 1991, is fitted with a Limbach L2000 80 hp engine and was fitted initially with a 56 × 46 fixed-pitch wooden propeller. In the climb the engine only produced 2,700 rpm and 2,900-3,000 rpm while at full throttle in level flight. The Limbach L2000 is rated at 80 hp (3,400 rpm) for 5 minutes during take-off, and 72 hp (3,000 rpm) continuously thereafter. Because the propeller was unable to make the best possible use of the available power the engine was effectively under-performing, producing only 65 instead of 80 hp at sea-level and less than 72 hp at altitude. In this case the solution was a prop with less pitch which would increase the climb performance with little effect on the cruise speed. In fact, for an aircraft such as the KIS, weighing around 1,000 lbs (453 kgs), climb would be increased by approximately 22 feet per minute for each additional shaft horsepower developed.

In order to decide on the most suitable propeller, first you need to work out the pitch angles, and this can be done either by the 'drawing method' of physically drawing the parameters of pitch against πD, or by the more accurate 'calculation method'. This is achieved by a simple formula:

$$\text{Tan of } L = \frac{P}{2 x \pi x R}$$

where L = angle of the blade at that station
P = pitch of the propeller
π = 3.14
R = distance from the propeller centre along the blade

After deciding on the best pitch angles for a particular engine, it is necessary to match these to blade area which in turn will match the chosen pitch to the engine. The important thing to remember is that for any increase in pitch the blade area must be reduced to compensate, and vice versa. Ken Fern has built up a tabulation of popular propellers for popular homebuilt/engine combinations—see the accompanying table.

Wooden propellers are still the most popular, even for state-of-the-art homebuilts such as the Rutan LongEze. In fact there are many advantages in using a wooden propeller on engines up to 180 hp, not least being the cost which is generally about one-third of that of an equivalent metal prop. Moreover wood is very strong along the grain and there is little likelihood of a wooden propeller flying apart; it is also very forgiving and flexible, having a high damping factor and being able to absorb a lot of vibration. Because wood is also about one-third of the weight of an equivalent metal prop, there are also fewer gyroscopic forces to foul up the engine bearings, and although some flywheel effect is lost on VW engines turning below 3,000 rpm above this speed there is no problem. If the worst happens and your homebuilt should nose over, a wooden prop also tends to break whereas a metal prop will bend and put harmful stresses on the engine crankshaft. The only real disadvantage of the wooden prop is in rain or hail—with tip speeds of up to 400-500 mph, the innocent raindrop becomes as hard as a stone, and if you fly long enough in the rain the tips of the prop will become damaged. Fibreglass tips have been tried, rather unsuccessfully, to help prevent this, and some props have metal strips incorporated on the blades.

The most economic wood to use if you intend to

Popular propellers for popular homebuilt/engine combinations

Prop diameter×pitch (inches)	Engine	Aircraft type
54×30	VW1600	Evans VP.1
54×32	VW1600	Taylor Monoplane/Evans VP.1
56×26	VW1600	FRED
54×34	VW1600	Tipsy Nipper
56×28	VW1600	Luton Minor
52×48	VW1834	Rand KR.2
52×42	VW1834	Brugger MB.2 Colibri/Monnet Sonerai 2
54×36	VW1834	Tipsy Nipper
72×42	A.65 Continental	Jodels/Wolf Boredom Fighter
72×44	A.65 Continental	Minicab/Jodels
70×48	RR 0-200	Jodels
70×50	C.90/0-200	Jodels/Emeraude
60×66	C.90/0-200	Taylor Titch/Rutan LongEze
79×40	C.90/0-200	Replica Plans SE.5a
69×55	C.90	Jodels
61×65	C.90/0-200	Taylor Titch
53×40	Arrow	Bensen Autogyro
64×40	Rotax 532	Assorted microlights/ultralights
72×46	Norton Rotary	Experimental propeller
62×66	Lycoming 0-290	Rutan LongEze
60×36	Jap 99	Luton Minor
69×48	Walter Minor	Currie Wot

Compiled from data provided by Ken Fern Propellers

make your own prop is Brazilian mahogany which is easy to work with and readily available from most timber merchants. It is important to get straight-grained wood and also to ensure that it is Brazilian mahogany and not some of the cheaper types available. Spruce, pine, maple and beech can also be used, but they are more expensive and hard to work with. Alternatively, laminations of mahogany and Parana pine give a beautiful and eye-catching contrast. However, as with all material used in any part of a homebuilt project, it should always be checked for quality by an expert or authorised inspector before any work is done with it—precautions now will prevent hours of despondency later on!

It is not the purpose of this book to give a detailed description of the methods used in making your own prop—booklets such as Ken Fern's do this satisfactorily and in detail. Propeller-making has been described as a 'black art', but for anyone with basic skills—and anyone tackling the construction of their own aeroplane must have these—the manufacture of your own propeller is quite a feasible task.

The fitting and maintenance of a wooden propeller also requires some comment. Installation is best done when the weather has been dry—if it is damp when the prop is fitted, the wood may shrink in drier weather and leave you with a 'floppy prop'. It is also important to tighten the bolts evenly in stages, but not to over-tighten them. Whatever, the bolts should be slackened and re-tightened every couple of months, the tracking being checked at the same time. It is also a good idea to check the prop bolts regularly during the early stages of test-flying.

A further advantage of the wooden prop is that the inevitable repairs can be done quite easily. Before flying it is always advisable—with switches off, of course—to wiggle the tip of the blade to check for bolt tightness. Any cracking of the finish should also be noted because water could penetrate, eventually causing a split to develop. If the blade is chipped it can be filed out and repaired, and such small repairs should not affect the balance—larger ones will however need a balance check. In short, propellers are like everything else in homebuilding—if in doubt, consult an expert before proceeding any further.

CHAPTER 9

Organisations around the world

AMATEUR-BUILT OR homebuilt aircraft organisations have themselves graduated from an amateur status in many countries to look after the interests of aircraft and their operators on behalf of official government bodies. Such organisations I am sure always conducted their business in the most professional of ways, but times have changed and in many countries the appropriate body looking after homebuilt aviation will now have full-time administrative staff, albeit still ably supported by a vast army of voluntary helpers.

In Britain, for instance, the Popular Flying Association (PFA) has offices at Shoreham Airport in Sussex manned by eight paid administrative and engineering staff. They are supported entirely by the income from subscriptions of PFA members together with small profits obtained from thc sale of goods and other commercial ventures, but are responsible for the growing needs of the 7,000-plus members the PFA now boasts.

Despite these full-time paid officials, it is still the voluntary staff who make the organisation tick. Without voluntary inspectors to make the required periodic inspections of homebuilt projects, the construction of homebuilt aircraft would be an entirely different proposition. Running the PFA's annual international Fly-In, formerly at Cranfield and now at Wroughton, requires a year of planning, not to mention the provision of hundreds of volunteers to carry out anything from aircraft marshalling to sign writing and cleaning of toilets!

But this British 'army' fades into insignificance when compared to that on which the Experimental Aircraft Association (EAA) can call to help run its big week-long Oshkosh and Sun'n'Fun Fly-Ins in the USA. The EAA's influence, in the form of regional Chapters, had helped it to spread not only to every State of the USA and every Canadian province, but also to the five continents of the world, making it the world's largest organisation representing not only the interests of the homebuilder but also covering other aspects of sport aviation.

France also has a large and thriving homebuilt organisation, the Reseau du Sport de l'Air (RSA), based in Paris but with membership throughout all French Departements and quite a sizeable international membership, particularly in countries with French ties from colonial days such as Algeria and the New Caledonia islands.

NB Contact addresses for the majority of major national homebuilt organisations are given in Appendix 5.

Great Britain

Popular Flying Association (PFA)

The Ultra-light Aircraft Association was founded in 1946 and from this the name and status was changed in the 1950s to the Popular Flying Association, but with similar aims and objectives (see Chapter 3). Membership is open to anyone with an interest in light aviation, pilot and non-pilot alike, particularly those interested in homebuilding, kitplane construction, aircraft design, aircraft restoration, sport and recreational flying, vintage aircraft, gyroplanes, ultralights and microlights (although these last two categories have their own specialist organisation, the BMAA—see below).

Local PFA branches, known as Struts, have been established throughout Great Britain, and these now number 46 from the Highlands to Cornwall and from Northern Ireland to Ipswich. Struts have even operated for expatriots in Germany (Dusseldorf) and Brunei, and there are two specialist rotorcraft Struts.

These Struts are the lifeblood of the PFA as they provide local forums where members can meet on a regular basis and get to know fellow homebuilders. The first Strut was founded in the late 1960s when some PFA members in the Sussex area met at a local public house and decided that it would be a good idea to form a local club to promote PFA activities in the area. A symbolic word was sought to describe this type of club, and the name 'Strut' was decide upon and has stuck.

When a PFA member begins to build, as well as the help and guidance he gets in an official form from PFA's headquarters and engineering staff, much of the more down-to-earth and practical help will usually come from contacts and friends in the local Strut. Here members can not only discuss problems, help each other, share experiences and provide local knowledge on sources of materials, components and services such as welding, but also, and probably most importantly, receive the support and encouragement often needed to help a project along to its conclusion. Strut meetings will also feature film shows, guest speakers, visits to see projects, social events such as barbecues and, in come cases, the organisation of their own fly-ins. The following Struts regularly organise their own fly-ins each year:

Wessex Strut	– Henstridge, Somerset
North Western Strut	– Barton, Manchester
Southern Strut	– Shoreham, Sussex
N Lancs & Flyde Strut	– Squires Gate, Blackpool
Cornwall Strut	– Lands End, St Just
Devon Strut	– Dunkeswell, nr Honiton, Devon

From the point of view of the organisation of the PFA's big annual international rally and fly-in, formerly at Sywell, Leicester, then Cranfield and now at Wroughton, many Struts organise voluntary teams from within their own membership to help with a particular aspect of the rally's running. It should be said that many of the PFA's and Struts' members are not actively involved in home aircraft construction, but simply have an active interest in this type of light and sport aviation.

The other equally important element of the PFA is PFA Engineering. Through negotiations and continuous discourses, the PFA has obtained the privilege of recommending the issue of 'Permits to Fly' for amateur-bult aircraft and some vintage/classic aircraft within defined criteria, as follows:

1. All-up weight less than 2,000 lbs (907 kgs)
2. Maximum engine size of 180 hp either as a single or shared (two) power-plant(s)
3. Maximum stalling speed of 60 mph (96 kmph), with power off in the landing configuration
4. No more than two seats
5. Not less than 500 hours' construction time

This authority is exercised for the benefit of PFA members by their full-time Engineering Executive who have delegated powers from the Civil Aviation Authority.

When a PFA member decides on which aircraft he is going to build—and there are reams of information on this available from the PFA including their list of 'Approved designs' and 'Designs currently under survey' (see the table overleaf)—he must complete a registration card with the aircraft type, plan/kit number, proposed engine and maximum take-off weight and return this to the PFA with a £30 registration fee. This will then be

Part of the homebuilts and veteran/vintage aircraft parking area at the PFA's Cranfield rally in 1988, with the characteristic hangars of the College of Aeronautics behind. (Author)

entered in the PFA's Projects data-base and a constructor's serial number will then be issued as well as the constructor's log-book in which the various stages of inspection of the aircraft are recorded in duplicate. This duplicate copy is then returned to the PFA Office and, in the event of the project changing hands before its completion, the PFA will then have tangible proof of its history.

Approved aircraft for the homebuilder in Great Britain

Aircraft of the following types have been approved by the PFA in this country. All information is presented in good faith, but there is no guarantee that a Permit to Fly can be issued.

Acrosport 1
Acrosport 2
Aerosport Scamp
Andreasson BA 4B†
Avid Flyer
Bede BD 4†
Boredom Fighter†
Bowers Fly Baby
Cassutt Racer†
Cavalier SA 102.5†
CFM Streak Shadow
Chilton DW 1
Colibri MB-2
Colomban Cri-Cri
Comper CLA7
Condor
Cosmic Wind*
Cozy
Currie Wot
DAL Tuholer†
Davis DA2A
EAA Biplane
Evans VP-1†
Evans VP-2
Falco F8L
Falconar F10
Falconar F11
Fisher Koala Cub
FRED
Hatz CB-1
Heath Parasol*
Isaacs Fury
Isaacs Spitfire
Jodel D9†
Jodel D11†
Jodel D18†
Jodel D119†
Jurca Sirocco
Jurca Tempete
Kitfox 1, 2 and 3†
Kittiwake 1*
Loisir*
Luton Major*
Luton Minor
Luton Minor 3 Duet*
Midget Mustang
Minicab CY 201 JB-01
MiniMax†
Monnett Moni†
Monnett Sonerai 1†
Monnett Sonerai 2†
Oldfield Baby Lakes†
Osprey
Pazmany PL1
Pazmany PL2
Pazmany PL4A
Piel Emeraude
Pietenpol Aircamper
Pitts Special S1
Plumb BGP-1 biplane
Practavia Sprite*†
Quad City Challenger†
Quickie 1
Quickie 2
Quickie 200
Rand KR 2†
Rans S4†
Rans S5†
Rans S6†
Rans S9†
Rans S10†
Renegade Spirit
Replica SE5A
Rollason Beta
Rutan Long-Eze*
Rutan Varieze*
Starlite†
Steen Skybolt
Stephens Akro
Stitts Playboy
Stolp Starduster 2†
Stolp Starlet
Stolp V-Star
Sunderland S-18
Taylor Monoplane†
Taylor Titch
Thorp T-18
Tipsy Nipper†
TSW-2
Turbulent†
Vans RV 4†
Viking Dragonfly
Volmer Sportsman
Wagabond
Wag Aero Cuby
WAR FW 190†
WAR Sea Fury†
Whittaker MW5
Whittaker MW6
Whittaker MW7
Wittman Tailwind
Woody Pusher
Zenith 100
Zenith 200, 250

† Mandatory PFA modifications must be incorporated
* New plans are not readily available for these aircraft. Second hand plans may be available, but potential builders should take care to ensure that these have been supported by amendments from the designer.

Aircraft currently under survey

Avid Speedwing
Bushby Mustang 2
BX2 Cherry
Carlson Sparrow
Celebrity
Christavia
Circa Nieuport II
Coot Amphibian
Corby Starlet
DK1 Der Kricket
Early Bird Jenny
Falconar F12
Flaglor Scooter
Fisher Classic
Fisher Super Koala
HAPI Cygnet
Jungster 1
Kingfisher
Kitfox 4
Kolb Twinstar
Lancair
LM-1X
Lobet Ganagobie
Marquart Charger
Macair Merlin
Menestrel 2
Minicoupe
Mosler Pup
Murphy Rebel
5151 Mustang
Pelican Club
Piel Saphir
Pober Pixie
Pulsar
Pottier P80
Rans S7
Rutan Variviggen
Sindlinger Hurricane
Smith Miniplane
Smyth Sidewinder
Sparrow Hawk
Turner T 40
Vans RV3
Vans RV 6
WAR Thunderbolt
Windwagon
Ultimate 100/200
Zenair CH 600
Zenair CH 701

Reproduced with permission of the PFA. Correct to January 1992.

Another document that the newly registered homebuilder will receive is the 'PFA List of Approved Inspectors'. Within the ranks of the PFA there are a surprisingly large number who are suitably qualified to act as Inspectors. They carry out, on a voluntary basis, the task of supervising the construction and reconstruction of members' aircraft, provided that they are within the criteria of the PFA's remit from the CAA. These Inspectors are categorised into their specialities, either fixed-wing aircraft or gyroplanes; their particular fortés, be it wood, metal or both, engines, composites, or whatever, are listed against their names; and there is a geographical break-down of names to help you locate your 'local man'. The PFA also points out that besides their list, any Licensed Aircraft Engineer is normally acceptable provided that his licence is valid in the appropriate category. Also, by special arrangements a member serving with HM Forces may use a station technical officer with the relevant experience.

The Inspector will also carry out the annual renewal check on the aircraft once it has flown, with the owner being able to do the maintenance, thus saving considerable sums of money as against having to use commerical aircraft engineering and overhaul companies.

Britain has sadly fallen behind in light and homebuilt aircraft design, and some of the blame for this is often placed at the door of the PFA and its 'conservative' attitude towards anyone with a new idea, and its restrictive criteria on aircraft size and power. Certainly when compared to the prolific output of homebuilt and kitplane designs of US origin, Britain's contribution has been pitifully small. Chapter 7 describes the struggle encountered by Ivan Shaw in this respect. Other notable examples of British homebuilt designs are John Isaacs's Fury and Spitfire replicas (Chapter 7), the Taylor Monoplane and Titch (Chapter 3), the FRED and the CFM Streak Shadow (Chapter 15). There are a few other one-offs, but this diminutive list speaks for itself!

In its defence, unlike the EAA in the USA whose role is more 'advisory' and puts the onus for design and construction upon the builder himself or herself, the PFA is the guardian of the homebuilt movement, a responsibility to be treated with professionalism and respect. However, within this authority PFA Engineering can be criticised for a lack of innovative foresight in the 1970s and '80s, a fact that is demonstrated by looking at the rows of homebuilts at each year's big fly-in. Part of this conservatism may have been due to too high a workload and too small a staff. It should be remembered that the PFA in Britain operates under the CAA whose rules are widely accepted as being far stricter than the equivalent FAA ones in the USA. The PFA finds it very difficult to persuade the CAA 'to move forward' in many areas – microlights are a case in point in 1992.

In this context it should, of course, be mentioned that PFA Engineering will also advise on and vet members' new designs, providing guidance and checking on the integrity of the structure. Inspectors will also provide innovative and freethought on new or accepted designs, and on modifications that a builder may wish to make.

For his or her annual membership fee (£27.00 per annum for a standard UK and overseas membership in March 1992) the PFA member will receive bi-monthly copies of its colourful and informative house journal, 'Popular Flying', and will be able to take advantage of the many services and activities listed in the preceding pages.

The current Chairman of the PFA is Ray Delves ARICS, and the Chief Engineer Francis Donaldson BTech CEng MRAeS. There are also two Vice-Chairmen, one of whom is designated Secretary and Treasurer. The Association is run by an elected Executive Committee totalling 15 members and every quarter a National Council meets consisting of this Executive Committee and a delegate of each Strut and certain Groups representing a membership currently numbering over 7,000.

British Microlight Aircraft Association (BMAA)

This is the governing body for microlight (ultralight or ULM) flying in Great Britain, formed in 1979 as the British Minimum Aircraft Association (soon to change to the British Microlight Aircraft Association), and a CAA Approved organisation for dealing with many aspects of the airworthiness procedures pertaining to such aircraft. The BMAA can now supervise the construction of homebuilt and kitplane microlights for 'Series' aeroplanes, ie those that conform to Section 'S' of the British Civil Airworthiness requirements. However, in the past all types of microlight construction have been controlled by the PFA and many still are—subsequent renewals of 'Permits to Fly' cannot be done by the BMAA.

Microlights fall into two basic categories: flex-wind or weight-shift (2- or 3-axis control), as used by hang-gliders; and fixed-wing or conventional 3-axis control. For the purpose of airworthiness requirements, the CAA considers a microlight to be: 'A one or two seat aeroplane whose empty weight shall not exceed 150 kg (330 lbs) and whose wing loading shall not be less than the weight divided by 10 in square metres'. This wing area rule was introduced to prevent the design and production of high-speed machines.

To permit two-seater machines to be used in the training role and to be made stronger, a new definition came into effect on 11 October 1988 which defined a microlight built after this date as: 'A one or two seat aeroplane whose maximum total weight authorised (MTWA) shall not exceed 390 kg (860 lbs) at take-off and whose wing loading at MTWA shall not exceed 25 kg (63 lbs) per square metre nor shall the fuel capacity exceed 50 litres (11 imp gals)'.

The freedom—and disasters—of the early days of microlighting in Britain in the late 1970s led in 1981 to the introduction of legislation. it was rather like the Flying Flea fiasco all over again. The addition of an engine to a hang-glider makes it an aeroplane under the definitions of the Air Navigation Order, administered by the CAA. What the PFA does for homebuilts the BMAA does for microlights, with a membership of over 3,800 and with an estimated 2,000 microlights operating in Britain. A close working relationship exists between the BMAA and the CAA—the former deals with routine inspection and checks flying on microlights under an inspectorate/check pilot organisation which is approved by the Authority. Also the BMAA deals on the CAA's behalf with recommendations and administration of pilot licensing and instructor rating.

The joining fee for the BMAA is £3.00, with a standard membership then being £25.00 per annum (at February 1991 rates)—there are also overseas and family memberships available. For this a member receives the bi-monthly magazine 'Flightlines' as well as intermediate newsletters and bi-monthly technical bulletins. Access is available through the BMAA to specialist insurers for third-party liability, to advice on technical matters from a full-time Officer; and to legal advice, particularly in relation to the status of a second-hand microlight which a member may be considering purchasing. Like the PFA there is also the regional camaraderie through local clubs, fly-ins and much more, including some of the most economic pilot training available today, with the BMAA authorised to recommend the issue of Private Pilot Licenses (A) Group D. The current BMAA Chief Executive Officer is Brian Cosgrove.

United States of America

Experimental Aircraft Association (EAA)

Founded in January 1953 by Paul Howard Poberezny (see Chapter 3) at a meeting at Curtiss-Wright (now Timmerman) Field in Milwaukee, USA, membership rapidly expanded from six to 31, all local. By 1971 this figure had become 29,025, and in 1991 over 120,000 worldwide.

The EAA group in Milwaukee was formed with the purpose of aiding and assisting amateur aircraft builders, but quickly took on the additional task of promoting all aspects of sport aviation, the preservation of the USA's aviation heritage of personal flight, and the promotion of aviation safety. By October 1953 the word had spread, and on the West Coast Ray Stits (see Chapter 3) had contacted the Milwaukee group and requested permission to form a branch based at Riverside, California. This became EAA Chapter No 1, the first of more than 700 worldwide that now exist to provide local support for the homebuilder, sport aviator and others.

It was through the pages of magazines such as *Flying* and *Mechanix Illustrated* that people got to hear about the EAA; by 1955 Paul Poberezny had modified the original Corben Baby Ace design and through the columns of *Mechanix Ilustrated* readers were given a series of articles on how to construct one. The Baby Ace was also adopted in 1955 by the EAA 'Project Schoolflight' aviation education programme which encouraged schools, under the administration of the EAA, to construct Baby Ace homebuilts. An estimated 100 projects were completed and flown.

The EAA's magazine *Sport Aviation*, a direct descendant of the earlier *Experimenter*, first appeared in January 1958. For the 7th Annual EAA Fly-In convention in August 1959, the EAA moved from Milwaukee to Rockford, Illinois, their home for several years before the move to Oshkosh, Wisconsin, in August 1971 (see Chapter 10). In the meantime the EAA Air Museum Foundation was incorporated in April 1962 and over the years has developed into one of the world's finest privately owned aviation museums, now housed in a prestigious and imaginative building at Oshkosh and displaying on rotation about 70 aircraft of more than 200 sport, light and homebuilt aircraft in the EAA's inventory.

Realising that many EAA members had interests beyond homebuilts, in 1971 three EAA Divisions were established to cater for more specialised interests: the Antique/Classic Division; the International Aerobatic Club; and the Warbirds of America. The Ultralight Association was added in 1981. Each of the three original Divisions have 'add-on' memberships to the basic EAA membership.

The EAA has always prided itself on its lobbying role with the Federal Government in Washington DC on behalf of its members and the private flying fraternity in the USA. An early success on behalf of its ultralighters was in 1983 when it successfully petitioned the Federal Aviation Administration (FAA) for exemption permits for flight training in two-seater ultralights. In 1984 they received FAA approval to issue additional Mogas/auto fuel certificates (STCs) for a wide range of light aircraft—101 separate aircraft models eventually became eligible for EAA Auto Fuel STCs.

The EAA's achievement have been monumental both nationally and internationally, and the election of Paul Poberezny as President of the Commission Internationale des Aeronefs des Construction Amateur (CIACA) was an added example of this esteem. CIACA is the committee of the Federation Aeronautique Internationale (FAI) which represents the interests of amateur builders and antique aircraft owners on a worldwide basis. The British PFA and many other national amateur aircraft organisations are also represented on the CIACA.

The most recent statistics from the EAA in 1991

The aircraft camping area at Oshkosh in 1990—these pilots arrived early to secure their plots. Note the home-from-home flamingos! (Author)

in respect of the USA indicate that on their Amateur Built Registry there are now over 13,000 operating aircraft plus about 600 racing aircraft. This growth started from 2,865 amateur aircraft in 1971 to 7,496 at the end of 1981. Overall, EAA membership nationally and internationally is 123,000 with about 6,000 members in each of the three Divisions.

If someone wants to build an aeroplane in the USA they have to adhere to FAA Advisory Circular 20-27C, 'Certification and Operations of Amateur-Built Aircraft' (see Appendix 2). The EAA has Technical Counsellors (TCs) (see Appendix 3 for details of the EAA's TC Program) within its Chapters who will visit aircraft under construction, and although they may give advice and be as helpful as possible, they do not sign logs and do not actually do formal 'inspections'. Also, the FAA does not recognise their work. Basically there is only one inspection of a homebuilt in the USA, prior to its first flight, and there are no formal inspections by the EAA or any government body prior to this. The onus is very much on the builder himself, or herself to keep good and accurate records of the construction, workmanship and methods and to satisfy the FAA Inspector of the aircraft's integrity. The Inspector will then, if satisfied, issue an Air-

The EAA's Museum at Oshkosh.

worthiness Certificate enabling the builder to carry out test-flying, exploring any particular avenues the Inspector may require. The test-flight programme must include 25 hours' flight-time, provided that a type-certificated engine and propeller combination has been used. Once this has been completed, the aircraft builder/owner must then apply to the FAA for amended operating limitations. For this he must submit his flight-test log.

The profusion of one-off and new homebuilt designs in the USA presents its own problems, but again the onus is on the designer/builder to prove to the FAA the airworthiness of the aircraft, and again the FAA's mandate is to be sure that the aircraft is airworthy prior to flight. For a new design or new engine/propeller fit, the FAA requires the Flight Test Programme to last 40 hours.

American homebuilt and kitplanes must be placarded as 'Experimental' as a result of this system. When the FAA issues its unlimited Airworthiness Certificate to a homebuilt, it imposes a limitation that further inspections must be carried out at 12-month intervals, but the builder can be certificated as the 'repairman' for the aircraft and can carry out the condition inspection himself. Again the onus is very much on the builder!

A growing complication within amateur-built aircraft circles identified by the EAA and FAA was the growing popularity of the kitplane. For this reason a change occurred to FAA certification of these types of homebuilt in 1987 requiring more than 50 per cent of the fabrication and 50 per cent of the assembly to be carried out by the builder. The '51 per cent rule' thus came into being and is now an accepted part of homebuilding in the USA. The same cannot be said of Britain where the CAA's Safety Regulation Group have issued an Airworthiness Information Leaflet to try to regulate such kits as either amateur or professional by having an 'hours-to-build' cut-off point (see Appendix 1). This takes no account of each builder's skills and threatens to impose considerable CAA charges in some cases; one well-known British homebuilder has commented, 'It would appear that US kit imports are giving the CAA an even bigger headache than the Flying Flea gave the old ARB almost 60 years previously'.

What happens under the EAA/FAA system in the USA does not apply to other national EAA organisations in other countries. Here the EAA is usually the forum for homebuilders in name and aspiration, but frequently each particular country's government aviation department makes its own rules and regulations for homebuilders (see, for instance, under Norway below).

Paul Poberezny finally retired as President of the EAA in August 1989 after 36 years, although he has moved sideways to become Chairman of the EAA Board of Directors. Paul's son, Tom, has taken over the day-to-day running as Senior Vice-President.

France

Réseau du Sport de l'Air (RSA)

France is probably the 'mother figure' of European homebuilt aviation. Historically the work of Henri Mignet in the 1930s established the enthusiasm and the means for the French man in the street to try to start building and flying, first with his Mignet HM.8 and then the HM.14 Pou-du-Ciel or Flying Flea. In 1934 the Réseau des Amateurs de l'Air (RAA) was founded as a central organisation to look after and promote the interests of Flea builders – few people had dared to believe such an organisation could exist, least of all the French administration.

Notwithstanding, the RAA flourished and although the 'Flea fiasco' followed and it was to disappear officially, followed by the war and the occupation, it has lit the fire in many Frenchmen, a fire that was to be re-kindled immediately with the cessation of hostilities.

Many Fleas survived intact beyond 1939-45 and it is claimed that the first flight by an amateur-built aircraft after the Liberation was by Maurice Guerimet from Auxerre in his HM.14 No 147, but there were many others. Robert Guidon, the President of the Pou-du-Ciel Club at Valenciennes, called for the formation of a Pou-du-Ciel Club of France. This aroused much interest and a meeting was arranged for 24 November 1946, sponsored by the Valenciennes Pou Club and the *Amicale d'Aviation Légère de Lyon* (Friends of Light Aviation in Lyon)—they proposed the formation of a national group in France to support the interests of amateur aircraft builders. A national meeting was thus organised in Paris in 1947 when the Réseau du Sport de l'Air was officially founded, and although Mignet himself and some of his supporters wanted to see him installed as the RSA's first President, the displeasure felt in many quarters about the pre-war Flea fiasco meant that Pierre Lacour was elected to the position. Georges Beraud helped manage the RSA through its formative years until 1971 when Louis Cariou took over the Presidency, a post he still holds.

Post-war France was a hive of aeronautical activity, partly a result of the homebuilding 'bug' generated by Mignet and the RAA but also as a result of considerable government support for the revival of the country's aircraft industry, pilot training and the flying club scene. Chapter 3 and the table of French homebuilts clearly illustrates this hive of homebuilt activity, all of the aircraft now being officially registered in the F-P . . . series (F-W . . . is the test

One of innumerable unidentified French-built examples of the Mignet HM.14 Flying Flea. (Pierre Gaillard, Author's Collection)

registration prior to ascribing to the F-P . . . status) and being issued with a Certificat de Navigabilité Restreint d'Aéronef (CNRA). The first CNRA 'permits' were introduced for homebuilts in 1938, then in 1951 a new revised CNRA came into existence looked after by Services Officiels—in 1955 this was expanded to encompass gliders, and in 1962 a further revision took place, introducing a relaxation of restrictions for amateur aircraft designers and constructors. CNRAs were issued to homebuilts being flown for sport and pleasure and not for hire or reward. Like the EAA in the USA and the PFA in Britain, the RSA in France is the official representative body for homebuilders campaigning at government level for their rights and those of the sport aviator and in turn helping to administer homebuilding.

A homebuilder in France has to have his aircraft inspected during construction and before its first flight at five different stages has to satisfy an Inspector representing the Director General of Civil Aviation (DGAC) on these counts. The stages are:

1. The techniques used and the airframe structure prior to covering
2. The aircraft with instruments and accessories in place
3. The assembled aircraft with control surfaces operational and in place
4. A final check of the completed aircraft to grant the temporary test flight authorisation
5. A check to ensure that the aircraft has basic equipment in place, eg restraint harnesses and instruments such as ASI, artificial horizon, compass, altimeter, etc

This technical control of homebuilts is dealt with by the DGAC/Bureau Veritas but builders who want an opinion from the RSA can send their construction 'dossier' to the RSA initially for evaluation (a model dossier is given in Appendix 4). Provided that the RSA is happy with it, they will then forward it direct to the DGAC. A Provisional Authorisation to Fly will then be issued to a homebuilt, which has to complete endurance flights within a 20 km (12.1-mile) radius of the home airfield, to complete 15 hours of test flying, and to have completed 50 landings. Provided this and everything else is in order, the Bureau Veritas in Paris will then issue the CNRA.

The RSA therefore plays an advisory role for the French homebuilder and is a forum for ideas, new designs and the promotion of homebuilding. It has a Technical Commission dealing with general problems but the individual builder or designer is technically responsible for the aircraft he builds. A unique innovation controlled by the RSA is the distribution, in the form of completion grants, of 100,000 francs annually to designers and builders of new homebuilt prototypes and standard designs which incorporate innovations or design improvements. This relatively small sum is nonetheless looked upon enviously by homebuilders in other nations and, whether by design or chance, France continues to support a proliferation of new homebuilt designs every year, and also has one of the strongest homebuilt movements.

The RSA has permanently manned headquarters in Paris looking after a current membership of about 3,000 in France plus many others in countries around the world. In 1991 there were about 1,050 homebuilt aircraft registered in the F-P . . . series, about 150 autogyros and 50 ULMs (microlights), and the RSA has records of another 1,300 under construction. The growth in aircraft numbers has

A cross-section of types now flying or under construction in France by RSA members

Aircraft	Country of origin	Number of seats	Engine	Type	Construction
Sport aircraft					
JODEL D9 'Bébé'	F	1	VW	low-wing	wood/fabric
DRUINE 'Turbulent'	F	1	VW	low-wing	wood/fabric
BRUGGER 'Colibri'	CH	1	VW	low-wing	wood/fabric
GATARD 'Poussin'	F	1	VW	low-wing	wood/fabric
NICOLLIER 'Menestrel'	F	1	VW	low-wing	wood/fabric
MIGNET HM 360	F	1	VW	'Flea'-type	wood/fabric
CROSES 'Pou-Plume'	F	1	VW	'Flea'-type	wood/fabric
EVANS VP.1	USA	1	VW	low-wing	wood/fabric
LUTON 'Minor'	GB	1	VW	high-wing	wood/fabric
STERN ST 80	F	1	VW	low-wing	wood/fabric
FOURNIER RF 4 or RF 7	F	1	VW	low-wing	wood/fabric
RAND KR 1	USA	1	VW	low-wing	wood/foam/resin
QUICKIE	USA	1	Onan	'Canard'	composite
NICKEL 'Astérix'	F	2	Ami 8	high-wing	wood/foam/fabric
POTTIER 'Bouvreuil'	F	1	Cont-Lyco	low-wing	wood/fabric
POTTIER P 70 or P 80	F	1	VW	mid or low	metal
COLOMBAN 'CriCri'	F	1	2 JPX	low-wing	metal
HEINTZ 'Mono Z'	F	1	VW	low-wing	metal
PARKER 'Teenie Too'	F	1	VW	low-wing	metal
WATSON 'Windwagon'	USA	1	1/2VW	low-wing	metal
PAZMANY PL 4	USA	1	VW	low-wing	metal
MONNETT 'Moni'	USA	1	KFM	low-wing	metal
VANS RV3 or RV4	USA	1 or 2	Cont-Lyco	low-wing	metal
Touring aircraft					
JODEL D18-D19	F	2	VW	low-wing	wood/fabric
J.P. MARIE J.P.M.01	F	2	VW	low-wing	wood/fabric
NICOLLIER 'Ménestrel II'	F	2	VW	low-wing	wood/fabric
RAND KR2	USA	2	VW	low-wing	wood/composite
BRANDLI 'Cherry'	CH	2	VW	high-wing	wood/composite
VIKING 'Dragonfly'	USA	2	VW	'Canard'	composite
POTTIER P 170	F	2	VW	low-wing	metal
POTTIER P 180	F	2	VW-Conti	low-wing	metal
POTTIER P100 or 105	F	2	Conti	low-wing	metal
JODEL D 112-D119	F	2	Conti	low-wing	wood/fabric
JODEL D 150	F	2	Conti-Lyco	low-wing	wood/fabric
JODEL 140	F	4	Lyco	low-wing	wood/fabric
JODEL DR 1050	F	3	Conti-Lyco	low-wing	wood/fabric
PIEL 'Emeraude'	F	2	Conti-Lyco	low-wing	wood/fabric
PIEL 'Diamant'	F	3	Lyco	low-wing	wood/fabric
PIEL 'Saphir'	F	3	Lyco	low-wing	wood/fabric
DENIZE 'Raid-Driver'	F	1–4	Conti-Lyco	low-wing	wood/fabric
DRUINE 'Turbi'	F	2	Conti	low-wing	wood/fabric
FOURNIER RF 6	F	2	Conti	low-wing	wood/fabric
COUPE JC 01	F	2	Conti	low-wing	wood/fabric
FALCO F 8L	USA	2	Conti-Lyco	low-wing	wood/fabric
PAUMIER 'Baladin'	F	2	Conti-Lyco	low-wing	wood/fabric
OSPREY 'GP4'	USA	2	Conti-Lyco	low-wing	wood/fabric
ADAM RA 14	F	2	Conti	high-wing	wood/fabric
CROSES 'Criquet'	F	2	Conti	'Flea'-type	wood/fabric
LEDERLIN 380 L	F	2	Conti	'Flea'-type	wood/tube/fabric
WITTMAN 'Tailwind'	USA	2	Conti-Lyco	high-wing	wood/tube/fabric
DURUBLE 'Edelweiss'	F	2–4	Conti-Lyco	low-wing	metal
HEINTZ 'Zénith' or 'TriZ'	F	2–3	Conti-Lyco	low-wing	metal
ZODIAC CH 600	CAN	2	Conti-Lyco	low-wing	metal
LUCAS L 5	F	2	Conti-Lyco	low-wing	metal
THORP 18	USA	2	Conti-Lyco	low-wing	metal
BUSHBY 'Mustang II'	USA	2	Conti-Lyco	low-wing	metal
CHASLE YC 30	F	2	Conti-Lyco	low-wing	metal
VANS RV 6	USA	2	Conti-Lyco	low-wing	metal

GRINVALDS 'Orion'		F	4	Conti-Lyco	low-wing	composite
CO-Z 'Cozy'		USA	2	Conti-Lyco	'Canard'	composite
HAMILTON 'Glasair'		USA	2	Conti-Lyco	low-wing	composite
NEICO 'Lancair'		USA	2	Conti-Lyco	low-wing	composite
Amphibian						
VOLMER 'Sportsman'		USA	2	Conti-Lyco	high-wing	wood/fabric
PEREIRA 'Osprey I or II'		USA	1 or 2	Conti-Lyco	mid-wing	
TAYLOR 'Coot'		USA	2	Conti-Lyco	mid-wing	wood/fabric
Aerobatic aircraft						
JURCA 'Tempête'		F	1	Conti-Lyco	low-wing	wood/fabric
K.S. AIRCRAFT 'Jungster I'		USA	1	Conti-Lyco	biplane	wood/fabric
PITTS S 1		USA	1	Conti-Lyco	biplane	tube/wood/fabric
STEPHENS 'Akro'		USA	1	Conti-Lyco	mid-wing	tube/wood/fabric
ACRODUSTER 1 or 2		USA	1 or 2	Conti-Lyco	biplane	tube/wood/fabric
PIEL CP 750		F	2	Conti-Lyco	low-wing	tube/wood/fabric
JURCA 'Sirocco'		F	2	Conti-Lyco	low-wing	wood/fabric
C.A.P. 10		F	2	Conti-Lyco	low-wing	wood/fabric
STARDUSTER TOO		USA	2	Conti-Lyco	biplane	tube/wood/fabric
STEEN 'Skybolt'		USA	2	Conti-Lyco	biplane	tube/wood/fabric
ACRO SPORT		USA	1–2	Conti-Lyco	biplane	tube/wood/fabric
Racing aircraft; Formula 1						
PIEL CP 80		F	1	Continental	low-wing	wood/fabric
M.P 205 'Busard'		F	1	Continental	low-wing	wood/fabric
TAYLOR 'Titch'		GB	1	Continental	low-wing	wood/fabric
LUTON 'Beta'		GB	1	Continental	low-wing	wood/fabric
CASSUTT III		USA	1	Continental	mid-wing	tube/wood/fabric
CONDOR 'Shoestring'		USA	1	Continental	mid-wing	tube/wood/fabric
OWL 'racer'		USA	1	Continental	mid-wing	tube/wood/fabric
BUSHBY 'Mustang 1'		USA	1	Continental	low-wing	metal
Racing aircraft; Formula V						
WITTMAN V		USA	1	VW	mid-wing	tube/wood/fabric
MONNETT 'Sonerai'		USA	1	VW	mid or low wing	tube/metal/fabric
SOUTHERN 'Renegade'		USA	1	VW	mid wing	tube/wood/fabric
Replicas	*Scale*					
NIEUPORT 17 or 24	(1/1)	USA	1	Conti-Lyco	biplane	wood/fabric
S.E 5A	(7/8)	USA	1	Conti-Lyco	biplane	wood/fabric
ISAACS 'Fury'	(4/5)	GB	1	Conti-Lyco	biplane	wood/fabric
JURCA 'Mustang'	(2/3)	F	1	Conti-Lyco	low-wing	wood/fabric
JURCA 'Mustang'	(3/4)	F	1 or 2	Conti-Lyco	low-wing	wood/fabric
JURCA 'FW 190'	(3/4)	F	1 or 2	Conti-Lyco	low-wing	wood/fabric
ISAACS 'Spitfire'	(7/10)	GB	1	Conti-Lyco	low-wing	wood/fabric
HAWKER 'Hurricane'	(5/8)	USA	1	Conti-Lyco	low-wing	wood/fabric
WAR 'FW 190'	(1/2)	USA	1	Conti-Lyco	low-wing	wood/composite
WAR 'P 47'	(1/2)	USA	1	Conti-Lyco	low-wing	wood/composite
WAR 'Corsair'	(1/2)	USA	1	Conti-Lyco	low-wing	wood/composite
WAR 'Zero'	(1/2)	USA	1	Conti-Lyco	low-wing	wood/composite
Gliders/powered gliders						
R. ADAM RA 10 S		F	1	Planeur léger	high-wing	wood/fabric
MARSKE 'Monarch'		USA	1	Planeur léger	loose-wing	wood/composite
MAUPIN 'Woodstock'		USA	1	Planeur	high-wing	wood/fabric
DEBREYER 'Pélican'		F	1	Motoplaneur	shift-wing	wood/fabric
FOURNIER RF 5		F	2	VW	low-wing	wood/fabric
NOIN 'Sirius'		F	1	Motoplaneur	high-wing	wood/composite
Ultralights						
PIEL 'Onyx'		F	1	20 hp	'Canard'	wood/fabric
GUERPONT 'Biplum'		F	1	20 hp	biplane	wood/fabric
TISSERAND 'Hydroplum'		F	1	40 hp	seaplane	wood/composite
CROSES 'Airplume'		F	2	40 hp	'Flea'-type	wood/composite
LANG 'A.P.O.U.A.L.'		F	2	40 hp	trike/flexwing	tube

Information supplied by the RSA

been steady from about 530 in 1978, through the 800 barrier in 1985. Membership has also grown by an average of about 250 each year since 1978. A typical cross section of homebuilt types built in France is given in the table on pages 126–7.

Regional Groups operate in France much as the PFA Struts and the EAA Chapters. One of the most active is in south-west France where the Centre National RSA de Montauban, *Ateliers Amateur de Montauban*, has been established during the 1980s thanks largely to the work of Charles Roussoulieres. This is a permanent facility funded by city, regional and national funds, and the RSA and their regional group, where homebuilders can be taught the skills of aircraft construction. In this prolific 'factory' a builder can construct part or all of his aircraft under expert guidance and, if building an established aircraft design such as a Jodel D.18, utilise the jigs already available there. Training courses are run at the centre for homebuilders from around France and also from other countries including Tunisia and Morocco. Their speciality, as with much of the French homebuilt fraternity, is wooden construction—examples of the two-seater VW-powered Jodel D.18 design have literally poured out of the Montauban 'factory' door in the last five years and have contributed considerably to the RSA's statistic of 1,050 homebuilts flying. Other notable types to be built at Montauban include the prototype of the side-by-side two-seater Nicollier HN.700 Menestrel (Minstrel) II, which first flew there in June 1989; a brace of four Sequoia F.8 Falcos is under construction, utilising common jigs; a J.3 Kitten ULM; other Jodels; an Emeraude; a Brugger MB.2 Colibri; and even a few metal aircraft including the Acroduster (tubular metal fuselage structure and wood/fabric wings) and a Pottier P.180.

Montauban is the pride of the RSA and has proved, with suitable voluntary and financial support, that it meets a growing demand in France for homebuilders of all ages. For this reason plans are at an advanced stage for another such facility for metal aircraft at Moulins, in central France, and a centre for composite construction has already been established at Verdun.

The Regional Groups of the RSA organise fly-ins each year, but France's tour du force is the RSA's International Fly-In held on the last weekend of July currently at Moulins (Montbeugny) airfield, where as many as 800 aircraft gather, at least one-third of them homebuilts (a very high percentage when compared to Oshkosh or the PFA rally) (see Chapter 10). An RSA Museum is also operational at Brienne-le-Chateau airfield, containing examples of many early French homebuilt types including the Adam RA-14 Loisirs, Leduc RL-19 and Williams Motorfly. The more modern jets housed there are part of the Musée Aeronautique de Champagne, now believed to be in the process of disbandment. Also associated with the RSA are the various country-wide 'branches' of Les Ailes Anciennes, whose interest is the preservation and operation of vintage and veteran aircraft, part of France's rich aviation heritage, and part of the Federation Français des Aeronefs de Collection (which can be contacted at 12 Rue Léon Cogniet, 75017 Paris, France).

The RSA publishes an excellent bi-monthly maga-

The international flavour of homebuilding—an American-designed and Norwegian-built Bowers Fly Baby homebuilt at the French fly-in at Brienne-le-Chateau, accompanied by several Swiss homebuilts. (Author)

zine, 'Les Cahiers du RSA', and one enlarged issue each year contains a complete pictorial review of the previous year's fly-ins. The annual subscription for normal membership of the RSA, including receipt of 'Les Cahiers', is 390 francs.

The Vice-President is currently Jacques Avril and the Secretary General Robert Granger, part of a controlling executive committee of 16 which also includes two Technical Counsellors, Jean Pottier and Henri Fékété.

Belgium

Flemisch Amateur Aircraftbuilders (FAA); Belgian Aircraft Homebuilders (BAH); Réseau du Sport de l'Air de Belgique (RSAB)

To quote one of Belgium's current homebuilt aircraft enthusiasts, 'To find some excuse for the present trio of organisations in such a small country, suffice to say that the Belgian amateur aviator is very much an individualist—being helped is a true dishonour!' This may go some way to explain the complexity of both the history of homebuilding in Belgium and the present diversity of organisation there.

Belgium's first homebuilders after the First World War were few and operated without any control or central organisation. M. Poncelet was one of the first of these in 1923 when he designed and built his own glider that set a world flight duration record. The later motorised version of this, the SABCA Poncelet Vivette 0-BAFH, is preserved in the AELR Museum in Brussels. Henri Mignet's influence in Belgium was considerable, first with his HM.8 and then inevitably with the HM.14 Pou-du-Ciel (Flying Flea).

Immediately after the Second World War frustrated amateur aviators in Belgium founded the first formal Belgian homebuild organisation, 'Les Amis du Pou-du-Ciel' (APC), with lawyer M. Gossieau as its first president, M. A. Watteyne as the head of its 'Technical Committee', and publishing a bimonthly magazine *L'Aeronef* for its members. Indeed, as early as February 1945 the fourth edition of *L'Aeronef* had already been published, including details of a tricycle undercarriage arrangement for HM.14s.

Although the APC was predominantly Flea-orientated and had the motto 'Let's Fly Our Fleas', in 1945 it was still illegal to fly a non-certified aircraft in Belgium. The APC therefore undertook to convince the Belgian Air Ministry to allow them to fly, and in 1946 the latter issued a new set of regulations officially allowing the construction of homebuilts, but not yet approval for them to fly. Under pressure from 98 Flea builders and fliers in Belgium, the Authorities capitulated and in July 1947 homebuilts in Belgium could officially fly provided it was within a 5 km (3-mile) radius of their home airfield. An official system of registration was also started with the 00- . . . system, projects being registered numerically and sequentially, although frequently many, many years before completion. Flea-mania subsequently diminished, probably because of Mignet's departure from Europe, the introduction of more stringent regulations for construction and operation of amateur aircraft, and the advent of new homebuilt designs such as the Jodel D.9 and the Druine Turbulent. As a result of this decline the APC disappeared in the early 1950s.

Paul Poberezny was invited to visit Brussels in 1966 and officially launched EAA Chapter 258 in Belgium. The initial euphoria promised by the vast range of new homebuilt designs now available via the EAA and from the USA soon faded when it was evident that the Belgian 'Service du Material Volant' (SMV) would not accept their construction and flight in Belgium just because they had flown in the USA.

It was from this 'watershed', though, that the regulations currently governing homebuilt aircraft in Belgium originated. The Belgian 'Service Technique de l'Aéronautique' (STA) had relatively liberal regulations initially, but soon became more restrictive. In 1973, for instance, the STA's general Technical Specifications only permitted a few specific single-seater homebuilt types to be built, such as the HM.290 and 293 (Fleas), the Turbulent, Jodel D.9 and Tipsy Nipper; for two-seaters or other single-seaters a full Airworthiness Certificate was asked for and the only affordable examples in this category were the Jodel D.112/117 and the Piel Emeraude.

In 1981 the regulations changed and the Evans VP-1 and VP-2, the EAA Acrosport and Jurca MJ2 Tempete were added to the official list—the scope was expanded so that homebuilders could now build any design provided they could supply a full stress and flight characteristic analysis. However, this was not as liberal as it might first appear because the comprehensiveness of the data required by the STA was phenomenal. They provided an alternative, however—Belgians could build a 'test airframe' to be tested to destruction at the DTA's (Direction Technique de l'Aéronautique) laboratories! It was not just new designs that suffered from these problems, but also modifications to the few established designs of the Belgian 'list'. A major achievement was approval for the construction and flight of two Rutan VariEzes in the 1980s—otherwise today's Belgian homebuilt aircraft inventory is very staid. About 100 homebuilts have been registered there since the official register commenced, but of these only about 25 have actually flown, with a mere 12 still active.

A Belgian homebuilder has to submit to a rigorous inspection process from DTA officials during construction. Apart from the initial clearance to commence construction of a specific type, about three or four inspection stages are required on the airframe alone—and not just before covering. All materials must be 'released' with the appropriate paperwork, all welds have to be carried out by a certificated welder, following which they have to be magnafluxed, then all accessories, such as control cables, fuel tanks, seat belts, instruments, etc, have to be thoroughly inspected. Come the end of construction, a pre-flight inspection is required and if everything is OK an 'ARCA' (Restricted Permit to Fly) is issued for the aircraft, but *not* for the builder. The aircraft can now be test flown, but only by a professional test pilot. It has to complete 75 hours of test flying, including 150 landings, not more than 5 km (3 miles) from the test airfield, then if this stage is completed satisfactorily a Permit to Fly is issued, allowing the aircraft to fly freely within Belgium. The flight test requirement is reduced to 50 hours and 75 landings if the homebuilt is fitted with a certificated engine such as a Lycoming or Continental. If the Belgian homebuilt pilot wants to fly his aircraft outside Belgium he has to obtain written clearance from the authorities of any country to be visited and also obtain a Belgian 'International Rating' for his PPL.

These criteria are, however, open to discussion with the DTA and, as one Belgian homebuilder told me, 'the trick is to have the right arguments to defend your case—I made the first flight of my homebuilt myself and got my Permit after only 25 hours test flying because my aircraft was one of the established and approved Belgian designs of simple construction, and everything went according to plan during my 25 hours flying. The DTA is very strict but, with the right engineering arguments put to them, open to any idea.'

EAA Chapter 258, based in Grimbergen, did not flourish, so in 1977 some of its members formed the Belgian Aircraft Homebuilders (BAH) with Paul Verbruggen as its first President. It was not a success and in 1984 the Flemish members of the BAH decided to form their own homebuilt organisation, the Flemish Amateur Aircraftbuilders (FAA), which, with more local and committed membership, is thriving in the 1990s and holds a regular annual fly-in, held at Zoersel (east of Antwerp) in 1991.

It was not until 1991 that the French-speaking members of the BAH founded their sister organisation in Belgium, the Réseau du Sport de l'Air Belgique (RSAB), with Alex Beghin, former secretary of the BAH, as its first President. BAH still exists, but EAA Chapter 258 ceased to operate in Belgium in 1985.

Republic of Ireland

Society of Amateur Aircraft Constructors (SAAC)

Irishman Richard G. Robinson of Newberry Hall in Co Kildare had a significant role to play in the formation of both the PFA in Britain and the RSA in France after the war. Using the Irish version of his name, Risteurd Offac Rorbin, he wrote an article that suggested the possibilities of re-establishing the pastime of homebuilt aircraft construction and flying. It was published in *Flight International* in Britain in 1946 and was then translated into French and published in *Les Ailes* in France shortly afterwards. It is more than a coincidence that the first formal meeting to found the ULAA (the PFA's predecessor) was in 1946 and that the RSA was founded in 1947 following an initial meeting in 1946. Blarney or not, Richard Robinson is still alive and an active observer of the rapidly changing world of homebuilt aeroplanes.

In Ireland it was Henri Mignet once again who was responsible for the first serious outbreak of homebuilding following the translation of his book *Le Sport de l'Air* into English by the Air League. Robinson and his father, John, were involved in the construction of a Flea, one of an estimated six or seven Irish examples. Robinson takes up the story: 'In those days builders worked in complete isolation from each other—and from the aviation authorities, such as they were—so it's hard to confirm the exact numbers of projects started. Maybe one or two were finished, but the others were stopped by the grounding of the Flea in the UK and then the outbreak of war. It was claimed that one flew, but if it did get airborne it was in a fast taxi mode, and certainly none flew within the ordinary meaning of the word.'

Two Fleas were flown from Phoenix Park, Dublin, in 1936 as part of the Cobham Flying Circus, and one even aspired to the Irish civil register as EI-ABH, built by W.H. Benson and members of the Dublin Amateur Flying Club.

After the war things were very slow to get going on the homebuilt front, and it was not until 1972 that Michael Donohue started to build an Evans VP-1, which first flew in 1975 and was registered EI-AYY; the aircraft is based at Weston where Donohue still flies it. The interest this aircraft aroused prompted Donohue to consider the formation of an official organisation for homebuilders in Ireland, and in 1978 the Society of Amateur Aircraft Constructors (SAAC) was founded.

Due entirely to Donohue's dedication and hard work, the SAAC is now a flourishing and respected organisation with over 100 members. It is run entirely on a voluntary basis by an elected commit-

The Flying Flea built by John and Richard Robinson at Carbury, Co Kildare, photographed in 1938. (Dick Robinson)

tee and officers, and has no offices or premises of its own. The SAAC has negotiated with the Irish aviation authorities and has been granted the authorisation to issue Certificates of Airworthiness for homebuilts on behalf of the authorities. Homebuilders must be members of the SAAC and register their project with them before commencing construction.

There appear to be no arbitary restrictions on Irish homebuilders and any design is acceptable as long as it has flown and been excepted elsewhere. This gave rise to an interesting situation with C. Lavery and C. Donaldson's composite kitplane, the Aero Composites Sea Hawker, which was built and successfully flown in the Republic in 1987. Then one of them moved to Northern Ireland and wanted to base the Sea Hawker there and operate it under a PFA 'Permit to Fly'. However, the design was not PFA 'Approved' so the aircraft had to remain on the Irish register, although being operated out of Northern Ireland.

There are about 10 homebuilts flying in Ireland now, several of them Heintz Zeniths, all-metal two-seater homebuilts. On 17 April 1985 Zenith EI-BKM first flew at Sligo after three years' work by five unemployed youths working under an Irish

Tony Murphy's Murphy Sprite which he built in Ireland between August 1979 and December 1985. It is powered by a Rolls-Royce 0-240 130 hp Continental. (Author)

Youth Employment Agency training programme, supervised by Niall Greene and with considerable assistance from the aircraft's designer in Canada, Chris Heintz. A second Zenith was built under a similar scheme at Drogheda, County Louth, starting in 1986. On 18 December 1985, after six years' construction, Murphy Sprite EI-BOY first flew, a customised version of the Practavia Sprite all-metal two-seater homebuilt, a British design that was first promoted by the magazine *Pilot* before the Practavia company took over. Tony Murphy was the constructor and a major influence in the Irish homebuilt movement until he was tragically killed whilst flying the Sprite in 1988.

One of the biggest difficulties facing homebuilders in Ireland is obtaining materials and parts. Virtually everything has to be imported with consequent hassle, delay and expense. As an example, a package of 'released' plywood from Britain that would have cost £60 over the counter there ended up costing £100 in Ireland, plus delivery costs.

The SAAC publishes an occasional mimeographed newsletter, organises weekend education workshops, lectures and film shows, visits places of interest to its members and organises a small annual fly-in. Groups of members have also flown to PFA and RSA rallies.

The Netherlands

Nederlandse Vereniging van Amateur-Vliegtuigbouwers (NVAV)

Founded in 1970, the Dutch homebuilt aircraft organisation had many years of hard work and negotiation with the Dutch government's Department of Civil Aviation (RLD) to even recognise the existence of homebuilding and the flying of homebuilt aeroplanes in Holland. Only in 1985 did the RLD give official recognition to the NVAV after an exhaustive investigation of the latter's technical knowledge and quality control programme in relation to certain selected homebuilt projects.

Dijkman Dulkes constructed the first post-war homebuilt in Holland, totally unofficially. This was the Dykhastar, a small single-seater high-wing wood/fabric tail-dragger powered by a 35 hp converted DAF car engine, which he flew from the beach at Wijk aan Zee to Rotterdam on 10 September 1969; he was promptly arrested by the police and the plane impounded. The RLD refused to grant the first Dykhastar a Certificate of Airworthiness and it was not until 1982 that Dulkes, having re-built the Dykhastar to a low-wing configuration, was presented with an official C of A for his aircraft by the RLD at the NVAV's 6th annual fly-in at Lelystad airfield.

An early President of NVAV, who did much of the early groundwork in making the organisation the respected and responsible organisation it is today, was Wolanda Verlaan. The current President is Marien Weijenberg, an employee of the Fokker Aircraft Company, who is also building a four-seater Velocity kitplane.

There has been a change of emphasis within the NVAV in recent years, brought about by the availability of good, practical kitplanes. The idealists from the earlier days, many of whom started complicated homebuilts which failed to materialise into completed aircraft, have now been very much superseded by the realists, although with the technical support now available from the NVAV it is far easier for the 'idealist' element to fulfil their ambitions.

There are now between 90 and 100 homebuilt projects under way in Holland, many of them nearing completion. However, there are still only seven or eight indigenously produced homebuilts flying including the Dykhaster, a Pottier P.80S and an Evans VP-1.

Technical matters relating to homebuilt projects are split into four categories by the NVAV, the work in these categories all being carried out on a voluntary basis by NVAV members on behalf of RLD:

1 TI - Technical inspections of an aircraft in the construction phase up until just before its first flight
2 TV - The actual first flight and flight test programme
3 TO - Technical maintenance programme after receipt of an aircraft's C of A during its subsequent years of operation
4 TK - Quality control/assurance on procedures involved with inspection

The NVAV holds an annual fly-in at different venues, that in 1991 being at Midden Zealand. There are no longer restrictions on foreign amateur-build aircraft flying in Dutch airspace—in 1982 the NVAV negotiated a two-month dispensation to allow such foreign homebuilts to fly to Holland.

Switzerland

RSA Suisse (RSAS)

Homebuilding in Switzerland has been very much influenced by the French organisation, the Réseau du Sport de l'Air, and in its formative years was concentrated in the French-speaking parts of the country around the airfield at Ecuvilliens. Not surprisingly, therefore, homebuilding in Switzerland comes under the control of the RSA Suisse which was founded in 1963 by Samuel Chuard and Ing Louis (Coco) Cosanday.

Cosanday was one of Henri Mignet's most ardent disciples and built several versions of his tandem-wing Flying Flea, his first being in 1939, a tandem-wing glider version, followed by a HM.19 and a HM.290. He also advised other early builders and test-flew their aircraft.

The people in the German-speaking part of Switzerland started construction of homebuilts separately from the others and formed a Chapter of the EAA, the EAA (Suisse). Membership and the number of projects grew steadily in the 1960s and '70s to the extent that the Swiss Aviation Authorities (BAZL) were forced into charging builders for their services in the supervision of homebuilts. In 1986, to simplify supervision, control and organisation, the RSA Suisse and the EAAS were integrated as the RSAS, which is entirely autonomous and independent of the French organisation. In 1991 the RSAS had 480 members, about one-third French speaking and the other two-thirds German. There are about 60 homebuilts actually flying, all of which are registered in the Swiss HB-Y . . . series, and there are 90 aircraft under construction, many of them kitplanes. A few builders are non-RSA members and deal directly with BAZL for inspection and certification.

It is only quite recently that the RSAS has taken over the larger part of control of inspection and certification from the BAZL, although the latter plans to delegate complete control to the RSAS before too long. To operate this system the RSAS has appointed 'Counsellors' or 'Bauberater' to oversee the building of a project, and then 'Test-Flight Counsellors' or 'Testflug-Berater' for supervision of the test-flight programme. Special training meetings are held each winter and spring for these counsellors to ensure that they are maintaining standards and are kept abreast of new developments, modifications and technologies. It is on their say-so that the final inspection, checks and weighing of a homebuilt aircraft are carried out and signed off before the BAZL Inspector is called in to make his inspection and issue a Permit.

Because of the diversity of types and experience, the RSAS has four groups of 'Bauberater' who operate in Switzerland:

1 Those responsible for prototypes
2 Those responsible for types built in Switzerland for the first time but already flying in other parts of the world
3 Those responsible for well-known types already flying in Switzerland
4 Those responsible for vintage aircraft restoration and reconstruction

As in Britain, the RSAS can only look after less powerful and smaller projects, those of 180 hp engine capacity or less and those whose gross weight does not exceed 2,646 lbs (1,200 kg). The '51 per cent rule', as operated in the USA, also applies, but the RSAS can supervise four-seater homebuilts. The BAZL takes a keen and active interest in category 1, the prototypes, regardless of the RSAS, and is said to be generally discouraging of sophisticated and fast homebuilt/kitplanes unless a builder can demonstrate considerable building and piloting skills for this type and can show detailed stress analyses for the new types. The BAZL's investigations have already shown up some weak points in certain designs and the BAZL has readily made recommendations to their designers.

Head of the RSAS Technical Commission is Max Brandli, well known in European homebuilt circles for his wood/composite design, the BX-2 Cherry, seven examples of which are now flying in Switzerland, Germany and France. Brandli told me, 'We operate under the rules of FAR 23 and JAR 22 in Switzerland although it depends on a particular engineer how deeply he goes into his study on a particular design—however, the Swiss people have a reputation for meticulous and precise engineering skills. Need I say more?'

Brandli also explained more details of the Swiss scene: 'Microlights and ultralights are banned in Free Switzerland although the heavier ones (more than 20 kg/m^2) can be flown in our "experimental" category. One of the main reasons for this is concern and legislation over noise levels. Every new homebuilt that is not an exact copy of a predecessor has to be subjected to a "noise test programme" and although in some instances the RSAS is permitted to do these tests, usually the BAZL is involved and they charge about SFr1,000 [approximately £250] each time a test is carried out.

'Another charge made by the BAZL to homebuilders' projects is for certification and even though they may be assisted by the RSAS, a standard Group 3-type homebuilt will attract a charge from the BAZL of between SFr 800 and 2,000 [£200 to £500].'

The current President of the RSAS is Bruno Vonlanthen and their Treasurer is Ernest Grünig. A news bulletin, the 'RSA-News', is published three times a year, there is an Annual General Meeting (General Assembly) held each March, there are spring and autumn fly-ins and the big RSAS International Fly-In held each August, in 1990 at Birrfeld and 1991 at Ecuvilliens. The RSAS has no central clubhouse, hangar or office facilities, but one of its most active groups in the Grenchen area meets on the first Tuesday of every month at the Airfield Restaurant at Grenchen.

A final piece of interesting information from Brandli: 'In Switzerland builders don't always need to use special aircraft grade materials, except where a designer specifies it. Even plywood doesn't need to be "released" and can be checked and approved by an individual builder. However, evidence has to be produced to the RSAS Counsellor or BAZL, as appropriate, that sample glued joints have been inspected and tested.'

Italy

Club Aviazione Popolare (CAP)

Until relatively recently the Italian authorities and aviation regulations just did not recognise that there was such a thing as the homebuilt aeroplane if you wanted to fly it. Build it, yes, but licence and fly it? Definitely 'No'! To illustrate this phenomenon, the first 'modern-day' Italian homebuilt, the work of Antonio Fedrigoni from Verona in northern Italy, although built mainly in the lounge of his fifth-floor flat in Verona, was in fact completed, registered, flown and hangared in Switzerland.

This was in the early 1970s and the aircraft was a British-designed tandem, two-seater high-wing wood/fabric Luton LA-5 Major. Fedrigoni, an economics graduate who became the manager of a factory producing plastic kitchenware, was a member of the EAA and started construction in 1966. In 1969 three Swiss technicians inspected the construction but condemned parts of it. By 1972 Fedrigoni had re-worked much of the wooden airframe and roaded it to Fribourg in Switzerland for its pre-cover inspection. It passed, and by February 1973 the LA-5 Major had received its Swiss registration (HB-YAH), flown its test time and received an appropriate Certificate of Airworthiness. It was then flown to Lugano in Switzerland, close to the Italian border.

In 1970 the Club Aviazione Popolare (CAP) was founded in Italy, initially to help and officially represent those restoring and flying vintage and veteran aeroplanes. As a forum for solving technical problems it was an important first step, but its main objective was to present a unified front to overcome the bureaucratic resistance of the aviation authorities in Italy to such restoration and flying activity, and the total lack of any parameters and regulations under which such activity could take place. The CAP organised its first national fly-in at Vizzola Ticino in September 1973.

Despite Fedrigoni's pioneering construction, the first wholly indigenous Italian homebuilt was an Evans VP-1 (I-CAPA) built by Giuseppe Blini and Gianni Tieppo which, after several years of intensive lobbying and hard work, was officially permitted to carry out test-flights in Italy in 1974.

Annual fly-ins continued to be held by the CAP each year at Vizzola Ticino but the fourth, in 1976, was the scene for great celebration amongst its members because the Italian Civil Aviation Authority had just published what is universally accepted as the CAP's greatest achievement, the Specification No 15, which covers the technical procedures a homebuilder has to follow in order to get the Special Certificate of Airworthiness for his aircraft.

In 1980 the Italian CAA issued a further set of rules, Specification No 40, which detailed their requirements on the subject of test-flights for homebuilts. The flood gates had now been opened and by 1986 the CAP could boast 300 members, about 100 homebuilt aircraft projects under way and about 65 homebuilts flying. These included VP-1s

Antonio Fedrigoni from Verona with the first 'modern-day' Italian homebuilt, a British-designed Luton LA-5 Major. (Author's Collection)

'One of the finest homebuilt Falcos in the world'—Bjorn Eriksen's verdict on Jan Waldahl's appropriately-registered example, nearing completion but awaiting an engine. (Author)

and 2s, VariEzes and LongEzes, KR-2s, a Volmer Sportsman, Skybolts, Zeniths and a Teenie Two, as well as indigenous designs such as the San Francesco 66L and the RD 95AV 'Asso'. The restoration side of the CAP's activities also flourished. By 1991 membership had topped the 600 mark and there were over 100 completed homebuilts flying in Italy, as well as many microlights. Italian homebuilts have been flown to several European fly-ins including the PFA's at Cranfield and the RSA's at Moulins in France.

Norway

EAA Chapter 573

One of the many worldwide Chapters of the Experimental Aircraft Association (EAA), the EAA Oslo Chapter 573 looks after the interests of Norwegian homebuilders, although the control and construction of projects is still firmly in the hands of the Norwegian Central Aviation Administration (CAA).

Homebuilding has been taking place in a small way in Norway since the beginning of flying itself, but it only really gained in popularity both in numbers and in terms of legality with the birth of the EAA in the USA in the 1950s. But it was not until 1976 that homebuilders in the Oslo area founded their EAA Chapter 573 which became a countrywide forum in subsequent years with some members as far north as the Svalbard islands in the Arctic Ocean at 80° North, close to the North Pole. There are now about 400 members in Chapter 573 and an estimated 90 homebuilts are under construction, with 20 flying.

One of Norway's most prestigious homebuilts is the Sequoia Falco LN-JAN built by seaplane pilot Jan Waldahl at Sandane. Started in 1981, it has taken over 10,000 hours of work to complete in the subsequent 11 years. In the opinion of Norway's other Falco builder, Bjorn Eriksen, Waldahl's homebuilt Falco is 'one of the finest homebuilt Falco's in the world'.

Many of Norway's current crop of homebuilts are in fact US-designed kitplanes. There are no restrictions on the import of basic timber for homebuilt projects in Norway, but with the profusion of kitplanes, builders have to be careful because there is a ban on the importation of ready-made wood laminations such as spars.

Norwegian builders are not permitted by their CAA to carry out any welding on their projects; that has to be undertaken by a CAA-certified welder. The CAA also have to inspect projects at critical stages such as pre-covering and, once a project is completed and flying, an annual inspection has to be carried out on the aircraft at a CAA Certificated Repair Station, whose charges can be astronomical.

EAA Chapter 573 is devoting much of its efforts at present to change this last requirement and to set up the necessary administrative, engineering and control organisation to take over the task from the CAA. As Jan Waldhal says, 'Who likes a dirty mechanic crawling all over your pride and joy once a year?'. Attitudes within the Norwegian CAA seem very entrenched and the EAA feels that this change will require many more years of hard lobbying to convince the authorities.

Australia

Sport Aircraft Association of Australia (SAAA)

Originally the Ultra Light Aircraft Association of Australia, founded in 1956, homebuilding in Austra-

The Corby Starlet, an Australian-designed homebuilt. (Air-Britain)

lia is now under the auspices of the SAAA, a national non-profit-making organisation of individual enthusiasts whose aims and objectives are to promote and assist, for educational, recreational and research purposes, the design and/or construction and operation of amateur-built aircraft of all kinds (sporting, microlight/ultralight, rotorcraft, replica, etc) and the restoration, reconstruction and maintenance of vintage, ex-military and historical aircraft.

The current membership is about 2,000 spread throughout the vastness of the six States of this major sub-continent. The president is Kim Jones, and the SAAA is administered from permanent headquarters at Clifton Hill, Victoria; it publishes an excellent bi-monthly magazine, *Airsport*. The annual national fly-in is held each March at Mangalore.

The various States conduct monthly Divisional meetings split as follows: New South Wales/ACT; Victoria/Tasmania; Queensland; South Australia/ Northern Territory; and Western Australia. There is also a Federal Technical Committee which liaises between the officials of the Australian Department of Transport (Air); the current SAAA Federal Technical Officer is Clive Canning (see Chapters 10 and 17 about his epic flight from Australia to England in a homebuilt).

Homebuilding is quite prolific in Australia and dates from 1910 when Houdini built and flew his Voisin biplane at Melbourne. Several pre-war Flying Fleas are known to have been built, and after the war, like the British and US homebuilt movement, that in Australia got going in the 1950s with French, British and American designs such as the Jodel D.9, Luton Minor and Stits SA-6A. By 1980 there were 257 homebuilts registered in Australia, and some of these were examples of Australia's indigenous homebuilt designs, the Corby CJ-1 Starlet, which had been designed by John Corby, a consultant aero engineer from New South Wales. The prototype was built by ten members of the Latrobe Valley Division of the Ultralight Aircraft Association (now the SAAA) and flew for the first time in 1972.

Since then SAAA membership and the numbers of homebuilts under construction and completed have mushroomed. Several other indigenous designs have also materialised, including recently the Australian Light Wing, a two-seater kitplane (also available as a complete manufactured aircraft), which first flew in 1986 and was the work of Howard Hughes in New South Wales.

Only very recently (1990) have SAAA Inspectors had the freedom to start workshop and project-stage inspections, and these were initially conducted jointly with Australian CAA regional airworthiness personnel. This authority has come after many decades of discussion but still only relates to accepted designs, the CAA being entirely responsible for 'first of type' designs.

Argentina

EAA Chapter 722

One of the most active South American countries as far as homebuilt aircraft are concerned is Argentina. Homebuilding received a major boost here thanks,

Aerial view of an EAA convention at San Pedro, Argentina.

once again, to Henri Mignet. In 1935 a group calling itself 'The Circle of Henri Mignet Aviators' was formed and more than 20 HM.14 Pou-du-Ciels (Flying Fleas) were built, including those by M. Bardin, the Frigoni brothers, Roberto Gallardo and U. Pallich.

When Mignet was ostracised from Europe, he first travelled to Argentina in 1947, settling in Alta Gracia, near Cordoba. There he tried to establish two of his tandem wing designs in commercial production but by 1951, partly due to political intrigue, he abandoned the idea and moved across the border into Brazil to try afresh there. One of Mignet's 'disciples' from early post-war France, Jean de la Farge, who had constructed one of the first Mignet HM.293 single-seater homebuilts, also moved to Argentina in 1950 where his uncle was the French attaché. There he started to construct a unique and personalised homebuilt version of the Flea, 'La Pulga', in 1960. Another French Flea fanatic, Emilien Croses, visited Argentina in 1962 and guided several local builders in the construction of a Croses EC-3 Pouplume, one of the very first true microlights (ultralights). He established a company there with a view to mass-producing Pouplume kits for homebuilders in the Americas, but he was about 20 years ahead of his time and the company foundered.

All this activity, together with considerable influence from the USA, contributed to a small but active interest in homebuilts, and several aircraft, mostly Flea-types, were built and flown. In 1980 the national homebuilt group of Argentina sought and received affiliation to the EAA as their Argentina Chapter 722. Before this a small organisation called APEX promoted homebuilding, but in the 1970s they became a small, almost introvert circle of enthusiasts. The 1980 affiliation to the EAA gave APEX and other homebuilders a new lease of life, a significant move for such a large, distant and sparsely populated country.

Political troubles, raging inflation and difficulties in buying or acquiring essential components have been some of the problems faced by homebuilders in Argentina. In some Government circles there have been moves to restrict severely such activities but, undetered, homebuilding is flourishing on a limited scale.

Each December or January (summer in Argentina) the EAA Chapter 722 organises its national fly-in, an event that moves around the country from venue to venue. In 1983 the second such fly-in was held at Junin, near Buenos Aires, when 41 'show aircraft' flew in together with 10 antiques, 12 classics, 11 experimentals/homebuilts and eight microlights/ultralights. A single-seater Pazmany PL-4 LV-X80 built by Roberto Gilli was that year's Grand Champion. 1985's and 1987's fly-ins were at San Pedro, and 1986's at Mercedes.

A mixture of French and US-designed homebuilts are being flown and built in Argentina ranging from Jodel D.9s to QAC Quickies and including several Flying Flea variants including the Croses EC-6 Criquet, Bowers Fly Baby, Spezio Tuholer, Bensen autogyros and many more. These aircraft are registered in a special sequence, LV-X . . ., and there are also believed to be several unofficial groups flying unregistered aircraft in parts of the country. EAA Argentina also now has its own grass airfield and country club!

Microlighting (ultralighting) is also popular in Argentina, with an annual championship. Branch 23 of the Ultralight and Branch 12 of the Antique and Classic Divisions of the EAA operate here and work together with EAA Argentina Chapter 722.

An Argentinian homebuilt Rotax-powered one-place helicopter designed by Augusto Cicaré was bought to the EAA's Oshkosh Fly-In in 1990, which helps to symbolise the growing stature and outward-looking nature of homebuilding in Argentina in the face of many difficulties.

Former Soviet Union

All Union Amateur Designers and Pilots Federation (AUADPF)

The recent momentous political changes that have brought about the demise of the Soviet Union will almost certainly have both good and bad effects on the potential for development of homebuilt aircraft within the newly independent states of the former Union. Severe economic problems will undoubtedly be detrimental to any large-scale homebuilt aircraft activity in the short term, but the new freedom from Communism and autocratic rule will create an environment in which aviators' self-expression through homebuilding will be eminently more possible.

Homebuilding has in fact been active in the Soviet Union for at least the last ten years, almost a contradiction in terms under Communism, but a rapidly growing pastime, where microlights/ultralights are the backbone of this kind of aviation; a flick through the pages of Jane's *All The World's Aircraft* in recent years will reveal some of the developments.

In 1985 one of the first Soviet homebuilt aircraft fly-ins was held at the Crimean town of Planyerskoye, and just prior to this it was officially announced that an estimated 10,000 microlight aircraft were now flying in the Soviet Union. Whether an additional zero may have slipped in to this figure is a matter for speculation.

However, also in 1985 it was announced that a system of training and licensing was to be introduced for microlight pilots; the note also added that homebuilding would remain at a relatively low level of activity and that any new designs would most likely emanate from universities and technical colleges, and as supplementary activities at the country's aerospace manufacturers. This is most likely to be similar to the controlling influence that was introduced in the West following the upsurge of interest in microlighting and the many often fatal accidents that occurred.

Soviet rules on flying homebuilts were relaxed around 1984 and designers and builders were permitted to test-fly their own aircraft, whereas pre-

The smallest homebuilt in the USSR, designed by Viktor Dmitriev. It weighs 105 lbs, has a 16½-foot wingspan, is 11 feet long and is powered by a single-cylinder 40 hp engine. (Author's Collection)

'Is one-half scale of Siberian Yak . . . covered with same!' (Robruchka)

viously this had had to be done by State licensed test pilots. Flying was also allowed in certain designated areas, well clear of airports, cities, power stations, dams and foreign borders. Homebuilt aircraft were permitted to be flown in a 3-mile radius from their base, not above 1,000 ft and provided that visibility was 3 miles or more.

Aircraft displayed at Planyerskoye in 1985 were basic but varied, including the all-metal two-seater Horizon-3, built by soil engineer Viktor Pivovarov. The Lithuanian Cheslav Kasonas displayed a microlight with an empty weight of only 182 lbs and an AUW of 230 lbs. Also in 1985 the Third All Union Competitive Parade of Ultralight Homebuilts was held near Kiev at the DOSSAF (the USSR's State Sporting Association) Sport Centre airfield at Tschaika. A report of this event in the Russian magazine *Trud* (Work) indicated that a strict jury would inspect the homebuilts. Participants also had to take their aircraft to a special stand where their centre of gravity was examined. Finally, professional test pilots from the Ministry of Aircraft Industries played their part. During the show there were also seminars and conferences.

Just four years later, through the columns of the German hang glider magazine *Drachenfleiger*, came further reports of an extremely active homebuilt aircraft movement in the USSR, again concentrated on microlights but also including some more substantial aircraft. 1989 also saw the Soviet Union begin the first official 'production' of light sport aircraft. A Government plan called for 900 hang gliders and microlights to be built by the Ministry of Aviation and at clubs and co-operatives. Several Ministry-appointed officially recognised 'heroes' led groups within the newly formed All Union Amateur Designers and Pilots Federation (AUADPF) with the chief test pilot of the Soviet Buran space shuttle, Igor Volk, as President. This was pre-Glasnost as well!

Further news has recently arrived from Lithuania and Latvia. In June 1991 the Lithuanian Vladas Kensgaila flew his enormous VK.8 Ausra (Dawn) homebuilt from Vilnius to the Swedish EAA Chapter 222 fly-in at Barkaby—the prospect of a Soviet homebuilt being flown to a fly-in in the West was unthinkable even in the late 1980s. Ivar Ozol is nearing completion of his Ozol IO-1 Latava homebuilt in Latvia. Powered by a British 90 hp Cirrus 1 engine, this is his fourth homebuilt. The 1990s could be an exciting time for homebuilders in the former Soviet states!

New Caledonia Islands

RSA du Nouvelle Caledonie

Illustrating the truly worldwide essence of homebuilt aeroplanes, the French protectorate islands of New Caledonia in the Coral Sea midway between Australia and Fiji prove that geographical isolation is no deterrent to the homebuilder.

There is a small but active group of RSA (France) members here, many of them based in the capital of Nomea, building and flying homebuilts—a strong

Mont-Dore, New Caledonia, is an unlikely location to find a homebuilt 'replica' of a Mignet HM.14, the work of 60-year-old Lucien Saucede. (Author)

French flavour and influence is understandable. Jean-Claude Gerard has built an all-metal tri-gear Pottier P.180S, and in 1985 Alain Tourand completed and successfully flew a Jodel D.119. Perhaps the most interesting type to have flown, though, was on 10 March 1989 when Lucien Saucede flew his 'modern' Mignet HM. 14 Flying Flea, which is classified in the French ULM category. It is powered by a 24 hp Koenig SC.430 engine with electric starter motor, hand-carved wooden propeller, improved and sprung undercarriage, wooden wheel hubs to save weight, and a modern instrument fit. As Saucede explained: 'It flies well. We have increased the wing span by 60 cms and have had to replace the original prop with a larger one, and put a reduction drive on the engine as it turns over at 4,200 rpm. Our major difficulty here is that materials and parts such as plywood, glues, engine, instruments, etc, have to be imported from Europe. This certainly encourages us to fabricate as much as possible here—an interesting occupation!'

New Zealand

Amateur Aircraft Constructors Association Inc (AACA)

A handful of enthusiasts founded this Association in 1964 to encourage and support the development and utilisation of amateur-built aircraft for recreational, educational and research purposes. The AACA is split in to 18 Chapters throughout New Zealand, some with very few members and the biggest, Auckland, with around 80 members. All AACA members are required to join their local Chapter, each Chapter running its own affairs with its own selected officers. An AACA National Executive is elected by the membership from Chapter members annually, and in addition there is a part-time paid secretary to run the AACA's affairs. The current membership of the AACA is about 410 under the presidency of Evan Belworthy, with Bruce Small as National Secretary.

There are currently about 200 homebuilts flying in New Zealand, ranging from the traditional Taylor Monoplane and Jodel designs to more recent types such as Glasairs and Kitfoxes. There have also been a few indigenous designs such as the Andrews A-1 Special, ZK-BLU. Currently there are 188 homebuilt projects under construction registered with the AACA. All inspections during construction are done by authorised AACA Inspectors except the final one, but new laws are about to be adopted giving the AACA a system similar to the 'Experimental' category in the USA.

The AACA publishes a quarterly magazine for members, 'Sport Flying', and each year holds a national fly-in—usually in February or March—each time hosted by a different Chapter around the country and attracting upwards of 60 homebuilts/ kitplanes and well over 100 other light aircraft.

Canada

Recreational Aircraft Association Canada (RAA Canada)

In the mid-1950s homebuilding of aircraft became sufficiently popular in Canada for standards to be established by builders working with Transport Canada to guide and protect participants. The Ultralight Aircraft Association of Canada (UAAC) was founded in 1956 at Goderich, Ontario, by the late 'Hoppy' Hopkinson, and this provided the continuing platform for dialogue between the amateur aircraft-building fraternity and the Canadian government authorities in Ottawa. In 1967 the UAAC changed its name to the Experimental Aircraft Association of Canada (EAAC) which survived until the 1980s when the process of deregulation of the aviation industry and of homebuilding prompted the organisation to change its name once more to the Recreational Aircraft Association Canada (RAA Canada).

There were and still are many Chapters of the US-founded EAA throughout Canada and the present success of the RAA Canada owes a great deal to the strong support received from the EAA in the United States. The current President is Barry Miller supported by four full-time paid staff at the RAA's headquarters office in Ajax, Ontario. The regional Chapters have their own Directors, and within these regions are smaller, more localised Chapters to give members closer contact with fellow builders.

There are many indigenous Canadian homebuilt and kitplane designs but the RAA has a system of vetting designs (similar to the PFA in Britain) and not all homebuilts are approved for construction in Canada. Regulations which cover the whole spectrum of amateur-built aircraft, including aeroplanes, balloons, sailplanes, autogyros and helicopters, are all contained in Chapter 549 of the Transport Canada Airworthiness Manual. Certificated materials have to be used, stage inspections carried out, construction records kept and final authorisation received before a completed aircraft is flown. The RAA has qualified and approved Certified Technical Advisors (CTAs) throughout the country, with at least one in each Chapter, and they are vetted by the RAA's own Research & Engineering Group. Although many of the Chapters around Canada are affiliated to the RAA, some are not, so some Chapter members are not necessarily affiliated to the national RAA—but the RAA's objective is to bring 100 per cent of Chapters and their members under its wing. This is of increasing importance because Transport Canada (the government agency responsible for all aviation regulations in Canada) has stated quite clearly that it no longer has the resources to attend to the needs of private aviation. Regulations are in place, so it is the RAA's objective to make all necessary arrangements to act on its own behalf in representing the amateur aircraft constructors of Canada.

With the delights of US airspace beyond the 49th Parallel, temptations to fly south from Canada are great, if only for the cheaper fuel, but Canadian amateur-built aircraft require special authority to enter foreign countries, and although this can now be easily obtained, the RAA is the recommended centralised advisory body for such flights—also for regulations pertaining to the import of homebuilts from the US to Canada.

The RAA publishes its house magazine 'The Recreational Flyer' six times a year and members also receive *Canadian Aviation News*, Canada's national aviation newspaper, every second week. The RAA also advises on and makes available insurance for the homebuilt/kitplane aviator.

South Africa

Experimental Aircraft Association of South Africa (EAASA)

The first amateur-built aircraft in South Africa is a title claimed by the first heavier-than-air machine to fly there, a glider designed and built by John Goodman Household and flown for the first time from a farm in the Kerkloof area of Natal in about 1875. The first successful homebuilt aeroplane was a locally modified and built version of the Bleriot Monoplane which flew on 30 April 1911 at Highlands North, Johannesburg. According to the EAASA it was not until the early 1930s that homebuilding started again, the design and aircraft of Lewis Noble from Knysna being the most notable—it first flew in 1933 and continued to operate for several years. Simultaneously several Heath Parasols were built and successfully flown, which is more than can be said for Henri Mignet's ubiquitous HM.14 Flying Flea, several of which were built but which also contributed to the demise of homebuilding in South Africa due to the well-recorded design fault.

Post-war the situation was similar to that in Britain and the USA, with a propensity of cheap and surplus military aircraft available to sport avaitors. Limited homebuilding started again in the 1950s and when the EAA was formed in the USA several South Africans became members. One of these, Mike Spence, called a meeting in Johannesburg in May 1964 with the intention of starting a South African EAA Chapter, but it was not until 1969 that EAA Chapter 322 was finally born. In parallel with this a group of enthusiasts at Pietermaritzburg in Natal formed the Amateur Built Aircraft Association (ABAA), made contact with the South African Department of Civil Aviation and through their joint co-operation drafted rules by which amateur-built aircraft could be constructed in South Africa. Their work resulted in Document LS.1, which is still the basis of homebuilt aircraft construction today, albeit with minor modifications. As far as the more recent phenomenon of kitplanes is concerned, the '51 per cent rule' applies in the same way as in the USA.

The Department of Civil Aviation has an enlightened attitude and sanctions the EAASA to operate an Approved Persons Scheme whereby experienced homebuilders can sign out projects at critical stages of construction—this smoothes out bureaucracy and saves the builder money. Aircraft are issued with a 'Permit to Fly' upon completion, are restricted to VFR operations and cannot be used for hire or reward. A South African homebuilt/amateur-built aircraft is allocated a registration in certain sequences, eg ZS-U . . ., ZS-V . . . or ZS-W . . ., and this extends to vintage and special types of aircraft. Bob Ewing, a recent past president of EAASA, has a restored DHC-1 Chipmunk, ZS-URC, and he can do the maintenance on this aircraft as long as the work is signed out by an Approved Person in the aircraft's log-book.

There are now 11 Chapters that comprise the EAASA with a total membership of 810, a total of about 320 homebuilts/kitplanes built and flying and some 50-plus projects under construction including Kitfoxes, Rand KR.2s, two full-size Spitfire replicas, a LongEze, Pietenpol Aircampers, etc. These statistics do not include restorations, which come under the EAASA's wing and number around 100—these include 45 airworthy Tiger Moths, 17 Chipmunks and more unusual aircraft such as a Dragon Rapide and a Fiesler Storch.

One of the first 'modern' homebuilts to be completed was Tony Wills's Bowers Fly Baby, started at Pietermaritzburg in 1968—many others soon followed including John Buchan with his Falconar F-11 and Owen Pilcher with his Smith Termite. A unique South African homebuilt constructed in this 'hot-bed' of homebuilding was the one-off Crutchley Special all-metal monoplane, ZS-UHH, built by Steve Crutchley and powered by a VW Revmaster 2,100 cc engine.

The political history of South Africa has contributed in no small way to the difficulties of homebuilders and for many years virtually every item of material used in the construction of homebuilts had to be imported. This became increasingly difficult with the trade sanctions imposed against South Africa by the international community but, regardless, homebuilding has survived and even before the recent abolition of sanctions and political changes, was flourishing.

The Department of Civil Aviation has delegated a large measure of responsibility for the regulation and administration of sport aviation in South Africa to the Aero Club of South Africa. The Aero Club in turn has 10 sub-sections of which the EAASA represents homebuilt aircraft; because of the huge geographical area covered, the EAASA has established a permanent headquarters at Halfway House to co-ordinate affairs. This headquarters is not affiliated to the EAA in the USA as it is only concerned with the co-ordination of local activities as governed by the South African Air Navigation Regulations. Headquarters tries to monitor the well-being and 'health' of all 11 Chapters, and each year, usually on the Ascension Day holiday weekend in May, the EAASA Annual Convention is held, with over 20 such events behind it, 11 having been held at its current location at Margate, Natal. The highest attendance was more than 420 aircraft in 1987, and in 1991 the total was 350 of which about 40 per cent were homebuilts/restored/vintage aircraft.

The current President of the EAASA is Major Dave Becker, and the Senior Approved Person Anton J. Maneschijn.

A Bowers Fly Baby built at Pietermaritzberg, South Africa, by Tony Wills, the second of the type to be completed in South Africa and first flown in 1972. (Author's Collection)

Germany

Oscar Ursinus Vereinigung (OUV)

Surprisingly for such a traditionally industrious and aviation-minded country—at least the old West Germany—and one with such a large and active light aviation population, the same cannot be said of Germany's homebuilt and kitplane population. Construction of and flying of homebuilt aeroplanes in West Germany in the years since the Second World War has met with a constant struggle against bureaucracy. The authorities would not normally permit such activity until fairly recently although there has now been a veritable surge of activity, with an 'Experimental' category having been established for homebuilts similar to that established by the EAA in the USA. The founding of the OUV has also consolidated the status of homebuilding, as it negotiated with the authorities to permit and then to control homebuilding.

In 1991 membership of OUV numbered about 720 and they currently have records of about 50 homebuilts/kitplanes flying in Germany (virtually all are in the old West) and have records of 169 homebuilt projects under construction. Amongst these are reported to be five gliders, 10 motor-gliders, five gyrocopters and a small number of microlights/ultralights. The OUV has a permanent headquarters in Koblenz, where the current Director of the OUV Special Board is Otto Brertsch. An annual national fly-in is held, usually in mid-June, and this has also been at Koblenz in recent years. Homebuilts and kitplanes completed in Germany in the last few years have included several Neico Lancairs, Jurca MJ.5 Siroccos, and an indigenous LongEze-type composite design, the side-by-side two-seater Gemini D-EFAR.

Denmark

KZ & Veteranfly Klubben/EAA Chapter 655

One of the earliest recorded homebuilts in Denmark was the work of Hans Axel who built a Ford-engined single-seater to his own design at Sjaelland in 1929. Axel was also the first Dane to build his own plane after the Second World War, when he completed his Druine D.31 Turbulent OY-AMG in 1958, and then followed this by completing two more. Homebuilding was formalised in Denmark as a result, with permission from the Danish CAA for the homebuilding of certain type-certified designs, namely the Jodel D.112, Jurca MJ.2 Tempete and the D.31 Turbulent. Up until 1980 about 70 examples of these types were built by amateurs in Denmark although subsequently many of them were sold to pilots in Sweden so that only 10 D.31 and seven Jodels of the original batch are still on the Danish register.

The KZ & Veteranfly Klubben (KZ stands for Kramme and Zeuthen, who founded Skandinavisk Aero Industri in Denmark in 1937 and designed and built a whole range of different light aircraft in the subsequent 20 years) was founded in May 1969, and EAA Chapter 655 in 1979. The KZ Club worked originally as a club for vintage aircraft only, but Danish homebuilders asked them to organise and administer their 'experimental' types so that in 1980 the KZ Club, as EAA Chapter 655, received official permission after lengthy discussions with Mr Val Eggers, the new Director of the Danish CAA, to administer and control construction and operation of homebuilts on behalf of the Danish CAA. Magnus Pedersen was the founder and is the current Chairman. They could now build non-certified designs other than the Jodel and Turbulent; the papers governing this arrangement are Rules BL 2-2, which form the basis but have subsequently been amended and improved.

All homebuilts must comply structurally with FAR 23 sub-part A. The fuel system and engine installation must comply with specific rules in FAR 23 and these are supervised by 'Official Club Inspectors', comprising an expert group of five to seven people who investigate projects at the outset and give advice to builders, plus a group of 10 to 12 Inspectors who follow construction work through at specific stages. These Inspectors sign out each stage of construction but the final inspection has to be done officially by the Danish CAA. Each type must be static load-tested to at least 3.8g and the seat-belt attachment points loaded to 9g forward. A detailed test-flying programme has to be flown before the homebuilt is 'released' and registered in the 'Experimental' category. There also has to be an annual inspection and renewal of the Experimental Certificate of Airworthiness, these being done by Club Inspectors at no charge.

Homebuilts/restorations up to 6,000 lbs/2,720 kgs may be administered by the KZ Club; kitplanes have first to be approved by the Special Group and there is no '51 per cent rule', the decision as to whether it is a homebuilt or not being again the decision of this Special Group.

At present the KZ Club has 836 members, publishes an excellent quarterly magazine and year-book and hosts its big annual international rally each June at Stauning. The first 'Experimental' type to be completed and flown under the post-1980 system was the Rutan LongEz OY-CMT (since exported to Britain as G-BMIM). About 40 homebuilts are under construction, eight in the 'test-flight' stage and two, LongEz OY-BSM and Dragonfly OY-BHS, full 'Experimentals'. Opus 3, a LongEz is an interesting composite project by Kai Christensen now being test-flown.

Eastern Europe

Czechoslovakia, Poland, Hungary and Lithuania

Limited homebuilt activity took place in these countries prior to the era of Glasnost, but no formal organisations existed such as the PFA or EAA. There was considerable interest by aviators and observers of the homebuilt scene in the West, but little in the way of practical results.

Czechoslovakia saw several homebuilts (constructed in the 1960s, '70s and '80s, and visitors to the NVAV rally at Lelystad in Holland in May 1981 were very surprised when a little single-seater, the Verner W-01 Broucek (Beetle) OK-YXA, was flown in from Prague by its designer/constructor Vladslav Verner. Prior to this in the early '60s, at the Svazarm Aero Club, Zdeňek Rublić designed and built the Racek R-7 Seagull, an all-wood low-wing single-seater aerobatic monoplane fitted with a 160 hp Walter Minor 6-III engine; marked OK-80, it was first flown by aerobatic pilot Jiři Cerný at the end of January 1964, but was destroyed in a hangar fire in 1975. There were several other experimental-type aircraft built in Czechoslovakia, but they were mainly gliders fitted with motors. The authorities were none too supportive of such activities, though!

Verner started design work on his wood/fabric Broucek in 1963 and it was first flown by Rudy Duchon in 1970 fitted with a 45 hp Praga B.2 two-cylinder horizontally opposed air-cooled dual ignition engine. Verner then started the design and construction of a composite two-seater resembling a VariEze, but old age and the difficulty of building during the 1980s have meant the project's abandonment.

The best-known Czech homebuilt proponent has been Jan Šimũnek, an employee of the large Letov engineering company in Prague. In the same year that Verner flew to Lelystad, Šimũnek flew his SK-1 Trempik (Little Tramp) OK-JXA to the July Hobyflug '81 fly-in at Offenburg in West Germany. In 1982 he flew the Trempik to the RSA fly-in at Brienne, and the following year to the PFA rally at Cranfield. The Trempik started life in 1969 and was built with several components from a Bucker Bu.131 Jungmann and other aircraft 'spares' that Šimũnek had inherited from his father—this included its 75 hp Praga D engine. It flew for the first time (marked as OK-006) with Jirim Kobrlem at the controls at Brandys airfield on 19 October 1979, and after being handed to the State Aviation Inspectorate for a detailed practical examination, Šimũnek was able to fly it himself for the first time on 8 September 1980.

Homebuilding as such was operated under a cumbersome State organisation known as 'Svazarm', membership of which was open to only a selected few. Ways around the restrictions were found such as an agricultural co-operative offering microlight flying (for agricultural purposes, of course!). Other aircraft reported to be under construction in Czechoslovakia during the 1980s were an Evans VP-2, a Fournier RF-3 motorglider and two Polish-designed Janowski JB-2 Polonez homebuilts (a design developed from the J-1 Don Quixote. Since the advent of microlighting there has been considerable activity on this front as well, with many one-off designs.

On 17 March 1990 the Amateur Flying Association of Czechoslovakia was established under the chairmanship of Petr Tucek and is registered as an 'independant association of individuals, clubs and groups involved in the design, construction, restoration and flying of light aircraft, including microlights, hang gliders and model aircraft'. Simultaneously another club was formed in Czechoslovakia, thought to be a Czechoslovakian Chapter of the EAA.

Poland has a long aeronautical tradition and has produced several homebuilt designs. The best-known is Jaroslaw Janowski and Witold Kalita's J-1 Don Kichot (Don Quixote), work on which started in 1967 and culminated in its first flight on 30 July 1970. It was a wood/fabric single-seater tail-dragger with a high wing, and the prototype had a pusher 23 hp Janowski/Saturn 500B two-stroke engine. From this basic concept the Marco J-5 was derived (see Chapter 5), now being sold complete and in kit form in Europe as a composite single-seater motorglider type, powered by a 30 hp KFM 107ER engine.

Further evidence of an upsurge of homebuilding in Poland and other former 'Eastern Bloc' European countries was seen at the French RSA rally at Moulins in July 1991 when the diminutive single-seater Turbulent-type homebuilt, the AT-1 SP-FMC, was flown in from Warsaw.

Hungary is another country where microlighting has literally 'taken off' in the last ten years. However, the same cannot be said for what we regard as true homebuilts. An exception was the little side-by-side two-seat reverse-stagger tri-gear wood/fabric biplane Famadar (Wooden Bird), designed and built in the 1980s by a group headed by Willy Simo. It was built by a group managed by Simo and was owned by the State Sporting Association, a half civil, half military organisation. The Famadar last flew in 1988 and when Simo subsequently died the

The AT-1, a Polish homebuilt flown from Warsaw to the RSA rally at Moulins in July 1991. (Author)

aircraft was grounded. This Sporting Association was disbanded with the big political changes taking place in Hungary during 1990, but Simo's widow was optimistic that her husband's creation might yet take to the air again in the newly liberalised environment.

Lithuania became one of the first three Soviet states, along with Latvia and Estonia, to achieve full independence from the Soviet Union on 6 September 1991. Earlier that year a Lithuanian homebuilt was flown to the West when Vladas Kensgaila from Vilnius flew his enormous two-seater Kensgaila VK.8 Ausra (Dawn) across the Baltic Sea to attend the EAA Chapter 222 fly-in at Barkaby, near Stockholm, Sweden. The Ausra is powered by a 360 hp Vedeneyev M-14P radial piston engine taken from a Yak-18 trainer and includes many parts taken from a variety of wrecked crop-dusters. Design of the aircraft started in 1987 and it first flew two years later—that same year it was flown to the fifth National Homebuilt Aircraft Convention at Riga, Latvia, where it was awarded the 'Best homebuilt' prize. A party of 30 other Lithuanian homebuilt

A Hungarian homebuilt, the Famadar (Wooden Bird), built by a team headed by Willy Simo. It last flew in 1988. (Laszlo Hemmert)

enthusiasts also visited Barkaby in 1991 for the EAA fly-in, arriving in a chartered Aeroflot Antonov An-24!

Other Countries

The countries so far detailed in this chapter and their respective homebuilt aircraft organisations are the most significant and interesting worldwide. The list is by no means exhaustive, but illustrates the diversity of rules, regulations and restrictions that face the homebuilder. They also illustrate the vast variety of homebuilt aircraft and organisations that embrace the word 'homebuilt'.

The EAA in the USA has the largest worldwide influence with Chapters in other European countries such as Sweden and Finland. There are also small homebuilt organisations in Greece and Spain.

Some of the former colonial countries in Africa have also seen homebuilding take place, such as Kenya with 'Pappy' Probyn's Jodel D.9 5Y-ALI, which has been flying for nearly 25 years, and the more recent Vans RV.3. North Africa has seen many homebuilts, Henri Mignet's influence in the 1930s and his later sojourn in Morocco being a major factor—a Pietenpol Aircamper TS-GNI has been built in Tunisia.

South and Central America and the Caribbean have also seen their share of homebuilts with considerable influence from the USA. Mr Uriel Bristol designed, built and first flew his BX-200 side-by-side two-seater at St Croix in the British Virgin Islands in July 1986 and is now selling kits and plans for the type, although he has now moved to North Lauderdale, Florida.

The Far East has great potential, particularly Japan and China. In South Korea the Institute of Aeronautical Technology has built the unusual composite two-seater microlight Blue Sky 3 with twin pusher 30 hp KFM engines.

See Appendix 5 for addresses of these homebuilt organisations world-wide.

CHAPTER 10

10 to 10,000—those big homebuilt events

ANY SPORTING ORGANISATION has its big get-togethers, be they annual, bi-annual or, in the cae of the world's amateur athletes, every four years at the Olympic Games. Quite naturally the homebuilt aircraft organisations around the world have their big events as well, providing a chance to meet fellow members, show off newly or part-complete homebuilts, pick up building tips, see what's new from the commercial suppliers, and many other benefits.

With aviators there is an added incentive at such events, which is simply to be able to fly in. Those who arrive by road are, of course, welcome and essential parts of such events, but it is not until you have experienced the excitement of the preparation, the early morning alarm call, checking your plane out and then actually navigating and flying yourself to a homebuilt aircraft fly-in, that you can appreciate the thrill and sense of achievement when your destination airfield hoves into view.

Some of the earliest homebuilt aircraft fly-ins were those organised in France by the Réseau des Amateurs de l'Air (RAA) in 1934–35. These were not so much a fly-in as a gathering of builders of HM.14 Pou-du-Ciels (Flying Fleas) and their supporters at which a few aircraft 'hopped' and 'flew'. The Paris (Orly) Flea meet in October 1935 organised by the French magazine *Les Ailes* was a classic example.

Whether there are 10 or 10,000 aircraft gathered at such events makes no difference—the spirit of conviviality in the common cause of support for homebuilt and sport aviation is the motivation. They also provide the show-case for each country's homebuilt organisation.

A group of RAA members in 1935 including de Roubaix, Dehove, Groene, Andre Thomas and, in the centre, Henri and Annette Mignet. (RSA, via Jacques Avril)

The Orly meeting of Fleas, with the mighty Kohler and Baumann example in the air. (Musée de l'Air)

Great Britain

It is hard to imagine a summer weekend in Britain now without a fly-in or air rally to attend somewhere; in fact on many weekends there are several such events. It has not always been that way, however, and when the Popular Flying Association (PFA) first decided to hold a national gathering for its members there were plenty of 'free' weekends.

Northampton's Sywell aerodrome was the venue chosen for the first formal fly-in and rally at which the PFA showed its flag. This was the Air League's event 'Flying For Fun' or F3, sponsored by the *Daily Express* and held on 13 and 14 September 1969; it featured aerobatics by Peter Philips in his Andreasson BA-4, the Army's 'Blue Eagles' Sioux helicopter display team, Air Training Corps glider displays and many other events including a fly-past of homebuilts by PFA members whose annual rally coincided with this event at Sywell. A long list of trade exhibitors were also lined up, including Rollason Aircraft and Engines, Southern Sailplanes, Campbell Aircraft with their Bensen gyrocopters, Beagle Aircraft with the Pup, Phoenix Aircraft with homebuilt kits of the Luton Minor and Major, Proctor Aircraft with their Kittiwake all-metal homebuilt, and many others. It was to be almost a light and sport aviation 'Farnborough'.

Unfortunately the September weather took its toll of the event which, although it went ahead, was poorly attended. Undaunted and still under the patronage of the Air League, plans were laid for the 'Flying For Fun Fair', or F4, at Sywell the following year, to be held on 11 and 12 July 1970. About 150 aircraft came and went throughout the weekend; Sywell aerodrome saw its movements total close to 1,000 for the two days, and there was a large turn-out by PFA members and their aircraft, who had declared the Saturday their 'Competitions Day'. Sywell Aerodrome Ltd and the Air Squadron were backers of the event and the line-up of British homebuilt aircraft was enhanced by the attendance of Bob Schnuerle, a member of the US Aerobatics team in Britain for 1970's World Championships at Hullavington, in his Pitts Special N1151H.

This first big PFA event was visited by a range of homebuilt, vintage and sport aircraft types that exemplified the state of homebuilding in Britain at the time:

G-ASCM	Isaacs Fury II now owned by M. Raper
G-AXGR	Luton Minor flown to Sywell from East Lothian in Scotland by 20-year-old David Spall who won the 'Most Commendable Flight' award, taking 12 hours' flying time to get there behind his 36 hp JAP-powered aircraft.
G-ASZY	FRED Srs.2 flown by Eric Clutton
G-AMAW	Luton Minor (Swalesong 1) flown by Jim Coates
G-AMVP	Tipsy Junior flown by A.R. Wershot
G-AXMB	Slingsby Twin-Cadet flown by E.W. Osbourne, a Cadet glider fitted with two 250 cc Villiers motor-cycle engines
G-AYAN	Slingsby T.31 Motor-Cadet fitted with a 1,600 VW engine
G-ARZW	Currie Wot flown by Ralph Hart from the Tiger Club, built by John Urmston and the subject of his well known book *Only Birds and Fools Fly*
G-ASRF	Gowland Jenny Wren, a tri-gear conversion of a Luton Minor
G-AWEP	Minicab flown by Stan Jackson from

Falconar F.9 G-AYEG and other homebuilts at the 'F5' PFA rally at Sywell, 17 July 1971. (Author)

	Lancashire
G-AVPD	Jodel D.9 flown by Stuart McKay, at the time editor of the PFA's magazine 'Popular Flying'
G-AWDO	D.31 Turbulent flown by Roy Watling-Greenwood and placed first in both the 'Best Homebuilt' and 'Concours d'Elegance' awards
G-AYFY	EAA Biplane built by H. Kuehling from Barry and roaded to the event but subsequently 'banned' because it was built from some non-released materials
G-AXVC	Tipsy Nipper flown by Air Commodore Christopher Paul
G-ABLS	DH.80A Puss Moth flown by Cliff Lovell and winner of the award for the 'Best-kept Vintage Aircraft'
G-ACTF	Comper Swift flown by Bill Woodhams
G-ABUS	Comper Swift flown by Keith Sedgwick (These last two were jointly awarded the prize for 'Oldest Ultra-Light')

An added fillip to the organisers of F4 was the arrival by air of a Royal participant, HRH Prince William of Gloucester.

The success of 1970's event soon had the PFA's rally-organising committee planning for F5 at Sywell in July 1971, the PFA's Silver Jubilee Year. This was to be Flying For Fun, Fair, and Frolic and it was just that, with around 250 aircraft being flown in. The PFA had virtually taken over the event as its official annual fly-in and rally, and already the name of the venue was becoming synonymous with the event. In 1972 came F6, and the PFA extended the event to three days between 14 and 16 July to enable the growing number of participants to arrive on the Friday and make a real long weekend of the rally. July 1973 saw the PFA back at Sywell, but having run out of original 'F' words to add to the event's title, simply referred to it as their Annual Rally and Fly-In. By this time the PFA was boasting a membership of 1,500.

And so through most of the 1970s Sywell in July became an annual pilgrimage for PFA members and their aircraft: 1974 saw 14 international visitors arrive, and the following year the number of aircraft flying into Sywell for the rally was up to 450. The next year's event, in the heat of the long, hot summer of 1976 saw it extended by a further day to include the Monday, with rally statistics giving a total of 475 visiting aircraft, an amazing 60 of which were overseas arrivals. The PFA could now quite justifiably call Sywell its International Rally.

That year Sywell also witnessed one of the high points in British homebuilt aircraft history when one of those overseas arrivals was Clive Canning in his all-metal two-seater homebuilt Thorpe T.18 VH-CMC, which with impeccable timing and not a little luck he had flown all the way from Australia. (See Chapter 17 for more detailed story of this historic homebuilt flight.) As well as the large 1976 Scandinavian contingent, the arrival of Clive Canning was really a feather in the PFA's cap and put the PFA, Sywell and, of course, Canning in the national headlines.

In the next two years, 1977 and '78, the PFA were back at Sywell in early July. The '78 event saw 372 aircraft fly in, but it was also a significant year in several other respects. It was the 50th Anniversary of the opening of Sywell aerodrome, on 29 September 1928, when a grand pageant attracting thousands of locals saw Alan Cobham and many other aviation personalities of the time setting the aero-

Clive Canning's T.18 VH-CMC flying a 'lap of honour' at Sywell in 1976 after its epic flight from Australia. (Clive Canning Collection)

drome on its way to a history that continues into the 1990s. It was also a sad year, as PFA members uttered the word 'Sywell' for the last time. So successful had these annual PFA International Rallies become that Sywell was now too small for the event to be held safely, particularly when one of the cross runways had to be used for aircraft parking, and if the wind was at 90° to the main runway, operations by many PFA aircraft were marginal.

A move north to Leicester East Aerodrome was made for 1979's PFA International Rally between 6 and 9 July. More space for aircraft and camping was claimed, but anyone who looked down on that 1979 rally on the Saturday afternoon from the air would have wondered 'what space?'. A significant arrival at this first Leicester rally was Rudi Kurth from Switzerland flying his Rutan VariEze, the first to be completed in Europe and certainly the first time the type had been seen in Britain. An incident at Leicester in 1981 when a microlight flipped over on to its back in very strong cross-wind conditions —without serious injury to its pilot—emphasised that, regardless of the lower turn-out at the PFA Rally that year because of poor weather, this new venue was far from ideal, particularly when 750 light aircraft were to fly in over one weekend.

So it was to the College of Aeronautics airfield at Cranfield in Bedfordshire that the PFA moved in 1982 for their 14th Rally. That year's rally was also designated the 'Premier Rally' of its type in the world by the Commission Internationale d'Aeronefs de Construction Amateur (CIACA), whose President was also the PFA's own president, David Faulkner-Bryant. Cranfield was seen as the ideal venue for the PFA's growing fly-in and rally: centrally located, but not too far from London, with cross runways including hard and grass examples, acres of grass for aircraft parking, commercial displays, parking and camping, and excellent on-site permanent accommodation, part of the College of Aeronautics and the Cranfield Conference Centre.

A happy association between the PFA and Cranfield blossomed, then died during the 1980s. Like Sywell before it, the venue's name became synonymous with the event until the developers tolled the death knell. Relations between the authorities at the host airfield and the PFA became less amicable and there was strong local hostility from residents in Cranfield village to 'all these small planes'. It was not helped in 1990, the last year the PFA were at Cranfield, when an arriving Cherokee crashed on finals, landing in the back garden of a nearby house, killing the plane's three occupants. It was neither a PFA-type aeroplane, nor were its occupants PFA members.

Nonetheless the PFA's achievements at Cranfield are remarkable, helped mainly by a dedicated yet generally small army of voluntary member helpers, who, as at all such events around the world, work long and hard throughout the preceeding 12 months to make 'their' rally a success. Their work over the weekend of the rally, most recently under the leadership of Rally Committee Chairman Richard Sykes, is quite remarkable and a credit to these PFA members.

The years 1982 to 1990 at Cranfield saw the rally grow to a regular 1,000-plus aircraft attendance, as can be seen from the table overleaf. This demonstrates that the PFA now has the distinction of hosting the largest aviation event in terms of numbers of aircraft outside the USA. It was sad, therefore, that when the PFA shut up shop at

A long line of composite 'canards' at Cranfield in 1987, with two factory-built speed canards from West Germany interloping. (Author)

Cranfield in 1990 it was for the last time; industrial development on part of the airfield was already well in evidence and the space that had been an asset in 1982 was now at a premium.

The PFA hosted its 22nd successive rally, the July 1991 International Rally and Fly-In, at RAF Wroughton near Swindon, Wiltshire. This airfield's history goes back to 1938, when it opened for flying in April 1940 as No 15 Maintenance Unit. It is now home of the Aeronautical Collection of the Science Museum and of two active service units, an RAF hospital and the Royal Naval Air Yard. Wroughton thus opens a new chapter, and is the fourth venue for the PFA's rally.

Cranfield in 1989, showing the trade exhibitors' tents and the Battle of Britain Memorial flight Lancaster beyond. (Author)

Year	Total aircraft attendance	Homebuilts attendance	Foreign attendance	Notable occurrences
1982	697	104	44	Two British-built VariEzes appeared.
1983	728	68	49	Jan Šimůnek and Jaroslav Kamaryi flew their Czech homebuilt SK-1 Trempik Ok-JXA to the rally. Yves Duval from Rennes displayed the first Cri-Cri seen at a rally.
1984	1,010	110	88	Large numbers of microlights on display for the first time. Cornelis Petrus flew the Dijkhaster PH-COR from Lelystad, Holland, the first Dutch homebuilt.
1985	945	119	88	First Italian homebuilt, LongEz I-MEZE, flown by Gianni Zuliani from Bergamo. Jan Šimůnek returns from Czechoslovakia in the Trempik, this time with colleague Vladislav Verner in another Czech homebuilt, the Brouchek W.01 OK-YXA.
1986 (PFA 40th Anniversary)	875	121	63	First Irish homebuilt, the Tony Murphy's Murphy Sprite, and the arrival of Peter Magnuson from Madrid in Spain in a LongEz he built in the USA. Busiest Sunday, with 495 aircraft arrivals.
1987	1,183	130	114	First Puffer Cozy and first Glasair (Soren Schmidt from Gottenberg.) 110 Jodels flew in.
1988 (40th Anniversary of the Jodel)	820	148	67	First Rutan Defiant, twin-engined composite homebuilt, flown in by Don Foreman. Serge Darroux arrived from Senegal in W Africa in Robin HR.100 6V-AEK. First Jodel D.18 seen, flown by Tugdual Bertho from Pontivy.
1989	1,100+	116	65	Three Kitfoxes appeared. First British-built Puffer Cozy, and Ivan Shaw won two awards with his unique TwinEze. A Sorrell Hiperbipe imported from the US flown in, one of many US homebuilt imports starting to appear in Britain.
1990	1,185	122	66	Two examples of Mark Brown's Starlite composite kitplane displayed as well as the first two-seater Pulsar from the same designer. Phil Boyer flew in to Cranfield from New York via Rekyavik in his Cessna 340. Pete Bish arrived from Hungary in a Piper Pacer. First Glasair III completed outside the USA on display.

Wroughton in Wiltshire was the venue for the PFA's rally in 1991. Björn Eriksen's Falco taxis past some of the hundreds of visiting aircraft. (Author)

The RSA rally at St Junien in 1976: this is the first French-built example of the Brugger MB-2 Colibri. (Author)

France

Ever since the founding of the Réseau du Sport de l'Air (RSA) in 1947, it has held a 'Rassemblement National'. Each year a different airfield around France has been the venue, the local Aero Club in association with the local town and its Chamber of Commerce and Syndicat d'Initiative supporting the event. For non-French aviators or non-RSA members to establish where each year's event was to occur was a task worthy of Sherlock Holmes! After all, it was a National Rally, so why should foreigners want to know its whereabouts . . ?

During the 1970s information started to leak out of France. The 1970 Rassemblement was held at Bergerac in the Dordogne. For the 24th event in 1971, the RSA convened at Cambrai in north-east France, guests of the Aero Club de Cambrai. This was only a stone's throw from Britain, so a couple of British-registered aircraft and their pilots made the flight for the weekend to join a small international contingent of several Swiss, a Belgian and a Swedish aircraft. A total of 160 aircraft flew in and, of these, 64—40 per cent—were homebuilts. France has become renowned for its individualistic and innovative homebuilt aircraft movement, and this high percentage of homebuilts attending each RSA rally is symptomatic of this.

Cambrai, as well as being host to Jodels, Jurca Tempetes and Siroccos and Emeraudes, demonstrated a fact that every RSA rally before and since has confirmed, that the tandem-wing designs derived from Henri Mignet's Flying Flea are still very much alive in France and being successfully and safely flown. Other unusual and one-off designs were also to be expected—the Estivals ED.3 (F-POIN), the Lederlin 380L (F-PMET), the Holleville RH-1 Bambi (F-PDPZ), and the Lucas L.4 (F-PKFU) were some.

The wanderings around France continued. In 1975 the RSA was at Laval in southern Normandy, in '76 at St Junien near Limoges. In 1977 it hosted the Gyro Club de Champagne at the ex-USAF NATO airfield at Brienne-le-Chateau, about 120 miles east-south-east of Paris, then 1978 saw a move to the south-west of France, to Brive, and then the following year back to Brienne.

These annual moves meant that the logistics of organising each rally started afresh each year, and in almost typical French fashion they were charming, informal, seemingly disorganised but always friendly and interesting events. A succession of new homebuilt designs continued to appear, and the RSA rally became rather like the big Paris couturiers' annual display of new fashions, when any designer/home builder with a new aircraft 'revealed' his new protégé. As homebuilding became more popular and larger numbers of foreign visitors flew to these RSA rallies, many of the small club airfields were really too small and unable to cope with 3-400 light aircraft suddenly descending on them.

With the move to Brienne for the second time in 1979, the RSA realised the merits of this enormous disused airfield. Mme Lumbreras, the airfield's owner, also went to considerable efforts to make the RSA welcome and one of the two hangars on the airfield was seen as just the location for the museum of French homebuilts which the RSA wanted to establish.

So, as with 'Sywell' and 'Cranfield' in the British vocabulary, so the name 'Brienne' soon became synonymous with the big annual French RSA rally and fly-in. The 1979 event there also recognised the event's growing international importance and was

Brienne's characteristic hangars provided the backdrop for the RSA's big annual fly-ins between 1979 and '87. A MH.1521 Broussard taxis out. (Author)

also billed as the '1st Rassemblement Européen'. Attendances were, however, smaller than at the equivalent British PFA rally, the RSA usually attracting an average of 500 aircraft to each event at Brienne—as with all their National rallies, though, the proportion of homebuilts in the total aircraft attendance was always high, at between 30 and 40 per cent. For the last weekend each July, the usual timing of the RSA rally, the innovative designs continued to flourish.

The isolation of Brienne from any nearby large towns produced the drawback of accommodation problems for the sudden influx of visitors. If one was camping there was no problem, but there was no good hotel nearby. By 1987, the last year that the RSA held their Rassemblement at Brienne, use of the airfield was also presenting a problem. Security was difficult and the good relations with the owner were wearing thin. This, combined with the isolation, decided the RSA to move on, and in 1988, for the 41st Rassemblement National and 10th Rassemblement Européen, the venue shifted south to Moulins at the very geographical heart of France.

In conjunction with the Moulins Chamber of Commerce and Industry and the City Council, the relatively new Moulins (Montbeugny) airport was made available to the RSA for the weekend of 28–31 July 1988. A single 4,264-foot (1,300 m) concrete runway, small parallel grass strip, terminal building, control tower and small hangar were all the facilities, but in typical RSA fashion, learned over many years before Brienne, the rally made itself instantly

The first RSA rally held at Moulins in 1988. (Author)

Roaded from Spain, A. Hernandez Garcia's Monnet Moni homebuilt EC-YAF was the first Spanish homebuilt to be seen at an RSA international rally. Moulins, 1988. (Author)

at home, helped by the beautiful weather, the attractions of the large and historic nearby town of Moulins, and the dedication of the RSA's Committee under Louis Cariou.

About 700 aircraft flew in for the first RSA rally there in 1988, including aircraft of 14 nationalities. One of the first Vans RV-4s (an all-metal tandem two-seater low-wing monoplane design very popular in the USA) to be seen in Europe, and built by Raymond Yves Deroche, made its debut; several other US types were also seen at an RSA rally for the first time, including the Avid Flyer, Avid Amphibian and the Country Air Karatoo. A pair of Brugger MB.2 Colibri wood/fabric single-seaters were flown to Moulins from Italy, and a Monnet Moni motorglider was roaded in by A. Hernandez Garcia from Spain. The 'poor-man's VariEze', the French RJ.02 Volucelle, a wood/fabric/foam two-seater 'canard' design of Roger and Jean-Claude Junqua (see Chapter 11), was very much in evidence, as well as the diminutive and unusual single-seater Chudzik CC-01 composite canard. In true French tradition there were plenty of Flying Fleas, including the HM.1000 Balerit being demonstrated by Henri Mignet's son, Pierre Mignet.

Another successful RSA rally took place at Moulins in 1989 with another 700-aircraft attendance, 250 of them homebuilts. The Jodel D.18, the 'new' two-seater Jodel design intended for a VW, Limbach or JPX engine, was very much in evidence, with 13 examples (two of the tri-gear D.19 version included) being flown in. An Aerodis G.802 Orion four-seater 'pusher' kitplane was back on the scene and three Brandli BX-2 Cherrys attended (see Chapter 13). The Nicollier HN.700 Menestrel II debuted, as well as the Australian-built Sadler Vampire.

Moulins also hosted 1990's RSA rally, despite thunderstorms and a lower attendance, and they were back there again in 1991 with their inimitable blend of the new and unusual in French homebuilt aeroplanes.

United States of America

Mention a big homebuilt aircraft event and thoughts may immediately spring to North America and the doyen of fly-ins, the event-to-end-all-events, the Experimental Aircraft Association's (EAA) Oshkosh Fly-In Convention. There are hundreds of other smaller events organised by the EAA, the Antique Aircraft Association (AAA) and similar organisations throughout the USA—and Canada—but other than Oshkosh there are really only two other 'big ones'; the EAA's Sun'n'Fun, held at Lakeland, Florida, each April; and in mid-July the EAA's North-Western Chapters' big fly-in at Arlington, Washington State.

Oshkosh—millions of words and several books have already been devoted entirely to the world's biggest aviation event, the Oshkosh Fly-In. Regularly attracting nearly a million visitors during the week-long event, aircraft attendance is usually well in excess of 12,000, and the host airfield, Wittman Field, handles an estimated 60,000-plus aircraft movements during the event, making it the busiest airport in the world and far exceeding the movements for the same period at the world's busiest commercial airport, nearby Chicago's O'Hare.

What started as a modest fly-in for the fledgling group of 31 EAA homebuilt aircraft enthusiasts, Paul Poberezny's newly-founded homebuilt aircraft movement, in September 1953 at Curtiss-Wright Airport at Milwaukee, has turned into a staggering air show with major commercial involvement.

But has it been a victim of its own success? There are those who would argue that the statistics speak for themselves, and that since one of the EAA's declared aims is air education, to have nearly one million people looking at and being entertained by aviation must do inordinate good in this respect. The counter argument is that by its very size and commercialism the event no longer caters for the grass-roots homebuilder and aircraft restorer, and that attendance at Oshkosh is more of an endurance test than a week of sports aviation fun.

It is a case of everyone to their own—the EAA members who year-in, year-out take their annual holidays to coincide with Oshkosh and then spend all their time carrying out the volunteer duties of marshalling, trash collection, crowd control, managing the camp-sites, etc, would have it no other way. The rows of arm patches on their jackets, one for each year they have been to Oshkosh, bear evidence of their total dedication to the cause. Then again, some EAA members would not be seen dead at Oshkosh—they like to fly their homebuilt and sport aircraft in an unhurried, unrestricted rural ambience, and the frantic air-traffic pattern at Oshkosh totally precludes this unless you arrive in June and leave in September!

Before Oshkosh, Curtiss-Wright was the venue between 1953 and 1959, then the EAA moved to Rockford, Illinois. The last EAA Rockford Fly-In attracted 300,000 people and almost 10,000 aircraft, and the EAA saw the need for a permanent site where facilities could be built that would serve them, their members and the fly-in not just for one week a year, but throughout the year. As a result Oshkosh, Wisconsin, was selected in 1970, and the first EAA fly-in there was held in 1971, the year that the EAA's three associate Divisions were established to represent the widening interest beyond just homebuilt/experimental aircraft.

Any critics of the EAA would do well to visit the EAA's Aviation Center and Air Museum, opened in 1983 at Wittman Field and now unanimously agreed to be one of the finest air museums in the world. It was as far back as April 1962 that the EAA Air Museum Foundation was formed and the official opening and dedication was the culmination of over 20 years' work. In 1984 the Voyager round-the-world aircraft was displayed at Oshkosh; that same year 750,000 visitors passed through the Oshkosh gates during Fly-In week, and 14,000 aircraft flew in to celebrate the EAA's event dedicated to the 'Freedom of Flight'. Also in 1984, and for the second year running, Oshkosh was named as one of the top 100 tourist attractions in North America. Two years later, for the 34th EAA Oshkosh Fly-In Convention, the aircraft visitors' total topped the 15,000 mark during the week, although to put the event into proportion only just over one-tenth (1,741) were what are described as 'show planes'—the homebuilts, antiques/classics, warbirds and aerobatic aircraft. The 1986 event saw the opening of Pioneer Airport at Oshkosh, located

The EAA's Oshkosh Convention—the 'big one'. (Ken Ellis Collection)

Sun'n'Fun '91—a DC-3 on amphibious floats dwarfs part of the display area, while a new Lake Seafury stands in the foreground. (Author)

directly behind the EAA Aviation Center, a real grass airfield designed to re-create the barnstorming era of flying, and where some of the EAA's valuable antique aircraft can be flown in an appropriate setting.

Each year sees new homebuilt and kitplane aircraft unveiled at Oshkosh. In 1990 it was the year of Neico's four-seater Lancair IV, a fast (329 mph at 25,000 feet) composite kitplane powered by a 350 hp Continental TSI0-550A, eclipsing the new 'stretched' Glasair II-S series kitplanes. At the opposite end of the scale was Randy Schlitter's new RANS S-12 two-seater microlight.

Oshkosh is many things to different people. It has grown from its homebuilt aircraft roots to attract enormous crowds and exude commercialism. The old adage still applies, though, that if you claim to like aeroplanes you owe yourself at least one visit to the world's biggest aviation 'happening', Oshkosh.

Sun'n'Fun is a relative youngster compared with Oshkosh. This EAA fly-in at Lakeland, Florida, has grown in size and popularity almost faster than Oshkosh. Largely the product of dedicated hard work by Sun'n'Fun's Executive Director, Billy Henderson, it is a similar cocktail of flying, homebuilts, sport aviation, workshops, commercial displays, warbirds, socialising and most other things under the sun associated with aviation. And it is the sun that is also one of the attractions—now held each

The Sun'n'Fun Foundation Air Museum at Lakeland is open all year round as an air education centre. A recent addition to its growing collection is this beautiful Command-Aire 3C3. (Author)

April, Sun'n'Fun is one of the first of the year's big aviation events and in the pleasant, usually sunny, warm and hospitable Southern environment it is a great place to banish those winter blues.

First held in 1974 as a regional EAA fly-in, the following year it was re-named the Mid-Winter Sun'n'Fun and, remarkably, by 1978 it had become the second largest fly-in in the USA, a week-long event at which over 4,000 aircraft flew in and 16,000 entered the gates. In 1980 the decision was taken to move Sun'n'Fun to March, and by 1984, the 10th anniversary of the event, 480 'show aircraft' were registered and the attendance topped the 100,000 mark. As with Oshkosh, permanent facilities first started to appear at the western end of Lakeland's municipal airport, and plans were made for the future to build a permanent museum and air education centre, opened in 1989. Other buildings for the antiquers, the FAA, the press and media and many others were constructed, as well as hard standings for tents and marquees during Sun'n' Fun week.

Yet another date shift occurred in 1988 when Sun'n'Fun was moved to the second week in April, to take advantage of the slightly better weather and the improved accommodation situation in the area. By this time the total attendance was up to 197,000 people, 20,830 aircraft movements during the week, and a total of 902 'show aircraft'. The economic impact on Lakeland of Sun'n'Fun was conservatively estimated at over $13,075,000.

With his team of over 1,000 voluntary helpers, Billy Henderson led the 'show plane' total to the 1,000-plus for the 15th annual Sun'n'Fun in 1989, and the total attendance to 226,000 people. Most of the major homebuilt aircraft, kitplane and ancillary supply companies are represented at the event, which exudes a less hurried, less commercial and more friendly atmosphere to my way of thinking than Oshkosh. Everything the homebuilder could want to see is at Sun'n'Fun these days, and many new types continue to make their debuts at the show. The 17th annual Sun'n'Fun in 1991 did it all over again during the April Florida sunshine, and set more new records in every category.

Arlington is the least well known of the three top US EAA fly-ins but like Sun'n'Fun has shown remarkable growth in the ten years of its existence. Hosted by the EAA at the ex-Second World War Navy airfield near Arlington, Washington State, it is probably the most 'thoroughbred' of the three fly-ins in terms of homebuilts—very few warbirds arrive here. Held over a long weekend each mid-July, Arlington's significance can be seen by looking at a map of North America. It is 2,000 miles east to Oshkosh, including some of the most rugged terrain in the Continent. The whole of the Pacific Coast of the USA, the Seattle conurbations and the Canadian cities of British Columbia are all reasonably accessible, and this is combined with a local preponderance of homebuilt and kitplane manufacturers—Stoddard-Hamilton is actually on the other side of the field, Wheeler technology to the south at Gig Harbor, Richard Van Grunsven with his Vans series of all-metal homebuilts not far away and, to the east, the Avid Flyer and Kitfox factories.

This is part of the reason why over 40,000 people visited 1990's Arlington fly-in, a 30 per cent increase on 1989's figure. It is the same cocktail of exhibitions, seminars, displays, camping, sport aircraft and 'plane-speak' that both Oshkosh and Sun'n'Fun dish up, but is even more informal and less hurried than Sun'n' Fun. Arlington can also boast its firsts, and at 1990's event Murphy Aviation, the Canadian manufacturer of the Renegade Spirit biplane kitplane, unveiled their Rebel all-metal three-seater recreational high-wing tail-dragger. Even the FAA's Deputy Administrator was present to hold discussions with participants, a measure of the importance the organisation attaches to this fast-growing West Coast show. It is the hard work of local EAA stalwarts Jim and Betty Scott that has helped Arlington to its esteemed position, and the No 3 position for EAA fly-ins in North America.

Details of other fly-ins organised by respective countries' homebuilt aircraft organisations can be found in Chapter 9.

CHAPTER 11

Case studies: wood and fabric homebuilts

PERHAPS ONE OF the most straightforward and simple-to-construct wood and fabric homebuilts is the TEAM Minimax, but this comes into the British microlight category and is dealt with in Chapter 16.

As befits the material with which man has worked and engineered for longer and in more ways than any other, wood was the primary material chosen for many of the first homebuilt aircraft designs, particularly in Europe. Most people have some experience of working with wood; it is a 'softer', more approachable and less intimidating material than metal or composites and is the material that many would-be homebuilders have already fashioned and fiddled with in the making of flying model aeroplanes. The relevance of this latter point is that a surprisingly large number of homebuilders cut their teeth in the world of aviation with models, long before they developed an interest in the real thing.

Any potential homebuilder should be aware that although a design might be intended primarily to be built of wood—in other words, that the airframe or structure is wooden—there are many other materials and elements in its construction. Metal fittings are as important, if not more so, than the wood itself in many cases, for attached to them are control wires, ailerons, engine, seats, undercarriage, bracing wires and many other essentials. So before embarking on a wooden homebuilt, one needs to be sure that these 'peripherals' can also be handled.

Engine, systems and instruments also need to be dealt with if the homebuilt is to be completed and flown, although if a particular aspect seems daunt-

Bud Evans's classic homebuilt design. This British example of an Evans VP-1, PFA/7029, G-BEIS, is under construction in the summer of 1980. (Ken Ellis Collection)

ing, remember that few homebuilts would reach completion without help from outside sub-contractors, and this is nothing to be disheartened about or ashamed of. Welding, for instance, in the construction of the engine bearers (if there are any) has to be carried out by a CAA Certified welder, and on something as important as this, peace of mind to know that the work has been done by a true professional is worth a lot. Although appearing basic, many homebuilt designs belie their complexity although the difficulty of a project very much depends on the builder's personal aptitude and experience.

In 1968 W.S. 'Bud' Evans designed his single-seater wood/fabric VP-1 Volksplane in the USA (soon to be re-named just the Evans VP-1 when Volkswagen objected to the name, even though the aircraft was intended to be powered by a converted VW car engine). The design was advertised as one that any competent modeller could build, and with its square-shape, boxy fuselage, constant section/constant chord wing and open cockpit it looked straightforward and became one of homebuilding's most significant designs. The PFA in Britain soon adopted the Evans VP-1 as its 'Approved Minimum Aeroplane' for first-time builders in the early 1970s and many were started, and quite a few completed and flown, but some projects were abandoned. It may be like a scaled-up model, but that scaling-up process introduces many new factors, not least of them being that the finished product is going to be carrying you or your test-pilot into the air. That responsibility demands a special security of construction.

Jodel D.18 and D.19

One of Europe's enduring and classic light aircraft designs is the Jodel 'family'. Joly and Delemontez's single-seater D.9 (see Chapter 3) was their answer to the 'minimum aeroplane' in 1948, 20 years before Bud Evans. The basic Jodel design was developed and refined in many forms and by many companies and individuals subsequent to the D.9's first flight. Commercially produced Jodel developments are still being manufactured, as are homebuilt versions, and one of the latest—and proving most popular amongst homebuilders—is the side-by-side two-seater Jodel D.18 tail-dragger, and its tri-gear variant, the D.19.

Few sport aviation enthusiasts, at least in Europe, can have failed to notice that 1988 was the 40th anniversary of the first flight of the Jodel. This undoubtedly helped to stimulate interest in the D.18, but already D.18 builders throughout Europe and particularly in Britain and France could be numbered in hundreds.

Today the D.18 is comparatively 'old hat' in the homebuilt world and it is difficult to pin down exactly why the design has caught the imagination of so many homebuilders in the 1980s and '90s. This two-seater wood/fabric homebuilt is intended to be powered by a Volkswagen engine (or modern equivalent) whereas the earlier two-seater Jodel designs such as the Jodel D.11 series were for 65 hp to 100 hp Continentals or other similar types which are not quite as easily obtainable in Europe as the ubiquitous Volkswagen.

Perhaps the grass-roots homebuilder will always prefer to build with the tried and tested wood/fabric combination and this, combined with the quality, efficiency and reliability that the name 'Jodel' evokes, and the chance to fit a converted VW engine at modest cost, has helped the D.18 to its popularity.

It was Frenchman Alain Cauchy, teamed with the surviving partner of the Joly/Delemontez duo, Jean Delemontez, who considered in the 1970s the

The prototype Jodel D.18 on display at Brienne-le-Chateau in July 1985. (Author)

possibility of designing and building a slightly larger two-seater version of the Jodel D.9 to be powered by a VW engine. On 6 July 1979, at Persan-Beaumont airfield, the prototype of the Delemontez-Cauche DC-1 (F-PFYU) first flew, powered by a converted 1,600 cc VW car engine. At 24 ft 3 in (7.39 m) it had a slightly larger wing-span than the Jodel D.9, mainly due to the increased width of the fuselage to accommodate the side-by-side seating. It had the characteristic Jodel wing, with the zero dihedral centre-section, and cranked-up wing-tips, part of the reason for the Jodel's safe efficiency in the air, with their excellent cruise performance and good slow-speed handling.

In short this was the birth of the latest Jodel marque, because shortly after the first flight it was unveiled at the French RSA's annual rally at Brienne-le-Chateau and was so well received that it inspired its creators to refine the design with a view to making plans available to other builders.

Construction of the Jodel D.18 prototype was undertaken by Ateliers Amateur de Montauban in south-west France (see Chapter 9) under the leadership of Jean Costes but with considerable input from Cauchy and Delemontez. Costes first flew the prototype D.18 (F-PYQM) at the Centre d'Essais en Vol at Toulouse on 21 May 1984. Unfortunately, on 8 July, whilst being demonstrated at Montauban to Gerard Perrin, President of the Federation National de l'Aeronautique, the prototype D.18 crashed, but without serious injury to the pilot or destruction of the aircraft. In five months the prototype had been rebuilt and was displayed at the Paris Salon at Le Bourget and at the RSA rally at Brienne in the summer of 1985. Since then, plans and building licences for D.18s have been sold in large numbers by Avions Jodel from their headquarters in Beaune, France.

Any person interested in building a D.18 would be advised to contact The Jodel Club based in Britain, a forum for all pilots, builders and aficionados of the whole Jodel series, and which now boasts a membership of over 800 throughout the world. The Club can be contacted c/o Chris Parker, Brooklands, Church Lane, Brafield-on-the-Green, Northampton, England NN7 1BA.

The second D.18 to fly was that of Eric Adillon at Edons in France on 10 May 1985, and it is estimated that by late 1991 there were nearly 50 examples flying in France, several in Britain and more under construction.

Construction of the D.18 has to be undertaken from plans only, with no parts kits available, although The Jodel Club has negotiated the supply of some wood kits, some metal fittings kits and a canopy/cowling/panel/instrument kit to assist builders. Another British homebuilt parts supplier, Barry Smith of Aero Engines & Airframes, has advertised engine mounts for sale, and Peter Cawkwell from Airflow Fibreglass top and bottom cowlings. In France, Societé Aeronautique Bourguignon (SAB), a subsidiary company to Avions Jodel, is selling fabricated metal parts and canopies for the D.18.

The homebuilder should be warned, however, that the D.18's drawings, although to a highly professional standard and of excellent quality, are in French, and anyone with no prior knowledge of aircraft construction could find themselves out of their depth. Here again The Jodel Club has come to the rescue of English-speaking builders with guidance notes and translations and the chance of meeting contacts within the club who have had translations done and started constructing Jodel D.18s, including Bert Jarvis from Portmoak in Scotland who was the first British builder to complete one.

The aim of Cauchy and Delemontez all along has

A Jodel D.18 (foreground) alongside a D.126 (85 hp Continental A.85) at Brienne in July 1987. (Author)

The wing ribs and outer 'cranked' section of the D.18 wing, box spar top right. (Author)

been to produce an economic two-seater homebuilt that will have superior performance with a relatively small engine. Like all Jodels before it, the construction is lightweight yet strong and the builder must have this at the front of his mind continuously during construction. With accurate building and restraint in the fitting of heavy old-fashioned instruments and radio equipment, the target empty weight of 551 lbs (250 kg) and all-up weight of 1,014 lbs (460 kg) should be easily achieved.

The D.18's wing uses a NACA profile 43013.5 for the centre section with the tip profiles evolved; the latter have some twist, whereas the rectangular centre section has none. A single box-spar is 200 mm wide by 164 mm high (yes, these French drawings are metric), or 7.9 in by 6.5 in, for the zero dihedral centre section. Four 25 mm (1 in) longerons make the four corners of the 'box' and within it plywood cross-braces at 45°, 2.5 mm (1/10 in) thick for the centre section and 15 mm (1/17 in) thick for the tapering box in the 'cranked' outer portion of the wing, make up the structure. This is one of the more difficult parts of a D.18's construction and for this reason many French builders have taken advantage of Ateliers Amateur de Montauban (see Chapter 9 under RSA) for help with the jigs and even completely fabricated spars.

More conventional construction is used for the rest of the wing, involving the threading of constant section wing ribs on to the spar. The leading edge is partially boxed-in using 1.2 mm (1/21 in) ply curved around from the upper front edge of the main spar to within 140 mm (5.5 in) of the lower surface of the spar, this ply being used to maintain the wing profile. Rectangular ailerons are fitted into the cranked-up part of the outer wing and have a 2° twist built into them with oblique ribs making a 'warren girder'. These are covered with fabric, as is the rest of the wing structure once control wires, pulleys and fittings have been attached. It is a one-piece wing, so requires a workshop at least as long as the wing-span—7.5 m (24 ft 7 in). The span is slightly shorter than the similar and older Jodel D.11 series (the wing section is also different from the D.11), but the fixed cantilever tubular main undercarriage legs which have rubber in compression for springing and are attached to the front of the wing main spar, are similar in concept to the D.11. Recommended wheels are 350 × 6 with brakes; some examples—including the prototype—have been fitted with fibreglass wheel spats and undercarriage leg fairings.

The fuselage construction of the D.18 is conventional, having a rectangular wooden section with a rounded back; it is 1.0 m (3.28 feet) wide across the cockpit. Both side frames are constructed flat on the work-bench using 15 mm (3/5 in) square longerons—doubled up at the front—and 7 mm × 15 mm (¼ in × 3/5 in) vertical stiffeners, with the slab sides covered in 2.5 mm (1/10 in) and 1.2 mm (1/20 in) ply. The turtledeck behind the cockpit position is mounted on 10 mm (2/5 in) ply frames covered in the same 1.2 mm ply as the underside of the fuselage. There are four bulkheads and the stern-post. The single-piece canopy is mounted on a tubular steel frame which is hinged at the back of the cockpit and opens like a clam shell behind the pilot's head, being held open by two gas-struts. An ingenious locking device at the canopy front fastens it down, but also allows the canopy to be partially opened for extra ventilation when taxiing—this really needs to be thoroughly checked as unfortunately I witnessed a D.18 crash in France caused by the canopy opening and detaching just after take-off.

In common with many of its predecessors, such as the Jodel D.9, D112 and the DC-1, the D.18 has an all-flying tail of approximately 2 m^2 (21.5 square feet) and providing about 20 per cent of the wing area, a generous allowance making for stability and considerable flexibility of the centre of gravity position. It has a single spar, a boxed-in leading edge and is covered with fabric. The traditional all-moving rudder with no fin has a single vertical spar with the leading edge again boxed in with

1.2 mm (1/20 in) ply and covered with fabric.

Fitting out a D.18 is claimed to be straightforward. The small tailwheel is mounted on a steel spring blade and is linked to the rudder pedals for ground handling. The total tankage is 65 litres (14+ imperial gallons) with 35 litres of this in the alloy front tank positioned behind the firewall, and the remaining 30 litres in a similar tank behind the seats. Both tanks are held firm with sheet metal straps and are covered with felt to reduce drumming and echo noises when the engine is running. Two stick control columns protrude from the cockpit floor and are wire-and-pulley linked to the control surfaces. The rudder bars are made of mild steel tubing with toe brakes. Cockpit fit is the individual's choice, although close attention must be paid to weight.

One of the D.18's main plus-points is its potential use of the converted VW car engine. Although the careful conversion has to be undertaken, the engine is cheap and readily available, and also has a smaller front profile, giving the D.18 its characteristic more pointed nose than its older sister-ship, the D.11 series. The French prototype D.18 was fitted with a 1,600 cc VW modified to 1,700 cc, and a variety of engines has since been fitted, some builders using basic 1,600 cc engines whilst others have gone for the commercially manufactured VW developments from Limbach and JPX with ratings as high as 2,050 cc, but always in the power range 45 to 60 hp. It is likely that the lightweight four-cylinder four-stroke Rotax 912A may also have been flown in a D.18 by the time of publication.

Those important engine mounts are made from mild steel tubing of either X18 or A37 specifications, being welded together by a Certificated CAA (or equivalent) welder. The recommended prop (although this is the choice of the builder based on his performance requirements) is wooden and 1.38 m (4½ feet) in diameter with a spacer recommended for the shaft to bring it forward of the two streamlined glass fibre cowling halves.

As with all homebuilt designs, innovation soon follows and a tri-gear version of the D.18, the D.19, appeared very soon afterwards. Jacques Vion from Marennes in France was the first to complete and fly a D.19—his 1,835 cc JPX-powered aircraft took to the air on 3 February 1987. Construction took about two years and the equipped aircraft has an empty weight of 244 kg (538 lbs), a cruise speed of 173 kmph (105 mph) and a maximum speed of 195 kmph (118 mph).

Whether the D.18 (and D.19) is a beginners' aircraft for the home-builder is very much a matter of opinion. Certainly it is not as straightforward or as cheap to build as the Minimax (Chapter 16), but of the available two-seater wood/fabric designs it certainly rates as managable, particularly with the support a builder can now obtain from his membership of The Jodel Club, as well as the large number of British and French builders. If the language barrier with the plans creates a problem, you can

A D.18 structurally complete on display in the RSA hangar at Brienne in July 1986. (Author)

The second Jodel D.19, built by Jacques Vion at Marennes in France and completed in 1991. Vion is now building a larger version, the D.20, with the assistance of Jean Delemontez. (Author)

even buy the *Aviator's English/French Dictionary*, published in England by the Cranfield Press.

Delemontez is now in his 70s, and his and Cauchy's latest 'baby', the Jodel D.18, has become one of the wood and fabric classics of European homebuilding in a very few years. Notwithstanding, Delemontez is now working on a new enlarged version of the D.19, the D.20, in association with Jacques Vion.

Junqua RJ.02 Volucelle and RJ.03 Ibis

French homebuilders have made the world of wooden homebuilts very much their own. As well as the Jodels there are the Druine Turbulent, Turbi and Condor, the many Piel designs such as the Emeraude, many Mignet designs, the more recent Nicollier designs, the Jurcas, and so on.

With the popularity of the 'canard' designs of Burt Rutan in homebuilding it was perhaps inevitable that, shying away from the 'mysteries' that some see in composites, a wood/fabric canard design would emerge. And where else would this happen than in the 'land of the wood/fabric homebuilt', France.

Roger Junqua from Bordeaux in western France, now in his 70s, was the driving force behind France's answer to the VariEze and the LongEz, the proof-of-concept Volucelle and its more recent derivative, the Ibis. Like the Jodel D.18, the Volucelle and Ibis are intended as two-seaters powered by the ubiquitous VW engine, and again like the D.18 they have attracted a great deal of attention and have become very popular in a relatively short space of time. A measure of this popularity can be gauged from an article about the designs which appeared in the June 1989 edition of the American magazine *Kitplanes*, following which Junqua received around 200 enquiries, mostly from the US and Canada but also from Brazil, Taiwan, Australia and South Africa. French and European enquiries have been equally buoyant and in Britain the RJ.03 Ibis design is under survey by PFA Engineering.

It was an attempt to blend the methods of the traditionalist and modernist that in 1980 first tempted Roger Junqua to ponder, 'Why not design a canard to be built in the traditional way from wood and fabric?'. He also felt that for many first-time homebuilders the mix of new materials (composites) used in all other available canard designs, together with the burden of learning the handling and flying qualities of canard designs, put off many would-be builders. If one of these elements could be made more familiar, then the design might receive a degree of popularity.

Aiming also to keep the construction as simple and as economical as possible, Junqua arrived at the basis for his new homebuilt design, the Volucelle. Joining Junqua in part of the design work, and more importantly with the construction of the prototype, were his son Jean-Claude (an executive jet pilot based in Geneva) and friend Jean-Yves Andreazza. To prove the basic design, a technique used by the most accomplished professionals, the construction of a one-quarter-scale radio-controlled model, was used as an initial proof of concept. It was then put on display in July 1983 at the RSA rally at Brienne. Meanwhile, first wood was cut and the fuselage soon completed.

Simplicity of construction is the essence of the Volucelle. The wing (rear) is constant chord, constant section with zero dihedral—set up one jig for

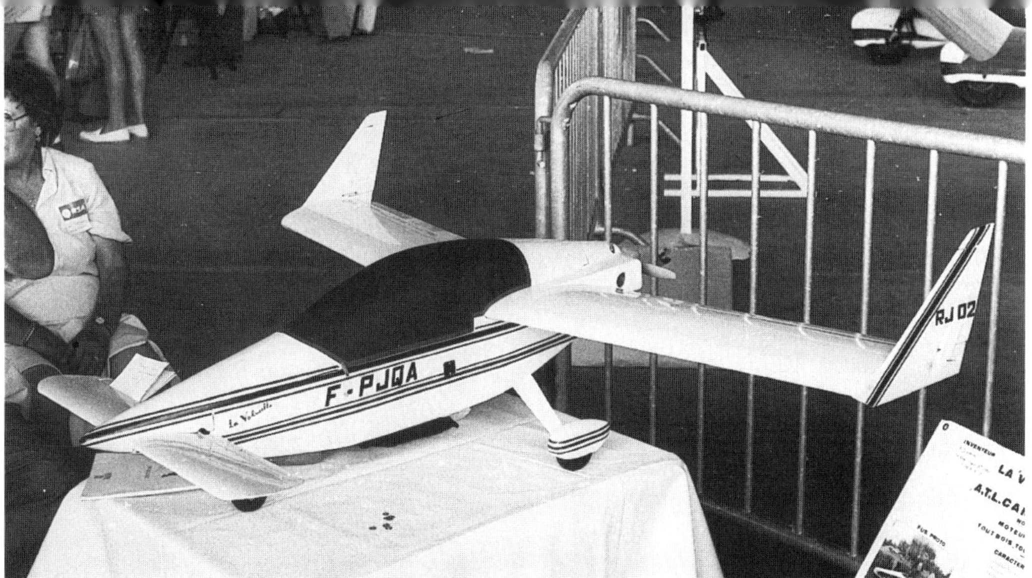

The model of Roger Junqua's RJ.02 Volucelle displayed at the RSA rally at Brienne in 1983. (Author)

the first wing rib to be cut from ply, and the rest are almost identical. Junqua reckons that they can all be made in one evening's work.

The Volucelle and Ibis do make concessions to the 1980s and '90s in their construction; the basic spar and ribs are wood but the spar and wing leading edge are filled by the vacuum method of composite foam on a Styrodur base, giving strength but lightness. The control surfaces are the same with a foam core in a ply casing, as is the 2.13 m (7 ft) canard with its full-span elevators and a tiny winglet fitted under the tip of the canard to prevent flutter.

Tandem seating with the rear seat slightly higher than the front gives an air of a military trainer. The seating position is also more upright than in some other canards which Junqua believes enhances the pilot discipline of 'good look-out'. Apart from that the sill level of the canopy is at chest level and, with the leading edge of the wing (rear) level with the rear seat position, the pilot in the front seat has an almost helicopter-like view.

Fuselage construction is also simple with fuselage sides laid out on a flat workbench and then joined together with formers. The basic structure level is on a horizontal plane with the lowest part of the cockpit; the forward and rear fuselage decking and the sides adjacent to the cockpit areas are then built up from this level. The rear bulkhead is also the firewall for the rear-mounted VW engine. The Volucelle prototype initially only had controls fitted for the front seat, but there was provision for an easy conversion to dual control. Floor-mounted control columns are linked to the control surfaces by push-pull tubes. The canopy hinges to one side, being held shut by a pair of clips; the throttle lever is on the right-hand side of the cockpit.

The first flight was made in July 1986 with a converted 1,600 cc VW car engine rated at 51 hp, giving a slight penalty of weight but not cost, the basic-equipped empty weight of the prototype being 230 kg (507 lbs). This means that the Volucelle has a payload for pilot and passenger weighing 87 kg

The RJ.02 Volucelle prototype with Jean-Claude Junqua in the front seat. (Author)

An RJ.03 Ibis partially complete, showing the simplified fuselage construction. (Author)

(192 lbs), plus full fuel capacity of 54.5 litres (12 gals). The prototype's VW had run many hundreds of hours before being fitted to the aircraft and was therefore not as efficient as a new engine might be—like the airframe, Junqua intended it only to prove the concept. Nonetheless, a calculation of performance figures was made and a range of 726 km (440 miles) at an economic cruise speed of 190 kmph (115 mph) were proven—the never-exceed speed is 266 kmph (161 mph) and the stall with flaps down is 99 kmph (60 mph). A CNRA Certificate of Airworthiness was granted for the Volucelle in December 1986.

Already in that year the Junquas had started work on the 'production' homebuilt development of the Volucelle, the RJ.03 Ibis, which has similar basic overall dimensions but a larger, sleeker fuselage that can accommodate two 1.9 m (6 ft 3 in) tall occupants and incorporates design modifications following experience with the Volucelle. Once plans were completed, three French builders started construction of Ibis prototypes. One of these was 29-year-old technical college technician Geraud Lafage. By July 1988 Lafage had spent seven months of spare-time work on his Ibis and had completed the basic wooden structure including the

The RJ.03 Ibis structurally complete in the summer of 1989—the outer wings can be detached for ease of storage and economy of space during construction. (Author)

Roger Junqua, his wife and Jean-Claude at the RSA Moulins rally in 1990. The Ibis is almost complete and ready for its first flight. (Author)

undercarriage. Wheel spats are suggested by Junqua as a way of increasing efficiency and good looks but the basic power unit is still the 1,600 cc VW, although presumably the similar JPX and Limbach VW variants could also be used as in the case of the Jodel D.18.

An unfortunate accident occurred in August 1990 when Jean-Claude Junqua and a friend were flying the Volucelle from a 610 m (2,000 ft) high grass strip in very hot conditions. The aircraft experienced considerable turbulence and wind-shear near some trees close to the runway and the aircraft crashed, both occupants fortunately surviving. Junqua told me afterwards that the subsequent investigation completely vindicated the engine and airframe; site and conditions were responsible, but it was a timely reminder to take extreme care in the operation of two-seater homebuilts, no matter how aerodynamically efficient they may be on relatively low power.

Undaunted, the Ibis programme has continued and plans are now available to builders around the world; a prospectus is available in English and plans in English will also soon be available; and there is even one in Chinese! The successful first flight of Lafage's prototype took place on 19 May 1991 and a full Certificate of Airworthiness for the type was granted in February 1992.

The main intention is to sell plans for the Ibis to other homebuilders, but Junqua would also like to market components such as the canopy, fuel tank, undercarriage and also possibly kits of ready-cut timber for the wings; he is waiting to see what the demand for this might be. The first indications are good for this innovative wooden 'poor man's VariEze'.

Falco, the Ferrari of the Air

The epitome of the wooden homebuilt aeroplane is the Sequoia Falco. Alfred Scott of Richmond, Virginia, took over the rights to the famous Italian Stelio Frati's design and created one of the elite aeroplanes in the world of homebuilts. That this aircraft, with its smooth, pleasing and aerodynamic lines is also constructed almost entirely of wood is a tribute to both the design and this form of construction.

The Falco can also fall into another homebuilt category, that of the kitplane, because although the first British-built Sequoia Falco was built from plans almost entirely from scratch, the Sequoia Aircraft Corporation now manufactures and sells a series of very comprehensive component kits.

While described with words such as 'elite' and 'Ferrari', the Falco also has another attribute of its class, that of expense. Norwegian Falco builder Björn Eriksen estimated the cost of his Falco at £50,000 and says, 'I rate it as an above average project both in terms of complexity—and of cost!'. A first-time builder should be warned of this before taking on a Falco homebuilt project, although having said this, for the builders of the first British Falco,

Neville Langrick, Bill Nattrass and Ray Holt, it was their first homebuilt.

It was June 1955 when the prototype Falco first flew in Italy, the latest of several designs that Frati had accomplished. Seventy-six of them were built commercially in the next eight years in Italy by Aviamilano, Aeromere and Laverda. In the 1950s, when the Falco was in production, Piper were building the Tri-Pacer (hardly a comparison!) and whilst the Falco was known then as an expensive 'bird', it was undoubtedly ahead of its time and has continued to enrich the European light aviation scene ever since.

The Falco (Hawk) design required considerable re-engineering from the original by Scott in the late 1970s, but his subsequent constructional drawings are praised by every Falco builder I have talked to. When his Construction Manual was published several years later, this was similarly praised. It is partly this and partly the aura surrounding the design that may account for Sequoia's sale of about 650 sets of plans worldwide, about 530 of them in North America but 60 to British builders and another 60 around the world to places such as Australia, South America, Germany, France, Holland, Denmark and even Italy!

The first homebuilt Sequoia Falco to fly did so in June 1982, constructed by Laurence Wohlers of Tucson, Arizona. The first Falco built from Sequoia kits flew two years later, built by David Aronson of Minneapolis, Minnesota. When the Langrick/Nattrass/Holt Falco flew in England on 6 June 1988 it was the 16th to fly and the first 'true' homebuilt Falco to fly in Europe, although German, Herbert Müller, had extensively re-built a crashed factory-built Falco before this, using Sequoia plans.

Why choose such a potentially difficult aircraft for a first-time project? Langrick and Nattrass (Holt was only to join the project later) wanted a two-seater, and Langrick, having seen a factory-built example, had a yearning to fly one. Their choice narrowed down to a Monnet Sonerai or the Falco—the Falco won and they bought a set of Sequoia's plans which they considered were so good that even an inexperienced first-time builder could work from them without trouble. Langrick was a self-employed chartered surveyor and Nattrass was a former RAF airframe rigger who was then working as an engineer for David Brown Tractors in Huddersfield.

It was off to Doncaster Sailplane Services in November 1982 to buy the first bundle of spruce to make the tailplane ribs. Like many other homebuilders setting off on a first project, the tail seemed the best part to start with, in case construction should turn out to be a disaster and it had to be thrown away. It was not, however, and working in their respective homes in Yorkshire, they put together a large quantity of wooden assemblies for wings and fuselage in the first six months.

It was time to decide where they could start to assemble the aeroplane and Langrick's 20 ft × 20 ft (6.1 m × 6.1 m) double garage was chosen as it was well equipped, had central heating and was also sociable as far as family and friends were concerned. Initial assembly was quick, includ-

G-BYLL, Europe's first Sequoia Falco—a true thoroughbred. (Gordon Bain)

Björn Eriksen's Falco fuselage at an early stage of construction at Bodo in Norway. (Author)

ing the fuselage which is built in one piece and then cut in half! That is how they built them in the factory in Italy and for the homebuilder with a space problem it is also an excellent bonus. The cut is made at fuselage 'station 8', just behind the cockpit, the two halves subsequently being connected tightly by 12 bolts.

For the one-piece Falco wing, with a span of 26 ft 3 in (8 m), the Langrick garage was not big enough, so a small diversion from aircraft construction ensued whilst they built a 28-foot (8.5 m) long 'shed' at the bottom of the garden in which to construct the wing. This shed was fitted with a long flat table and they acquired dozens of joiner's clamps to build the laminated main spar. The wing itself was built in a vertical position with the spar supported on jigs and the ribs then fitted in place from the centre outwards. The single main spar runs from wing-tip to wing-tip, whilst the aft spars are separate and only as long as each wing half. Another point is that although the wing ribs are made in one piece, they have to be cut up to be glued in place on to the forward and rearward faces of the main spar. Construction of the basic wing, without skinning, took Langrick and Nattrass about three months.

A T-shaped extension then had to be built on to the 'shed' because, although the fuselage is designed to be cut in half, it has to be in one piece when first mated to the wing for making triangulation and dimensional checks. (The Sequoia manual

Attachment of the tail to the rear fuselage of Marcel Morrien's Falco under way in Holland. (Author)

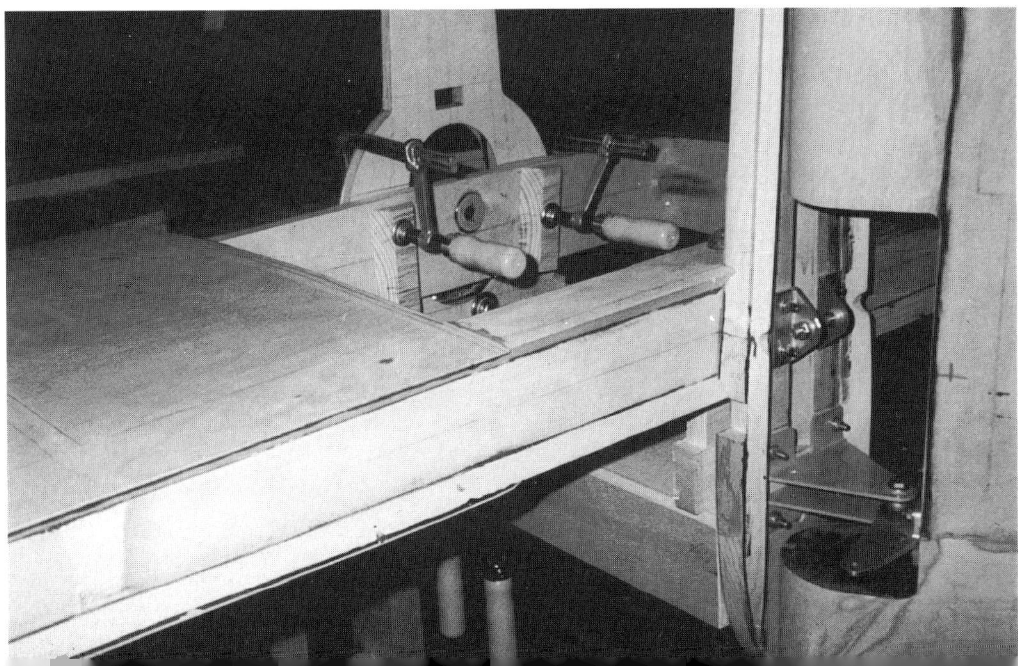

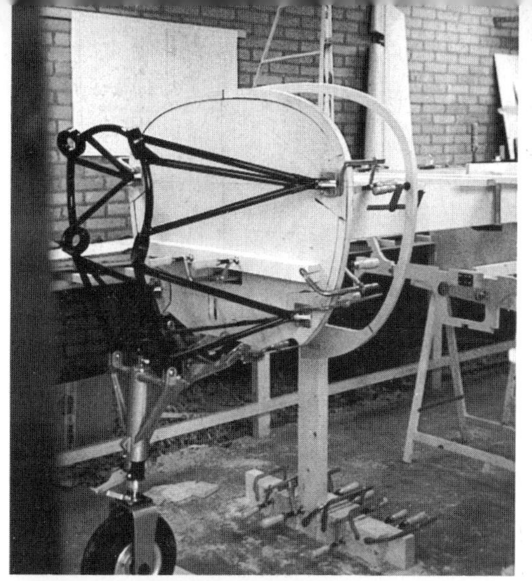

Left *The forward fuselage of Morrien's Falco set up on a substantial but temporary jig which ensures accurate and true construction.* (Author)

Below *The Falco fuselage is designed to be detached at 'station 8' which eases workshop space and transport problems.* (Author)

Bottom *The wings of Eriksen's Norwegian Falco being covered; the main one-piece spar is prominent.* (Author)

G-BYLL fits very snugly into the specially made workshop in Neville Langrick's garden. (Author)

recommends that builders have adequate workshop space for this, but at the time that Langrick and Nattrass were building, the manual had not yet been produced.)

Interest started to wane and enthusiasm flag after 18 months of quite concentrated building effort. The cockpit area of the fuselage and wing were set up on trestles for installation of flaps and ailerons; there is washout and dihedral on the wing and this has to be carried through in the shape of the control surfaces, proving one of the most difficult aspects of the whole project.

A 150 hp Lycoming 0-320 engine from a scrapped Sud Aviation GY-80 Horizon was acquired but had to be shipped to Standard Aero in Canada for a complete rebuild. In retrospect Langrick and Nattrass consider it would have been better to buy a new one and also to have opted for a fuel-injection engine rather than the carburetted one, because Sequoia provide a bottom cowling kit and that has to be extensively modified to accommodate the carburettor bays and air intake.

Many minor details turned into major tasks and the first flight date seemed to be drifting further and further away. Despite despondency, Nattrass continued to churn metal fittings out from his workshop, including hinges, bellcranks, pulleys, control column hardware and rudder bar.

Washout and dihedral continue into the flying controls—to achieve accuracy, the flaps and ailerons were built direct on to the wing of the Langrick/Nattrass/Holt Falco, later G-BYLL. (Author)

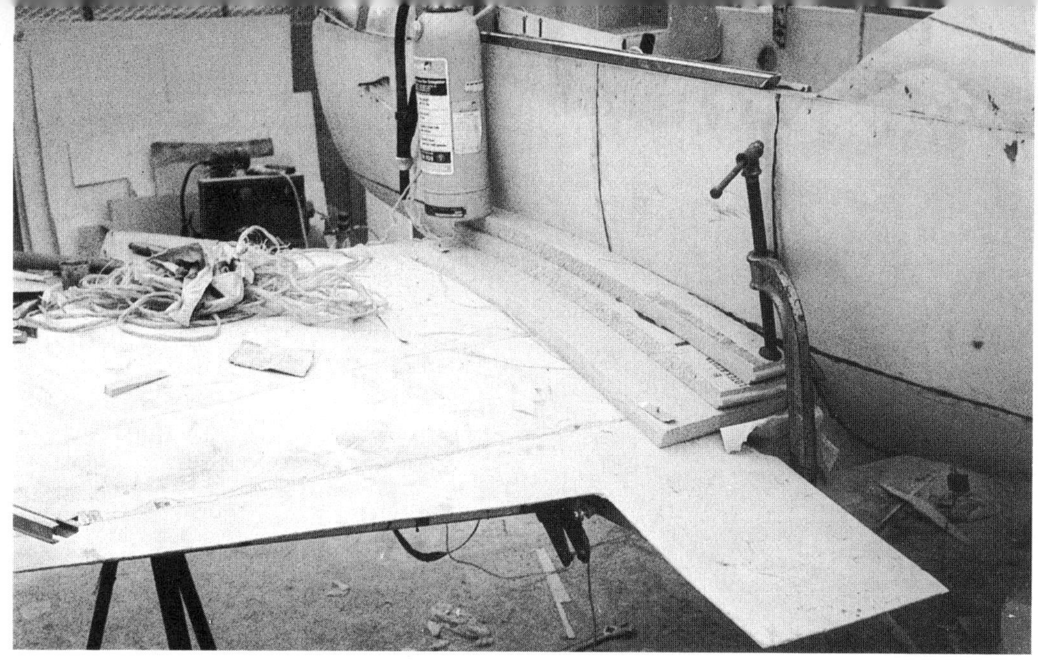

Attachment of the inner wing skin to the main structure on Bob Sothcott's Falco, being built near Hull, England. (Author)

Langrick takes over the story with some very timely advice: 'Many homebuilt and kit manufacturers claim their aircraft can be built by the "average" craftsman. I truly believe that had it not been for Bill Nattrass's skill gained from a lifetime of experience, our Falco project would have foundered. My only experience prior to starting the project was to get A-level woodwork. This had taught me the basics about tools and materials but an undertaking like this is a whole new ball-game. For instance, there's the glueing and bending of wood, which is quite difficult and requires considerable self-discipline to learn—it's like serving an apprenticeship. Even if a complete Falco kit had arrived in a big box with the spars and other major components already fabricated [this is now reality thanks to the Sequoia kits], construction would have still been a daunting task.'

Nattrass's *pièce de résistance* was the fabrication of the main gear and the undercarriage retraction

Some of Bill Nattrass's handiwork on the control system fitted into the wooden fuselage framework at a relatively early stage in the project. (Author)

Ray Holt's main contribution to the Falco was the cockpit upholstery and avionics—his work matches the perfection of the rest of the aircraft. (Author)

system. Getting it to fit correctly into the fuselage/wing module was, he insists, definitely the most difficult part of the whole project (it is now possible to buy a Sequoia kit for the undercarriage to speed builders through this major obstacle). There was a kit available at the time for the nosewheel landing gear, a cast aluminium construction—nobody in their right mind should try to make this themselves. They also bought the canopy, canopy frame, engine mounts and several other parts from Sequoia.

Undercarriage and canopy fitted, wings and forward fuselage mated, and the Falco started to resemble a finished aircraft. It was a moment of encouragement, but at a point when the builders' resources were considerably depleted. At this stage land drainage contractor Ray Holt joined the team, giving a much-needed injection of encouragement and cash, necessary for the detailed final assembly and fitting out. Holt also had a large workshop, so everything was moved there. The airframe was turned completely upside down and the process of skinning, covering and finishing all the undersides took up the next six months. Glass fibre seats were also fabricated at this time and Holt got stuck in to the work of painting, upholstery and avionics for which they had agreed he would be responsible.

As inexperienced first-time homebuilders, the trio admitted afterwards that they had not really taken a lot of care with weight-saving. In their defence, though, they claim that if they erred at all it was on the side of safety—using sufficient rather than skimpy quantities of glue, and cutting wood just outside the pencil line rather than exactly on it. They also began to realise that no matter what aircraft you build or fly it cannot be 'all things for all men'. Quoted weights and performances do not always correspond with every flying experience. For instance, in the Falco you cannot fly two people, weekend baggage, full fuel, autopilot, full avionics and still be able to do aerobatics! However, you can come close.

The Falco trio also rejected the use of the 'bathroom scales' method for weighing their project. 'It has to be done professionally on an aircraft like this,' they insist. In fact, the final weight was 1,293 lbs (586 kg), well within limits but still considerably heavier than the weights reported for many US-built Falcos.

Langrick took on the job of the instrument panel and its wiring, one which, although no electrician, he found easy thanks to Sequoia's excellent drawings and colour coding. He was also able to do this part of the work in the lounge at home. Preparations for painting started at the end of 1987 with the tedious process of rubbing down the ply skinning, filling, rubbing down and undercoating. A professional auto-sprayer applied the final coat of twin-pack epoxy paint.

Final assembly was carried out at Sherburn airfield to the east of Leeds, a job expected to take a month but which ended up taking six! A further blow to the trio occurred at this stage when Nattrass suffered a heart attack and stroke. A speech loss resulted from the latter, and although he was soon able to receive visitors in hospital, it made the job of identifying many of the bits and pieces he had made extremely frustrating and difficult. He was discharged from hospital after several months and was able to join Langrick and Holt during the final weeks of pre-flight checks at Sherburn.

The first flight drew closer and the question of a test pilot had to be resolved. Sequoia's Alfred Scott stresses it, and the trio of Yorkshire builders endorse it, that even if you are an experienced pilot and you have spent the last 5½ years of your life building this aeroplane, this does not necessarily qualify you to be the test pilot, particularly on a relatively 'hot' ship like the Falco. Sherburn Aero Club's CFI, 'Jacko' Jackson, ex-commanding officer of the Battle of Britain Memorial Flight, accepted the invitation to do the test-flying of G-BYLL, now registered as such as a tribute to the work that Nattrass had contributed to the project. In the early morning of 6 June 1988 the Falco lifted into the air amidst an odd feeling of apprehension and excitement amongst the three ground-bound builders. When G-BYLL landed the apprehension turned to relief and then elation in a private and very fulfilling moment.

The gear was left down during the 20-minute flight which was declared nearly perfect with the exception of a slightly heavy port wing, corrected by fitting a trim tab to the starboard aileron. Six hours of test-flying was safely completed by Jackson in the next fortnight, but the disappointing hurdle of getting the 'Permit to Fly' from the PFA by the time of Cranfield '88 was not quite crossed so the Falco's 'big time' debut had to wait for nearly a year until Cranfield '89 when they were awarded the Air Squadron Trophy for the 'Best Homebuilt'. In the meantime Holt and Langrick had flown the aircraft on a 3,000-mile round trip to the Malta Air Rally, winning the Concours d'Elegance trophy and gaining valuable experience into the true performance of their aircraft.

Some of the inevitable questions at the conclusion of any homebuilt project were more than pertinent in respect of this Falco. The builders have no idea at all about the number of hours the project took—Nattrass retired from his full-time job during the 5½ years the project was under way, after which he worked nearly full time on it, averaging at least five hours a day. Langrick took two years off work and worked more than full time on the project, and when Ray Holt joined the team he was averaging at least a 100 hours a month. To this one has to add the sub-contracted items, the bought-in items and the inestimable value of Nattrass's engineering skills. Langrick found the project a heavy financial burden, hurting a lot at the time but in retrospect worthwhile. They felt considerable relief with the project's completion and estimate the overall cost at 1988 prices was very approximately £45,000. Langrick also considers that it would take

Cranfield '89—Ray Holt and Neville Langrick, with Europe's first Sequoia Falco to be completed, were winners of the Air Squadron Trophy for the 'Best Homebuilt'. (Author)

any disciplined homebuilder working on his own on a plans-built Falco and with a fair degree of skill about 10 years to complete it. Obviously with Sequoia now having an inventory of 29 different kits available for purchase, and assuming a builder had the requirement and finance to use them, a Sequoia Falco could be completed much more quickly.

There is always a domestic and social side to any homebuilt aircraft project that many builders ignore at their peril. As well as paths strewn with abandoned projects (when the enthusiasm runs out), these paths are also strewn with marital breakdowns, stress and tension. Langrick remained a married family man throughout the time he worked on the project, but declares that he will never get involved with a homebuilt aircraft again, and this says a lot about the sacrifices he had to make during the 5½ years. He says that the further they got with the project, the more he tended to develop a kind of tunnel vision in which the aeroplane became the over-riding interest in life to the exclusion of almost everything else. The only consolation for wives in that predicament is that at least they know where their husbands are!

These three entirely different and basically wooden homebuilts are the tip of a very large iceberg. As well as two-seaters, many single-seaters, replicas and biplanes can be built. If wood, sawdust and glue turn you on, this type of homebuilt could be for you.

CHAPTER 12

Case studies: metal homebuilts

THE OBVIOUS COROLLARY of the wooden homebuilt is that built from the other standard basic material used in aircraft construction throughout aviation history, metal. For some reason metal has not proved as popular a medium in which to construct homebuilts, at least as far as European builders and designers are concerned. Here the USA predominates, although it does not have it all quite its own way as one of the following case studies from France shows.

Metal construction can be split roughly into two categories:

1 Sheet metal/riveted construction such as the Thorpe T.18 Tiger, the Zenith designs of Chris Heintz in France/Canada, the RV designs of Richard Van Grunsven from Oregon, USA, and the French designs of Jean Pottier.

2 Tubular metal construction, usually of the fuselage, with fabric covering and either metal and wood or all-wood/fabric wings, such as the Wittman Tailwind, Lou Stolp's Starduster and Starlet series of homebuilts, the EAA AcroSport biplane, and the single-seater EAA Pober Pixie.

These are but a small selection of homebuilt types in the 'metal' category, and Britain has not been entirely left out. The Mitchell Proctor Kittiwake (prototype G-ATXN) first flew in May 1967, intended for use as a glider tug. Plans were made available and a further example was completed as a Royal Navy training project at RNAS Lee-on-Solent in 1971 (see Chapter 6). From the Kittiwake, one of the co-designers, Roy Proctor, went on to design the two-seater Petrel, and there was also a two-seater version of the Kittiwake. The Practavia

A Heintz Zenith 130 homebuilt at the RSA's Moulins rally in 1989. Designed by Chris Heintz, it is a popular sheet metal project for homebuilders worldwide. (Author)

Jim Waller's first British-built Thorpe T.18 at Cranfield in 1987. (Author)

(earlier Pilot) Sprite was another valiant attempt to get homebuilders interested in construction of homebuilts through the pages of the magazine *Pilot* (then under a different ownership from the current magazine of the same name). Several were completed and flown, including the Murphy Sprite in Ireland (see Chapter 9).

Other diminutive all-metal homebuilt designs from around the world have been the Pazmany designs (see Chapter 6), Cal Parker's Jeanie's Teenie and the Teenie Two, the WindWagon, Morey Hummel's Hummel Bird powered by half a VW engine (two cylinders only instead of four), the Monnett Sonerai, the Davies DA-2, the sleek Bushby/Long Midget Mustang racer (see Chapter 3) and the microlight Brutsche Freedom 28 (254 lbs/115 kg empty).

Thorpe T.18 Tiger

One of the first and subsequently most popular all-metal homebuilts, the T.18's enduring quality has been demonstrated many times by record-breaking flights such as that of Don Taylor from the USA and Clive Canning from Australia (see Chapter 17).

Whilst few have been built in Britain, Jim Waller's T.18, G-BLIT, built near Southampton was the first and has established the design as PFA Approved. The design's pedigree over 30 years, combined with the pedigree of the designer, John Thorpe, make the PFA's seal of approval almost unnecessary and also beg the question as to why so few T.18s have been built in Europe, whereas in the USA the type proliferates.

John Thorpe learned his basics at the Boeing School of Aeronautics in Oakland, California, in the 1930s—he was also an excellent pilot. His first design in 1931, the T.1, a two-seater light aircraft, never went beyond the study stage, and the same applied to the T.2. However, the T.3 in 1933 was a large four-seater all-metal retractable (see Chapter 2). Thorpe was the Preliminary Design Engineer on the Lockheed P.2V Neptune and, whilst with Lockheed during the Second World War, he developed the single-seater T.10, which became known as the Lockheed Model 33 'Little Dipper' designed for flying infantrymen. The 'Big Dipper' followed, but neither was adopted by the military.

In 1945 Thorpe developed the 'Big Dipper' into

John Thorpe in 1984. (Don Downie)

his all-metal T.12 Sky Skooter and a small production line was started at Van Nuys airport, California, first with a 65 hp Lycoming, then with 100 hp Continentals. Two Sky Scooter kits were exported to Australia. Thorpe's designs continued to appear: the high-winged AOP T.13, whilst he was working for Fletcher Aviation in California in 1950; the Fletcher Defender FD-25A in 1951 during the Korean War; and the Fletcher Utility FU-24 (developed from the T.15), used and built extensively in New Zealand for top-dressing fertiliser. From 1956 to '58 after leaving Fletcher, Thorpe did the preliminary design work for Piper's ubiquitous PA-28, the Cherokee. On his own he then designed for George Wing a twin-engined Sky Skooter, the T.17, that ended up as a side-by-side high-performance retractable twin with two 180 hp engines which went into limited production as the Wing Derringer.

It was in 1960 that Thorpe substantially completed his drawings for the T.18 homebuilt design and put plans of the type on sale for builders, a revolutionary design at the time for a homebuilt, with a performance better than most equivalent factory-produced light aircraft. Bill Warwick, an experimental machinist at Northrop Aircraft, teamed up with Thorpe and, as soon as Thorpe had completed a drawing, started cutting metal to fabricate the component. It took Thorpe three years to complete the drawings and Warwick about the same on the construction, with a slight time-lag. Fitted with a 180 hp Lycoming 0-360, Warwick's T.18, the prototype N9675Z, flew for the first time on 12 May 1964. During the aircraft's development Thorpe built his own example (N18JT) and with meticulous attention to detail and weight saving made it one of the best and fastest of a rapidly expanding fleet of T.18s, mainly in North America.

Typical figures quoted for the enclosed-cockpit T.18 (there were several open-cockpit versions built that were soon converted to cabin types because of considerable buffet in the cockpit) with a 180 hp engine are a maximum cruise speed of 175 mph (282 kmph) and a range of 500 miles (805 km) with two-up and full fuel. Obviously Don Taylor's and Clive Canning's record-breaking T.18s (Chapter 17) were modified as far as tankage is concerned, and although Thorpe has said 'You can't put in any deviation to the T.18 design and must keep to tolerances on the drawings', there have been many modifications to the basic design over the years, including several retractable undercarriage versions.

Thorpe himself sold more than 1,600 sets of plans and believes that between 500 and 600 of the type are flying worldwide, including more than a dozen in Australia where another 50 are said to be under construction. Copies of Thorpe's T.18 tooling were sent to Australia to help with this effort.

Thorpe eventually gave up selling plans for the T.18 but several builders and organisations took over, with Ken Knowles and Ken Brock, both in California, selling plans, bills of materials and many prefabricated parts. Lu Sunderland of Apalachin, New York, developed a wider/longer-fuselage version and these were incorporated in the version sold by Knowles. Knowles also sold plans for a folding-wing version which Sunderland designed, so that

Bill Warwick with the first T.18. (Don Downie)

John Thorpe with his personal T.18 under construction at Van Nuys, California. (Don Downie)

one person could convert his T.18 from road-towing to flight-worthy status in 5 minutes with only two tools. The wings of Thorpe's original could be detached but were in one piece which required the removal of seven major fixing bolts and the control systems, and was a day-long job for three men.

Ken Knowles has been selling parts and sub-assemblies for the T.18 since 1970 and has really put the aircraft into the realm of the 'kitplane', as his complete package with all pre-formed metal components, including the fuel tank, sold for $10,500 in 1985. The skins are all pre-punched from templates ready for drilling, a job he does by hand with a hammer and a special punch. There must be 2,000 matching holes, but Thorpe considers that this matched-hole tooling minimises gross errors and in

An early T.18 flown without a canopy—there was considerable buffeting. (Don Downie)

Ken Knowles with hammer and scribe marking matched hole drill points in a T.18 skin under a template. (Don Downie)

the process helps the builder to finish his aircraft. The Knowles version of the T.18 also incorporates a leading-edge modification that is claimed to reduce the stalling speed by 10 mph and increase the maximum speed by a similar amount. The Thorpe is another homebuilt with cranked-up wing-tips similar to the Jodels in Europe. The folding-wing version is designated the T.18C, and the wide-body the T.18C-W. Plans for the T.18 (or S.18 now) are available from Lu Sunderland's 'Sport Aircraft', and the Thorpe T.18 Builders & Owners Association still flourishes, producing a quarterly newsletter.

Thorpe's aim all along with the T.18 was to produce an efficient homebuilt which would enable anyone mildly interested and proficient in metal-work to bring their project to fruition. It is an all-metal design that requires no jigs and, as both Knowles and Thorpe waggishly remark, 'has no curing temperature problems' (a reference to wood and composite homebuilts). Virtually the whole airframe can be assembled with either Monel pop rivets or with standard AN 470 AD or AN 426 AD rivets. The brochure that Ken Knowles has produced for prospective T.18 builders cautions: 'Building an airplane is no small task but it can be assembled by anyone who has average skills and above-average persistence. If you're a person who's willing to stick to a job until it's finished and if you enjoy the satisfaction of creating a thing of beauty with your own hands, then you can build a T.18.'

The suggested starting point of the construction of a T.18 is the ailerons, which are not too demanding in terms of skill, not too large in case you make a mess of the job first time around, and also give you valuable experience of the techniques used for the rest of the construction process. It is worth remembering that even professional aircraft builders, particularly where metal is involved, do not make a perfect part every time, so that metal in the scrap bin is nothing to be ashamed of or disheartened by. The main control surfaces are made from sheet metal skin and the ailerons, rudder and stabilator tabs will take up about 25 square feet of a standard 30-square-foot sheet.

British T.18-builder Jim Waller, who started off with these parts, says: 'This gave me an important psychological boost—there was always something to look at as I signed it out and it also made for easier storage and cash flow. I was able to keep and fly my previous homebuilt, a Tipsy Nipper Mk III, until well into the project and the cash I got from selling it enabled me to finance my navcom, engine, propeller, canopy and paint job. If I'd started on the fuselage I would have had a major outlay with little to show for it.'

Fuselage construction of a T.18 follows this sequence:

1 Drill the centre-punched holes in the skins with a No 40 (2.5 mm/0.98 in) drill. Trim to scribe lines and file the edges smooth.
2 Drill the holes in frames, bulkheads, etc, with a No 40 drill.
3 Pin the fuselage together with 3/32 in clecos. (A 'cleco' is a temporary positioning pin used in

sheet metal work, removed with cleco pliers once the metal is formed and fixed in place.) Drill the holes out to the rivet size with a No 30 (3.264 mm/0.1285 in) drill, removing the 3/32 in clecos and replacing them with ⅛ in clecos as you drill out the holes.

4 Start with the firewall and work back 72 inches. Countersink all holes for flush rivets.

5 Take fuselage apart. Deburr all the holes and countersink them into the stringers except where the part on the outside is .040 or thicker. If the skin or doubler is .040 thick or thicker on the outside, countersink it for rivets. Reassemble the fuselage and dimple it with a draw dimple set or a side dimple set and rivet.

The wing skins for the T.18 are designed to be formed from a single sheet of 0.32 Alclad. The original basic Thorpe version had a one-piece wing, but the Sunderland/Knowles versions with folding wings make variations to this specification.

Another British builder who started a T.18 did initial component fabrication the hard way, using only hand tools, because he did not want to disturb his neighbours, his workshop being in the living room of his flat! Hand drills were used, frame flanges were bent with rubber hammers on wooden frames held on his lap, and hand-held lever snips were used for all metal cutting, the noisiest tools being his Whitney punch and pop-rivet gun.

Thorpe T.18 Tiger builders and pilots class themselves as part of homebuilding's elite. Many of them have been around for over 20 years and with the large number of the type completed and flown, John Thorpe's design must currently rank as one of the most successful of all time. It is a fitting tribute to the T.18's designer that the development of his T.12 Sky Skooter design, the T.211, went back into commercial production with Thorp Aero Inc at Sturgis, Kentucky, in 1991, not for the US market, due to product liability concerns, but for export. The first three aircraft were delivered to Britain, Germany and Brazil respectively, and the T.211 received full British Certification in July 1991.

France's metal master—Jean Pottier

In the country that is alleged to be the world's premier producer of wood/fabric homebuilts, it may seem incongruous to find a prolific designer of all-metal homebuilt designs. And not just a designer, for they can be ten-a-penny, but also one whose ideals and ideas have been taken up by many hundreds of French homebuilders to the extent that Pottier designs rival the Jodel D.18 in terms of homebuilders' output.

Pottier was born at Lessay near Cherbourg in 1945 and became a professional aeronautical engineer with Aerospatiale in 1981, working in the same factory as Mike Colomban, designer of the diminutive twin-engined single-seater Cri-Cri. Model-making was that familiar starting point for his interest in aviation, which extended to sailplanes and gliders before, in 1969, he released details of his P.50 Bouvreuil (Bullfinch), a wood/fabric single-seater low-wing aerobatic tail-dragger suitable for engines between 65 and 90 hp. Robert Jacquet assisted him with this design and Swiss builder Michel Sugnaux was the first to complete a P.50,

The first example of the Pottier P.50 Bouvreuil (Bullfinch) to fly was built by Michel Sugnaux in Switzerland. (Jean Pottier)

The Besneux-Pottier P.70 prototype, Jean Pottier's homebuilt metal design which first flew on 19 July 1974 with a 40 hp VW engine. (Pierre Gaillard)

HB-YBF. Other designs were already in the pipeline—a flying wing, a biplane, a formula one racer and a glider, the JP.15, developed as the Kit Club, one of the few homebuilt glider designs around.

The real turning point in Pottier's homebuilt career came in 1973, when he declared that traditional wood/fabric materials were outdated for easy-to-build, practical and inexpensive homebuilts, and despite his growing experience with plastics and composites, he felt that they presented too many pitfalls for the inexperienced builder. Metal was the available alternative, so he set about designing a light aircraft that employed this method of construction, yet was straightforward to build.

Alain Besneux from Laval teamed up with Pottier to produce the prototype of this new aircraft, the P.70, which had a slab-sided, rather squarish all-metal fuselage, mid-wing, open cockpit, tailwheel undercarriage and a 40 hp VW engine for power. It took about 400 man-hours to build and flew for the first time on 19 July 1974. It proved the concepts held by Pottier and he improved this basic design into the P.70S which incorporated principles of design and construction that all his subsequent metal homebuilt designs have followed:

1 Use of flat sheet metal and L-shaped corner pieces or sections

The main components for the wing of a Pottier P.80S laid out ready for assembly. (Author)

2 Assembly work done by riveting with blind rivets and glue bonding on all joints, to give a high standard of joint withstanding all possible wear and tear
3 All designs capable of being modified and developed. Only a minimum of metal bending and forming is necessary in the basic designs
4 Sheet metal covering joined by overlapping instead of edge-to-edge, preventing the inevitable movement in joints associated with the latter method
5 Use of piano hinges for everything that has to move: control surfaces, flaps, flight control mechanisms and pedals. Such standardisation is cheap and avoids the expensive machined components which many homebuilt designs specify
6 Simple leaf-spring undercarriage requiring virtually no maintenance. A system of rigid controls used for ailerons, elevators and rudder

These axioms imply an aircraft with an angular fuselage, visible rivets and ridges from the overlaps, all of which reduce performance. However, Pottier is not concerned by this because he maintains that they represent only a few per cent reduction and to the majority of homebuilders it is not much to pay for a 400-hour construction time, minimal tooling and the requirement for few specialist skills. By 1985, from Pottier's range of four basic metal homebuilt designs, 30 aircraft had flown and a further 150 were under construction, mainly in France. By 1990 those figures had more than doubled and the P.180S and P.80S designs were under survey by the PFA and yet to fly in Britain.

A Pottier P.80S fuselage showing the clecos—temporary fixing pins—holding the top fuselage sheet in place. (Author)

The P.70S is a modified tri-gear version of the original Besneux-Pottier aircraft, designed for engines between 40 and 75 hp and, with the top of this range, cruising at nearly 150 mph (248 kmph) over a distance of 250 miles (413 km).

Developments of the single-seater P.70S soon followed: the tandem two-seater tri-gear P.170S and then, a few years later, the single-seater tri-gear P.80S and its two-seater derivative the P.180S. This latter has become one of the most

A tandem two-seater mid-wing P.170S under construction, showing the basic nature of Pottier's designs. (Author)

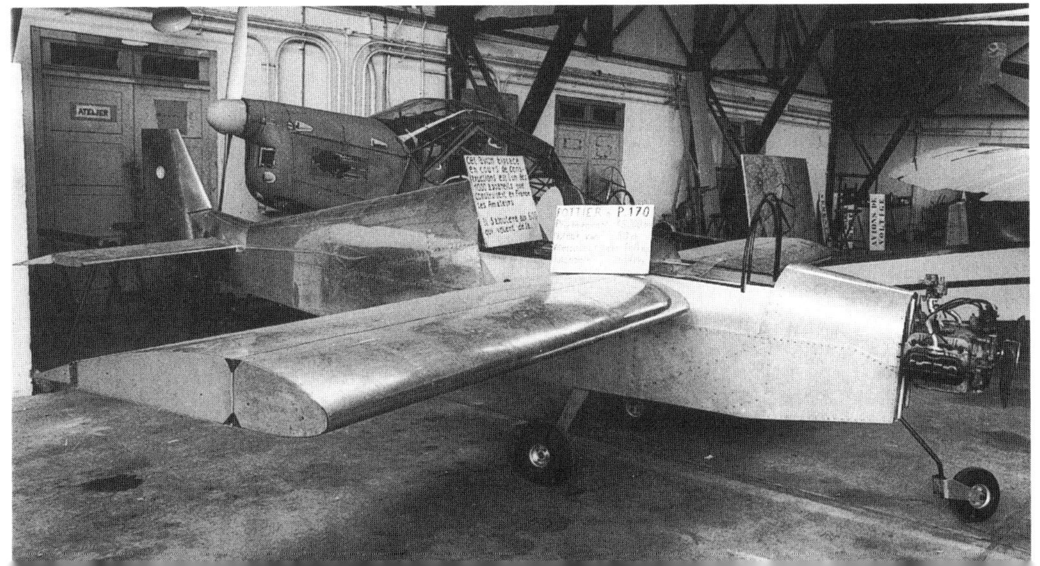

popular Pottier designs, having a cabin width of 3½ feet (1.07 m), a wing-span of 21¼ feet (6.48 m), and a squarish rectangular-shaped wing in plan-form with a NACA 4415 constant-chord profile of 4 feet (1.22 m). The tail surfaces are controlled by semi-rigid cables and whilst some examples have manually operated flaps, many builders have opted for electrically-powered ones. Despite the copious pop rivets and overlapping sheet metal, a very smooth finish can be achieved.

The spring-steel main undercarriage is quite easy to make or buy in and robust and practical for either hard surfaces or grass/dirt operations, particularly with the large mainwheels and toe-operated brakes. A lockable hand brake is used for parking. The nosewheel has altered with design evolution and the flexible metal shaft has now been replaced by a telescopic leg with rubber bungees. Power-plants are again the builder's choice, but in France many P.180S builders have opted for the JPX 1,830 cc VW conversion rated at 60 hp. Between the engine firewall and the instrument panel is fitted the 10-gallon (45-litre) reinforced fuel tank.

The P.180S is entered over a reinforced wing panel at the root of the port wing; a one-piece moulded canopy hinges upwards to one side from the starboard side, allowing first the passenger and then the pilot ample access to the large cockpit. The P.180S sits well on the ground with excellent forward visibility and on an uneven airfield the undercarriage gives adequate flexibility and damping of bumps. An average ground run and into a climb at a rate of between 400 and 500 fpm will bring you to 2,000 feet quickly enough, where the throttle can be eased off and the aircraft trimmed for a 3,000 rpm/105 mph cruise and a fuel consumption of about 5 gph. Even at full rpm in the climb the cabin noise is not excessive, but individual aircraft can vary considerably from builder to builder. A standard exhaust muffler can be fitted for cold weather flying and some P.180S builders have gone to great lengths to improve the cabin ventilation for hot weather to prevent a cockpit greenhouse effect!

Controls are positive and easy to move through the floor-mounted stick and, although the P.180S is not one of the most responsive homebuilts, it has to be remembered that this is a modest two-seater for weekend flying and not a Pitts Special. However, the pilot has to keep his wits about him as the relatively short wing-span causes a quick attitude change because of the minimal lateral inertia. Directional stability must also be watched as the aircraft is sensitive to turbulence compared to the majority of modern training aircraft. Another effect of the short wing-span is sensitivity to any asymmetrical loading—if your co-pilot is overweight, you will need plenty of control force to keep on the straight and narrow. In a clean stall at around 45 mph the wings remain reasonably level, but with the stick hard back the onset of the stall is indicated by continual, moderately loud vibrations of the airframe with quite a pronounced wing drop until the nose drops and a standard stall recovery is executed. Landing with 30° flaps, it is best to maintain a steeper-than-average approach, keeping a little power on and maintaining about 70 mph. Reducing the power over the threshold there is good forward visibility and the aircraft will sit on the runway quite positively, rolling to a halt in calm conditions in about 400 feet. In short, the Pottier P.180S is a 'real' practical aircraft—if there are any doubts at all regarding Europe's most popular metal homebuilt.

Jean Pottier continued work throughout the 1970s and '80s on a variety of other metal homebuilts and also, despite a period of ill-health, a microlight. With Jacques Challard he built the three-seater, high-wing Bede BD.4-like Pottier P.100TS over a period of three years, its first flight being at Les Mureaux on 16 October 1980. More than 4,000 man hours were devoted to the P.100TS, a 100 hp Continental-powered aircraft, including work by several teenagers from the local school. A four-seater development, the P.110TS, has also been designed by Pottier, but a prototype has yet to appear.

Throughout the 1980s Pottier was extremely busy supporting the hundreds of builders who had bought plans from him. A 'work-aholic', he has designed and developed a completely new series of metal homebuilt designs using similar ideals and constructional techniques to the 100-series, these being his 200 series of kitplanes, the P.210 single-seater, P.220 side-by-side two-seater, P.230 2 + 2 (but more realistically a three-seater), and P.250 tandem two-seater. All of these are tri-gear all-metal kitplanes which are being sold by Pottier and his Avions Pottier at Les Mureaux near Paris, and come in four sub-kits. Orders at the end of 1990 were keeping Pottier extremely busy with 12 kits delivered and orders for 12 in preparation. In addition to the four models mentioned, a four-seater, the P.240, to be powered by a 150 to 180 hp Lycoming, will also soon be available.

The first public airing of the Pottier 200 series of homebuilt kitplanes was at the Austrian homebuilt fly-in at Wels in mid-June 1990. This was followed by the 'big one', the RSA's annual fly-in at Moulins in July 1990. Charles Biré from Cholet had the distinction of being the first builder to complete a Pottier P.230S 'Panda' (F-PACB), the three-seater version, which first flew on 5 May 1990. It took approximately 2,000 man-hours to complete, at an estimated cost of £23,000, excluding the 100 hp Continental C-90 engine. Some composite components are included in the kit for wing-tips and parts of the tail, but it is still 95 per cent metal. The

The first Pottier P.230S metal kitplane was built by Charles Biré and flew for the first time in early May 1990, at Cholet, France. (Jean Pottier)

smaller P.210/220 and 250 are all designed to be powered by 65 hp JPX engines.

Lamar Steen's tubular-metal marvel

As wood and fabric are to French homebuilding (with the exception of Pottier), one could almost ascribe the tubular metal fuselage with fabric covering as the characteristic American form of homebuilt construction. This was before the advent of composites when, during the burgeoning US homebuilt movement, there seemed to be little apprehension or 'consumer resistance' to construction of the welded steel-tube fuselage frame. The list of US-designed homebuilts with such construction is

A Pitts Special with a steel-tube fuselage frame. This example became G-MINT when completed. (Ken Ellis Collection)

almost endless: the Wittman Tailwind, the Pitts Special, the EAA Biplane, AcroSport and Pixie, the Bakeng Duce, Corben Baby Ace, the various Lou Stolp designs, Spezio Tuholer, Hatz Biplane, WagAero Cuby, etc, etc. This last-mentioned type, a modern-day homebuilt version of the Piper Cub introduced before the Super Cub was made available again in kit form by Piper, may hold part of the secret to the popularity of this type of construction, as many post-war American pilots were weaned on aircraft such as the Cub, Taylorcraft and Aeronca with similar fuselage construction. Bend a Cub and all that was required was a quick visit to the 'blacksmiths' to straighten it out and re-weld the tubular steel structure. Familiarity was the by-word for these commercial types, so the same type of construction for homebuilts presented no problems at all.

Wings were inevitably wood and fabric, although some types had metal spars and wooden ribs or various other wood/metal combinations. For the American homebuilder, the home 'tig-weld' set was to become almost part of the garage and workshop furniture of most homes long before it did in Europe.

Lamar A. Steen was an aerospace teacher in a Denver, Colorado, high school and started work on the design of a tandem two-seater aerobatic biplane in June 1968. It was to be built as a class project in the manual-arts high school, so simplicity of construction was a primary aim. Work on the prototype started on 19 August 1969 and on and off over the next 15 months many thousands of hours and an estimated $5,000 were put into the project before the prototype of the aircraft, now called the Steen Skybolt, N11NN, made its first flight at Denver in October 1970.

The prototype was fitted with a 180 hp Lycoming HO-360 and, with a 24-foot (7.32 m) wingspan and a length of 19 feet (5.79 m), was a fairly large aircraft. It was the first two-seater aerobatic homebuilt biplane design and immediately attracted considerable interest, Steen initially selling sets of plans for $50. In 1971, after the prototype had flown about 150 hours, Steen flew the Skybolt to Oshkosh where he was awarded the 'Best Chapter or School Project' award.

The Skybolt, a 'simple' design with symmetrical airfoil but stressed for +12g and −10g, is a braced biplane with a single interplane strut on each side and N-section centre-section struts. The welded tube fuselage and wire-braced tail unit are built from 4130 chrome molybdenum steel tube with fabric covering and there is a trim tab on the port elevator. The fuel tank is located between the front cockpit and the firewall and has a 24-gallon (110-litre) capacity, there is the option to install an 8-gallon (37-litre) additional tank in the centre section of the upper wing.

The upper and lower wing sections are differ-

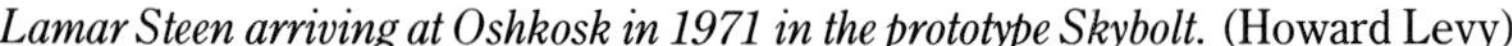

Lamar Steen arriving at Oshkosk in 1971 in the prototype Skybolt. (Howard Levy)

A Skybolt under construction in Phoenix, Arizona. (Don Downie)

ent—the upper wing has a zero dihedral whereas the lower has a 2° 30′ dihedral—and there is sweep-back on the upper wing only. Two wooden spruce spars form the main structure of the wings with wooden built-up ribs and fabric covering. Frise ailerons feature on both upper and lower wings, streamline-section landing and flying wires are used, and there is a cut-out in the centre section of the upper wing for ease of access to the front cockpit. A fixed tail-dragger-type undercarriage is fixed to the fuselage by side-Vs and half axles with rubber bungee suspension. The mainwheels have hydraulic disc brakes.

At one stage Steen set up Steen Aero Lab to sell fuselage, wing and tail kits to builders; he sold about 1,200 tail kits. More recently sales of plans for the Skybolt have been taken over by the Stolp Starduster Corporation at Flabob, California, so 20 years on they are still available and still as popular as ever amongst homebuilders. An estimated 4,000 sets have now been sold and Steen thinks that over 600 Skybolts are flying in at least 22 countries. His prototype is still around and has clocked up over 1,000 hours and been put through exhaustive stress tests similar to those required for FAA certification in the USA. One structural problem emerged quite early on, that of stabiliser flutter. With modifications to the bellcrank control system, however, these were rectified, and Steen amended the plans and set out airworthiness directives to all plans purchasers prior to this.

Steen's Skybolt is a PFA Approved design in Britain and several have been built; the first, G-BFHM, was built by Bill Penaluna at St Just in Cornwall and first flew in 1978.

An American Skybolt builder, Don Bennett from Salem, New Jersey, took six years to complete his project in one section of a three-car garage, and first flew it on 17 June 1981. He is a carpenter by profession so he found the wings relatively 'average' to construct. He also had a working knowledge of welding so enjoyed a head-start as far as the fuselage was concerned. (British builders should note that airframe welding has to be carried out by a Certificated CAA welder.)

The top wing contains 24 ribs and the bottom 22—Bennett turned out a total of 48 ribs in 48 nights—and the leading edge has a 0.020-inch 2024-T3 wrap-around aluminium skin. There is a lot of work in a Skybolt which is why he took so long to complete the aircraft. He acquired its 180 hp Lycoming from a scrapped Piper Cherokee.

With plenty of flying experience, including many hours in a Cessna 140, Bennett decided to do the maiden flight himself, so after quite a few high-speed taxi runs he felt confident that the aircraft wanted to fly and took it around the circuit. All he needed to do was to tighten the tail wires, and since

The modified Skybolt built and flown by Eric Schilling. (Don Downie)

doing so he confesses that it handles and flies as nicely as any other aircraft he has flown, and that the hands-off flight is outstanding. He sticks to simple aerobatics even though he has fitted an inverted system to his Skybolt, but finds it responsive and capable of very quick recoveries. In the last ten years he has flown nearly 300 hours in the Skybolt with a couple of 'long' trips to Oshkosh and one to Florida.

Another American, Eric Schilling, was also smitten by the Skybolt and has carried out modifications to the design: a three-piece top wing with a 5-foot (1.52 m) centre section; different strut bracing from the fuselage to the outer part of this new centre section, all of which considerably improves cockpit visibility; different flying wire arrangements; aileron hinges moved forward to make more of a frise rigging; and ailerons 'fatter' at the projected trailing edge of the wing, creating a surface that does not let the airflow break away from the wing.

The most significant 'mod', though, is a new linkage arrangement whereby all four ailerons can be deflected downwards by 10° to produce flaperons, allowing the pilot to see the runway on finals. The stall with the flaperons up is now 50 mph (82 kmph) but with them down only 40 mph (66 kmph). Schilling's aircraft is officially the Skybolt II and is available in plan form from Stolp at Flabob or as a modification, welded-up to retrofit existing Skybolts.

Schilling did not start building his Skybolt until he retired from commercial flying in 1976 at the age of 60. With over 23,000 hours in his log book he knows a good aeroplane when he flies one and thinks Lamar Steen got it just about right, a fact to which the hundreds of other Skybolt homebuilders will doubtless also testify. Unfortunately, as it is a homebuilt it cannot be used for commercial dual instruction, but many builders have nonetheless incorporated dual controls and front-seat brakes. Schilling sums up his modified Skybolt as 'a biplane with the easy-handling landing characteristics of a Stearman, beautiful visibility and much simpler than a Pitts'.

The Skybolt is, as Don Bennett of New Jersey found out, a kind of early 'composite'—a blend of woodworking and metalworking skills! There are still many other similar homebuilt designs available, and if you are prepared to qualify as a Certificated Welder and are a passable carpenter as well, such a project may be for you.

CHAPTER 13

Case studies: wood and foam composite homebuilts

ONE OF THE largest aerial machines is a gas-filled airship, basically a large void filled with a lighter-than-air gas. Imagine a material that appears solid yet is filled with voids, even if this is only ordinary air. The search by aircraft designers and constructors for the ultimate lightweight yet strong material almost inevitably led to foam rubber. One can imagine a 20th-century aeronautical engineer sitting in his bath, pondering the lightweight structure problem, then '*Eureka*'—foam!

As detailed in Chapter 4, Ken Rand and Stuart Robinson in the USA were two of the first to see the potential of this material as far as small homebuilt aircraft were concerned. George Pereira was another pioneer, in the building of the hull of his Osprey 2 amphibian.

Urethane foams have become an accepted part of many lightweight structures—not just in the homebuilt aircraft world—in a very short space of time, and are basically used for filling and shaping a homebuilt's structure. Many people's first attempts at working with this material produce clouds of urethane dust, the material being extremely soft; indeed, a thin layer of dust can be removed simply by running your finger over the surface of the foam. Thus experiments need to be conducted either in the open or in a well-ventilated and builder-protected workshop.

Cutting the basic sheets to rough shape is the first exercise and this can be done with bench saws, hand saws, hacksaws and knives, but the secret is to use a blade with very fine teeth and to cut deliberately and very slowly—a fine-toothed hacksaw blade is probably the best tool, with the teeth facing away from you (backwards) and held at a very shallow angle to the surface of the foam. A steel rule or other guide should be used to keep the cut straight and true, or chunks of foam will soon be gouged out.

Several passes with the blade will be required to start a cut, but once commenced it should be seen through to the end. A piece of 2 in × 1 in softwood timber could also be used as your guide, and will help to keep the blade vertical for a good, straight cut.

With a basic shape achieved it is time to refine the shape to allow for hinges, blocks on the wooden airframe structure and other obstructions. Place the foam over the obstruction so that an impression is made, then cut out the unwanted foam, testing your final shape in position before you consider gluing it permanently in place.

A '5-minute' epoxy glue is probably best as this will soon enable you to continue working but will also enable some last minute adjustment in position before it finally sets. The golden rule with all homebuilding applies here as well: use your glue economically but not *too* economically; use too much and it becomes messy and wasteful; use too little and you could be building yourself a disaster.

Clamping the foam lightly in place will ensure good contact between the parts, but it is important to remember not to clamp too tightly. If glue oozes out of any joints or cracks, this is best wiped off with a paper towel as soon as possible because if you try to sand it away once it dries you could pull out chunks of foam.

If the dust of cutting foam seems messy, then the dust of shaping and sanding is worse. It is really more like sculpture than building. First roughly shape the foam to the approximate contours required, then sand it to achieve the exact contour; finally deal with small details such as cut-outs. It is most important to consider personal safety and eye protection—a face mask and gloves are essential for anyone working on or close to this material.

There will most likely be plywood 'frames' such as wing leading edge ribs or fuselage frames and decking to indicate the rough shape of foam required, and it is best to get this shape to within about 1 cm (½ in) of the correct finished shape. For critical shapes, such as the leading edge of the airfoil, it is best to cut out a plywood template to ensure that when you start sanding the shape achieved is exactly right. Once the foam has been secured in position, and the assembly secured in something like a WorkMate, it is down to the laborious and dusty business of sanding, which, if climatic conditions permit, is best done outside—but away from the washing-line!

The initial rough sanding can be done with a surofoam plane but, like the cutting mentioned earlier, it has to be done delicately and in continuous strokes otherwise the foam will be gouged. All the time the excess dust needs to be removed with something like a feather duster.

The next process requires a 'sanding stick', basically some straight 2 in × 1 in timber with a grip, to which is attached the smoothest abrasive paper you can find. Like all other work with the foam, small, gentle movements are necessary with the sanding stick; as you move it to and fro, listen for the scraping noise that comes when you cross a wooden rib and this will help to eliminate any over-enthusiasm. It is messy but it is quick, and one builder I spoke to working on the horizontal stabiliser part of the tail took only 2 hours sanding from rough to finished surfacing.

Finally comes the glassing over of the foam, which some builders think is even worse than foam sanding, but others quite enjoy. Microballoons—minute spherical glass bubbles—are used to fill any small irregularities in the surface. First the microballoons are added to epoxy resin and hardener, thoroughly mixed and made thick enough that the mixture does not sag or run—five parts glass to one of resin is about right. First it is essential to fix firmly the part being worked on and to cut the glass cloth required. The resin mixture is then squeezed over the raw foam to seal the air in the foam and act as the base surface on which to lay the glass cloth. It is best to do a whole surface at any one time, such as an upper wing surface, to lay the cloth at 45° to the wing chord, and to cover any surface with a continuous piece of cloth.

Cleanliness is difficult but important, and none of the mixture must be allowed to get on to components or structural members. Also the glass cloth must adhere directly to all spars and rib surface. The laying-up of the cloth on to the resin mixture—or micro—is quite a labour-intensive job on a wing or even the tail, so willing hands should be enlisted to assist. Once the cloth is on the micro, the squeegee is used to press it on to the micro, to ensure that it is fully impregnated and all wrinkles are removed. Then a further thin layer of resin is applied over the surface, lightly pressing all the time but being careful not to press out all the resin. The weave in the cloth should be visible and there should be no white areas; these will have air trapped under the cloth and must be removed by adding a little extra resin and re-squeegeeing.

A second layer of cloth then has to be applied, particularly if you are building in Britain where the additional strength of this second 'skin' is recommended. This will be at 90° to the first layer of cloth and, on a wing, at 45° to the direction of chord so that a criss-cross, strength-forming bias is achieved. The same process is repeated for this second layer as for the first, but before application you should ensure that the first is perfect. Finally, a coat of resin is applied to the exterior surface and it is finished.

Further sanding down is then necessary once the skin has hardened to achieve the smooth, finished shape you require.

Obviously the application of the second layer of cloth and resin increases the weight of your structure, but this may be a small penalty to pay for the added strength and security it gives, particularly if your homebuilt, such as a WAR fighter replica, is to be used for aerobatics.

Using foam and resins is an easy, quite labour-intensive but quick method of achieving shape for your homebuilt. In the USA, some homebuilts have used this material and method for load-bearing structures, but this is not permitted in Britain where a conventional skeletal wooden structure forms the basis of the load-bearing structure throughout. Specific brands and types of cloth and resins are available from which the builder may choose; ensure that they are approved for your specific application.

Mark Parr's WAR FW.190 replica

Like the Steen Skybolt in the previous chapter, with its blend of metal and wood construction, the popular half-scale replicas of Second World War fighters that were marketed by War Aircraft Replicas of Santa Paula, California (since the crash of their P.51 prototype they are believed to have gone out of business), are also a blend of construction techniques—old and new. They typify the wood/composite homebuilts whose basic structure is a conventional wooden truss but whose ultimate shape and part of its strength result from the use of urethane foam, high-strength laminate fabric and epoxy covering. Like any modern homebuilt there are also the inevitable metal fittings for control pulleys, the roll-bar for the cockpit, the undercarriage, hinges, engine mounts, etc.

The replica homebuilt offers the builder the chance to build his own aeroplane but at the same time to express some more personal bravado and extrovert tendancies. Chapter 7 has shown the 'odd-balls' and some of their ideas, together with the insatiable quest for replicas amongst home-builders.

When Mark Parr, a mechanical engineer from Guernsey in the Channel Islands, first started building his WAR FW.190 replica in 1980 he was only 22 years old. He and his three brothers had been keen radio-control aeromodellers and Mark and his eldest brother Peter both had PPLs and a share in a Cessna 172. The inevitable 'bug' bit them—if they could build and fly radio-controlled aircraft, why not go up a scale and actually build a *real* aeroplane. They had seen the first WAR FW.190 replica built in Britain by Mike Searle at Elstree, liked the idea of flying a 'fighter'—the performance possible and its aerobatic capability—so had soon sent off to WAR for their set of plans.

WAR's plans at the time were adequate but not fantastic. They were full-size blueprints of the aircraft, from which components were supposed to be scaled off—if the paper shrank slightly, as it did with the Parrs' drawings, inaccuracies could creep in. Such plans are also very unmanageable in the workshop. Notwithstanding, they got stuck into the work of constructing the basic wooden spruce/plywood framework with the enthusiasm that most new builders possess. Being located on Guernsey added a further difficulty in obtaining materials, but these were overcome. WAR themselves produced a small number of components such as the engine cowling, glassfibre fuel tank, wheels (standard go-kart wheels), the spinner, the wooden three-bladed Fahlin propeller, canopy and engine bearers, and Parr purchased these, the worst part being the staggering freight costs to get them from California to Guernsey.

By 1981 all structures were assembled and, minus undercarriage, the aircraft was propped up on milk churns (Parr's father runs a dairy farm in Guernsey) in the farmyard. The retractable undercarriage showed every sign of being very difficult to make, so they decided to sub-contract it out with a delivery time of six months hence. After 18 months they got it back, but only 50 per cent complete, so finished the work themselves.

A comprehensive instrument fit was decided upon despite the FW.190's small cockpit. The layout design and fitting was an extremely fiddly process, as were any adjustments, because once the foam/resin/cloth filling and covering had been done, it is almost like hermetically sealing the contents. The foam—acquired from Cool-Lag, a refrigeration company in England—was 'slabbed' on to the wooden framework with microballoons and two layers of bi-directional glass cloth, then squeegeed over the sanded and shaped foam. There followed endless days and nights of rubbing down and filling, then rubbing down and filling again, all of this process taking most of 1982.

Very few original Luftwaffe FW.190's survived the war, but at the time one was preserved in the museum collection housed at RAF St Athan in South Wales. Parr thought a look at this might prove a useful insight into the construction of their half-scale

Mark Parr's Guernsey-based WAR FW.190 half-scale replica G-SYFW is finished in the colours of the aircraft flown by Josef Wurmheller who served on the Eastern Front. (Author)

replica—it didn't, as it happens, but it was an interesting trip!

Being former modellers, the Parrs were able to maintain the high standard of construction through to the final finish. Spray painting was done with an airbrush to give a professional touch, especially to some of the finer details. The colours were chosen almost at random from a book about the FW.190 and were those of an aircraft flown on the Eastern Front by Josef Wurmheller. Because of Guernsey's occupation by the Germans during the last war, out of respect the swastikas of the original scheme were omitted from the tail markings. Its British civil registration is G-SYFW.

The outer panels of the mainplanes or wings can be separated just outboard of the undercarriage. To get the 'Wulf' from the farm to the airport, these were detached and in April 1984 it was towed slowly on its own undercarriage wheels the couple of miles along public roads for final assembly, systems checks, weighing and first flight.

One of homebuilding's major dilemmas concerns the maiden flight and test-flying. Half the builders you speak to will tell you that 'I've built it, therefore I'm going to fly it'—the other half will tell you, 'I'm only a pilot and not experienced enough to be a test pilot'. Long before completion it is worth considering this problem because if you have chosen the latter option, your test pilot may want to familiarise himself with the project during its latter stages. Whichever option you have chosen, do not allow yourself to be rushed into the first flight, because it is important to make sure that both you and your aircraft are completely ready for it. Comprehensive engine and fuel-flow tests are vital, as well as the important weight and balance determinations—all necessary before that vital 'Permit to Test Fly' is issued.

Mark Parr decided to test-fly his Wulf himself. He had limited tail-dragger experience so took time off to attend the Aeros Flying Club at Gloucester (Staverton) Airport who at the time were doing tail-dragger courses on their Bellanca Citabria. This completed, he felt considerably more confident, although it must be said in retrospect that even this was not really enough. However, everything was complete and it was now a case of waiting for the weather. With Guernsey having only one airport and a very busy one at that, to get the timing right for the first flight was difficult. Good weather, light winds down the single east/west runway, a quiet spot in the traffic pattern and the aircraft and pilot 'psyched up' and ready to go. The evening of Tuesday 29 May 1984 met all these criteria, so after some very fast runs during which the tail lifted and Parr could get a feel for the aircraft, he considered himself confident to take to the air.

Back to the apron for a final chat with his brothers—and a television camera crew from the BBC who were coincidentally in the island to cover a visit by the Queen Mother—and taxi clearance was given to line up and take off. The fire tender was on the field as a further precaution. Full power and away, and after quite a long run the small group of friends and airport workers saw Parr lift the Wulf off the runway for a short time; but then, with some rather erratic movements, he put the aircraft back down again apparently rather heavily, with a swaying from one main wheel to the other and with one of the wing-tips almost touching the runway.

There was no apparent damage, thankfully, and Parr taxied back to the apron for a conference with his brothers. It seems that the Wulf had been exceptionally sensitive in pitch, which had surprised Parr, and with discretion being the better part of valour, he had decided to abort the flight, think about the situation some more and then try again. He had also, within seconds of his first take-off, had to execute his first landing in the aircraft, and with the pressure of the moment it was not one of his best.

Now knowing what to expect, the second attempt went like clockwork and he climbed ahead to about 3,000 feet for some basic manoeuvres, returning for a perfect landing after about 20 minutes. That was enough flying for one day, as it was time to crack a bottle of champagne in celebration and give that 'on-the-spot, heat-of-the-moment' account of his feelings to the BBC. The 1,000 hours-plus of building time had come to a successful conclusion.

The 5-hour test flight programme was soon completed, undercarriage retracted in flight for the first time, the few snags that cropped up rectified and the application for a full 'Permit to Fly' despatched to PFA Engineering and received back in time for Parr to fly north across the English Channel to 1984's PFA Rally at Cranfield where he was awarded the Pooley Sword for the 'Best Replica'.

The main stages in the construction of Mark Parr's WAR FW.190 half-scale replica are best followed by reference to the series of pictures, taken by Parr himself, on pages 195–201.

Quite a few FW.190s have now been completed and flown in Europe. WAR has also produced similar half-scale plans for the P-47 Thunderbolt, the Hawker Sea Fury, the F-4U Corsair and the P.51 Mustang.

The world's first WAR Sea Fury to be completed and flown was built in Hampshire between 1981 and 1985 by Peter Pykett. He confesses to preferring the construction of a homebuilt to the flying. His first homebuilt was an Evans VP-1; he sold his Sea Fury about a year after its first flight, then started construction of a full-scale Hawker Hurricane replica.

The WAR FW.190 is a good illustration of the

WAR's half-scale replica of the P-47 Thunderbolt employs the same basic design and construction techniques as the FW.190. (Author)

difference between it and some US-built examples of aircraft. The wings of some American examples are built with the resin-impregnated foam forming structural elements—the PFA, before approving the design for construction in Britain, stipulated that all structural members, such as the wing ribs, had to be of wood, the foam and resin only used as a filler.

A sobering incident relating to this took place on 4 February 1989 when Peter Nieber, then President of WAR Aircraft Replicas, was killed near Tracy, California, whilst testing WAR's new P.51 replica. A witness to the crash reported that he made a high-speed pass with the gear extended and then went quite tightly around the circuit and retracted the gear for the first time, ready for what appeared to be a long straight pass. At about 1 mile from the

The world's first WAR Sea Fury to be completed and flown was built by Peter Pykett of Andover, Hampshire. The first flight took place on 24 February 1985 at Thruxton. It took four years to build, using only WAR plans and no kit parts, and is powered by a 100 hp Continental 0-200 engine with a two-blade McCauley prop, both taken from a Cessna 150. (Author)

runway threshold the starboard wing appeared to 'flutter' violently for about a second; the aircraft stabilised, but then pitched up and went into a wing-over which resulted in a dive into the ground from several hundred feet. The engine was running at the time of impact. The inference is structural failure. The FAA made a full investigation for the National Transportation Safety Board (NTSB).

WAR which sold plans and components for all five of its half-scale replicas, no longer trades.

The Brandli BX-2 Cherry

Using identical construction methods to the WAR replicas, with a wooden framework and foam/glassfibre/resin shaping and covering, is the BX-2 Cherry, a lovely two-seater design from Switzerland designed by Max Brandli who is now head of the RSA Suisse Technical Commission in Switzerland (see Chapter 9). The prototype (HB-YBX) first flew at the Swiss Air Force base at Payerne on 24 April 1982 after an estimated 5,000 hours of design and constructional work. In 1985 Brandli was awarded the prestigious FAI Henri Mignet Diploma at Delhi in India for his work on the Cherry. In early 1991 his prototype had accumulated 1,100 hours of flying in 1,720 flights, and he had sold 140 construction licences and sets of plans around the world, including Britain where the type should soon receive PFA Approval. At least seven aircraft are now flying, including five in Switzerland and one each in Germany and France, with others nearing completion in Holland, Austria, Sweden and Australia.

The engine chosen is the 65 hp Continental A-65 with a fixed pitch propeller, and the lighweight structure, retractable undercarriage and efficient aerodynamic shape result in excellent performance on relatively low power, and economy of operation. With a wealth of flight experience on the prototype, Brandli quotes an average cruise speed at 75 per cent power of 125 mph, consuming 3 gph with a range of 575 statute miles at 65 per cent power. In addition, to comply with Swiss regulations, it is a very quiet aircraft and is roadable, wings and tail being easily detached so that when it sits on its trailer it is only 6½ feet (1.98 m) wide.

Between 3,000 and 4,000 man-hours' building time is Brandli's estimate for a beginner on a Cherry. Again the undercarriage and retraction mechanism—as on the WAR replicas—is potentially the most difficult feature to construct and install. As a two-seater alternative in wood and foam, and with Brandli's excellent and rapid builder back-up and support, the BX-2 Cherry is certainly worth considering.

Max Brandli's prototype BX-2 Cherry, a neat two-seater homebuilt. (Author)

Building the WAR FW. 190 half-scale replica (*photos by Mark Parr*)

1. The basic wooden spruce fuselage frame, set up in plywood jigs on the workbench, was the first structure to be built. The space heater just visible behind caused problems because of differential heating of the workshop, causing the fuselage frame to twist—it then had to be re-set.

2. The tail was constructed next and attached to the rear of the fuselage frame, to the outside of which 1/16 in ply webbing has been stuck; its darker colour is where it has been painted with sealant to protect the wood from resin.

3. The main spar and rear spar of the wing structure with its plywood ribs. The leading edge fore-ribs are a ply/foam sandwich; all the gaps will be filled with foam to create the finished surface. Aileron fittings are in place.

4. The aileron bell crank and control rods in place in the wing. All fittings such as this have to be in place before the foam is cut and put in place prior to the application of the resin/microballoon and cloth covering.

5. The engine bearers were bought from WAR as Parr considers them one of the aircraft's most vital components. The relatively simple attachment to the square box front end fuselage firewall is evident.

6. The main circular body of the front fuselage is now built up and the metal firewall and cowling clips attached.

7. Structurally complete and just pre-foaming. The engine—100 hp Rolls-Royce Continental 0-200 taken from a scrapped Aerospatiale Rallye—is in place as well as all other control mechanisms, undercarriage, fuel tank, electrics and hydraulics.

8. Design of the instrument panel in progress with a trial template to juggle with positions for optimum arrangement of the comprehensive 'fit' that Parr was to install.

9. The electrically operated undercarriage mechanism and hydraulic mainwheel brake tubes. The picture also shows the inward-folding retraction method and the attachment plate bolted to the front main spar.

10. Urethane foam sheets (8 ft × 4 ft) leaning against the workshop wall and the tail and rear fuselage with the foam slabbed on to the wooden frame. The fuselage foam is cut from templates on the drawings, then roughly shaped before being fitted and glued to the wooden frame for final shaping and sanding.

11. The port wing in the foreground with the foam covered in microballoon epoxy resin and unidirectional cloth, two layers of which were applied at 45° to the chord of the wing and at 90° to each other. The foam slabbing of the fuselage has not yet been resined and clothed.

12. Mark's brother Peter hard at work in the workshop during the seemingly endless task of sanding and rubbing down to achieve the final shape.

13. All filling, foaming, resin work and sanding/shaping complete, only the painting and spraying is now required for completion. The dark colour is as a result of the microballoons from the final coat of slurry.

14. The comprehensively equipped cockpit after fitting out with a central Edo navcom incorporating a VOR, a DI, turn/slip, altimeter, VSI, compass, ASI, accelerometer, rpm gauge, EGT gauge and oil temperature/pressure gauges. On the right-hand side panel are fuel contents and pressure gauges, plus an ammeter, as the Wulf is fitted with a small battery. (*Author*)

15. One disadvantage of such a small, single-seater homebuilt with few detachable inspection panels is maintenance or adjustment. After several flights Parr had problems with his stall warning light, and the only way to get at it was to 'dive' into the cockpit head first and, using a torch for light, try go adjust the offending item. (*Author*)

16. What homebuilding is all about—for the majority anyway. Several hours under his belt and confident to close in on a camera ship, Mark Parr's half-scale FW.190 could be real were it not for the out-of-scale head of the pilot! However, some builders do prefer the building experience to the subsequent flying experience! (*Author*)

17. The finished product after more than 1,000 man-hours of work and estimated cost—at 1984 prices—of about £9–10,000. The final accolade at the PFA's Cranfield fly-in in July 1984 was when Parr, here leaning on the rear fuselage, was awarded the Pooley Sword for 'Best Replica'. Gerard Titeca's WAR FW.190 from Belgium was also at Cranfield that year, its nose just visible behind Parr's G-SYFW. (*Author*)

CHAPTER 14

Non-kit composites—Rutan's VariEze and LongEz

THE NAME RUTAN crops up time and time again when talking of homebuilts, and Chapter 4 has shown how he was largely responsible for the materials and shape 'revolution' in homebuilding with the VariEze.

The composite VariEze, unlike most of the more conventional wooden and metal aircraft, has no wing ribs, and the spar, such as it is, is a convenience rather than a necessity. With the composite aircraft operating in its normal performance envelope, the maximum stresses are small compared to the design loadings and will give the structure a long fatigue life; cracks cannot form across individual layers of the glass/composite structure. The surface is smooth, totally non-absorbent to water, and durable. It is also easily patched and repaired in case of damage.

Rutan's 100 per cent composite construction as exemplified by the VariEze should not be confused with the mixed wood/composite construction method described in the previous chapter. There can be differential stress with this latter—not so with the true composite.

Composite structures are also quieter—the foam core is a natural sound deadener—and there is no tendency for the airframe to 'drum', as it does in a frame and cloth-covered or metal aircraft. Moreover, novice builders of composite homebuilts who have already built more conventional aircraft almost universally admit that composites are a far quicker method of construction—however, the builder does have to 'learn' the new technology.

Terms such as 'hot-wire cutting', 'lay-up', 'epoxy resin', 'slurry', 'squeegeeing' and many more enter the homebuilder's vocabulary for the first time and are as an essential part of the composite construction process as rivets are to metal homebuilts and spruce to wood.

Some of the tips and do's and don'ts of working with foam have already been detailed in Chapter 13, and polystyrene foam is also the basis of composite structures in homebuilts such as the VariEze. Often abbreviated to just 'styrene', the blocks in which it comes have to be cut and shaped by a method called 'hot-wiring'. This type of foam should not be confused with polyurethane foam or 'urethane', which is generally softer and easier to sand than 'styrene'. There is also 'blue foam' or 'Clark foam' of higher density, which is also easy to sand.

Cutting styrene is best achieved with a hot-wire tool. This is a length of stainless steel wire stretched between two arms, like an archer's bow, and connected up to an electrical power supply. The wire heats up and slices through the foam like the proverbial hot knife through butter. Using a cooler wire and slower rate of cut is better and less prone to mistakes than a hot/fast cut combination and, like any process it is best to try it out first on a piece of scrap foam before launching into the centre of a big block. Templates have to be made from either plywood or sheet metal/aluminium, the latter being preferable for accuracy of cut.

The templates can be nailed to each end of the block of foam if something like an aileron is in production and, once the foam is levelled and firmly weighted, two operators, one holding each end of the bow, can pass the bow slowly through the foam with the wire resting on the template. If you start with the top surface, once it has been cut from the foam block, the bottom surface is a repeat performance: replace the cut-off part of the block to make it square again, turn it over and pass the wire-cutter slowly over the template once more. A little sanding of the surfaces at the end of these processes will smooth any lag lines or irregularities left by the hot-wire.

Both simple and very complicated parts can be cut in this way, the dimensions and shape of the all-important templates being taken from the particular homebuilt's plans. It is a relatively easy task

A British-built example of Rutan's VariEze flown by Tim Bailey. (Ken Ellis Collection)

Mike Melville (left) and Dick Rutan mixing epoxy when working on their two LongEzes. They built their two ships together to 'prove out' the plans. Mike and his wife Sally completed their LongEz in 1,200 man-hours, including overhauling the engine, developing a new engine mount and baffling, and even installing a tape-deck! (Don Downie)

but, like many jobs, careful and time-consuming attention to preparation pays off as the actual job then proceeds quickly and efficiently.

The personal protection mentioned in Chapter 13, such as gloves, face-mask and eye protection, is equally important for any builder doing this type of composite construction. The next stage of sealing the porous foam and the wet lay-ups involves the use of chemicals—further warnings to any responsible builder should not be necessary. It is all a matter of common sense.

Resin and a catalyst are the two components of the epoxy resin used for glassfibre in a homebuilt—like the glues you buy from a do-it-yourself shop, with one tube of glue and the other of hardener. But before a foam part is 'glassed' it has to be sealed, and this is done with a slurry, a mixture of epoxy and catalyst with those tiny glass sphere microballoons stirred in to reduce the weight and give a pasty consistency.

This sealing slurry is poured over the foam and squeegeed into it, to make a smooth non-porous surface, help the bonding of the glassfibre and reduce sanding. Composites are messy! This coat has to be allowed to become tacky, usually in about 3 or 4 hours, then it is time for laying on the glassfibre cloth. There are two main types, and on Rutan plans these are referred to as BID and UND (bi-directional and uni-directional) cloth, referring to the threads of the weave.

Once the cloth is laid over the surface of the part, it is essential to remove any wrinkles before mixing up a batch of epoxy and squeegeeing this on to the cloth. You will know when the glassfibre cloth is properly 'wetted' because its colour changes. More epoxy should then be worked into the cloth and must be squeegeed out, otherwise you will end up with a part that is too heavy when it sets. This process is repeated for a second layer, when the resin is applied first before the cloth. Suggestions for the direction of laying up the cloth are given in Chapter 13. Some experts in composite work also suggest pouring microballoons over the finished surface to help reduce irregularities and any necessary filling later.

As soon as this work is complete you can think about the final processes of priming and painting. Firstly it will be necessary to sand the surface lightly; this can be done manually or with a power tool, although lightness of touch is essential because you must avoid sanding away the micro surface and getting down to the weave of the cloth. If you do penetrate the cloth by mistake, then some slurry or even the primer may be enough to fix it.

One US builder claims that you can get this far in the construction of a LongEze wing in 45 minutes! However, he doesn't say how much preparation time is necessary to reach this stage. Whatever, the end product is an incredibly strong, lightweight, smooth and beautifully shaped piece of aircraft.

As you might imagine when working with resins and epoxies, workshop temperature is important. A British builder spent the first two months of his VariEze project insulating and installing heating in his workshop. It's the old adage again—plenty of time spent in adequate preparation pays off with speedy progress later in the project.

Working on a small piece such as an aileron or even a wing is comprehensible, but what about the fuselage with all those curves and crannies? Well, it is really just the same. To make a squarish shape with rounded corners, such as you find with the VariEze fuselage, it is a case of putting together pre-shaped sides of foam to make up a box structure. To form the initial right-angle (or whatever) from the sheets of foam, it is best to hold them together initially with toothpicks or pieces of small dowel. Backing blocks can then be stuck in place and the joint then has to be sealed up with tapes of BID cloth in exactly the same way as on the flat surface described earlier. These tapes are strips of cloth cut from a larger roll, and when the line of the joint is prepared the tapes are thoroughly soaked in resin mix and squeegeed along the join. A second tape is laid over this and finally both tapes are wetted out before a lightweight dacron cloth strip or 'peel-ply' is put over the top of the join just like the previous two strips. This is used to give a 'toothy' finish to the glassfibre epoxy lamination for subsequent application of glassfibre/epoxy layers. Again, it is important to work out all bubbles from under the peel-ply.

After about 8 hours, this peel-ply strip lives up to its name when it is peeled slowly off once the resin has cured. This is the primary bond process, because in many instances it will be necessary to repeat this process again on top for the secondary bond to give even greater strength to the join.

The exterior and interior of the fuselage box can then be dealt with in the same way as described earlier for an aileron or similar, with laying up over the basic foam.

Vacuum-bagging is another method for ensuring that the composite structure has more glass, less bulk and therefore more strength—it means laying up a piece of glassfibre, putting an impermeable plastic film over the part, sealing it from the outside air and sucking all the air out. However, if there is too much resin in one part and you cannot feel the weave of the cloth, then the part is too 'wet' and will probably end up being more prone to failure than a lighter, thinner part. The vacuum pump has to be kept going for as long as the resin takes to cure.

Finishing off the basic structure of the VariEze, or a similar composite homebuilt, all made up in the manner described above, starts with hand-sanding

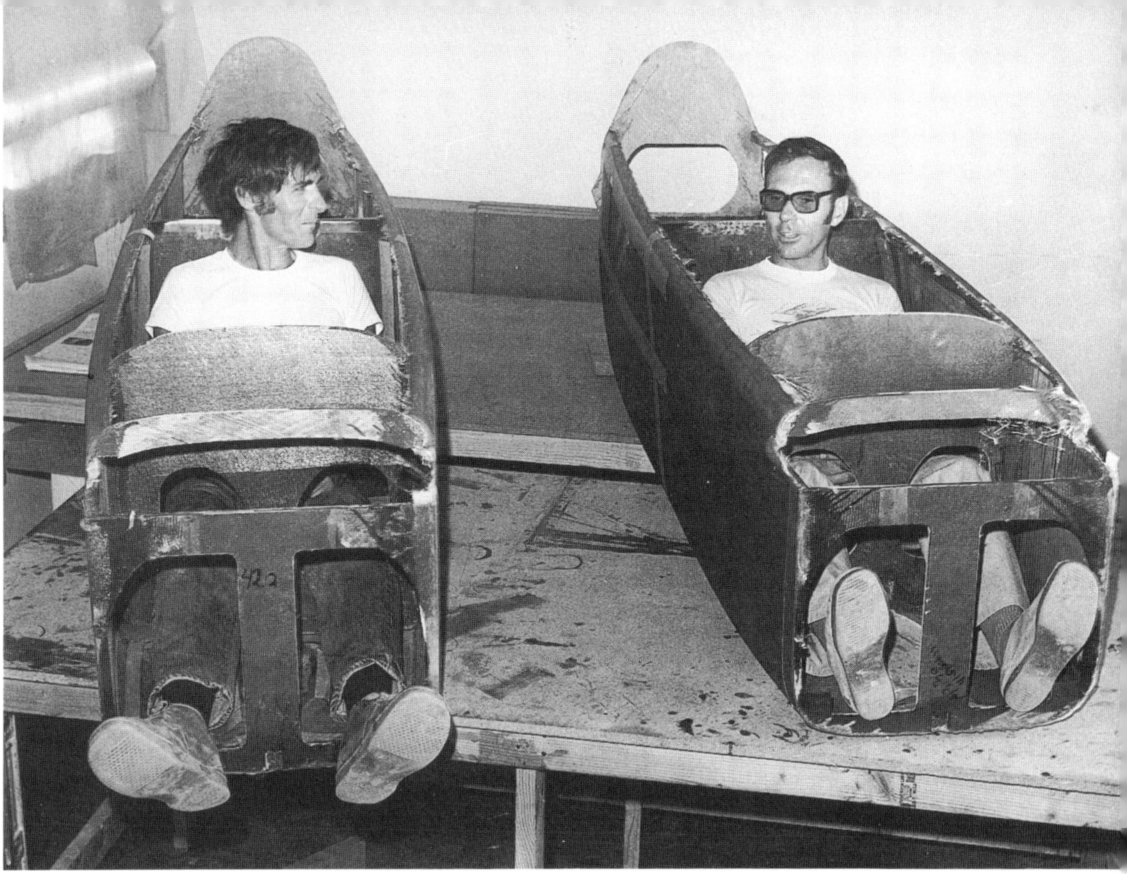

Rutan and Melville sit in the fuselages of their LongEzes during early stages of building. (Don Downie)

LongEz builder Marshall Gage of Whittier, California, with his project under way in his garage. (Don Downie)

and cured laminate before a primer is applied, usually a two-part liquid that requires a catalyst just like the epoxy resin system. Primer generally has a very short usable life, measured in minutes, although its useable life can be extended by adding up to 30 per cent by volume. Then with the primer in a good compressed-air-power sprayer, it can be sprayed on to the surface in smooth back and forth movements. As with all composite techniques, it is best to do a practice run with the spray gun on a spare piece of material first. As an alternative, the primer can be brushed on by hand; if there are any dry spots on the surface you may anyway have to squeegee the primer down into the weave of the fabric. After the first coat of primer has become tacky, a second coat is applied, followed by subsequent coats as necessary before it is time to sand these smooth, again ensuring that it is done gently so that no new 'valleys' are created on the surface, and that the underlying weave is not exposed.

Then it is time for painting, again preferably with the spray gun. Most commonly available paints can be used and the finish should be 'glass smooth'; you can understand why another well-known composite kitplane manufacturer uses the word 'glass' in the name of their aeroplane. Rutan just coined a term for the speed and simplicity of composite, mouldless construction: once you have got some experience under your belt, it is 'very easy'—or, as we all now know, VariEze!

Another composite construction technique that can be very useful to know about for both small and large parts, and one that many of the 'big boys' in the kitplane world use to churn out their composite kits, is the use of moulds. It is a particularly useful method for making engine cowlings, fuselage deckings, etc. A 'female' mould is required, and this can be made from wood or, more commonly, from glassfibre-reinforced plastic or foam blocks glued together with layers of glassfibre cloth laid up over them to give rigidity. This is achieved just as above only this time it forms the concave side of a mould instead of the convex or flat exterior surface of a component.

A brief résumé of the stages in moulding is as follows:

1 Cut out the layers of Kevlar cloth—or similar—in the dry mould to ensure that they will be the right size once laid into the wetted mould.

2 Apply a layer of mould-release material to the surfaces of the mould.

3 Pour resin into the mould and brush it all over the surface.

4 Apply a layer of cloth and ensure that it is thoroughly sticky with resin.

5 Wet the cloth by the application of resin, having first practised on a small throw-away piece because Kevlar cloth has different characteristics from glassfibre cloth.

6 Apply a second layer of cloth, followed by as many layers as you require for the particular part you are fabricating—a cowling could be four or five—in exactly the same way, wetting out each layer. Overlapping of cloth layers can be done to form a joint, and it is best to overlap the edge of the mould.

7 Using a small hand-roller such as a paint-roller, roll the whole inside surface of the mould to work out any air from the weave of the cloth.

8 Peel-ply may need to be applied if a secondary bonding is required for the part you are making in order to add stiffening, or at bulkheads.

9 Lay a release breather film, which contains millions of tiny holes and comes in a sheet, into the mould on top of everything else. This is required because it is best to vacuum-bag the mould to draw out all the excess resin and the breather will allow this excess to be removed—the peel-ply would allow too much out.

10 Trim the breather film just below the top edge of the mould.

11 Vacuum-bag the whole mould as described previously; if it has been laid up correctly you will see the excess resin squeezing out through the holes in the breather film.

12 After the part has properly cured it can be removed from the mould; the exterior surface should be glassy and smooth.

14 Cleaning up the part and the mould (if it is to be used again) are the final tasks.

New plans for the VariEze and the LongEz have not been available for a long time. However, there are still plenty of copies around if these types of homebuilt attract you, combined with the fact that both are PFA Approved. Another advantage is that so many examples have been built around the world that there is a fountain of information and advice on their construction and operation.

The same goes for the Quickie and its two-seater version the Q.2, designs which were spawned at the same Mojave location and at the same time as the VariEze. The Tri-Q is another version of the Quickie with a tricycle undercarriage instead of mainwheels housed in the wing-tips. Similar to the Quickie in looks only is the two-seater Dragonfly,

The finished product—in this case a two-seater Quickie Q.2. (Ken Ellis Collection)

originally marketed by Viking Aircraft in the USA and for which plans and kits are now available from Mosler Airframes & Powerplants of Hendersonville, North Carolina. Another composite 'canard' design is Nat Puffer's Cozy, a three-seater design that originated in the USA but which is now marketed in plans form from Germany by Cosy Europe; a Cozy has been built and flown in Britain (see the picture on page 73). Similar in looks is Dan Maher's four-seater canard, the Velocity, although this is a kitplane.

The list of these composite types is almost endless and very confusing. Companies and designs come and go, names change, plan-built types suddenly become kitplanes, and they are not limited to just canard-type designs by a long shot. Composites are different—but their mystery should now be history.

CHAPTER 15

The purposeful Pulsar—a composite kitplane classic

IF THE WORLD of moulds and vacuum-bagging all seems too remote to contemplate, you can be sure that the 'wily' homebuilt entrepreneur will not have missed a trick. Requiring some composite work in the form of joining parts, but not anything like the amount of work required by even the VariEze and LongEz, is one of the nicest and most economic composite kitplanes around, the Aero Designs Pulsar, Mark Brown's classic from Texas introduced in Chapter 5 and shortly expected to become a PFA Approved design. The following description is extracted from Aero Designs' brochure for the basic Pulsar; in 1991 the Pulsar XP was introduced with the more powerful 80 hp Rotax 91Z engine. Certain basic modifications to Aero Designs' basic kit may be required by the PFA in Britain.

Aircraft design textbooks always start off with the same obvious point (because it is important). Every aeroplane is a compromise. If you want to go faster you sacrifice some wing area and raise the stall speed. If you want to go faster, you get a bigger engine and sacrifice economy. If you want better manoeuvrability, you sacrifice stability. If you try to get it all, you get disappointment.

The Pulsar does not violate these basic principles but it has one thing that gains a plus in every area. It is light in weight. That allows it to go faster with less wing area and keep a slow stall speed. Also it gives the Pulsar outstanding manoeuvrability with light responsive controls while maintaining exceptional hands-off stability. Other benefits of the light weight are a startling take-off and climb performance and realistic trailerability. Weight is such a big factor in the quality of an aeroplane that it is the best measure of good engineering. Beyond this obvious factor the Pulsar is backed by 15 years of professional engineering analysis and testing. All primary structures meet FAR part 23 design requirements, and all joints made by the builder have a minimum margin of safety of 2.0.

The majority of the Pulsar structure is a top-

Mark Brown flying the prototype of his two-seater composite Pulsar kitplane. (Author)

quality premoulded sandwich composite made with pre-preg glass skins and a structural foam core. The skin material is called 'pre-preg' because the glass cloth is pre-impregnated with high-temperature epoxy and then quick frozen for shipping and storage. The advantage of pre-preg is that the quantity and distribution of resin in the cloth is precisely controlled to eliminate excess weight and provide a guaranteed strength to the finished part. In fact, pre-preg composites are so reliable in strength and durable in service that they are certified by the FAA for use in commercial airliners.

Composite parts made with pre-preg skins also have a great advantage in thermal stability. After the high-temp resin is over-cured as part of the process, the parts are not affected by solar heating. This means that you can paint the Pulsar any colour you desire and still not worry about thermal damage in the sun. This structure also has very good fatigue properties. At the load levels present in the Pulsar the fatigue life is technically infinite.

Damage tolerance is a big advantage of composite aeroplanes in general. The tough resilient outer skin supported by the stiff inner foam core will resist dents better than .04 inch aluminium. Even if a dent or puncture is sustained it is easily repaired. When protected from ultraviolet radiation with a carbon black primer under the paint, a composite aeroplane has a technically infinite life span. It is not affected by the sun, rain, salt water or even most chemicals. In fact, composite materials are used for industrial acid vats.

Some composite aeroplanes do not have a reputation for being particularly light in weight. This is because some types of composite materials have a rather poor strength-to-weight ratio due to excess resin. Also, a composite part made with a mouldless process requires a great quantity of body filler which adds considerable useless weight. The light weight of the Pulsar is a direct result of using the most advanced composite materials and processes available today.

The Pulsar was designed to be as fun and easy to build as it is to fly. First of all every part that you need to build a Pulsar is included in the kit—only the paint and upholstery are left to the builder's preference—even the cups to mix the epoxy are included. Second, any part that requires any special tools or skills is pre-fabricated. No welding, machining or shaping is required. The control system is ready to install and all hardware is included and identified. Best of all, the Pulsar is simple—does not have any complex systems or close tolerance structures. Also it comes with very detailed construction manuals with pictures on every page. Nothing is left to the builder's imagination.

All the premoulded composite parts are made with an internal joining flange so no wet lay-ups are required. The inherent stiffness of the sandwich structure along with the moulded joining flange eliminates the need for assembly jigs because the shell maintains its own shape. Structural adhesive is simply spread on the flange and the parts held together with tape until cured. The resulting joint is five times stronger than the basic shell and ten times stronger than is required for ultimate flight loads. All important dimensional information is pre-marked on the shells so measuring mistakes are eliminated.

The only internal structures in the Pulsar are the bulkheads to support the landing gear, the wing and the pilots. All these bulkheads are cut from a flat sheet of sandwich composite using full-size patterns supplied in the kit; a hand-held electric sabre saw cuts this material very easily and quickly. The bulkheads are bonded into the fuselage with fillets of epoxy and glass tape to form a very strong continuous structure. Attachment points for the wings and landing gear are reinforced by embedding aluminium plates in the bulkhead structure.

The engine installation is greatly simplified by the design of the mounting system. The lower half of the cowling is structurally bonded to the fuselage and reinforced to support the engine loads. Two cross-beams are bonded and glassed into the cowling, then the engine is shock mounted to the cross-beams. This system is a true bed mount which eliminates the complex geometry and interference problems of the standard welded steel tube truss. Also eliminated are the four complex mounting points for the truss. The bed mount is simpler to align, structurally stronger, lighter in weight and much less expensive than the common steel truss. This unique feature is representative of the cost effective simplicity of the Pulsar.

The fuel tank is equally simple and efficient. The flat sandwich composite material is used to form the bottom and back of the tank while the fuselage shell itself forms the sides, top and front. The sandwich composite material in the fuselage and flat panel is fuel proof and fire proof, but in addition to this the tank is sealed with a special process to guarantee a perfect permanent tank. The fuel filler cap is bonded and sealed into the top of the fuselage, while the fittings for the sight-tube-type fuel gauge are bonded and sealed into the tank.

The canopy is another uniquely simple feature in the Pulsar design. The canopy frame is premoulded so that the canopy is a guaranteed close fit on the fuselage. When the canopy is bonded and glassed to the composite frame it forms a very solid unit which rolls forward on three unique tracks embedded in the fuselage shell. Unlike most canopies that have four points of motion that always bind, the three-track system is always free and smooth. It is analogous to building a four-legged stool and trying

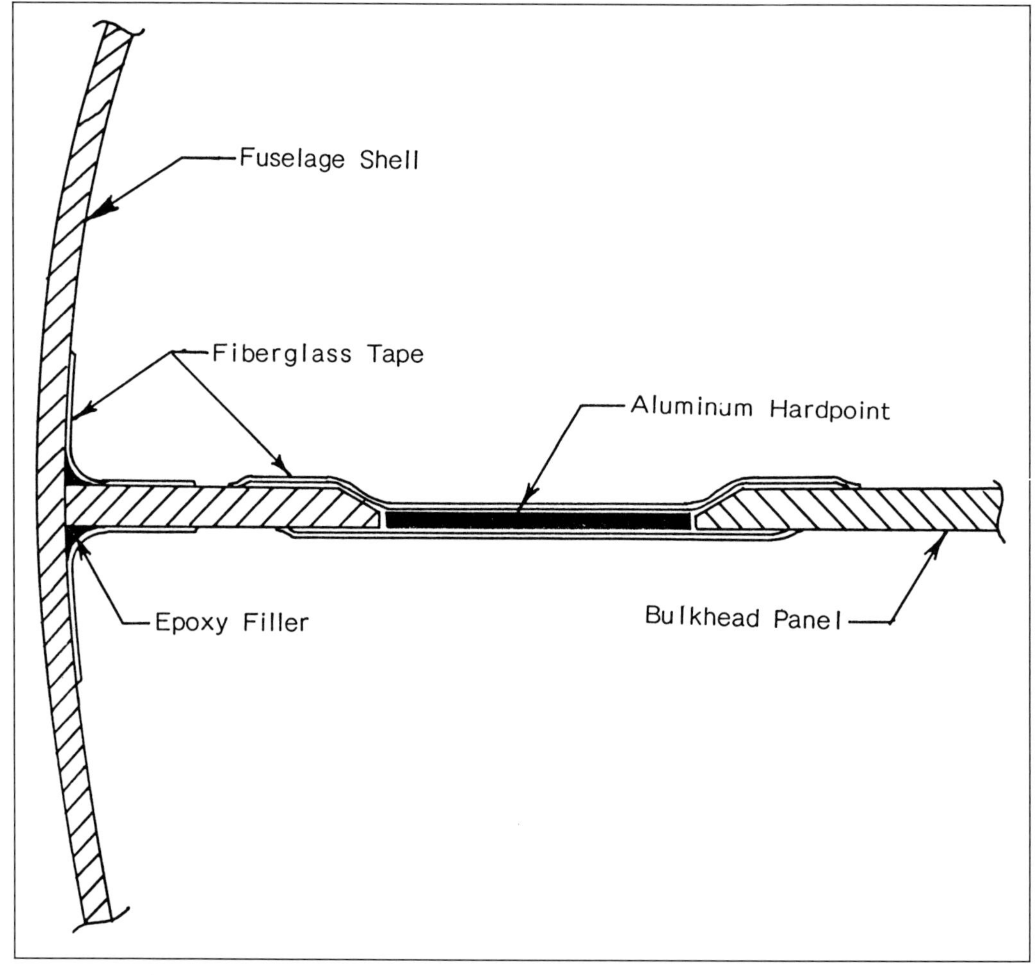

Bulkhead and fuselage assembly in the Pulsar. (Aero Designs)

to get all four legs to touch an uneven floor at the same time, compared with building a three-legged stool for the same floor. When the canopy is closed, it engages alignment pins so that only one latch is required to keep it closed.

The landing gear is a premoulded uni-directional composite leaf type that attaches to the fuselage shell through ears that are glassed on to the gear. This type of gear is very flexible so it absorbs normal bumps easily, but it is also extremely strong so that it can deflect almost flat if necessary to decelerate the aeroplane and pilot to a safe load level.

The horizontal and vertical stabilisers are premoulded in two parts like the fuselage and are assembled by the same simply flange method. The vertical stabiliser is bonded and glassed directly to the fuselage, while the horizontal stabiliser is bonded to an aluminium spar tube which then slides into a splice tube bonded into the fuselage. With this design the horizontal stabilisers are quickly removable for trailering if your trailer will not accommodate a 7 ft 10 in width.

The time it takes to build a Pulsar will vary considerably depending on the experience level of the builder and the degree of perfection he desires in the details. The average construction time will be 600 hours, which is about 9 months if you work 2 hours per day and 8 hours at the weekend. For first-time builders the Pulsar is ideal because it is one of the simplest kits on the market. The construction manuals cover every detail in a step-by-step format in non-technical language, large margins of safety are designed into all areas that are assembled by the builder, and the premoulded shells make the Pulsar easy and quick to build.

The only part of the Pulsar that it not premoulded glass composite is the wing, which is made from the

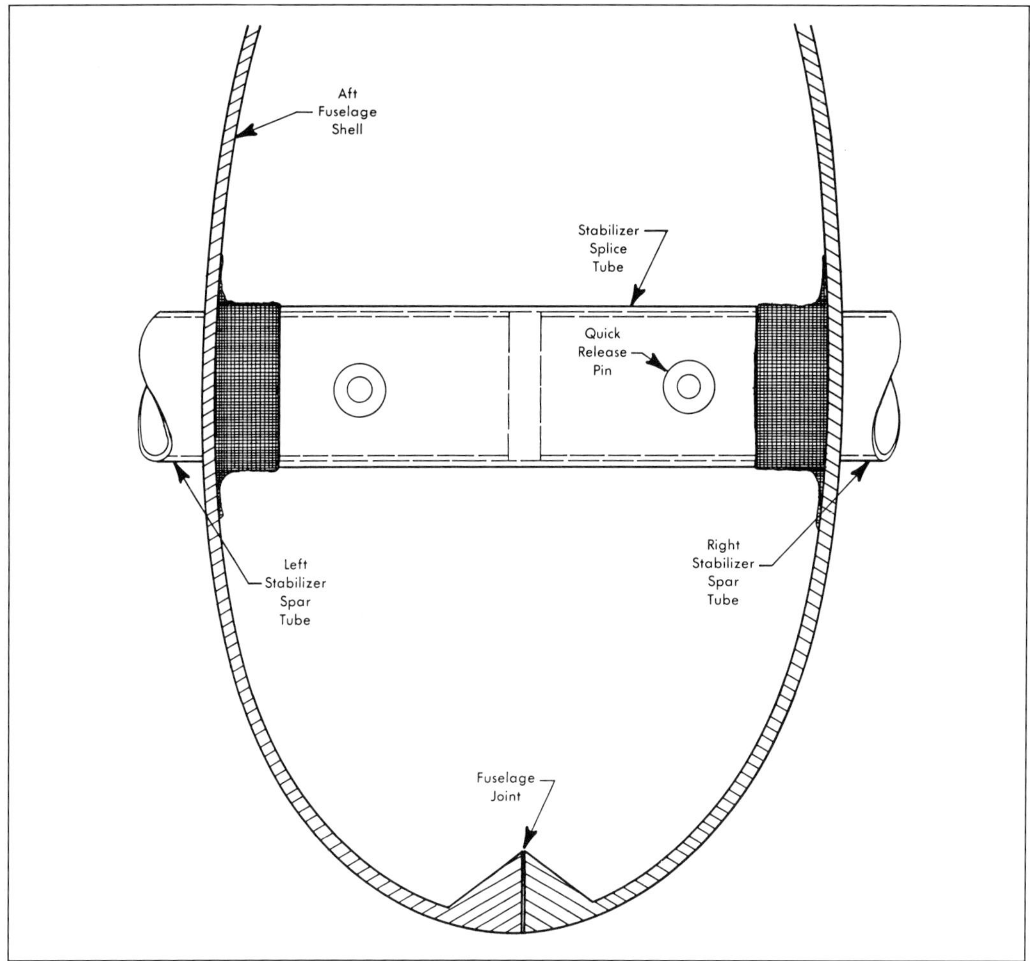

Details of the Pulsar's stabiliser arrangement. (Aero Designs)

most advanced composite of all—wood! The complex matrix of unidirectional fibres and interlocking cell structure of wood makes it a natural composite, and even though it has been largely overlooked in recent years due to the excitement over the man-made composites, wood remains one of the most efficient materials ever designed. It has been proven in aircraft all the way from the Wright Flyer to the sleek Falco. Of course, for compound curves like those of the Pulsar fuselage, wood is rather difficult to form, so the moulded composites are preferred. But for a flat wrap application like wing skin, plywood is ideal; it is unsurpassed in ease of bonding and workability and has a cost advantage of ten to one over moulded composites.

Most people think that modern composites are stronger than wood, but in the case of a wing skin, where the primary load is shear, wood is equal to glassfibre composite for the same weight. Glass is four times stronger, but also four times heavier, so the strength-to-weight ratio is identical. Wood is also very efficient for pure bending applications like wing spars if the wing loading is fairly low. However, for greater load intensities, unidirectional glassfibre is more efficient. The Pulsar uses a unique combination of both materials for a very strong lightweight spar. The basic spar is machined from certified aircraft sitka spruce because of its light weight, flexibility and outstanding bonding characteristics. Then the centre section and inboard spar are reinforced with unidirectional glass caps to take the higher load intensity. These glass caps are cut from high-strength pressure-cured laminates and bonded to the spruce spar at the factory.

Since wood is about four times more flexible than glassfibre composites and ten times more flexible than aluminium, a wooden wing provides a very smooth ride through rough bumpy air. However, up until a few years ago no paint was available that would flex with the wood, and the resulting cracks in the finish exposed the wood to its only natural enemy, moisture. Many older aeroplanes experienced this problem and developed what is commonly called dry-rot (this term is somewhat misleading because the spores that deteriorate the wood are only started when the wood is wet for an extended time; once the spores are started they will continue to attack the wood even after it is dried out). Labelled with this problem of 'dry-rot', wood lost a lot of support for use in aircraft, but following the introduction of very flexible finishes like polyurethane enamel, the wood could effectively be protected from moisture and given a life span as long as modern composite materials or aluminium. In fact, in the presence of salt water or unfiltered ultraviolet radiation, wood will outlast either composite or aluminium.

Bonding wood is also much easier and more reliable than in the past. The old adhesives required tight joints and considerable clamping pressure to develop adequate strength. With modern thixotropic epoxies, joints are less difficult because the thickened epoxy will fill the gaps and still be stronger than the wood itself and only light contact pressure is required. Overall, the wooden wing is actually easier to build, lighter in weight and just as strong and durable as a composite wing would be. Also, since plywood is about one-tenth of the cost of moulded composite and the wing surface area of the Pulsar is greater than the rest of the kit put together, the wooden wing is a major factor in the economy of the Pulsar kit.

Construction of the Pulsar wing requires no jigs because all the ribs are precut from 1-inch thick foam with the wing twist built in. The ribs are simply bonded to the spars with epoxy. Then the 1/16 in birch plywood is bonded to the spars and ribs. Since the plywood is fairly thin it wraps around

Cross section of the Pulsar fuselage at the cockpit. (Aero Designs)

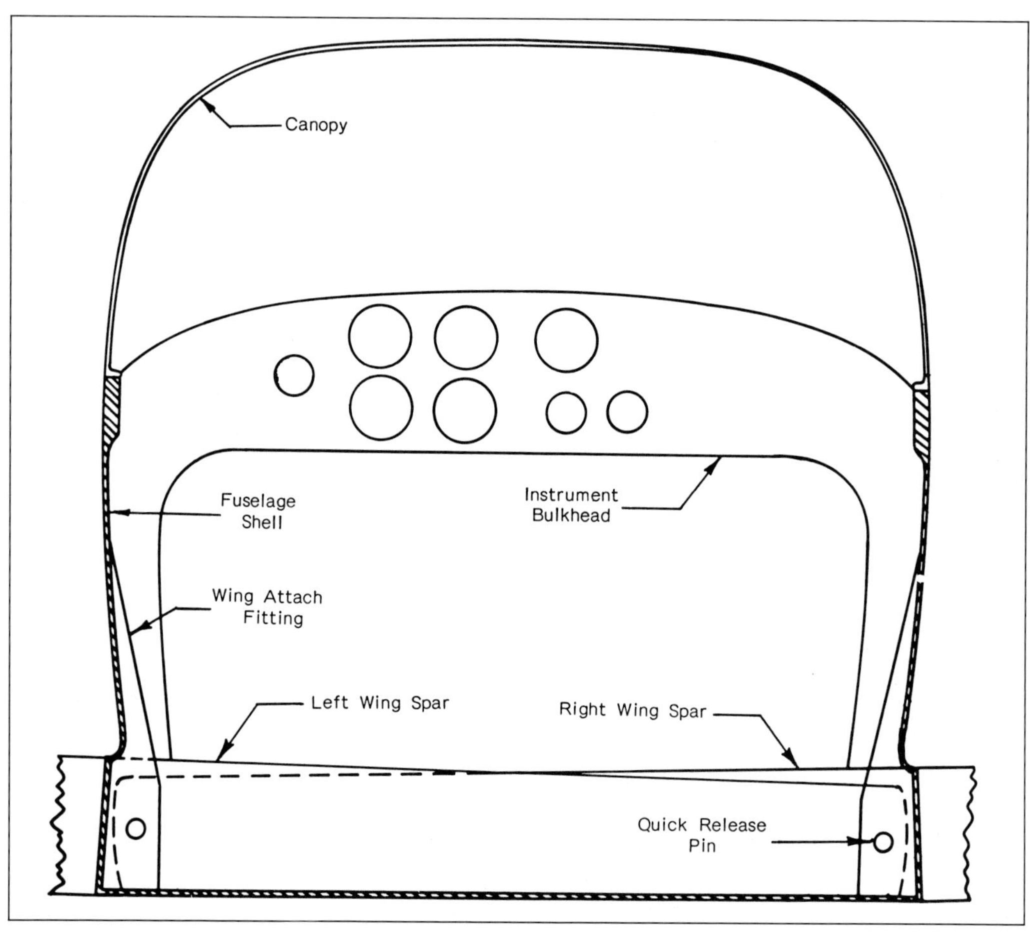

the leading edge very easily. The 8-inch rib spacing and wide rib surface provide such solid support to the wing skin that the wing contour is very smooth. After four coats of primer-surfacer and one coat of polyurethane enamel most people will think you have a glass wing.

The Pulsar wing design incorporates a simple high-strength system of wing attachment that allows detachment in less than 10 minutes for realistic trailerability. Aluminium plates are bonded and glassed to the wing spar and fuselage shell; during the initial wing assembly, the plates are line drilled so they will always match up. Then 5/8 in diameter shear pins are installed through the plates. Since the spars overlap for the entire width of the fuselage, all the wing bending loads are transmitted through the shear pins so that only pure lift loads are transmitted to the fuselage. This system is so simple and reliable that its been used for many years in sailplanes which are trailered for almost every flight.

The Pulsar cockpit is designed for creature comfort and efficient use of space. The seat is reclined only 35° to provide the best piloting position as well as the most comfortable angle for uniform support of the pilot's back and legs, and relief of the stress concentration on the pilot's posterior, thus making long flights more comfortable. The centre-mounted control stick and armrest can be used from either seat; this arrangement not only greatly simplifies the control system but actually provides a control feel superior to the standard centre stick or yoke. This is because the pilot's arm is supported by the armrest which provides a solid reference surface to gauge control motion. A good analogy is trying to aim a target rifle from a free-standing position compared with using a tree fork to steady your aim. That is why the F.16 fighter uses a sidestick. Another advantage of the side stick for a very lightweight aeroplane like the Pulsar is that is magnifies the control forces into an optimum range for good feel.

The rudder pedals are installed to fit a particular pilot but are adjustable (within limits) with turnbuckles on the rudder cables. If large adjustments are necessary they can be made most easily in seat cushion thickness. The brake pedals are located just inboard of the rudder pedals for heel operation. The brakes are cable actuated bands on steel drums and have proved to be very smooth and effective, not to mention simple and low in maintenance.

The cockpit is designed to accommodate two 170 lb people up to 6 ft 2 in tall. Heavier pilots up to 220 lbs can be comfortable if the passenger is smaller than 130 lbs. The cockpit width is a comfortable 39 inches at the elbows and a little wider than a Cessna 150 at the shoulders. The maximum leg room is 46 inches from the seat back to the rudder pedals, and the cockpit height from seat bottom to canopy is 40 inches. Pilots taller than 6 ft 2 in would have to modify the seat bottom to lower the seat.

Behind the seat is a sizeable baggage area that can hold up to 40 lbs with two 150 lb pilots or 20 lbs with two 170 lb pilots.

The instrument panel is all shock mounted and is large enough to accommodate a full IFR package. However, to be consistent with the simplicity and economy of the Pulsar, only standard VFR instruments are supplied in the kit.

Since the design goals for the Pulsar centre around simplicity and economy, which depend on light weight, the engine selection is obviously very important. In fact, the performance and efficiency of the Pulsar would not even be possible without an engine like the Rotax 532*. At 85 lbs and 64 hp, the Rotax 532 has a power-to-weight ratio almost twice as high as a Lycoming, Continental or Volkswagen type engine. Of course, the reason that the 532 puts out so much power for its size is the two-stroke advantage; it produces power on every revolution of the crankshaft instead of every other revolution like a four-stroke engine. In addition to twice the power per revolution, a two-stroke can also safely turn more revs per minute because it has so few moving parts. The engine business basically boils down to how many times the piston pushes on the crankshaft per minute. Then, to keep the propeller turning at the most efficient speed, a very simple durable gearbox is bolted on. The gear ratio for the Pulsar is 2:1, so at 5,500 engine rpm (which is really loafing for a two-stroke) the prop rpm is a very efficient 2,750 rpm.

Besides the power-to-weight advantage, the two-stroke Rotax engine has two more pluses for the Pulsar. It is very simple and easy to work on, and is very economical to operate and purchase in the kit. These two pluses are actually related, since the complexity and number of parts in an engine directly affects the cost. Another influence on the cost of an engine is the volume in production; Rotax of Austria builds over 100,000 engines a year and they have been in business for 30 years [see Chapter 8].

The excellent reliability of the Rotax 532 has been established over many years in thousands of lightweight aircraft. A large part of this success is a result of liquid cooling. A two-stroke engine produces so much power for its size that heat build-up is the most serious challenge. To further complicate matters, the engine needs the most cooling when it is at full power during climb, just when the low

*Since this was first prepared, the 532 has been superceded by the Rotax 582, a similar but improved version.

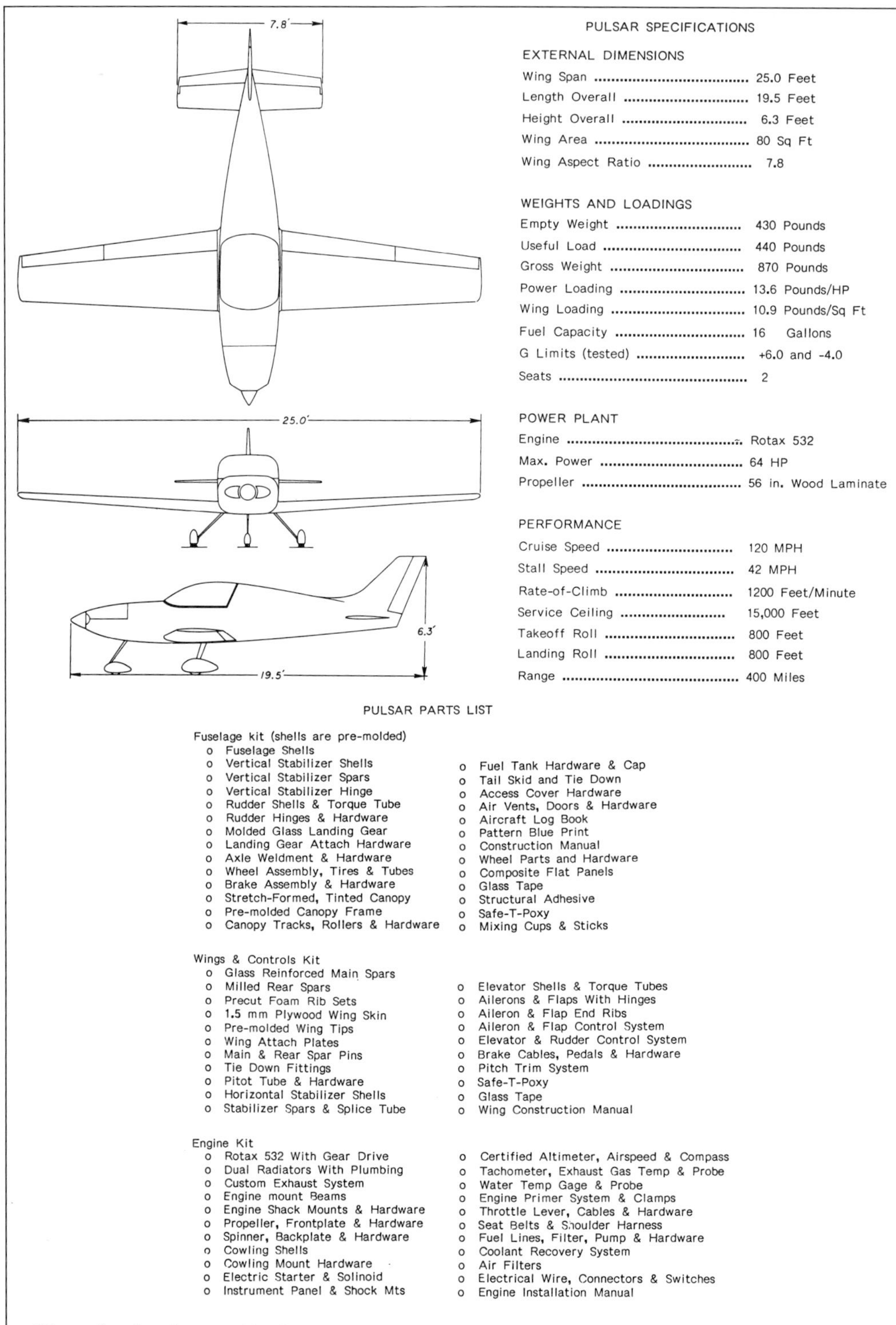

PULSAR SPECIFICATIONS

EXTERNAL DIMENSIONS

Wing Span	25.0 Feet
Length Overall	19.5 Feet
Height Overall	6.3 Feet
Wing Area	80 Sq Ft
Wing Aspect Ratio	7.8

WEIGHTS AND LOADINGS

Empty Weight	430 Pounds
Useful Load	440 Pounds
Gross Weight	870 Pounds
Power Loading	13.6 Pounds/HP
Wing Loading	10.9 Pounds/Sq Ft
Fuel Capacity	16 Gallons
G Limits (tested)	+6.0 and -4.0
Seats	2

POWER PLANT

Engine	Rotax 532
Max. Power	64 HP
Propeller	56 in. Wood Laminate

PERFORMANCE

Cruise Speed	120 MPH
Stall Speed	42 MPH
Rate-of-Climb	1200 Feet/Minute
Service Ceiling	15,000 Feet
Takeoff Roll	800 Feet
Landing Roll	800 Feet
Range	400 Miles

PULSAR PARTS LIST

Fuselage kit (shells are pre-molded)
- o Fuselage Shells
- o Vertical Stabilizer Shells
- o Vertical Stabilizer Spars
- o Vertical Stabilizer Hinge
- o Rudder Shells & Torque Tube
- o Rudder Hinges & Hardware
- o Molded Glass Landing Gear
- o Landing Gear Attach Hardware
- o Axle Weldment & Hardware
- o Wheel Assembly, Tires & Tubes
- o Brake Assembly & Hardware
- o Stretch-Formed, Tinted Canopy
- o Pre-molded Canopy Frame
- o Canopy Tracks, Rollers & Hardware
- o Fuel Tank Hardware & Cap
- o Tail Skid and Tie Down
- o Access Cover Hardware
- o Air Vents, Doors & Hardware
- o Aircraft Log Book
- o Pattern Blue Print
- o Construction Manual
- o Wheel Parts and Hardware
- o Composite Flat Panels
- o Glass Tape
- o Structural Adhesive
- o Safe-T-Poxy
- o Mixing Cups & Sticks

Wings & Controls Kit
- o Glass Reinforced Main Spars
- o Milled Rear Spars
- o Precut Foam Rib Sets
- o 1.5 mm Plywood Wing Skin
- o Pre-molded Wing Tips
- o Wing Attach Plates
- o Main & Rear Spar Pins
- o Tie Down Fittings
- o Pitot Tube & Hardware
- o Horizontal Stabilizer Shells
- o Stabilizer Spars & Splice Tube
- o Elevator Shells & Torque Tubes
- o Ailerons & Flaps With Hinges
- o Aileron & Flap End Ribs
- o Aileron & Flap Control System
- o Elevator & Rudder Control System
- o Brake Cables, Pedals & Hardware
- o Pitch Trim System
- o Safe-T-Poxy
- o Glass Tape
- o Wing Construction Manual

Engine Kit
- o Rotax 532 With Gear Drive
- o Dual Radiators With Plumbing
- o Custom Exhaust System
- o Engine mount Beams
- o Engine Shack Mounts & Hardware
- o Propeller, Frontplate & Hardware
- o Spinner, Backplate & Hardware
- o Cowling Shells
- o Cowling Mount Hardware
- o Electric Starter & Solinoid
- o Instrument Panel & Shock Mts
- o Certified Altimeter, Airspeed & Compass
- o Tachometer, Exhaust Gas Temp & Probe
- o Water Temp Gage & Probe
- o Engine Primer System & Clamps
- o Throttle Lever, Cables & Hardware
- o Seat Belts & Shoulder Harness
- o Fuel Lines, Filter, Pump & Hardware
- o Coolant Recovery System
- o Air Filters
- o Electrical Wire, Connectors & Switches
- o Engine Installation Manual

Three-view drawing, specifications and parts list for the Pulsar. (Aero Designs) speed and angle of attack cause minimum cooling. Even worse is the let-down where the engine suffers thermal shock from too much cooling just when it does not need much at all. The liquid cooling system of the 532 solves all these problems. The large radiators have enough capacity to easily cool the engine at high power and low speeds, while at high speeds the air flow through the radiator is restricted by the fine mesh of cooling fins which prevents overcooling. The air that cannot get through the mesh spills around the cowling to reduce cooling drag. With such a comfortable home as a Pulsar cowling the Rotax 532 should have a long healthy life.

The 532 is supplied in the Pulsar kit with an electric starter, 14 amp alternator, special Pulsar exhaust system, and dual carburettors.

Every active pilot who pays his own way struggles with the astronomical cost of general aviation. In fact, this problem is the driving force behind the upsurge of the kitplane market. The Pulsar solution is to attack every angle of the cost barrier simultaneously. First of all, the certified engine problem: a Lycoming or Continental engine can easily cost as much as a complete Pulsar. Even the overhaul cost can be several thousand dollars/pounds.

Hangar rent alone could pay for a Pulsar in just a few years. But with the Pulsar you can bring your aeroplane home with you on an inexpensive boat trailer and have the convenience of working on it in your own garage. In fact, you will eliminate another major fixed expense by doing your own maintenance and inspections, and will save several hundreds a year for the annual inspection and a considerable sum per hour on maintenance.

The operating cost for a Pulsar will average about half of what you would pay for most two-seater aeroplanes with similar performance. At economy cruise the Rotax will burn as little as 3.8 gallons an hour. Of course there is no oil to change, and tyres and brakes will last for years on such a light aircraft.

The old saying that 'an aeroplane will fly the way it looks' is not entirely true. If you see an aeroplane with a tiny thin wing you can be sure that it is a 'hot potato' in the traffic pattern and that you will need lots of room for take-off and landing. An aeroplane with a short fuselage and a small tail will feel touchy and unstable, and a boxy aeroplane with struts and wires is not going to win many races. By these examples it can be seen that flying qualities are an important aspect of the basic design, and the Pulsar was designed from the wheels up to be fun and easy to fly.

The most important influence on how an aeroplane flies is obviously the wing. The Pulsar has a very generous wing area for its weight which gives it a very slow and comfortable stall speed. In addition, it has 1½° of washout which provides the pilot with good roll control throughout the stall to prevent unintentional spins. The airfoil has a big effect on stall characteristics and the Pulsar uses the MS(1)-0313 which has a very gentle break. This airfoil is also very forgiving of surface imperfections whether caused by the structure, the paint or the insect population. The MS(1)-0313 also contributes to the speed because it has a maximum CL of 1.7 while maintaining a very low drag coefficient of .005 in cruise. With large flaps included for glide path control and even slower speed, the Pulsar is a real joy to take-off and land. At 45 mph, you've got plenty of time and runway to relax.

The wing design also plays a large part in cruise quality. The highly tapered planform reduces the rolling moments caused by gusts while decreasing resistance to roll inputs from the ailerons. The result is a much better roll rate when it is required and much less when it is not. The tapered wing also produces less drag for a more efficient cruise and improved climb performance. Completing the Pulsar's wing design is the differential frise-type aileron system, which reduces adverse yaw for much simpler turn co-ordination.

The next most important factor in aircraft handling qualities is tail volume, which is the length of the fuselage from wing to tail multiplied by the area of the tail. This, along with the position of the centre of gravity, determines the stability of the aircraft. The Pulsar has a very large tail volume due to the long fuselage and generous tail area. This design feature gives the Pulsar its uncommon stability, so in cruise you can trim it out and fly hands-off indefinitely (and slow map-readers won't end up practising unusual attitudes). The large stability margin also gives the Pulsar a very solid feel in manoeuvres, so the controls are not at all touchy and oversensitive. Even with such outstanding stability, the Pulsar is still very responsive and manoeuvrable because of its extremely light weight. In short, it stays where you put it hands-off, it moves gently with small control movement, and manoeuvres like a fighter with large control input.

One aspect of flying quality that is difficult to control but has a major effect on flying pleasure is rough air, and the Pulsar even has a solution to help here. First of all the wing loading is high enough that small gusts do not have much effect. Any weather suitable for a Cessna is suitable for a Pulsar. The big help is really in climb performance. The Pulsar is so light in weight that it climbs like an elevator; the rough air just does not have much time to bother you because you are above it in just a couple of minutes. Even on a hot summer day you can be up in smooth air before you know it, and you will have automatic air conditioning and the true airspeed boost to help you on your way. The Pulsar is a natural mountain aeroplane because it will take off at

7,500 feet better than most aeroplanes at sea level.

The Aero Designs' brochure's comparison of the Pulsar with the popular two-seater production light aircraft, the Cessna 150, is interesting. The empty Pulsar weighs less than half the Cessna 150, at 430 lbs (195 kg), although the latter's useful load is slightly more, 550 lbs (249 kg) compared to the Pulsar's 440 lbs (200 kgs). This is not a direct comparison, however, becuase the Cessna has to carry more fuel to feed its fuel-thirsty 100 hp engine—the Pulsar's current Rotax 582, rated at 66 hp, uses far less. The Pulsar will cruise at 125 mph (205 kmph) at 8,000 ft (2,440 m) using about 4 gallons (18 litres) of mogas per hour; if you can get the Cessna up to that sort of speed the flight manual says that it will consume 5½ gallons (25 litres) of avgas per hour, although I suspect that both these Cessna figures are optimistic, based on those I have flown. However, baggage capacity is greater in the Cessna and some may not like the 35° angle of rake of the Pulsar's seats. A big Pulsar bonus is the maintenance and hangarage costs—the Rotax engine is cheap to maintain and, with the detachable glider-style wings, the aircraft takes up a fraction of the space of a Cessna in a hangar, and even better, can be trailered home after 15 minutes unbolting the wings and loading. Finally the costs—well, you cannot get a new Cessna 150, or 152, but a reasonable second-hand one could set you back £20,000. The Pulsar kit will cost about $15,500 (approximately £8,150) plus air freight costs from Texas of about £1,000, but then there is your time and the costs involved in the kit construction plus a radio and any avionics required. My biased opinion, though, is that the Pulsar wins hands down in any comparison with a Cessna, a fact with which several British builders already agree.

In the air is where any aeroplane must prove itself, and although with any homebuilt there are different levels of equipment on board, propellers of different pitch and different weather/temperature effecting performance, depending on where the evaluation is carried out, the Pulsar stands out very well. External checks are few, save moving the control surfaces and checking hinges and holes. The seating is designed for the '95 per centile man' and the first impression is of a very sparce cockpit, the panel dominated by a central and apparently crude but totally effective fuel sight gauge. Five basic instruments are, on the left, the ASI, VSI, altimeter and compass, and three engine instruments on the right. On the left-hand side is the throttle and flap lever with the trim lever and control stick in the centre below the fuel gauge. Brakes are mechanical (cable, not hydraulic) heel-type, needed on the ground to steer the swivelling nosewheel. The taxi is straightforward, the high rpm and different note of the two-stroke engine soon becoming accepted. Stall speed is in the lower 40s (mph) and one would expect a best climb speed of 60—in fact with the cruise-pitch prop on the aircraft I flew, the climb

The first British example of the Pulsar at the PFA rally at Wroughton in July 1991. (Author)

recommended was a flat, fast 90 mph. Take-off is remarkably quick from a hard runway; with a touch of left rudder and with only the slightest back pressure on the centrally placed stick, the Pulsar is airborne at 65 mph and at 90 climbed at over 1,000 fpm. Up at 2,000 feet and set up with 75 per cent power and just over 6,000 rpm, the cruise speed of 125 mph came up in straight and level flight with no difficulty. The Pulsar flies nicely and although the controls are sensitive, they are not twitchy—a roll is smooth with only a little rudder required to compensate for yaw.

Power-checked for an evaluation of the stall, clean and straight and level, the right wing dropped quite sharply at 43 mph. The wings levelled quickly, however, when back pressure on the stick was released and we dropped less than 100 feet. With flaps down buffet was felt in the stick at about 40 and the same slight right wing drop occurred at 38. The Pulsar trims out well and, hands-off, a quick push of the stick is soon dampened out—at 7,000 rpm, which is still not full throttle, clean and straight and level, 130 mph is shown on the clock, although if this were maintained fuel consumption would rocket to over 4 gph. At a much lower 90 mph the rpm is 5,000 and fuel is consumed at only a miserly 2 gph.

Landing is also straightforward, with the good cockpit visibility helping in a busy circuit. Initially set at 5,000 rpm and 94 mph and then slowing slightly and the application of flaps, giving first 75 and then 65 over the threshold, the Pulsar gives a landing with which anyone used to a standard production tri-gear type, such as the Cessna 150, should have no trouble. As I suspected, the aircraft looks good and its performance matches this—remember that it is a 66 hp two-seater!

CHAPTER 16

Case studies: microlight homebuilts

FOR THE PURPOSE of airworthiness, the Civil Aviation Authority (CAA) considers that a microlight aeroplane is 'A one or two-seat aeroplane whose all up weight (AUW) shall not exceed 390 kg (860 lbs) and whose wing loading shall not be greater than 25 kg/m^2 (5.1 lbs/ft^2)'. Two-seater microlights can be flown, and are primarily used in the training role. See Chapter 9 for full details of the British Microlight Aircraft Association (BMAA).

The TEAM MiniMax

One of Britain's first Minimax builders was Peter Harvey from Dursley in Gloucestershire, who was 52 years old when he started building in January 1989. He is a surveyor by profession and later ran his own building company, although he is now by his own admission 'in semi-retirement'.

The Minimax is an all-wood/fabric single-seater low-wing kitplane/homebuilt monoplane of very simple design that has proved exceedingly popular with homebuilders throughout the world since the prototype first flew in the USA in February 1985. Wayne Ison is the MiniMax's designer and he started work on the project in August 1984, cutting the first wood in October. It was designed at the outset to be powered by a small 27 hp Rotax 277 (bigger engines have since been fitted) and to be classified either as a microlight or homebuilt (Experimental in the USA) aircraft. Subsequently TEAM (Tennessee Engineering and Manufacturing Inc) have developed comprehensive kits for the Minimax as well as developing the design into the HiMax (a high-wing version) and several other variants, including one on floats. MiniMaxes are being flown and built by the hundreds with sales in Canada, France, Italy (where a float-equipped version is flying), Sweden, Holland, South Africa, Norway and Japan. In Britain the design is now fully

Peter Harvey flying his completed TEAM MiniMax. (P. Harvey)

approved for homebuilding by the PFA for subsequent operation in the 'Microlight Category'.

Peter Harvey learned to fly at Gloucester (Staverton) airport in the early 1970s. He accumulated about 60 hours in his log-book on Cessnas and Piper Cherokees but found that the pressures of family life, pursuing his other hobby of off-shore powerboat racing, and flying were not all possible together, the latter being, he felt, an expensive luxury. With the family grown up and away from home, older and wiser, Peter re-married and settled down again. He decided he would like to start flying once more in about 1988 but was still staggered at its cost. He looked to the world of microlights for an aircraft design he could build himself but none of those commonly available in Britain at the time and within his price range appealed to him.

He therefore studied every conceivable piece of literature from Europe and North America that he could lay his hands on—books and magazines flooded into his Gloucestershire home. His evaluations eventually saw him decide that the MiniMax had the most possibilities, so he ordered a set of drawings, building instructions and a full structural analysis of the design from TEAM in the USA. At this time the MiniMax design was not PFA Approved, so everything had to go off to them for study. This took a considerable time, but Nick Sibley (then Assistant Chief Engineer with the PFA) was marvellous with help and advice, working out not only the mandatory modifications necessary to bring the MiniMax in line with British requirements but also the modifications that Harvey personally wanted to make to the design, and also thoroughly checking the complete stress analysis. The whole evaluation, decision and type approval process took two years, the PFA part of this taking about 6 months, their approval coming through just before Christmas 1988. On 22 January 1989 Peter started building.

He was by now more than familiar with the TEAM-supplied plans and construction manual; no would-be builder should rush into construction even when he has decided what aircraft he is going to build, and a cooling-off period for study of drawings and manual (if available) is very much recommended. It will help with an appreciation of the complexity and planning of the construction work, and can be used to draw up a work programme which, as well as giving the builder a cross-check on how things are going, also provides a chance to establish a materials and ordering schedule. From this in turn the builder will know what his approximate cash-flow requirement is going to be and whether he is going to have to start renting out the spare bedroom to make ends meet!

The MiniMax drawings, according to Peter Harvey, are 'very detailed and thorough, giving step-by-step instructions which would enable anyone who could build a model aeroplane to successfully build and complete a MiniMax. The whole thing is actually built like a model aeroplane but it's not as difficult because the detailed items are not too small and fiddly.'

His first major outlay after the plans was £150 on buying a second-hand garage to use as a workshop. This was a standard British garage approximately 18 ft × 9 ft 9 in (5.5 m × 3.0 m) which then had to be 'furnished' with a large flat-top workbench and power supply.

Peter had decided to build his MiniMax from plans using none of TEAM's kits, so his first major task was to obtain materials and parts with which to build (he thought it inadvisable to buy a kit because of the modifications and alterations that it might require). Scouring the country for materials of the correct specified size and quality took up an inordinate amount of time and money and, on reflection, it would probably have been as cheap to have bought the TEAM kit. Mainair in Lancashire, Tube Sales Ltd of Southampton, Robbins of Bristol, CSE Aviation Ltd at Oxford, and Chilbolton Sailplanes in Surrey were some of the main suppliers he visited and from whom he purchased materials. He also arranged for Tim Cox from Winterbourne in Avon to be his official PFA Inspector and, on reflection, he says that 'without his help, knowledge and thoroughness on every aspect of the project, the whole thing wouldn't have been possible'. An example of this, which may have appeared aggravating at the time, were the metal tail hinges. He admits to having difficulty in drilling straight holes in metal and had to make three sets of hinges before Tim Cox considered them suitable. 'A perfectionist—but no complaints whatsoever,' says Peter.

Peter followed the example of many first-time homebuilders by starting on the tail of the MiniMax because it is the smallest and least expensive part of the plane, and therefore the best on which to make any beginners' mistakes whilst low on the learning curve. This may not have been a good idea in one respect because it is not of uniform chord like the wings and is therefore more complicated. Nonetheless he considered himself a competent carpenter, part of the reason why he chose the all-wood MiniMax in the first place.

The only jig required for the project was used to build the wing-ribs—12 for each wing, 24 in all, which he built in one concentrated effort at his work-bench over a three-day period. These ribs are one of the most time-consuming aspects of the construction, but building the wing itself is quite straightforward, being a wooden truss and plywood structure for speed and simplicity of construction, each rib made from ¼ in square stock wood moun-

Left *The tail of Peter Harvey's MiniMax was tackled first as a trial to evaluate his construction aptitude.*

Below *The jig for the wing ribs; enough for one wing have already been made.*

Bottom *The MiniMax wing being constructed on a large flat table.*

Right *The fuselage sides ready to be joined together, just like a large model aeroplane.*

Below right *The completed fuselage ready for covering.*

(All photos, P. Harvey)

ted on 'C'-channel spars made of wood caps on plywood webs. The whole wing—each is about 12 feet (3.66 m) long—is built flat on the large work-table with no washout, which simplifies the process. Small leading edge riblets are stuck to the front of the spar and the leading edge is covered with thin ply. Full-span ailerons, which double as flaps, are attached to the trailing edge of each wing.

Fuselage construction is simple and just like that of a model aircraft, the structure being a braced box with plywood covering forward of the seat. Initially each fuselage side is laid flat on the work-table for setting out and glueing, and is then set up and the cross braces glued to form the box. Roll-over protection is incorporated in the turtledeck behind the cockpit. The wings slot into holes cut in the side of the fuselage, located with pins and bolts for the easy de-rigging that Peter wanted from his home-built. The tube-braced unsprung undercarriage is fitted to the bottom of the fuselage by turning it upside down on the workbench on a couple of trestles, and the unbraked wheels can then be added (a brake kit is available as an optional extra). Fabric covering of the wooden structure can then take place before it is sprayed, a job Peter let his auto-mechanic cousin Martin Hammond carry out.

Martin also took over the engine installation for Peter. The chosen power-plant was a standard hand-started 27 hp Rotax 277 single-cylinder engine fitted with a 2.58:1 reduction drive. The fuel tank was made by a specialist aluminium company in Cheltenham. The final weight of the MiniMax was 270 lbs (122.6 kg), considerably above the basic US kit version (230 lbs/104 kg), for Peter had over-sized some of the timbers and incorporated quite a few modifications; however, it was still well inside the maximum 330 lbs weight for microlights current at that time.

Nine months after cutting the first wood and with a special trailer built from the chassis of an old caravan, Peter's MiniMax was roaded to a grass airstrip at Badminton, to the north of Bath. Registered G-MVXZ, the blue and white aircraft was test flown by Eddie Clapham for the first time in very

Weighing the completed MiniMax and checking alignments. (P. Harvey)

blustery 15 knot conditions on 14 October 1989 when, despite the wind and worry, the flight of the first MiniMax to be built and flown in Britain went extremely smoothly. The only adjustment was the necessity for a trim tab on the elevator.

Peter's hopes were therefore realised with a sprightly little aeroplane that could take off from 150 feet (46 m) of grass and climb at 600 fpm; that had a very docile stall with no tendency to drop a wing; and that was economical to operate and provided safe and easy handling. These were Peter's main criteria when looking for a homebuilt design to build, criteria he believes the MiniMax meets well.

Peter's PPL 'A' licence had lapsed so the CAA suggested he should take a full PPL 'D' course to qualify him to fly the MiniMax. He did this under the

Eddy Clapham brings Peter Harvey's MiniMax in to a smooth landing at the end of its maiden flight at Badminton. (P. Harvey)

tuition of Will Knowles, a BMAA test pilot and instructor, as Weston Zoyland airfield near Bridgwater.

Test-flying took about 15 hours to complete, all done with the Rotax and with no problems except a broken throttle cable, when Peter was able to practise forced landings without power! Because the MiniMax handled so well, even with a 16 stone (224 lb) pilot in it, Peter decided to do a little experimenting by fitting a newly available lightweight Italian-made engine, the 34 hp Arrow 250GT, which produces 6,800 rpm. One of its beauties is that is comes with an electrical start and dual CD ignition to one plug and weighs only 10 lbs (4 kg) more than the Rotax. Allan Newton made a special wooden prop for the new engine with a 60 in × 41 in pitch (1.52 m × 1.04 m) but this proved to be a little too coarse, giving a cruise of 75 mph (124 kmh) and lengthening the take-off run by about 240 feet (73 m). Allan was asked to make a second prop with a 60 in × 38 in (1.52 m × 0.96 m) pitch, and this proved to be the further making of the MiniMax as far as Peter was concerned. A take-off run of only 150 feet (46 m) and a cruise of 70 mph (116 kmph) resulted.

By early 1991 Peter had done about 40 hours flying in the MiniMax, 25 of them with the Arrow engine. 'It's not possible to say how pleased I am with it,' Peter told me. 'I'm not a clever pilot, only wanting something safe and economical to play with. The handling is superb with its full-span ailerons and large tail surfaces. It has a large speed range with a 20 mph (33 kmph) power-on stall and a 90 mph (149 kmph) never-exceed speed, and for test purposes we have even done 110 mph (182 kmph) with no problems and no sign of flutter. It's the ideal little plane for an amateur like myself, especially as the landings are so slow, and when you do bounce, the airframe is very strong with no risk of damage. At first only a tail-skid was fitted but I did so many ground-loops when I was taxing it downwind that I've now fitted a steerable tailwheel.'

Peter was so pleased with the MiniMax that he and a colleague in Dursley decided to start importing MiniMax kits to Britain under the name of Ultralight Flying Machines (UFM) (see Appendix 6 for address).

As with any homebuilt aircraft project the builder has many thank-yous to deal out on completion. Deserving the greatest thanks, Peter thinks, is his wife, for her support throughout the building and her active involvement in always being ready to supply that extra pair of hands in the workshop when needed. PFA Inspector Tim Cox has already had his praises sung, but it is worth emphasising again the importance to the British homebuilt movement of this voluntary, yet totally professional and dedicated group of engineers who are always willing to advise and show a builder how to do those awkward or new jobs when he is stuck. Finally, thanks have to go to other contributors such as Peter's cousin, his BMAA flying instructor, his test pilot Eddie Clapham, and many more. You may make a few enemies building your own plane but more than likely, as Peter Harvey found out with his MiniMax, you make many more new aquaintances that can soon become lifelong friendships.

And the future? Peter is currently enlarging the garage workshop alongside his house to 20 ft × 14 ft (6.1 m × 4.3 m). No, it is not for a new car—he has been bitten, like so many homebuilders, by the bug, and intends to start building again, only this time a two-seater. Meanwhile he will continue to enjoy flying his single-seater TEAM MiniMax.

The CFM Streak Shadow

In case you are thinking that the world of kitplanes and homebuilts has little or no British involvement, David Cook and his company based in Leiston, Suffolk, CFM Metal-Fax Litd (Cook Flying Machines), are making sure that the Union Jack keeps flying, and in a big way.

The secret of this success is a development of the successful Shadow microlight, the Streak Shadow, a tandem two-seater design categorised as a homebuilt amateur-produced microlight aircraft in Britain, as an 'ultralight' in Europe, and 'Experimental' in the USA. It weighs in at 388 lbs (176 kg) empty and, with a total fuel capacity of 12 imperial gallons, has an endurance of 5½ hours at economic cruise and a range of 400 miles. It has wings that can be detached in 10 minutes for carriage on a trailer, and its predecessor, the factory-built Shadow, has been used for several epic flights, including two from Britain to Australia and one from Britain to India.

Is there a catch? Definitely not, and even pricewise the complete Streak Shadow kit is competitive with US kit imports (£11,800 basic plus VAT at 1991 prices). This may explain why CFM in 1991 had sold 170 aircraft including 40 kit versions of the Shadow and have also started to play the Americans at their own game by granting a production licence for Streak Shadow kits to be built under licence in the USA by LARON Aviation Technologies of Clovis, New Mexico. The Streak Shadow has thus become the only British-designed aircraft in production in the USA excepting the joint venture BAe/MDD AV-8A and Hawk T-45, both military aircraft.

David Cook is a little-recognised pioneer in the field of hang gliding and microlighting, although he has been involved in the business for nearly 20 years. When everyone else was flying Rogallo

The Streak Shadow two-seater kitplane differs from the earlier Shadow in having a shorter wing-span and larger engine. (Author)

The prototype Shadow first flew in 1983. (Ken Ellis Collection)

flex-wing hang gliders (the triangular type in which the pilot hangs on a tubular frame underneath and self launches), he pursued rigid-wing designs. His mentor and aide was Californian Volmer Jensen, whose aircraft he built and flew in this country, not the well-known Volmer Jensen VJ.22 Sportsman wood/fabric two-seater amphibian homebuilt, but the VJ.23 that became the first powered hang glider to cross the English Channel, with David as its pilot—it had a 9 hp engine and never got above 300 feet for the crossing!

That was in the pre-regulatory days of hang gliding and microlighting, but soon several countries, including Britain, published provisional airworthiness requirements for the sport and the future direction of microlighting then became clearer. Cook designed and built the prototype Shadow as a result of years of experience in designing and flying ultralight aircraft and first flew it in 1983. That year it set an FAI world speed record in its class of 78.5 mph (126 kmph) over a 3 km course, and the following year an FAI world distance record, the first of a long list of records and achievements for the aeroplane.

The basis of the Streak Shadow's design is the aviator's eternal dream of a high-strength structure with a low weight. Hang-glider-type construction was rejected in favour of an advanced specification bonded structure. Although a first look at a completed Streak Shadow leads one to believe that it has strutted wings, it is in fact a cantilever design, the struts having been added mainly for 'psychological security' but also to reduce wing root stress whilst taxiing on rough ground and in ground handling. The wing spar employs an 'I'-beam structure with a plywood shear web and pre-formed alloy capping pieces. Foam/glassfibre wing ribs are attached to the main spar, the leading-edge 'D'-tube being of plywood and the rear wing covering being polyester fabric suitably doped. Cable-operated three-stage flaps occupy the inboard part of the wing trailing edge and the ailerons are operated by push-pull tubes with immediate low-friction response. The Streak Shadow's body or fuselage is built from 'fibrelam', a specialist and robust material of exceptional strength, rigidity and light weight. The main undercarriage suspension is a steel-tube and glassfibre rod combination to which differential caliper brakes are added. The nosewheel is free-castoring. The engine, a 64 hp twin-cylinder liquid-cooled Rotax 532, is located at the rear of the fuselage in a pusher configuration, beneath the trailing edge of the wing.

Building a Streak Shadow kit is really a process of assembly from the pre-cut and pre-formed materials in the kit. Using CFM's excellent manual, instructional video and pilot/service notes, a builder of 'limited practical ability' can do this assembly with only readily available hand tools being required. Probably the most time-consuming part of construction is the finishing and fitting out, an area in which builder-preference inevitably creeps in but which provides the builder with a high level of satisfaction.

CFM have also divided the Streak Shadow's construction into four stages, producing appropriate 'Stage Kits' as follows:

Stage 1 FUSELAGE including the LANDING

The Shadow's Rotax engine at the rear of the fuselage. (Author)

GEAR—the monocoque fibrelam is pre-cut to shape, routed and drilled, the nose cone pre-formed and canopy screens pre-shaped. Hangar tubes are cut to length, coined and jig drilled. Wheels, tyres and tubes with complete brake assembly are included. The fuel tank components are pre-cut. The main items included are the rudder foot pedals, joy-stick and controls, hand primer bulb and filter, seat belts, ignition switch and all electrics (no instruments are included and the UK statutory minimum of ASI, altimeter, fuel gauge, tachometer and CHT or EGT gauge will all have to be purchased extra).

Stage 2 WING CONSTRUCTION—the main spar and 'D'-section are already factory produced, all foam wing ribs have been cut to shape by 'hot-wire' techniques, the rear spar, drag and compression struts are pre-shaped and the tubular tail-boom is

The forward fuselage of the Streak Shadow. (CFM)

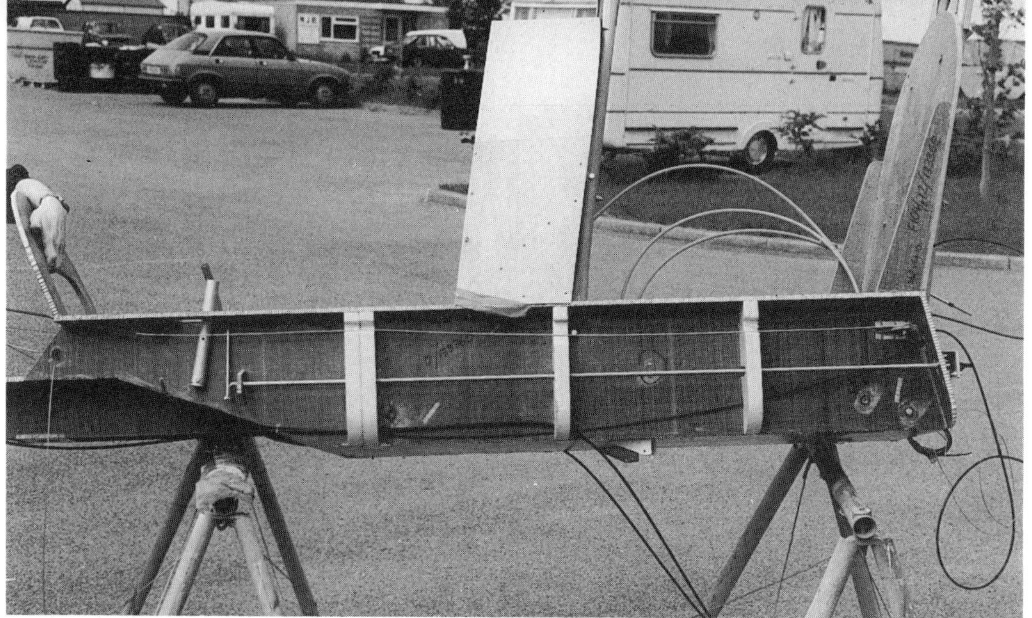

Main structural elements of the Streak Shadow fuselage. (CFM)

also included at this stage.

Stage 3 TAILPLANE CONSTRUCTION—the leading edge tubes are pre-bent to shape and everything else is provided for the tailplane, elevator, rudder and fin-post.

Stage 4 POWER-PLANT—the Rotax 532 is supplied complete with all ancillary equipment, the alternator, recoil hand-start system, sparking plugs, carburettor, exhaust unit, reduction drive unit and propeller.

CFM also make a point of reassuring potential kit customers that the factory-produced parts only require their edges to be dressed and smoothed, that all welding, both ferrous and non-ferrous, is completed, all tube bending complete, all foam parts (except the wing-tips) have been pre-formed, all bolts and other hardware are included, and bi-directional and uni-directional glass cloth is supplied; adequate polyester fabric for covering completes the package.

The completed cockpit of the Streak Shadow with the side stick evident. (CFM)

On the minus side, a Streak Shadow purchaser will not get in his kit from CFM the paint, polyester and spray filler, thinners, acetone, red hermetite, loctite, the cushions and the instruments, although, as might be expected, CFM will supply an add-on kit containing these items. Another small additional expense is that if the 'Stage Kits' are purchased separately, there is an additional cost of £300 over buying the four outright.

There are also different variants of the basic Streak Shadow kit that can be purchased depending on the seat and control requirements in the finished kitplane: Series B-D, tandem two-seater with dual controls; Series B, tandem two-seater single control with footwell; and Series B, tandem two-seater single control but without footwell.

CFM also make it quite clear at what stages a builder of one of their kits needs to get it checked and formally inspected by themselves or a qualified PFA Inspector. There are five identifiable inspection stages, although these do not all have to be carried out separately, with two visits sufficient to effect all four stage checks and the final inspection. These stages are:

1. Fuselage including undercarriage—when complete but before fitting of side panniers and nose cone.
2. Both wings, centre wing section and tail boom—when complete but before any part is covered.
3. Tailplane, elevator, fin-post and rudder—when complete but before any part is covered.

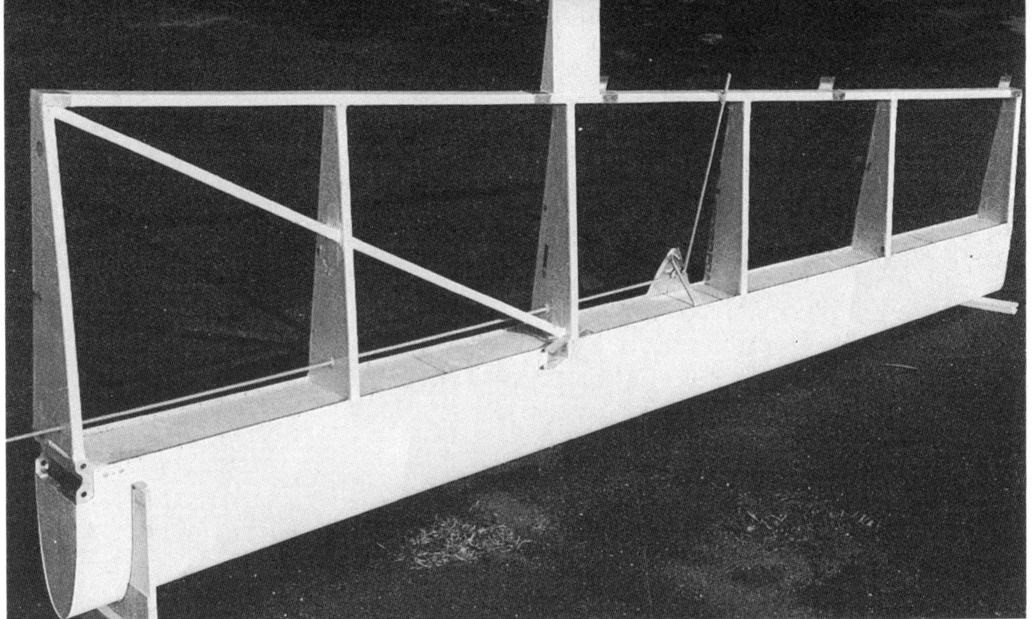

The wing construction of the Streak Shadow. (CFM)

4 Engine, fuel system, fuel tank and propeller—when fitted to airframe.
5 Complete aircraft—fully assembled, covered and rigged.

There is a high percentage of non-completions in the homebuilt aircraft world, especially when builders work just from plans, but also even with kitplanes. That CFM have got the cocktail correct with their Streak Shadow is demonstrated by the high completion rate for their kits. David Cook thinks it is at least 95 per cent!

An average builder should be able to complete a Streak Shadow kit in about 500 to 750 hours, although CFM do not like such figures to be quoted as each builder's aptitudes and motivations are different. One of the longer jobs is the preparation for painting and adding the skins to the fuselage 'pod', involving a great deal of stripping and rubbing down and taking in all about 40 to 50 hours. This can be reduced by careful removal of all excess smears of Araldite whilst it is still wet. It is also important to have a grease-free surface before any glueing takes place—even a fingerprint can damage the bond—so a treatment with acetone is advisable to degrease. Filling the leading edge of the wings and glueing the wing ribs in place may take as much as 20 hours, and all of these glueing and filling processes need to be done in a constant heat/humidity environment (21°C/70°F for 34 hours), so consideration should be given to workshop needs before embarking on the project.

Building your own plane has one objective, and that is to fly it upon completion. Sitting in the front seat of a Streak Shadow is a bit like sitting in a glider or helicopter with superb forward visibility, although if you are of exceptional proportions it may be a bit uncomfortable, particularly as regards the width. It is a conventional three-axis-control aircraft but with a side stick on the right-hand side that may take some getting used to. There are heel brakes on the rudder pedals which are extremely effective so that when you get used to them ground handling and taxiing are easy. The pull-start chord for the engine at the rear of the pilot's head is a bit awkward, although the Rotax starts easily and you soon discover the excellent power-to-weight ratio of the Streak Shadow and where part of its name comes from. To take off you hold the brakes on, apply full power, release the brakes, pull the stick back to lift the nosewheel off the ground and roll on the two rear mainwheels until the speed reaches about 60 mph (99 kmph); after a mere 300 feet (91 m) you will be off the ground maintaining 60 mph as the best climb speed and at a rate of 1,000 fpm (305 mpm), and this with two up.

David Cook frequently operates from the cricket pitch alongside his factory. Such operations are quite feasible, and because of the small fuselage side area they can carry on in quite strong cross-winds (25 knots at 90° is quoted as the limit by CFM). The controls feel quite heavy but this helps stability and you have to use some rudder to make positive, effective turns; the roll rate is good and it is an easy aircraft to stabilise in pitch.

At the 80 per cent cruise rate a speed of 100 mph (165 kmph) is possible, but throttle back to the economy 50 per cent cruise it is down to 75 mph (124 kmph). The never-exceed speed is 140 mph (231 kmph). It is impossible to spin the Streak Shadow and at the stall—about 30 to 35 mph (50 to 58 kmph)—there is no wing drop or instability either at full power or power off. There is no real need for flaps because of the excellent slow-speed

The Streak Shadow in flight.

handling, although they are fitted and are actuated by a lever behind and to the left of the pilot's head. Landing is easy and as soon as the nosewheel touches there is a negative angle of attack on the wing and the aircraft stays firmly put. With the application of the brakes, the landing roll is short and your local cricket pitch can really become your own airfield.

Renowned glider pilot Derek Piggott sums up the Streak Shadow: 'I can recommend the Streak if you you want to build your own aircraft and are not too wide across the bottom. It's a super fun machine with a very good performance and a worthy complement to the standard factory-built Shadow. Both types are easy and quick to rig and can live in their trailer at home instead of costly hangarage. They can be operated from almost any reasonably smooth field—even the Cook cricket pitch.'

Operating costs for the Streak Shadow are below £10 per hour including permit and insurance costs and a regular contribution to your Rotax replacement fund. You will need only a PPL 'D' licence to fly it solo or unsupervised with or without a passenger as it is in the microlight category, and once you have completed construction of your kit, CFM will carry out the flight testing for you at a cost of £100 prior to your application for a 'Permit to Fly'. (CFM will also do the stage inspections—you can even put your part-complete Streak Shadow on a trailer and take it to them!)

David Cook's creation is Britain's answer to the homebuilder's kitplane dream, totally professional and every bit as good as any American rival in its class. So for under £12,000 you too can build and fly the British CFM Streak Shadow kitplane.

CHAPTER 17

Homebuilt feats

'If you ask mountain climbers why they climb a mountain, the frequent reply is "Because it's there!" That's why we flew our Avid Flyer home-built and Mistral microlight to the North Pole.'

Hubert De Chevigny and Nicolas Hulot speaking on their return to France in 1987 after one of the most momentous flights undertaken in a homebuilt aeroplane.

THE OBJECTIVE OF most builders in building their own plane is also to fly it. There are exceptions—those who prefer the building process rather than the subsequent flying—but these are few. Having got through the traumas of the first flight and the flight testing, and having visited a few air rallies and fly-ins, one wonders what the homebuilder ultimately has in mind. Spreading his wings still further—or the contentment of just enjoying flying with the knowledge that his aircraft is almost part of him?

Such modest aspirations are commendable and normal. However, as in any sphere of life, there are those homebuilders who wish to stretch themselves and their machines to the limit. This 'stretching' is partly a personal thing but also, in the world of homebuilt aeroplanes, a way of proving their machine in the ultimate way. Depending on the aircraft type, the 'stretch' can take many forms. A flight from England to Italy in a TEAM MiniMax would be a major feat—indeed, such a flight in a QAC Quickie has been achieved, there and back in a day. Yet a flight to Italy by a Sequoia Falco might be regarded as perfectly normal, exactly the type of flight for which the aircraft was designed.

Across America

American George Bogardus (see Chapter 9 about the EAA) was one of the first post-war homebuilders and he also achieved a major aeronautical feat for the time, in 1947, by flying his homebuilt Little Gee Bee across the USA from Oregon to Washington DC.

Bogardus took over the editorship of a newsletter for amateur aviators in Oregon, which he called the *Triple 'A' Flyer*, from its previous editor Leslie LeRoy Long who had died. By 1946 the interest in homebuilding and amateur aviation had grown, particularly in Oregon—due to fewer restrictions there both pre and post-war compared to the rest of the USA—but also in other parts of the country, so Bogardus announced the re-organisation of the former Amateur Aircraft League under the new name of the American Airmen's Association in a re-named magazine/newletter *Popular Flying*.

The concern felt in Oregon, and expressed by members through the letters columns of the magazine, about the laws affecting the licensing and operation of homebuilts prompted Bogardus to drive from Oregon to Washington in April 1946 to meet CAA officials. He had some success and in October a letter was received from the CAA stating that in 1947 'X' Certificates for homebuilts would be issued for those homebuilt planes built before the war.

Bogardus started construction of his own homebuilt in the spring of 1947, a cocktail of bits from other aircraft but based mainly on a design by Tom Story, itself based on Long's Wimpy. In May 1947 the Little Gee Bee was granted an 'X' Certificate, and Bogardus and his companions amongst the AAA decided that it would be beneficial for him and their movement to fly the aircraft across the States to Washington DC to meet CAA officials in an attempt to improve the conditions under which homebuilders operated in the USA.

Bogardus took off from Beaverton airport, Oregon, on 11 August 1947. He followed the approximate route east that he had driven the previous

George Bogardus's Little Bee Gee homebuilt in which he flew from Oregon to Washington in 1947. It had a welded steel-tube fuselage, wooden wing structure, was fabric covered, and was powered by a 65 hp Lycoming 0-145. Below are early Oregon homebuilders' 'licence plate' and emblem. (Author's Collection)

year and stayed at AAA members' homes during the flight. He was soon landing at Brentwood airport, Long Island, to be met by Jack McRae, another AAA member, who on 25 August had taken off in his Cessna 140 in company with Bogardus in the Little Gee Bee for the final leg of the journey to Washington.

A successful meeting with both the CAA and the Civil Aeronautics Board (CAB) followed this epic flight, with the direct assurance from the former that a permanent category for homebuilts would be prepared and that in the meantime the 'X' Certificate would be granted to homebuilts and renewed every six months. Bogardus flew back west a pleased man and arrived in Oregon on 15 September. He and his homebuilt aeroplane had proved a point that was to form the foundation for all subsequent homebuilding activity in the USA.

Around the world

The performance and pedigree of John Thorpe's two-seater all-metal T.18 homebuilt design were established soon after the aircraft's maiden flight in May 1964 (see Chapter 12). At Hemet, California, Don Taylor built a Thorpe T.18, N455DT, which is now displayed in the EAA's Museum at Oshkosh, Wisconsin. But why should such a potentially active homebuilt be grounded in a museum? The answer is that it was the first homebuilt to be flown around the world. It was also the first to be flown to the North Pole (without landing), and serves as a fitting tribute to the power of and growing respect for homebuilt aeroplanes and of the courage and skill of builder and pilot Don Taylor.

It was in 1973 that Don Taylor and his Thorpe T.18 went into the record books, even though he gave up his first round-the-world attempt 4,000 miles short of his goal between Japan and the Aleutian Islands. He decided almost immediately that he would try again and, with the American Bicentennial looming, 1976 seemed a good goal to aim for. John Thorpe helped considerably in the re-design of the wing fuel tanks for the T.18, and provided a new cowling. Members of Taylor's local EAA chapters, Nos 92 and 448, helped raise finance for this re-build and later set the ball rolling with sponsorship for the flight. Mike Kensrue and his automatic welding equipment firm, MK Products, agreed to be a major sponsor, and Don Pridham joined the team of helpers. The start of the flight was scheduled for 1 August 1976 at that year's Oshkosh.

Now christened 'Victoria '76', the T.18 made it to Oshkosh for the scheduled start and, like clockwork, Don Taylor taxied out for take-off at 09.30 local time at the start of this epic flight; 5 minutes later the flight was under way. That first day saw 730 miles covered as Taylor landed at Burlington, Vermont, ready to clear customs before pressing on for Moncton, New Brunswick, Goose Bay, Labrador, and Sonderstrom, Greenland. The planned Greenland destination, Narssarssuag, was not available due to poor weather, so at 9,000 feet over the Greenland icecap, Taylor was a very relieved pilot when he found he was able to touch down at Sonderstrom, on the west coast, after 8 hours and 20 minutes in the air.

After a day's rest it was off on the 850-mile flight to Keflavik, Iceland. Taylor climbed to 15,000 feet in the T.18 to cross the Greenland icecap, and had to use his oxygen system. Then the next day it was Keflavik to Glasgow, followed by one of the shortest hops of the trip on the following day, 8 August, from Scotland to Leeds-Bradford (Yeadon) where the British part of sponsor MK Products have their factory.

Leeds to Venice, Italy, was the plan for the 9th, but after 700 miles and experiencing severe rain and ice conditions, Taylor decided to divert to Munich. He rested there for three days before flights on the 12th, 13th, 14th and 15th to Corfu, Greece, Larnaca, Cyprus, Diyarbakir, Turkey, and Tehran in Iran, where his problems started with officialdom and a damaged tailwheel. A day's break there to sort out the problems was followed by a flight across the Iranian desert to Zahedan in Iran, flying in severe turbulence, haze and on instruments for 500 of the 710 miles flown that day.

That break in Iran was to be Taylor's last for over a week. He flew from Zahadan to Karachi, Pakistan, on 18 August, from Karachi to Ahmadabad in India on the 19th, Ahamabad to Nagpur-Calcutta-Bangkok on the 20th, 21st and 22nd, then down the Malayan peninsula on a 770-mile, 5 hr 25 min flight to Kuala Lumpar on the 23rd, where he was able to get his laundry done by a fellow EAA member overnight!

Maintaining the momentum, and with clean clothing, Taylor pressed on on the 24th to Kuching in Malaysia, then on the 25th and 26th to Kota Kinabalu, Malaysia and Zamboanga and Davao in the Philippines, before the first part of the Pacific Ocean crossing.

Davao to Yap Island on the 27th was 900 miles and took 6 hours 38 minutes, Taylor's first experience on this trip of island hopping then, on arrival at Yap, of landing on a coral runway. On the 28th it was another 515 miles to Guam and the USAF base, which for three days was home-from-home for Taylor, and provided him with a much-needed rest before embarking on some of the longest legs of the flight.

On 1 September it was off from Guam to Truk, on the 2nd from Truk to Ponape, then on the 3rd the 7 hr 31 min, 1,030-mile flight to Wake Island; for a while he thought his ADF had failed until via his HF radio link to Guam he discovered that it was not him but the Eniwetok ADF itself which had broken down! A temporary repair was effected and Taylor had an ADF fix again. Wake picked him up from 400 miles away and he was there at the start of the flight's most troublesome sector.

He wanted to fly from Wake Island to Midway, but did not have permission to land at the Navy facility there. It was, however, the only practical routing, but in order to save embarrassment to the base commander at Wake, Taylor filed his flight plan from Wake to Honolulu but with every intention of

Don Taylor and his round-the-world T.18, now preserved in the EAA Museum at Oshkosh. (Don Downie)

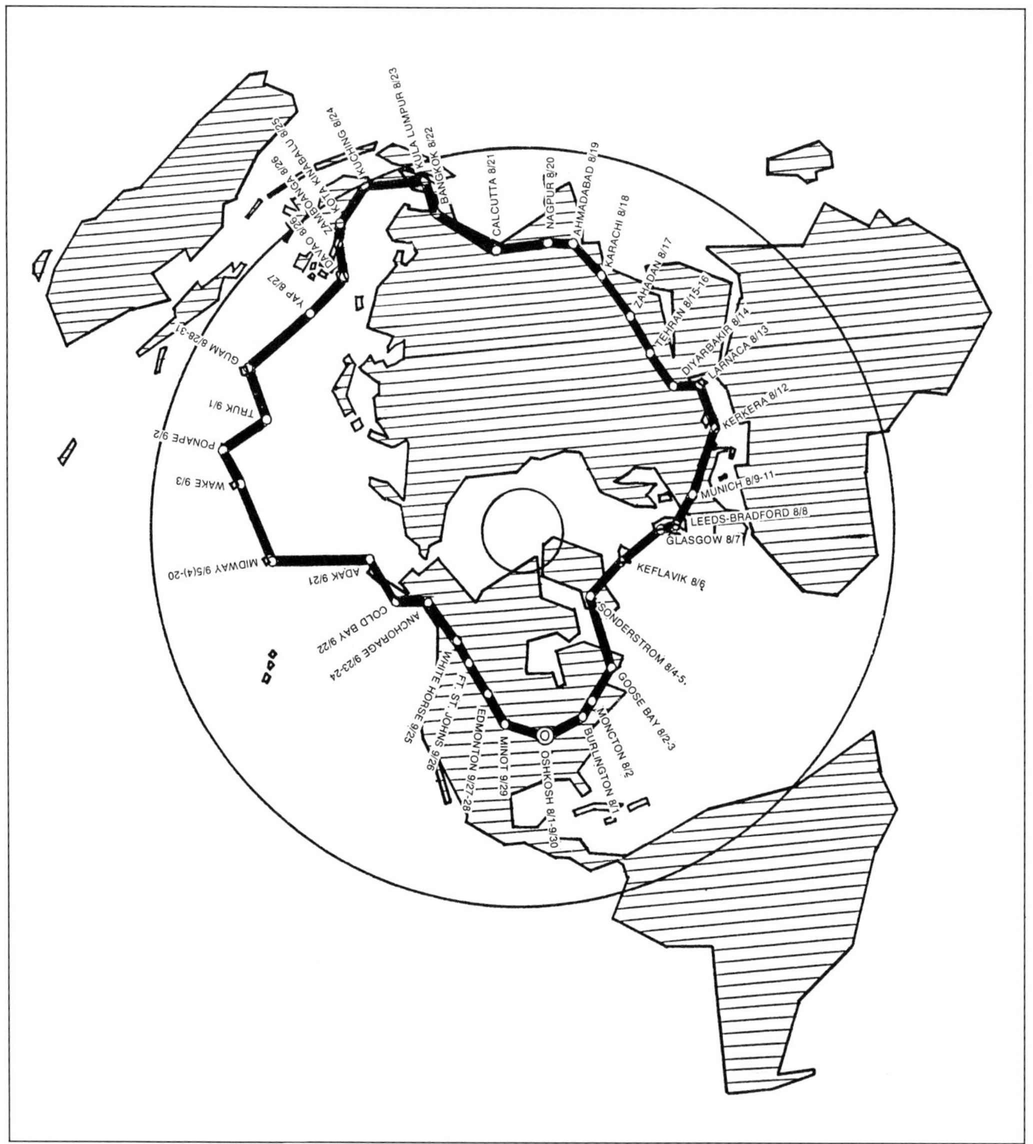

Don Taylor's round-the-world flight, 1 August–30 September 1976. (Map by Jack Cox)

getting permission to land at Midway. On 5 and 4 September, after 1,140 miles and nearly 9 hours flying across the International Date Line, he arrived above Midway, reported his position and was given landing instructions. This was the start of what Taylor later called 'the Second Battle of Midway', a 14-day hiatus that involved the higher echelons of power with the Joint Chiefs of Staff in Washington, the FAA and Congress!

As Taylor lost sight of Midway he began the 1,650-mile flight north to Adak in the Aleutian Islands, which was to be the emotional high point of the flight. This section between Japan and the Aleutians had been where he had given up his 1973 round-the-world attempt and he confessed to some apprehension: '. . . I did wonder—wonder if I would make it,' he confessed later. Thanks to some brilliant navigation in crosswinds varying from 10 to 50 knots, and with help from an RAF Vulcan crew and a Navy P-3 Neptune relaying accurate wind forecasts so that he could correct his track, when Taylor tuned in his ADF to see if he could pick up Adak it started homing in at once—and within 1° of the heading! With only half an hour's daylight left and after 11 hours of flying, Taylor landed the T.18 at Adak, just before the Aleutian fogs swirled in and closed down the airport. He felt fantastic. He had done it—he had beaten the Pacific and, whilst there was still some tricky flying ahead, it was 'all downhill' now.

On 22 September he left Adak for Cold Bay, Alaska, and then the next day on to Anchorage. A day's break, then on the 25th, 26th 27th and 28th he was getting near to home with flights from Anchorage to White Horse, Yukon, Fort St John, British Columbia, then Edmonton—then Edmonton again! He made a precautionary return there with a rough-running engine; this was the first mechanical problem with the engine on the whole flight. The cause was fouled plugs from the high lead content of the avgas he had been buying from the military on his Pacific crossing and with which his Lycoming engine could cope no longer.

The problem solved, Taylor flew back into the USA on 29 September and received the first of many cordial receptions that the following days and months would bring, at Minot, North Dakota. But the objective was Oshkosh, Wisconsin, so the next day, Thursday 30 September 1976, Taylor left Minot for the 690-mile flight east to Oshkosh. After a ceremonial low-level fly-by, Taylor and his Thorpe T.18 homebuilt touched down at Oshkosh at 1.48 pm amidst all the razmataz of EAA and media acclamation.

Over a period of 61 days, Don Taylor had flown almost 26,200 statute miles and broken four records in the National Aeronautics Association's category and class for piston engined aeroplanes between 1,102 and 2,204 lbs gross weight. His average speed was 168.6 mph for the trip, which took 171 hours of flying time.

Not content with this achievement, Taylor went on to fly his T.18 to the North Pole and back, as well as flights to Australia, New Zealand and the Bahamas, and back to California of course. His final tally with the T.18 was 29 world-class aviation records. When he donated 'Victoria '76' to the EAA Museum at Oshkosh he started building a second T.18 from, he claims, parts left over from the first project! And not content with that, in 1986 he started work on a composite Lancair 200 kitplane. A modest man who has come a long way since his pre-war commercial flying in Cubs and Porterfields and a 20-year military career as a fighter pilot that ended in 1962, Don Taylor proved what all homebuilders knew anyway, that their kind of aviation was as good, if not better, than any other.

Australia – Britain – Australia

Whilst Don Taylor was hitting the headlines in his Thorpe T.18, in 1976 another homebuilder was doing exactly the same thing in exactly the same type of homebuilt. Australian Clive Canning had set

Clive Canning sets off from Melbourne at the start of his flight to Britain in 1976. (Clive Canning Collection)

Clive Canning's Thorpe T.18 VH-CMC. (Clive Canning)

off from Moorabbin, Melbourne, Australia, on Saturday 12 June in his Thorpe T.18 VH-CMC to fly to Britain, with the intention of attending the PFA's annual international fly-in over the weekend of 2-4 July.

Canning had first learned to fly in 1958 and 1959 in Tiger Moths at the Royal Victorian Aero Club. He became interested in competition flying during the 1960s, and in 1967 purchased his first aircraft, a DHC-1 Chipmunk, and also qualified for a commercial licence, although with no intention of actually using it. He became interested in homebuilt aeroplanes after reading an American magazine and was soon a member of the Ultra Light Aircraft Association (ULAA, superceded by the SAAA—see Chapter 9) in Australia.

In April 1969 he started construction of his first homebuilt project, a Thorpe T.18, having looked for an aircraft with a high cruising speed without sacrificing range, one stable enough to practise instrument flying in, and one having possible aerobatic qualities as an additional bonus. With three years of intensive work behind him, Canning flew his T.18, VH-CMC, for the first time on 10 March 1972 at Latrobe Valley airfield, Victoria, and by 23 April had been issued with a full Certificate of Airworthiness by the Australian Department of Civil Aviation. VH-CMC was the 77th Thorpe T.18 to be completed and flown in the world. A week later Canning and his aircraft were awarded the Concours d'Elegance at the first ULAA National Fly-In at Latrobe Valley.

To cut his teeth on long-distance flying, later in 1972 Canning undertook a circumnavigation of Australia in his T.18, taking 52 hours to fly the 6,716 statute miles (11,081 km). By this time he had been elected Federal President of the ULAA and in this capacity attended international conferences of the FAI. At one of these he met David Faulkner-Bryant, Chairman of the PFA in Britain. The friendship struck between the two, and Canning's hankerings to emulate the early pioneers such as Hinkler and Sir Charles Kingsford Smith, helped the ideas about a flight from Australia to Britain to gel.

Working out data he realised that his T.18's fuel capacity would only give him a 780 nm range and that he also needed to increase the T.18's all-up weight. Consequently Thorpe repeated the exercise carried out for Don Taylor in the USA. The modifications were undertaken and detailed preparations for the trip made with the aim of departing from Australia 17 days before the PFA rally at Sywell. The last few days before ETD became a real strain as last-minute installations and preparations reached a frenzied pitch; all the approvals he required to cross or visit various countries had not arrived and with deteriorating winter weather in Australia and the need to fly VFR there, the pressures on Canning became immense.

Loaded with US dollars and every conceivable chart, Canning set off from Moorabbin as planned on 12 June in 'Charlie Mike Charlie', destination Great Britain. His itinerary took in Archerfield, Townville, Thursday Island, Timika, Ujung Pandang, Banjermasin, Pontianak, Singapore, Hatyai, Rangoon, Calcutta, Ahmadabad, Bandar Abbas, Bahrain, Homs (Syria) and Larnaca in almost 16 days of consecutive flying, apart from one day wasted waiting for Indonesian clearances at Thursday Island. Saturday 26 and Sunday 27 June were to prove the most traumatic days of Canning's flight, when the man-made terror of military jets attacking his home-built aeroplane far exceeded the worst frights experienced during flights through turbulent tropical weather. Syrian Air Force MiG.21s attacked Canning in 'CMC and he was forced to take the severest of diversionary action and land on a dirt track near the town of Homs to avoid them. Interrogation and overnight detention followed. Only Canning's signature on a letter of apology expedited his release, and whilst to apologise to his attackers was the last thing he wanted to do, he also wanted to get out of Syria and back in the air on his way to Britain.

Late afternoon on Sunday 27 June he was taken back to the Thorpe T.18 still sitting on the dirt strip and told to take off. Despite his protestations that his VOR was unserviceable, that he had no weather information and that he would be landing at Larnaca, Cyprus, in the dark, the Syrians were now very anxious to get rid of him. The 1 hr 20 min flight to Larnaca turned out to be almost uneventful, and the next day Canning took a well-earned rest and got 'CMC back into shape for his departure to Kerkyra, Corfu, on 29 June, then on to Marseilles on the 30th and finally to Shoreham-by-Sea, Sussex, on Thursday 1 July 1976. Later that day it was on to Redhill and to Canning's flight goal, arrived at Sywell, Northants, for the 1976 PFA International air rally.

One hundred hours of flying since leaving Melbourne saw Canning and his Thorpe T.18 at Sywell amongst 60 other foreign-registered aircraft arrivals at the rally, with a further attendance of 475 assorted British homebuilts and light aircraft (see Chapter 10). He was without doubt 'the star of the show'—nobody before or since had flown a homebuilt aeroplane so far to attend a PFA fly-in. But despite being so far from home, Canning was amongst many friends, part of the worldwide fraternity of homebuilding.

Three months to the day after arriving at Shoreham, Canning set off in his T.18 for the return flight to Australia. During those three months he travelled quiet extensively in Europe, flying 53 hours, visiting many places in Britain, but also flying to the RSA ralley at St Junien in France, and also to Holland.

His route back home followed the outbound one quite closely, but with one obvious difference—he steered well clear of Syria! Instead he routed to Crete, then to Cairo and down the Nile valley to Luxor and across the Red Sea to Saudi Arabia. However, Saudi Arabia was not much of an improvement on Syria because when Canning and 'CMC landed at Wejh, he was put under house arrest for three days. Only the efforts of an American Boeing 737 training captain, who was passing through Wejh and was interested to discover the owner of the little homebuilt on the apron, got things moving so that Canning was released—but he was still fined $500, allegedly for landing there without a clearance! But it was on to Bahrein and back on to his outbound route again through India and down to Thailand.

Back in Australia he routed from Darwin via Alice Springs, Leigh Creek and the headquarters of the Sport Aircraft Association of Australia (formerly the ULAA but which had changed its name while he had been away) at Mangalore before the last 60-mile hop to his home near Melbourne on 23 October 1976.

Powered by a trusty 150 hp Lycoming 0-320 E2A, Canning's Thorpe T.18 had taken 98 hr 35 min flying time to reach Britain and just over 96 hours for the return—average ground speeds were respectively 140.9 and 139 mph and fuel burn averaged 6.9 gph. Only once did he climb higher than 10,000 feet and that was to 11,500 feet over Egypt because of a large amount of military traffic at lower levels. He also picked up seven FAI world records in category C1B, the PFA awarded him their

Canning's SE.5 replica homebuilt—a total contrast to his T.18 and Rutan Defiant. (Clive Canning Collection)

Roderick Turner Memorial Award and, on his return to Australia, he received the highest accolade for aviation achievement, the Oswald Watt Gold Medal awarded by the Royal Federation of Aero Clubs of Australia. Previous recipients had been H.J.L. Hinkler in 1927, '28, '31 and '32, Charles Kingsford Smith in 1929, '30, '33 and '34, and Sir Reginald Ansett, the Australian airline pioneer, in 1975.

Canning's reaction to this? 'I was quite staggered really.' And a further summing up of the trip: 'While I do enjoy the satisfaction of having achieved a "first", is it not a little sad that a grandfather embarked on such an undertaking?' He was in his 50s when he made the flight.

Canning is still dedicated to the homebuilt aircraft cause in Australia in the 1990s. Since his flight to Britain and back he has built two more homebuilts, an SE.5A replica (VH-CIC) which won the 'Concours' prize at the SAAA's Mangalore '84 fly-in and, much more significant, a Rutan Defiant (VH-OOI) which was the 'Most Outstanding New Aircraft' at Mangalore in 1989 and also the first twin-engined homebuilt to be completed in Australia. Canning has also been at the forefront of the SAAA in their negotiations and dealings with the Australian aviation authorities over the licensing of homebuilt projects. He is the SAAA's Federal Technical Officer, supervising the system whereby SAAA Regional Inspectors are now authorised to carry out workshop and project stage inspections of homebuilt projects.

By kitplane to the North Pole

Don Taylor had done it before in his Thorpe T.18, becoming the first person to fly there in a homebuilt. But he had not actually landed there—in fact, few fixed-wing aircraft ever do land there because of its inhospitable terrain and climate. The place is the top of the world, the North Pole, and in 1987 two Frenchman flew there and landed, one of them in an amateur-built kitplane, an Avid Flyer, and the other in a commercially manufactured microlight, an Aviasud Mistral.

In its own way this flight in 1987 proved several things. It proved the determination and skill of the two pilots involved, Hubert de Chevigny and Nicolas Hulot, the integrity of the aircraft and engines which they flew, and finally the boundless possibilities of a modest homebuilt or kitplane.

All right, the aircraft they flew were specially modified and the trip attracted considerable sponsorship from the French postal service, *La Poste*. For Hubert de Chevigny, though, flying the Avid Flyer, it was his kitplane that would determine failure and success— and in the desolate and rigorous Arctic world in which they were flying, only success would be relevant.

Originally they had attempted the flight in 1986 in two French-designed microlights but had to abandon the attempt due to a crash and bad weather.

As with any flight, short or long, in temperate latitudes or at the Poles, preparation is the keyword to success. Even though the flight was to be in the late spring, the average temperatures were as low as −40° Celsius and this meant special preparations for both aircraft and pilots. The departure point was to be Resolute Bay on the Barrow Straits between Somerset Island and Devon Island in northern Canada at about 74° N. The flight was to cover 1,400 miles (2,300 km) with nearly 30 hours flying time over a period of 15 days; four nights would be spent camping on the ice, including one night actually at the North Pole.

Considerable amounts of equipment were needed, governed by the restrictions on payload of the aircraft; in particular they would have to carry sufficient fuel for the whole flight after departure from Resolute Bay, totalling 82½ gallons (375 litres), most of it in the specially modified belly pannier of the Avid Flyer, to feed the 65 hp Rotax 532 water-cooled engines with which both aircraft were equipped. Navigational equipment including a Global Positioning System (GPS) and HF radio; the batteries to power them and insulation of the aircraft were the main additional items. There was food for 16 days, tents, specially-designed clothing and what they thought might be essential, a rifle to defend themselves against polar bears, which in the end was never used.

The Light Aero Avid Flyer was chosen for its performance, its rugged construction and because it was a two-seater in the event of it having to operate as a rescue ship. Calculations during the Avid Flyer's construction showed that it had to carry an additional load of 141 lbs (64 kg), but because both seats might be required, additional fuel and payload could not be stowed alongside the pilot. The aircraft had to be fitted with wheel penetration skis to fly off snow or hard runways, and had to be able to operate safely in 80 mph (130 km) winds and crosswinds of up to 40 mph (66 kmph); modifications were required to the wings, undercarriage, fuselage, fuel tank, door, cabin heater, the special tear-drop-shaped blister beneath the fuselage and finally a ballistic parachute to comply with Canadian regulations. The North Pole Avid Flyer's gross weight topped out at 1,311 lbs (513 kg), and an empty weight of 500 lbs (227 kg)—the comparable statistics for a normal Avid Flyer are respectively 850 and 340 lbs (385 and 154 kg).

These special modifications to the basic Avid Flyer were designed and organised by Dean Wilson at Light Aero's factory. They were accomplished between January 1987 and the delivery of the

The specially modified Avid Flyer kitplane with the enlarged belly pannier for fuel and supplies for the historic flight to the North Pole. (Avid Aircraft Inc)

aircraft to Montreal, scheduled for 4 April.

Part of the flight's preparations involved detailed study of the weather patterns in the area of the flight. A 'window' during late April and early May was determined, so with delivery of their aircraft nearly three years of preparations completed, de Chevigny in the Avid Flyer and Hubot in the Mistral departed from Resolute Bay on 20 April. They arrived at the North Pole on 4 May, having camped seven times. All the way the relentless calculations of fuel used against distance travelled and fuel remaining continued—each aircraft was using about 3 gph (13.6 lph). A navigational error whilst their GPS system was inoperative nearly put paid to their success, they had to spend three days camped with no flying because they could not afford the fuel to fly into strong headwinds. When they did set out to fly, the ice-floe between their aircraft tie-down spot and the take-off strip started to crack!

They made it to the Pole with a mere ½ gallon (2 litres) of fuel left in the tank of each aircraft! A Canadian Twin Otter flew to retrieve the two intrepid adventurers and their aircraft. Asked later what they considered to be the hardest part of the flight, de Chevigny stated: 'It wasn't the weather or the temperatures but the continual necessity to be calculating'.

This was a team effort with a large back-up support group and the welcome addition of sponsorship. It therefore differs from Clive Canning's almost entirely solo effort in his Thorpe T.18 flight from Australia to Britain and back. Nonetheless, this French duo and their aircraft, particularly the Avid Flyer kitplane, notched up another world-

A historic shot of Hubert de Chevigny's homebuilt Avid Flyer in company with Nicholas Hubot's Mistral at the North Pole on 4 May 1987. (Avid Aircraft Inc)

beating feat for aviation and in particular homebuilt aeroplanes.

The ultimate aviation feat—by a homebuilt

As the Rutan Voyager slipped in to Edwards Air Force base in the cool of the morning on 23 December 1986 it was an emotional moment for many thousands of watchers around the world. Not least were the emotions of the two pilots on board Voyager, Dick Rutan and Jeana Yeager, who had piloted their remarkable 'homebuilt' Voyager for 9 days or 216 hours over a distance of 26,678 miles (44,000 km) to complete the first unrefuelled non-stop circumnavigation of the world by an aircraft.

That this final and ultimate feat in the world of aviation should be achieved by what was essentially a highly sophisticated yet fundamentally basic homebuilt aeroplane is a tribute to the level of achievement and esteem in which the world of homebuilt aviation now finds itself held. It is due also in no small way to the tenacity and skill of the two pilots on board, to the design work on the Voyager by Burt Rutan and, like the North Pole Avid Flyer but to a far greater extent, to the teamwork of hundreds of enthusiasts over many years.

The popular press picked up on the preparations for the round-the-world flight attempt early in 1982. At this time there were two 'rivals' at Mojave, California, the Rutans and, next door, Tom Jewett and his Quickie Aircraft Corporation with their 'Big Bird'. Apparently there was a race to be the first and Jewett was ahead. At least, he had the hardware in the form of his all-composite 'Big Bird' complete and flying—there was no race as far as Jewett and the Rutans were concerned. Unfortunately Jewett was later killed whilst test flying the 'Big Bird'—it then became a one-horse race, or at least a struggle against personal frustration, dwindling finances and the need to 'go for it'.

Much of the emotion around the world on that December Tuesday morning in 1986 as the live television coverage depicted the strange-looking aircraft winging its way to its historic and final landing was in the hearts of the world's homebuilt aircraft fraternity. Their sense of pride and admiration in the achievements of the new unofficial 'patron saints of homebuilt aeroplanes' was universal, and came from a deeper knowledge of the almost impossible and overwhelming problems and solutions achieved by the Rutans, Yeager and their team.

Voyager was the ultimate homebuilt aircraft experience; and it was without doubt a homebuilt aeroplane, as the word 'Experimental' stencilled on its fuselage side proclaimed. That this round-the-world achievement was accomplished by a homebuilt should never be forgotten. The era of the 'crank in his shed building an aeroplane' is over, the homebuilt and kitplane industry is now the spearhead of world light aviation, and the individual homebuilder's responsibility in this world should never be forgotten.

Tom Jewett's QAC 'Big Bird' at Mojave, California, in 1982 preparing for the attempt at a non-stop unrefuelled round-the-world flight. Jewett was later killed, leaving Rutan's Voyager as the only contender in the alleged 'race'. (Author)

Voyager roll-out at Mojave. (Don Downie)

Voyager taking off for the round-the-world flight. Note the nose-down attitude and wing-tips dragging. The photograph was taken at about the midpoint of the 11,000-foot runway at Edwards Air Force base, California. (Don Downie)

Voyager landing at Edwards after the round-the-world flight. (Don Downie)

Burt Rutan autographing photographs after the flight. (Don Downie)

Appendix 1

UK Civil Aviation Authority, Safety Regulation Group: Airworthiness Information Leaflet

SUBJECT TITLE Information and advice on the Procedures for the issue of a Permit to fly for amateur constructed aeroplanes.

NOTE: Guidance information applicable to Rotorcraft will be published in due course.

PURPOSE The purpose of this Leaflet is to advise those persons who are contemplating constructing an aeroplane from drawings or from a kit of parts. It covers procedures, conditions, and limitations associated with such an activity and also provides advice to kit manufacturers and importers of kits.

REFERENCE BCAR Chapter A3-7 and B3-7.

1 INTRODUCTION

1.1 Home built or amateur built aeroplanes whether they are designed and constructed by an individual, a group of individuals, or assembled from a bought out kit of parts, may be eligible for the issue of a Permit to Fly, issued by the CAA. Amateur built aeroplanes are not, however, eligible for the issue of a Certificate of Airworthiness as such a Certificate has international status and it guarantees standards of design and manufacture which can only be brought about by companies approved by the CAA for that purpose. Such an approval would not be approved or economically possible for an individual constructing an aircraft solely for his or her own recreation.

1.2 It is therefore necessary for the CAA to differentiate between kit aeroplanes and 'manufactured' aeroplanes, as clearly a kit can be supplied as anything from a collection of individual parts to an almost completed aeroplane, in an extreme case merely attaching the wings and empennage may be all that is necessary to complete the aeroplane. This latter case is undoubtedly a manufacturing activity and of course would need to be the subject of a full CAA certification investigation against internationally accepted design requirements, and the manufacturer of the 'kit' would need to have CAA approval. Such activity is not the subject of this AIL, but the dividing line between amateur construction and manufacturing has always been blurred. Some Authorities have adopted a rule which requires that the amateur constructor must have undertaken more than 51% of the total man hours needed to build the aeroplane. This has been apparently difficult to administer and does not allow amateur builders to 'finish' aeroplanes needing less than 51% of the man hours to complete! For these reasons more definitive rules are required.

2 RULES FOR THE AMATEUR CONSTRUCTION OF AEROPLANES There are pre-conditions to be met before a Permit to Fly may be issued for such an aeroplane. These are based on the amount of work needed to be performed by the amateur builder to complete the kit in accordance with the kit manufacturer's estimate of man hours required to assemble the kit.

The CAA may have need to comment on this estimate should the need arise.

The following categories apply:-

2.1 Aeroplanes built from plans or kits with a work content greater than 500 hours to complete.
Application is made through the Popular Flying Association (PFA) for a Permit to Fly, or directly to the CAA using form CA3.

2.2 Kit aeroplanes with work content less than 500 hours to assemble.

In this Category although the total hours to assemble an aeroplane from a kit must not be in excess of 500 hours, the amateur builder himself must have substantial involvement, i.e. in excess of 100 hours, in the assembly.

A complete kit assembled under these requirements must have been supplied from a CAA approved organisation and the design of the aeroplane substantiated against a suitable code of requirements by the approved organisation.

The approved organisation is responsible for monitoring the build standard as the assembly of the kit proceeds and is ultimately tasked with recommending to the CAA the issue of a Permit to Fly for each completed aeroplane.

Under this arrangement the PFA is not involved.

2.3 Aeroplane kits for which the amateur build time is not substantial, i.e. up to 100 hours approximately.

This situation is approaching that of an aeroplane manufacturer. Application for a Permit to Fly will not be accepted by the CAA or by the PFA. Kit vendors will be advised that the aeroplane must be type certificated against a suitable code of requirements by a CAA approved organisation.

3 THE ROLE OF THE PFA The PFA is a CAA approved organisation set up to monitor the design, build standard and quality of light aeroplanes which have been amateur built. It exists to allow a low cost route for amateur designers and builders to obtain a Permit to Fly for aeroplanes which are intended to be used for recreational purposes only.

Often a number of enthusiastic amateurs may get together to build more than one aeroplane of the same design for their own use. This position is quite acceptable, but the commissioned building of one or more aeroplanes by an individual for the owner would not be regarded as being in the spirit of the PFA remit because there would be commercial connotations associated with such activity.

4 THE ROLE OF THE PRIMARY COMPANY An approval may be granted in Group A1 to an organisation for the purpose of providing reports to the CAA in respect of manufacture and/or assembly and flight testing of kits and kit built aeroplanes in connection with the issue of a Permit to Fly.

The A1 primary company would be responsible for ensuring that:

(a) The design of the finished aeroplane complies with an acceptable code of requirements, i.e. Paper 98, JAR VLA, BCAR Section S, etc. Where it is not possible to show compliance a proposal of equivalent safety must be produced.

(b) The quality of each kit supplied meets an agreed standard.

(c) The finished amateur built aeroplane has been properly constructed and that the flight characteristics are satisfactory.

A recommendation from the primary company for the issue of a Permit to Fly for the amateur built aeroplane would be actioned by the CAA.

5 THE ROLE OF THE CAA AREA SURVEYOR When application is made directly to the CAA, the appointed CAA area surveyor will make recommendation for the issue of a Permit to Fly for a kit constructed aeroplane. Before he can do this he would need to be satisfied that the design, build and quality standards were acceptable and that it had satisfactory flying characteristics. This would involve specialist surveyors and the applicant would need to undertake to pay CAA charges.

6 DEMONSTRATION OF COMPLIANCE Whichever route is chosen by the amateur builder, demonstration of compliance with the appropriate requirements will be necessary.

This will involve in the main, depending on the type of construction, submission of calculations, performing structural tests and proof strength tests of each aeroplane in some cases, and flight test. The programme will be agreed by the investigating surveyor or PFA inspector for each project. Where an approved organisation is making the submissions in some cases a 'kit type approval' will be possible rendering 'series' proof tests unnecessary.

It is essential, before commencing the construction of an aeroplane that an application be made so that proper advice on required inspections, suitably of the facilities, etc. can be given to the amateur builder.

PFA Engineering, by Francis Donaldson, Chief Engineer, PFA

PFA HOMEBUILT AIRCRAFT DESIGNS

One of the objectives of the Popular Flying Association, is 'the encouragement of amateur design and construction of light and ultra-light aircraft'. PFA Engineering are often asked what the design requirements are for PFA homebuilt aircraft and what is involved in getting a new type of aircraft approved.

The design requirements and procedures have recently been formalised with the issue of the Terms of Approval of the PFA by the Civil Aviation Authority, and this attempts to describe the process.

Homebuilt aircraft which may be cleared for flight through the PFA must come within the following limitations:

Maximum take-off weight not to exceed 910 kg (2006 lbs)

Maximum stalling speed, power-off in the landing configuration not to exceed 60 mph EAS

Design dive speed not to exceed 250 mph EAS

Installed power not to exceed 180 BHP

It must be amateur-built, the work content on the part of the amateur builder being not less than 500 hours.

In some circumstances aircraft outside of these limits may be cleared through the PFA where individual permission is received from the CAA.

Once it has been determined that a design comes within the above limits, approval of the design is carried out by PFA Engineering by assessing the aircraft against the requirements of one of the following categories:

CATEGORY 1

An aircraft which can be shown to comply with the structural requirements of a CAA-approved published airworthiness code, e.g., BCAR Section K, FAR 23, BCAR 23, JAR VLA. This is the route applied to all new UK designs and, wherever possible, to overseas designs as well. This was the method used to clear such aircraft as the Isaacs Fury, Whittaker microlights and ARV Super 2. Whilst the requirements may initially look baffling, they do in fact provide an excellent step-by-step design guide.

While the aircraft is being built, the designer must submit to PFA Engineering a compliance checklist showing how the requirements are met, which will cross-refer to more detailed stress reports, proof load tests, material checks etc. which should be supplied. PFA Engineering will examine the drawings and verify the design submission, calling up modifications to the aircraft and additional analysis as deemed necessary, and all being well the prototype can then be cleared for flight test. A pilot familiar with the testing of such aircraft will be specified to carry out the initial flights and an evaluation of the performance and handling of the prototype. A development programme under the supervision of PFA Engineering is usually necessary to achieve the handling requirements of the design code. On satisfactory completion, the test pilot must submit a report to the PFA. The design is then recommended for the issue of an unrestricted Permit to Fly.

CATEGORY 2

An aircraft of a type which has been certificated by a recognised National Airworthiness Authority. This applies to the vintage production aircraft (e.g. D H Gipsy Moth, Aeronca Champs, Luscombe 8 series, etc) which are in some cases able to be cleared on PFA Permits to Fly. It also applies where a certified aircraft is also available in plan or kit form for amateur building, e.g. Pitts S1-S and Jodel D112. In this case PFA Engineering checks (by way of an examination by a PFA inspector) that the aircraft has been built to the same standard as the certificated design and that mandatory modifications and alterations have been complied with.

If an aircraft in this category is built or imported into the UK, and no previous example of that design has been approved by the CAA or evaluated by the PFA, then it will need to be flight tested under PFA supervision in much the same way as a prototype aircraft, to check that there are no hazardous performance or handling features. It is accepted that an aircraft of this type may not comply with the current UK flight requirements but it must be in line with standards in force at the time when the type was certificated.

CATEGORY 3

An aircraft of a design which has accumulated a considerable history of reliable and satisfactory experience. This category applies to a large number of homebuilt designs originating abroad, such as the Rand KR2 and Boredom Fighter, where the designer has not necessarily been able to supply detailed design and stressing information but the aircraft has nevertheless proved itself by satisfactory service over a number of years. Vintage military aircraft designs such as the Sopwith Pup and replica Fokker Triplane also fall into this category.

In this case PFA Engineering carries out an investigation into the service experience of the type by checking up on accident data, number of aircraft previously flown, airworthiness problems found in service etc., to check that there is sufficient evidence available on which to base a recommendation.

A simplified design survey of the aircraft is then carried out to ensure that no unduly hazardous or unusual features exist and to specify what minor modifications must be made in order to bring the aircraft into line with accepted UK practices. If major modifications are found to be needed, then the design is rejected.

The first UK example of the design is then flight tested under PFA Engineering supervision to check that the performance and handling is acceptable and in general agreement with the flight characteristics obtained previously overseas.

For all three categories of aircraft, once sufficient evidence has been obtained to recommend to the CAA that a Permit to Fly be issued, PFA Engineering write a report (an Airworthiness Approval Note) which describes the aircraft and its operating limitations and details the basis on which the design has been approved. This is submitted to the CAA along with the application for the initial Permit to Fly.

MODIFICATIONS TO HOMEBUILT AIRCRAFT DESIGNS

When a homebuilder wishes to build an aircraft which differs from previous UK examples of the type (or to modify an existing machine) this must always be authorised by PFA Engineering. In most cases, simple design changes can be processed by PFA Engineering and, following suitable testing, and Engineering Concession is issued which authorises the modification.

These points should be borne in mind in planning the details of your 'dreamship':

(a) The fact that the designer states on the drawing that a certain range of engines is acceptable, or that a retractable undercarriage may be fitted, does not automatically mean that this will be approved by the PFA. If this option has not been used before on a UK example, this will require a mini design approval programme of its own.

(b) For any significant home-brewed modifications which have not previously been tested overseas, the modification will have to be assessed against the current airworthiness requirements, even if the rest of the aircraft has been approved as a category 2 or 3 type. The argument that a modification can be approved on the basis that it is better than original, but still sub-standard by comparison with approved requirements, is occasionally applied. In general, however, the penalties in terms of weight and effort in fully complying with the requirements are only marginal and the aeroplane will be safer as a result. This approach also puts the PFA in a strong position should the approval of the modification ever have to be justified in a law court.

(c) If an aircraft type has been cleared in category 3, then the PFA may not possess detailed design calculations for the type, which means that carrying out apparently simple modifications may require an investigation into the whole structure to determine what are the reserve factors in the area to be altered and what will be the knock-on effects. Modification of these types must be treated with particular caution.

(d) When contemplating designing a modification, it is well worth getting in touch with PFA Engineering to find out whether a previous builder has already tried something similar, and hence avoid re-inventing something which may already have been developed. PFA Engineering do not in general advertise what optional modifications have been approved because, whilst we are satisfied that these are adequate as built, and may be just what the original builder wanted, we do not necessarily recommend that other people incorporate such changes or wish to imply that the modification makes for a better aeroplane.

Reproduced from *Popular Flying* by kind permission of the PFA

Appendix 2

US Department of Transportation, Federal Aviation Administration: Advisory Circular 'Certification and Operation of Amateur-Built Aircraft'

U.S. Department of Transportation
Federal Aviation Administration

Advisory Circular

Subject: CERTIFICATION AND OPERATION OF AMATEUR-BUILT AIRCRAFT

Date: 6/22/90
Initiated by: AIR-200

AC No: 20-27D
Change:

1. PURPOSE. This advisory circular (AC) provides guidance concerning the building, certification, and operation of amateur-built aircraft of all types; explains how much fabrication and assembly the builder must do for the aircraft to be eligible for amateur-built certification; and describes the Federal Aviation Administration (FAA) role in the certification process.

2. CANCELLATIONS. Advisory Circular 20-27C, Certification and Operation of Amateur-Built Aircraft, dated April 1, 1983, is cancelled.

3. BACKGROUND. The Federal Aviation Regulations (FAR) provide for the issuance of FAA Form 8130-7, Special Airworthiness Certificate, in the experimental category to permit the operation of amateur-built aircraft. Federal Aviation Regulations section 21.191(g) defines an amateur-built aircraft as an aircraft, the major portion of which has been fabricated and assembled by person(s) who undertook the construction project solely for their own education or recreation. Commercially produced components and parts which are normally purchased for use in aircraft may be used, including engines and engine accessories, propellers, tires, spring steel landing gear, main and tail rotor blades, rotor hubs, wheel and brake assemblies, forgings, castings, extrusions, and standard aircraft hardware such as pulleys, bellcranks, rod ends, bearings, bolts, rivets, etc.

4. DEFINITION. As used herein, the term "office" means the FAA Flight Standards District Office (FSDO), Manufacturing Inspection District Office (MIDO), or Manufacturing Inspection Satellite Office (MISO) that may perform the airworthiness inspection and certification of an amateur-built aircraft.

5. FAA INSPECTION CRITERIA.

a. The amateur-built program was designed to permit person(s) to build an aircraft solely for educational or recreational purposes. The FAA has always permitted amateur builders freedom to select their own designs. The FAA does not formally approve these designs since it is not practicable to develop design standards for the multitude of unique design configurations generated by kit manufacturers and amateur builders.

b. In the past, the FAA inspected amateur-built aircraft at several stages during construction. These inspections were commonly called precover inspections. The FAA also inspected the aircraft upon completion, before the initial issuance of the special airworthiness certificate, for the purpose of showing compliance with FAR section 91.42(b) (new FAR section 91.319), and again before issuance of the unlimited duration FAA Form 8130-7. After reassessing the need for these inspections, the FAA in 1983 decided to perform only one inspection prior to initial flight test.

NOTE: FAR Part 91 has been revised effective August 18, 1990. Both old and new FAR sections are referenced in this AC.

c. Since 1983, FAA inspections of amateur-built aircraft have been limited to ensuring the use of acceptable workmanship methods, techniques, practices, and issuing operating limitations necessary to protect persons and property not involved in this activity.

d. In recent years, amateur builders have adopted a practice whereby they call upon persons having expertise with aircraft construction techniques, such as the Experimental Aircraft Association (EAA) Technical Counselors (reference paragraph 6.(a)) to inspect particular components, e.g., wing assemblies, fuselages, etc., prior to covering, and to conduct other inspections, as necessary. This practice is an effective means of ensuring construction integrity.

e. The FAA has designated some private persons to act in its behalf in the inspection of amateur-built aircraft and the issuance of airworthiness certificates. These persons are known as Designated Airworthiness Representatives (DAR) and are authorized to charge for their services. These charges are set by the DAR and are not governed by the FAA. The amateur-builder may contact the local FAA office to locate a DAR.

f. In view of the foregoing considerations, the FAA has concluded that safety objectives, relative to the amateur-built program, can continue to be met by the use of the following criteria:

(1) Amateur builders should have knowledgeable persons (i.e., FAA certificated mechanics, EAA Technical Counselors, etc.) perform precover inspections and other inspections as appropriate. In addition, builders should document the construction using photographs taken at appropriate times prior to covering. The photographs should clearly show methods of construction and quality of workmanship. Such photographic records should be included with the builder's log or other construction records.

(2) The FAA inspector or DAR will conduct an inspection of the aircraft prior to the issuance of the initial FAA Form 8130-7 to enable the applicant to show compliance with FAR section 91.42(b) (new FAR section 91.319). This inspection will include a review of the information required by FAR section 21.193, the aircraft builder's logbook, and an examination of the completed aircraft to ensure that proper workmanship has been used in the construction of the aircraft. Also, the appropriate operating limitations will be prescribed at this time in accordance with FAR section 91.42 (new FAR section 91.319).

(3) An FAA inspector or DAR may elect to issue amateur-built airworthiness certificates on a one-time basis to the builder for showing compliance with FAR section 91.42(b) (new FAR section 91.319) and continued operation under FAR section 21.191(g). Under this procedure, the aircraft will be inspected by the FAA only once prior to flight testing. The airworthiness certificate will be issued, but its validity will be subject to compliance with the operating limitations. The limitations will provide for operation in an assigned flight test area for a certain number of hours before the second part of the limitations becomes effective, releasing the aircraft from the test area.

6. DESIGN AND CONSTRUCTION.

a. Many individuals who desire to build their own aircraft have little or no experience with respect to aeronautical practices, workmanship or design. An excellent source for advice in such matters is the EAA located in Oshkosh, Wisconsin. (See appendix 1.) The EAA is an organization established for the purpose of promoting amateur aircraft building and giving technical advice and assistance to its members. The EAA has implemented a Technical Counselors Program whose aim is to ensure the safety and dependability of amateur-built aircraft. Most EAA Technical Counselors are willing to inspect amateur-built aircraft projects and offer constructive advice regarding workmanship and/or design.

b. Any choice of engines, propellers, wheels, other components, and any choice of materials may be used in the construction of amateur-built aircraft. However, it is strongly recommended that FAA-approved components and established aircraft quality material be used, especially in fabricating parts constituting the primary structure, such as wing spars, critical attachment fittings, and fuselage structural members. Inferior materials, whose identity cannot be established, should not be used. The use of major sections (i.e., wings, fuselage, empennage, etc.) from type certificated aircraft may be used in the construction as long as the sections are in a condition for safe operation. These sections are to be considered by the FAA inspector or DAR in determining the major portion in FAR section 21.191(g), but no credit for fabrication and assembly would be given the builder for these sections. It is recommended that builders contact their local FAA office to coordinate the use of such sections.

c. The design of the cockpit or cabin of the aircraft should avoid, or provide for padding on, sharp corners or edges, protrusions, knobs and similar objects which may cause injury to the pilot or passengers in the event of an accident. It is strongly recommended that Technical Standard Order (TSO) approved or equivalent seat belts be installed along with approved shoulder harnesses.

d. An engine installation should ensure that adequate fuel is supplied to the engine in all anticipated flight attitudes. Also, a suitable means, consistent with the size and complexity of the aircraft, should be provided to reduce fire hazard wherever possible, including a fireproof firewall between the engine compartment and the cabin. When applicable, a carburetor heat system should also be provided to minimize the possibility of carburetor icing.

e. Additional information and guidance concerning acceptable fabrication and assembly are provided in AC 43.13-1A, Acceptable Methods, Techniques, and Practices - Aircraft Inspection and Repair, and AC 43.13-2A, Acceptable Methods, Techniques, and Practices - Aircraft Alterations. These publications are available from the U.S. Government Printing Office.

f. The builder should obtain the services of a qualified aeronautical engineer or consult with the designer of purchased plans or construction kits, as appropriate, to discuss the proposal if the aircraft design is modified during construction.

7. CONSTRUCTION KITS.

a. Construction kits containing raw materials and some prefabricated components may be used in building an amateur-built aircraft. However, aircraft which are assembled entirely from kits composed of completely finished prefabricated components, parts and precut and predrilled materials are not considered to be eligible for certification as amateur-built aircraft since the major portion of the aircraft would not have been fabricated and assembled by the builder.

b. An aircraft built from a kit may be eligible for amateur-built certification, provided the major portion has been fabricated and assembled by the amateur builder. Kit owner(s) may jeopardize eligibility for amateur-built certification under FAR section 21.191(g) if they allow someone else to build the aircraft. The major portion of such kits may consist of raw stock such as lengths of wood, tubing, extrusions, etc., which may have been cut to an approximate length. A certain quantity of prefabricated parts such as heat treated ribs, bulkheads or complex parts made from sheet metal, fiber glass, or polystyrene would also be acceptable, provided the kit still meets the major portion of the fabrication and assembly requirement, and the amateur builder satisfies the FAA inspector or DAR that completion of the aircraft kit is not merely an assembly operation.

CAUTION: Purchasers of partially completed kits should obtain all fabrication and assembly records from the previous owner(s). This may enable the builder who completes the aircraft to be eligible for amateur-built certification.

c. Various material/part kits for the construction of aircraft are available nationally for use by aircraft builders. Advertisements tend to be somewhat vague and may be misleading as to whether a kit is eligible for amateur-built certification. It is not advisable to order a kit before verifying with the local FAA office if the aircraft, upon completion, may be eligible for certification as amateur-built under existing rules and established policy.

d. It should be noted the FAA does not certify aircraft kits or approve kit manufacturers. However, the FAA does perform evaluations of kits which have potential for national sales interest, but only for the purpose of determining if an aircraft built from the kits will meet the major portion criteria. A list of these kits is maintained at the local FAA office for information to prospective builders.

8. REGISTRATION AND MARKING INFORMATION. Federal Aviation Regulations section 21.173 requires that all U.S. civil aircraft be registered before an airworthiness certificate can be issued. Federal Aviation Regulations Part 47, Aircraft Registration, prescribes the requirements for registering civil aircraft. The basic procedures are as follows:

a. A builder wishing to register an aircraft must first obtain a registration number assignment (N-number) from the FAA Aircraft Registry. (See appendix 1 for the address of the Aircraft Registry.) This number will eventually be displayed on the aircraft. It is not necessary to obtain a registration number in the early stages of the project. Builders intending to obtain a special number of their choice must submit a letter (see appendix 2) listing up to 5 possible registration numbers desired. Under FAR Part 47, a special registration number will cost $10 and may be reserved for no longer than 1 year. Renewal is necessary each year with an additional $10 fee. If a special number is being requested along with registration, an additional $5 fee is required. Although this reservation does not apply to numbers assigned at random by the Aircraft Registry, it is recommended that application for registration number assignment in either case be made 60 to 90 days prior to completion of construction.

b. To apply for either a random or special registration number assignment, the owner of an amateur-built aircraft must provide information required by the Aircraft Registry by properly completing an Aeronautical Center (AC) Form 8050-88, Affidavit of Ownership for Amateur-Built Aircraft (see appendix 3). The affidavit establishes the ownership of the aircraft; therefore, all aircraft information must be given. If the aircraft is built from an eligible kit, the builder should also submit a signed bill of sale from the manufacturer of the kit as evidence of ownership. If AC Form 8050-2, Aircraft Bill of Sale, is used, the word "aircraft" should be deleted and the word "kit" inserted in its place. (See appendix 4.)

c. After receipt of the applicant's letter requesting a special or random number assignment, the Aircraft Registry will send a form letter to the applicant giving the number assigned (this does not constitute registration of the aircraft), a blank AC Form 8050-1, Aircraft Registration Application, and other registration information. All instructions must be carefully followed to prevent return of the application and delay in the registration process.

d. The applicant must complete and return the white original and green copy of the Aircraft Registration Application (with N-number) to the Aircraft Registry as soon as possible, accompanied with a fee of $5 by check or money order payable to the FAA (see appendix 5). The pink copy of the application is to be retained by the applicant and carried in the aircraft as temporary authority to operate without registration for a maximum of 90 days or until receipt of AC Form 8050-3, Certificate of Aircraft Registration. If AC Form 8050-3 is not received in the 90-day period, the builder must obtain written authority from the Aircraft Registry for continued operation. However, if the recommendations in paragraph 8.a through 8.d above are followed, the applicant should have received AC Form 8050-3 before the airworthiness inspection.

9. IDENTIFICATION AND REGISTRATION MARKS. When applying for an airworthiness certificate for an amateur-built aircraft, the builder must show in accordance with FAR section 21.182 that the aircraft displays the nationality and registration markings required by FAR Part 45. The following is a summary of the FAR Part 45 requirements:

a. The aircraft must be identified by means of a fireproof identification plate that is etched, stamped, engraved, or marked by some other approved fireproof marking as required by FAR section 45.11. The identification plate must include the information required by FAR section 45.13.

b. The identification plate must be secured in such a manner that it will not likely be defaced or removed during normal service, or lost or destroyed in an accident. Aircraft built and certificated after March 7, 1988, must have the identification plate located on the exterior either adjacent to and aft of the rear-most entrance door or on the fuselage near the tail surfaces and must be legible to a person standing on the ground (reference FAR section 45.11.)

c. The name on the identification plate must be that of the amateur builder, not the designer, plans producer, or kit manufacturer. The serial number can be whatever the builder wishes to assign, provided it is not the same as other aircraft serial numbers.

d. The builder should refer to FAR sections 45.22 and 45.25, which define specific requirements for the location of registration marks on fixed-wing aircraft. The location of registration marks for non-fixed wing aircraft are specified in FAR section 45.27. These registration marks must be painted on or affixed by any means insuring a similar degree of permanence. Decals are also acceptable. The use of tape which can be peeled off, or water soluble paint, such as poster paint, is not considered acceptable.

e. Most amateur-built aircraft are required to display nationality and registration marks with a minimum height of 3 inches. However, if the maximum cruising speed of the aircraft exceeds 180 knots calibrated air speed (207 miles per hour), the registration marks must be at least 12 inches high. The builder should refer to FAR section 45.29, which defines the minimum size and proportions for nationality and registration marks on all types of aircraft.

f. The registration marks displayed on the aircraft must consist of the Roman capital letter "N" (denoting United States nationality) followed by the registration number of the aircraft. (Registration marks may not exceed five symbols following the prefix letter "N".) These symbols may be all numbers (e.g., N-10000); one to four numbers and one suffix letter (e.g., N-1000A); or one to three numbers and two suffix letters (e.g., N-100AB). Any suffix letter used in the marks must also be a Roman capital letter. The letters "I" and "O" may not be used. The first zero in a number must always be preceded by at least one of the numbers 1 through 9. In addition, the word "experimental" must also be displayed on the aircraft near each entrance (interior or exterior) to the cabin or cockpit in letters not less than 2 inches nor more than 6 inches in height.

g. If the configuration of the aircraft prevents marking in compliance with any of the above requirements, the builder should contact an FAA office regarding approval of a different marking procedure under FAR section 45.22(d). It is strongly recommended that any questions regarding registration marking be discussed and resolved with a local FAA inspector or DAR before the marks are affixed to the aircraft.

10. CERTIFICATION STEPS. The following procedures are in the general order to be followed in the certification process:

a. Initial Step. The prospective builder should contact the nearest FAA office to discuss the plans for building the aircraft with an FAA inspector. During this contact, the type of aircraft, its complexity and/or materials should be discussed. The FAA may provide the prospective builder with any guidance necessary to ensure a thorough understanding of applicable regulations.

b. Registration. Detailed procedures are in paragraph 8 of this AC. This must be done before submitting an FAA Form 8130-6, Application for Airworthiness Certificate, under FAR section 21.173 to an FAA inspector or DAR.

c. Marking. The registration number (N-number) assigned to the aircraft and an identification plate must be affixed in accordance with FAR section 21.182 and Part 45, Identification and Registration Marking. Detailed procedures are in paragraphs 8 and 9 of this AC.

d. Application. The builder may apply for a special airworthiness certificate by submitting the following documents and data to the nearest FAA office or to the DAR.

(1) Federal Aviation Administration Form 8130-6 (see appendix 6).

(2) Enough data, such as photographs or three-view drawings, to identify the aircraft.

(3) A notarized FAA Form 8130-12, Eligibility Statement - Amateur-Built Aircraft, certifying the major portion was fabricated and assembled for education or recreation, and that evidence is available to support this statement. Evidence will be provided to the FAA Inspector or DAR upon request. (See appendix 7.)

(4) A letter identifying the aircraft and the area over which the aircraft will be tested should accompany the application. (See appendix 8.)

11. AIRCRAFT INSPECTION. The applicant should be prepared to furnish the following to the FAA inspector or DAR:

a. An aircraft complete and ready to fly except for cowlings, fairings, and panels opened for inspection.

b. An Aircraft Registration Certificate, AC Form 8050-3, or the pink copy of Aircraft Registration Application, AC Form 8050-1 (with N-number).

c. Evidence of inspections, such as logbook entries signed by the amateur builder, describing all inspections conducted during construction of the aircraft in addition to photographic documentation of construction details. This will substantiate that the construction has been accomplished in accordance with acceptable workmanship methods, techniques, and practices. It is recommended that this evidence be documented in some form (e.g., the Service and Maintenance Manual available from the EAA).

d. A logbook for the aircraft, engine, and propeller to allow for review of service records and recording of inspection and certification by the FAA inspector or DAR.

12. FAA INSPECTION AND ISSUANCE OF AIRWORTHINESS CERTIFICATE.

a. After inspection of the documents and data submitted with the application, the applicant should expect the FAA inspector or DAR to inspect the aircraft. Upon a determination that the aircraft has been properly constructed, the FAA inspector or DAR may issue an FAA Form 8130-7, together with appropriate operating limitations. The applicant should expect the FAA inspector or DAR to verify that all required markings are properly applied, including the following placard which must be displayed in the cabin or the cockpit at a location in full view of all passengers. (Placard not applicable to single-place aircraft.)

"PASSENGER WARNING - THIS AIRCRAFT IS AMATEUR-BUILT AND DOES NOT COMPLY WITH FEDERAL SAFETY REGULATIONS FOR STANDARD AIRCRAFT"

b. Details concerning flight test areas are contained in paragraph 13. The operating limitations are a part of the airworthiness certificate and must be displayed with the certificate when the aircraft is operated. It is the responsibility of the pilot to conduct all flights in accordance with the operating limitations, as well as the General Operating and Flight Rules in FAR Part 91.

c. In the case of a limited duration airworthiness certificate, upon satisfactory completion of operations in accordance with FAR section 91.42(b) (new FAR section 91.319), in the assigned test area, the owner of the aircraft may apply to the local FAA office or a DAR for amended operating limitations by submitting another FAA Form 8130-6, along with a letter requesting amendment of operating limitations. Prior to issuance of the amended limitations and a new FAA Form 8130-7, the applicant should expect the FAA inspector or DAR to review the flight log to determine whether corrective actions have been taken on any problems encountered during the testing and that the aircraft's condition for safe operation has been established. Reinspection of the aircraft may be necessary.

d. Refer to paragraph 13d.(1) and (2) for the processing of unlimited duration airworthiness certificates.

13. FLIGHT TEST AREAS.

a. Amateur-built airplanes and rotorcraft will initially be limited to operation within an assigned flight test area for at least 25 hours when a type certificated (FAA-approved) engine/propeller combination is installed, or 40 hours when a noncertificated (i.e., modified type certificated or automobile) engine/propeller combination is installed. Amateur-built gliders, balloons, dirigibles and ultralight vehicles built from kits evaluated by the FAA and found eligible to meet requirements of FAR section 21.191(g), for which original airworthiness certification is sought, will be limited to operation within an assigned flight test area for at least 10 hours of satisfactory operation, including at least five takeoffs and landings.

b. The desired flight test area should be requested by the applicant and, if found acceptable by the FAA inspector or DAR, will be approved and specified in the operating limitations. It will usually encompass the area within a 25-statute mile radius (or larger depending on the type of aircraft) from the aircraft's base of operation or in a designated test area established by the local FAA office. The area selected by the applicant and submitted to the FAA for approval should not be over densely populated areas or in congested airways, so that the flight testing, during which passengers may not be carried, would not likely impose any hazard to persons or property on the ground. Advisory Circular 90-89, Amateur-Built Aircraft Flight Testing Handbook, contains recommended procedures for the flight testing of amateur-built aircraft. It is strongly recommended that amateur builders obtain a copy of this AC and follow its guidance.

c. The carrying of passengers will not be permitted while the aircraft is restricted to the flight test area. It is suggested that a tape recorder, for example, be used by the pilot for recording readings, etc. Flight instruction will not be allowed in the aircraft while in the flight test area.

d. In those instances where the unlimited duration special airworthiness certificate was issued, the operating limitations may be prescribed in two phases in the same document as follows:

(1) For the Phase I limitations, the applicant will receive from the certificating FAA inspector or DAR all those operating limitations, as appropriate, for the applicant to demonstrate compliance with FAR section 91.42(b) (new FAR section 91.319) in the assigned test area. This would further include a limitation requiring the owner/operator to endorse the aircraft logbook with a statement certifying when the aircraft has been shown to comply with FAR section 91.42(b) (new FAR section 91.319). The owner/operator may then operate in accordance with Phase II.

(2) For the Phase II limitations, the applicant will receive from the certificating FAA inspector or DAR all those operating limitations, as appropriate, to the issuance of an unlimited duration FAA Form 8130-7 for the operation of an amateur-built aircraft. Appendix 9 contains a sample of typical operating limitations that may be issued. For special conditions, these may vary for each aircraft.

14. SAFETY PRECAUTION RECOMMENDATIONS.

a. All Aircraft.

(1) The pilot should become thoroughly familiar with the brake tests, engine operation, and ground handling characteristics of the aircraft by conducting taxi tests before attempting flight operations. Liftoff is not permitted during taxi tests without an airworthiness certificate.

(2) Before the first flight of an amateur-built aircraft, the pilot should take precautions to ensure that emergency equipment and personnel are readily available in the event of an accident.

(3) Violent or acrobatic maneuvers should not be attempted until sufficient flight experience has been gained to establish that the aircraft is satisfactorily controllable throughout its normal range of speeds and maneuvers. Those maneuvers successfully demonstrated while in the test area may continue to be permitted by the FAA when the operating limitations are modified to eliminate the test area. All maneuvers satisfactorily conducted are to be documented in the aircraft logbook by the pilot.

(4) The operating limitations issued by the FAA inspector or DAR will require the aircraft to be operated in accordance with applicable air traffic control and general operating rules of FAR Part 91 as they apply to amateur-built aircraft. Those operators who plan to operate under Instrument Flight Rules are alerted to the specific requirements under FAR sections 91.115 through 91.129 (new FAR section 91.173 through 91.187).

(5) Depending on the intended operation under FAR Part 91, the following FAR sections may be applicable:

a. FAR Section 91.33(b) (new FAR section 91.205) Visual Flight Rules (day).

b. FAR Section 91.33(c) (new FAR section 91.205) Visual Flight Rules (night).

c. FAR section 91.33(d) (new FAR section 91.205) Instrument Flight Rules.

(6) Unless authorization to deviate is obtained from Air Traffic Control, any aircraft that will be equipped with a Mode C transponder shall have a calibrated airspeed/static pressure system to prevent an error in altitude reporting. (Reference FAR section 23.1323 and 23.1325.) The Mode C transponder must be tested and inspected per FAR section 91.172 (new FAR section 91.413).

(7) An emergency locator transmitter is required to be on board by FAR section 91.52 (new FAR section 91.207) upon release from the flight test area. Single-place aircraft are exempt from this requirement in accordance with FAR section 91.52(f)(9) (new FAR section 91.207).

b. Rotorcraft. The appropriately rated rotorcraft pilot should be aware of the following operating characteristics:

(1) Operators of rotorcraft having fully articulated rotor systems should be particularly cautious of "ground resonance." This condition of rotor unbalance, if maintained or allowed to progress, can be extremely dangerous and usually results in structural failure.

(2) Tests showing that stability, vibration, and balance are satisfactory should normally be completed with the rotorcraft tied down, before beginning hover or horizontal flight operations.

15. AMATEUR-BUILT AIRCRAFT CONSTRUCTED OUTSIDE THE UNITED STATES AND PURCHASED BY U.S. CITIZENS.

a. When a U.S. citizen purchases such aircraft, acceptable procedures for obtaining airworthiness certification for amateur-built operations are as follows:

(1) The previous owner should have conducted or had a condition/annual type inspection performed on the aircraft within 30 days of the new U.S. owner applying for certification. This inspection shall be recorded in the aircraft records.

(2) The previous owner should obtain documentation from their Civil Aviation Authority that verifies the aircraft is/was originally certificated in that country as an amateur-built, and that the aircraft meets the requirements of FAR section 21.191(g). This documentation should be furnished to the new owner.

b. The new owner of such aircraft shall present the FAA inspector or DAR with a properly completed FAA Form 8130-6, along with the following documentation:

(1) All letters and records of inspections called for in paragraph 15.a. (1) and (2).

(2) Proper documentation of registration in accordance with FAR section 47.

(3) A letter of request to accompany the FAA Form 8130-6.

c. The applicant should expect the FAA inspector or DAR to:

(1) Conduct a thorough review of all documentation called for under paragraphs 15 a and b.

(2) Determine the amateur-built eligibility of the aircraft presented.

(3) Inspect the aircraft like any other amateur-built aircraft, since these airworthiness certifications are considered original.

(4) If the aircraft is found to be eligible and inspection is satisfactory, issue the FAA Form 8130-7 with proper operating limitations. If the required flight time has not been met or there is some question regarding the aircraft's flight capability, the certificating representative may require flight testing.

(5) Advise that the condition inspection on the aircraft can only be performed by the original builder.

16. REPAIRMAN CERTIFICATION. The aircraft builder may be certificated as a repairman if the builder is the primary builder of the aircraft and can satisfactorily prove requisite skill in determining whether the aircraft is in condition for safe operation. This certification can be obtained by making application to the local FAA office after the satisfactory completion of required flight hours in the test area. Each certificate is issued for a particular aircraft. (See appendix 10.)

17. REFERENCE MATERIAL.

a. AC Forms. These forms may be obtained through the local District Office.

AC Form 8050-1, Aircraft Registration Application.

AC Form 8050-2, Aircraft Bill of Sale.

AC Form 8050-88, Affidavit of Ownership for Amateur-Built Aircraft.

FAA Form 8130-6, Application for Airworthiness Certificate.

FAA Form 8130-12, Eligibility Statement - Amateur-Built Aircraft.

FAA Form 8610-2, Airman Certificate and/or Rating Application.

b. Federal Aviation Regulations.

Part 21, Certification Procedures for Products and Parts.

Part 45, Identification and Registration Marking.

Part 47, Aircraft Registration.

Part 65, Certification: Airmen Other Than Flight Crewmembers.

Part 91, General Operating and Flight Rules.

Part 101, Moored Balloons, Kites, Unmanned Rockets and Unmanned Free Balloons.

Part 103, Ultralight Vehicles.

c. Advisory Circulars.

AC 20-126A, Aircraft Certification Service Field Office Directory.

AC 43.13-1A, Acceptable Methods, Techniques, and Practices - Aircraft Inspection and Repair.

AC 43.13-2A, Acceptable Methods, Techniques, and Practices - Aircraft Alterations.

AC 43-16, General Aviation Airworthiness Alerts.

AC 65-23A, Certification of Repairmen (Experimental Aircraft Builders).

AC 91-23A, Pilot's Weight and Balance Handbook.

AC 183-33A, Designated Airworthiness Representatives.

AC 183-35B, FAA Designated Airworthiness Representatives (DAR), Designated Alteration Stations (DAS), and Delegation Option Authority (DOA) Directory.

18. HOW TO GET PUBLICATIONS. The FAR and those AC's for which a fee is charged may be obtained from the Superintendent of Documents, U.S. Government Printing Office, Washington, DC 20402. A listing of FAR and current prices is in AC 00-44, Status of Federal Aviation Regulations, and a listing of all AC's is in AC 00-2, Advisory Circular Checklist.

19. PUBLICATIONS:

a. To request free advisory circulars, contact:

U.S. Department of Transportation
Utilization and Storage Section, M443.2
Washington, DC 20590

b. To be placed on FAA's mailing list for free AC's contact:

U.S. Department of Transportation
Distribution Requirements
Section, M-494.1
Washington, DC 20590

M.C. Beard
Director, Aircraft Certification Service

APPENDIX 1. ADDRESSES

EXPERIMENTAL AIRCRAFT ASSOCIATION, INC. (Telephone, (414) 426-4800); Mail to P.O. Box 3086, Wittman Air Field, Oshkosh, Wisconsin 54903-3086; Street address: 3000 Poberezny Road, Oshkosh, Wisconsin 54903-3086.

FEDERAL AVIATION ADMINISTRATION, AIRCRAFT REGISTRY. (Telephone, (405) 680-3116); Mail to Airman and Aircraft Registry Division, Mike Monroney Aeronautical Center, P.O. Box 25504, Oklahoma City, Oklahoma 73125; Street Address: 6500 South MacArthur Boulevard, Oklahoma City, Oklahoma 73169.

APPENDIX 2. SAMPLE LETTER FOR REQUESTING AN AIRCRAFT REGISTRATION NUMBER IN ACCORDANCE WITH FAR SECTION 47.15

xx-xx-xx
Date

FAA Aeronautical Center
FAA Aircraft Registry
P. O. Box 25504
Oklahoma City, Oklahoma 73125

Gentlemen:

This is a request for a United States identification number assignment for my home-built aircraft.

Aircraft description:

Make RIGHTWAY; Type (airplane, rotorcraft, glider, etc.) ROTORCRAFT; Model WHIZ-BANG; Serial number 001.

This aircraft has not been previously registered anywhere. (FAR section 47.15)

____ Normal Request - $5 (Fee attached)

X Special Registration Number Request - $10 (Fee attached)

CHOICES
1st 123TR
2nd 100TR
3rd 100R
4th 200TR
5th 300TR

____
Signature

APPENDIX 3. SAMPLE AFFIDAVIT OF OWNERSHIP FOR AMATEUR BUILT

U.S. Identification Number ____________

Builder's Name Joe Brown

Model Star Fire 1

Serial Number (required) 001

Class (airplane, rotorcraft, glider, etc.) Airplane

Type of Engine Installed (reciprocating, turbopropeller, etc.)
reciprocating

Number of Engines Installed 1

Manufacturer, Model, and Serial Number of each Engine Installed
Lycoming, 0-290D, 12395

Built for Land or Water Operation Land

Number of Seats 2

The above described aircraft was built from parts and I am the owner.

Address ____________

City ______ State ______ Zip Code ______

Telephone: Home ( )______ Work ( )______

____
(Signature of Owner)

State of ______

County of ______

Subscribed and sworn to before me this ____ day of ______, 19__

My commission expires ______.

____
(Signature of Notary Public)

AC Form 8050-88 (6-87)(0052-00-559-0003) Supersedes previous edition

APPENDIX 4. SAMPLE BILL OF SALE

*U.S. GOVERNMENT PRINTING OFFICE: 1977-774-297

FORM APPROVED:
OMB NO. 04-R0074

UNITED STATES OF AMERICA
DEPARTMENT OF TRANSPORTATION FEDERAL AVIATION ADMINISTRATION

KIT ~~AIRCRAFT~~ BILL OF SALE

FOR AND IN CONSIDERATION OF $ THE UNDERSIGNED OWNER(S) OF THE FULL LEGAL AND BENEFICIAL TITLE OF THE AIRCRAFT DESCRIBED AS FOLLOWS:

UNITED STATES REGISTRATION NUMBER N 23456

AIRCRAFT MANUFACTURER & MODEL
PRATT B-1

AIRCRAFT SERIAL No. 1

DOES THIS DAY OF 19
HEREBY SELL, GRANT, TRANSFER AND DELIVER ALL RIGHTS, TITLE, AND INTERESTS IN AND TO SUCH AIRCRAFT UNTO:

Do Not Write In This Block
FOR FAA USE ONLY

PURCHASER

NAME AND ADDRESS
(IF INDIVIDUAL(S), GIVE LAST NAME, FIRST NAME, AND MIDDLE INITIAL.)

Builder, Early A.
4397 Takeoff Road
Eloy, AZ 85335

DEALER CERTIFICATE NUMBER

AND TO EXECUTORS, ADMINISTRATORS, AND ASSIGNS TO HAVE AND TO HOLD SINGULARLY THE SAID AIRCRAFT FOREVER, AND WARRANTS THE TITLE THEREOF.

IN TESTIMONY WHEREOF HAVE SET HAND AND SEAL THIS DAY OF 19

SELLER

NAME (S) OF SELLER (TYPED OR PRINTED)	SIGNATURE (S) (IN INK) (IF EXECUTED FOR CO-OWNERSHIP, ALL MUST SIGN.)	TITLE (TYPED OR PRINTED)
Howard W. Pratt		

ACKNOWLEDGMENT (NOT REQUIRED FOR PURPOSES OF FAA RECORDING: HOWEVER, MAY BE REQUIRED BY LOCAL LAW FOR VALIDITY OF THE INSTRUMENT.)

ORIGINAL: TO FAA

AC FORM 8050-2 (8-76) (0052-629-0002)

APPENDIX 5. SAMPLE AC FORM 8050-1, AIRCRAFT REGISTRATION APPLICATION

FORM APPROVED
OMB No. 2120-0042

UNITED STATES OF AMERICA DEPARTMENT OF TRANSPORTATION
FEDERAL AVIATION ADMINISTRATION-MIKE MONRONEY AERONAUTICAL CENTER
AIRCRAFT REGISTRATION APPLICATION

CERT. ISSUE DATE

UNITED STATES REGISTRATION NUMBER N23456

AIRCRAFT MANUFACTURER & MODEL
PRATT-STEEN

AIRCRAFT SERIAL No.
001

FOR FAA USE ONLY

TYPE OF REGISTRATION (Check one box)

☒ 1. Individual ☐ 2. Partnership ☐ 3. Corporation ☐ 4. Co-owner ☐ 5. Gov't. ☐ 8. Non-citizen Corporation

NAME OF APPLICANT (Person(s) shown on evidence of ownership. If individual, give last name, first name, and middle initial.)

Pratt, Robert

TELEPHONE NUMBER: (602) 412-3785

ADDRESS (Permanent mailing address for first applicant listed.)

Number and street: 342 Teaberry

Rural Route: P.O. Box:

CITY	STATE	ZIP CODE
Somewhere	Arizona	85000

☐ CHECK HERE IF YOU ARE ONLY REPORTING A CHANGE OF ADDRESS

ATTENTION! Read the following statement before signing this application. This portion MUST be completed.

A false or dishonest answer to any question in this application may be grounds for punishment by fine and / or imprisonment (U.S. Code, Title 18, Sec. 1001).

CERTIFICATION

I/WE CERTIFY:

(1) That the above aircraft is owned by the undersigned applicant, who is a citizen (including corporations) of the United States.

(For voting trust, give name of trustee: ____________), or:

CHECK ONE AS APPROPRIATE:

a. ☐ A resident alien, with alien registration (Form 1-151 or Form 1-551) No. ____________

b. ☐ A non-citizen corporation organized and doing business under the laws of (state) ____________ and said aircraft is based and primarily used in the United States. Records or flight hours are available for inspection at ____________

(2) That the aircraft is not registered under the laws of any foreign country; and

(3) That legal evidence of ownership is attached or has been filed with the Federal Aviation Administration.

NOTE: If executed for co-ownership all applicants must sign. Use reverse side if necessary.

TYPE OR PRINT NAME BELOW SIGNATURE

EACH PART OF THIS APPLICATION MUST BE SIGNED IN INK.

SIGNATURE	TITLE	DATE
Robert Pratt	Owner	xx/xx/xx
SIGNATURE	TITLE	DATE
SIGNATURE	TITLE	DATE

NOTE: Pending receipt of the Certificate of Aircraft Registration, the aircraft may be operated for a period not in excess of 90 days, during which time the PINK copy of this application must be carried in the aircraft.

AC Form 8050-1 (8-84) (0052-00-628-9005)

APPENDIX 6. SAMPLE APPLICATION FOR AIRWORTHINESS CERTIFICATE (AMATEUR-BUILT)

Form Approved
O M B No 2120-0018

US Department of Transportation
Federal Aviation Administration

APPLICATION FOR AIRWORTHINESS CERTIFICATE

INSTRUCTIONS — Print or type. Do not write in shaded areas; these are for FAA use only. Submit original only to an authorized FAA Representative. If additional space is required, use an attachment. For special flight permits complete Sections II and VI or VII as applicable.

I. AIRCRAFT DESCRIPTION

1. REGISTRATION MARK: N23456	2. AIRCRAFT BUILDER'S NAME (Make): Pratt	3. AIRCRAFT MODEL DESIGNATION: B-1	4. YR MFR: 1990	FAA CODING
5. AIRCRAFT SERIAL NO: 1	6. ENGINE BUILDER'S NAME (Make): Lycoming	7. ENGINE MODEL DESIGNATION: O-290-D		
8. NUMBER OF ENGINES: 1	9. PROPELLER BUILDER'S NAME (Make): Sensenich	10. PROPELLER MODEL DESIGNATION: W76AM-2-50	11. AIRCRAFT IS (Check if applicable): IMPORT	

II. CERTIFICATION REQUESTED

APPLICATION IS HEREBY MADE FOR: (Check applicable items)

A	1		STANDARD AIRWORTHINESS CERTIFICATE (Indicate category)		NORMAL		UTILITY		ACROBATIC		TRANSPORT / GLIDER / BALLOON
B		X	SPECIAL AIRWORTHINESS CERTIFICATE (Check appropriate items)								

2		LIMITED								
5		PROVISIONAL (Indicate class)	1		CLASS I					
			2		CLASS II					
3		RESTRICTED (Indicate operation(s) to be conducted)	1		AGRICULTURE AND PEST CONTROL	2	AERIAL SURVEYING	3		AERIAL ADVERTISING
			4		FOREST (Wildlife conservation)	5	PATROLLING	6		WEATHER CONTROL
			7		CARRIAGE OF CARGO	0	OTHER (Specify)			
4	X	EXPERIMENTAL (Indicate operation(s) to be conducted)	1		RESEARCH AND DEVELOPMENT	2 X	AMATEUR BUILT	3		EXHIBITION
			4		RACING	5	CREW TRAINING			MKT SURVEY
			0		TO SHOW COMPLIANCE WITH FAR					
8		SPECIAL FLIGHT PERMIT (Indicate operation to be conducted, then complete Section VI or VII as applicable on reverse side)	1		FERRY FLIGHT FOR REPAIRS, ALTERATIONS, MAINTENANCE OR STORAGE					
			2		EVACUATE FROM AREA OF IMPENDING DANGER					
			3		OPERATION IN EXCESS OF MAXIMUM CERTIFICATED TAKE-OFF WEIGHT					
			4		DELIVERING OR EXPORT	5	PRODUCTION FLIGHT TESTING			
			6		CUSTOMER DEMONSTRATION FLIGHTS					

C	6		MULTIPLE AIRWORTHINESS CERTIFICATE (Check ABOVE "Restricted Operation" and "Standard" or "Limited" as applicable)

III. OWNER'S CERTIFICATION

A. REGISTERED OWNER (As shown on certificate of aircraft registration) — IF DEALER, CHECK HERE →

NAME: Howard W. Pratt	ADDRESS: 1320 West Street, St. Louis MO 41345

B. AIRCRAFT CERTIFICATION BASIS (Check applicable blocks and complete items as indicated)

	AIRCRAFT SPECIFICATION OR TYPE CERTIFICATE DATA SHEET (Give No and Revision No): N/A		AIRWORTHINESS DIRECTIVES (Check if all applicable AD's complied with and give latest AD No): N/A
	AIRCRAFT LISTING (Give page number(s)): N/A		SUPPLEMENTAL TYPE CERTIFICATE (List number of each STC incorporated): N/A

C. AIRCRAFT OPERATION AND MAINTENANCE RECORDS

X	CHECK IF RECORDS IN COMPLIANCE WITH FAR 91.173	TOTAL AIRFRAME HOURS: 0.00	3	EXPERIMENTAL ONLY (Enter hours flown since last certificate issued or renewed): 0.00

D. CERTIFICATION — I hereby certify that I am the registered owner (or his agent) of the aircraft described above, that the aircraft is registered with the Federal Aviation Administration in accordance with Section 501 of the Federal Aviation Act of 1958, and applicable Federal Aviation Regulations, and that the aircraft has been inspected and is airworthy and eligible for the airworthiness certificate requested.

DATE OF APPLICATION: XX-XX-XX	NAME AND TITLE (Print or type): Howard W. Pratt-owner	SIGNATURE: Howard W. Pratt

IV. INSPECTION AGENCY VERIFICATION

A. THE AIRCRAFT DESCRIBED ABOVE HAS BEEN INSPECTED AND FOUND AIRWORTHY BY (Complete this section only if FAR 21.183(d) applies)

2		FAR PART 121 OR 127 CERTIFICATE HOLDER (Give Certificate No)	3		CERTIFICATED MECHANIC (Give Certificate No)	6	CERTIFICATED REPAIR STATION (Give Certificate No)
5		AIRCRAFT MANUFACTURER (Give name of firm)					

DATE	TITLE	SIGNATURE

V. FAA REPRESENTATIVE CERTIFICATION

(Check ALL applicable blocks in items A and B)

A. I find that the aircraft described in Section I or VII meets requirements for		THE CERTIFICATE REQUESTED			
	4	AMENDMENT OR MODIFICATION OF CURRENT AIRWORTHINESS CERTIFICATE			
B. Inspection for a special flight permit under Section VII was conducted by		FAA INSPECTOR		FAA DESIGNEE	
		CERTIFICATE HOLDER UNDER	FAR 65	FAR 121, 127 or 135	FAR 145

DATE	DISTRICT OFFICE	4	DESIGNEE'S SIGNATURE AND NO	1	FAA INSPECTOR'S SIGNATURE

FAA Form 8130-6 (11-88) SUPERSEDES PREVIOUS EDITION

APPENDIX 7. SAMPLE ELIGIBILITY STATEMENT AMATEUR-BUILT AIRCRAFT

Form Approved
O M B NO 2120-0018

U.S. Department of Transportation
Federal Aviation Administration

ELIGIBILITY STATEMENT AMATEUR-BUILT AIRCRAFT

Instructions: Print or type all information except signature. Submit original to an authorized FAA representative. Applicant completes Section I thru III. Notary Public Completes Section IV

I. REGISTERED OWNER INFORMATION

Name(s): E.A. BUILDER

Address(es): # 4397 Takeoff Road (No. & Street) — Eloy (City) — AZ (State) — 85335 (Zip)

Telephone No(s): (602) 346-9123 (Residence) — (602) 346-1253 (Business)

II. AIRCRAFT INFORMATION

Model: Vari-Eze — Engine(s) Make: Lycoming

Assigned Serial No: EAB-1 — Engine(s) Serial No(s): 803399

Registration No: W1234B — Prop./Rotor(s) Make: Sensenich

Aircraft Fabricated: Plan ☐ Kit ☒ — Prop./Rotor(s) Serial No(s): 479638

III. MAJOR PORTION ELIGIBILITY STATMENT OF APPLICANT

I certify the aircraft identified in Section II above was fabricated and assembled by E.A. BUILDER (Name of Person(s) - Please Print) for my (their) education or recreation. I (we) have records to support this statement and will make them available to the FAA upon request.

— NOTICE —

Whoever in any matter within the jurisdiction of any department or agency of the United States knowingly and willfully falsifies, conceals or covers up by any trick, scheme, or device a material fact, or who makes any false, fictitious or fraudulent statements or representations, or makes or uses any false writing or document knowing the same to contain any false, fictitious or fraudulent statement or entry, shall be fined not more than $10,000 or imprisoned not more than 5 years, or both (U.S. Code, Title 18, Sec. 1001.)

APPLICANT'S DECLARATION

I hereby certify that all statements and answers provided by me in this statement form are complete and true to the best of my knowledge, and I agree that they are to be considered part of the basis for issuance of any FAA certificate to me. I have also read and understand the Privacy Act statement that accompanies this form.

Signature of Applicant (In Ink): Early A. Builder — Date: XX-XX-XX

IV. NOTARIZATION STATEMENT

FAA Form 8130-12 (4-89)

APPENDIX 8. SAMPLE LETTER TO ACCOMPANY APPLICATION FOR AIRWORTHINESS CERTIFICATE

To: (LOCAL FAA OFFICE) OR DAR) — Date: XX-XX-XX

In compliance with FAR section 21.193, I hereby request a Special Airworthiness Certificate for my amateur-built aircraft for the purpose of operating amateur-built aircraft. The aircraft description is as follows:

Builder: A. BROWN — Registration No: N6543
Model: T-BIRD — Serial No: 21
No. of Engines: 1 — No. of Seats: 2
Design Criteria; own design _____, plans ______, kit x

The aircraft has been completely assembled and the following has been accomplished:

Yes No — I enclose FAA Form 8130-6 which has been completed in Sections I, II, and III.

Yes No — I enclose FAA Form 8130-12, which has been completed in Sections I, II, and III by me and notarized in Section IV.

Yes No — I possess AC Form 8050-3 or the pink copy of AC Form 8050-1, signed and dated as evidence that I have complied with the registration requirements of FAR Part 47.

Yes No — I enclose a three-view drawing or photographs of the aircraft as required by FAR section 21.193.

Yes No — I have weighed the aircraft to determine that the most forward and aft center of gravity positions are within established limits. The weight and balance report is available at the aircraft, and a copy is submitted with this application.

Yes No — I have maintained a construction log for the project, including photographs taken during the construction. Log entries describe all inspections conducted during construction.

APPENDIX 8. SAMPLE LETTER TO ACCOMPANY APPLICATION FOR AIRWORTHINESS CERTIFICATE (CONT'D)

Yes No — The marking requirements of FAR Part 45 have been complied with, including permanent attachment of a fireproof aircraft identification (data) plate, permanent application of appropriate registration marks, and the word "EXPERIMENTAL" near each entrance.

Yes No — The following placard has been displayed in the cockpit in full view of all occupants (not required for single-place aircraft):

"PASSENGER WARNING - THIS AIRCRAFT IS AMATEUR BUILT AND DOES NOT COMPLY WITH FEDERAL SAFETY REGULATIONS FOR STANDARD AIRCRAFT."

The aircraft will be available for inspection at this location, and directions are as follows:

GOLD CITY AIRPORT HGR. 5
1400A AIRPORT ROAD
GOLD CITY, NEVADA

I request that the initial operating limitations be issued to permit me to operate the aircraft within the following geographical area for flight test:

____
____
____
____
____

My residence telephone number is: (XXX) XXX-XXXX
A daytime telephone number is: (XXX) XXX-XXXX

____
Signature (owner/builder)

APPENDIX 9. SAMPLE LIST OF OPERATING LIMITATIONS

THESE OPERATING LIMITATIONS SHALL BE ACCESSIBLE TO THE PILOT

EXPERIMENTAL OPERATING LIMITATIONS
OPERATING AMATEUR-BUILT AIRCRAFT

REG. NO. ____________ SERIAL NO. ________
MAKE ____________ MODEL ________

Phase I, Initial Flight Test in Restricted Area:

1. No person may operate this aircraft for other than the purpose of operating amateur-built aircraft to accomplish the operation and flight test outline in the applicant's letter dated __________ in accordance with FAR section 21.193. Phase I and II amateur-built operations shall be conducted in accordance with applicable air traffic and general operating rules of FAR Part 91 and the additional limitations herein prescribed under the provisions of FAR section 91.42 (new FAR section 91.319).

2. The initial ______ hours of flight shall be conducted within the geographical area described as follows:

____
____

3. Except for takeoffs and landings, no person may operate this aircraft over densely populated areas or in congested airways.

4. This aircraft is approved for day VFR operation only.

5. Unless prohibited by design, acrobatics are permitted in the assigned flight test area. All acrobatics are to be conducted under the provisions of FAR section 91.71 (new FAR section 91.303).

6. No person may be carried in this aircraft during flight unless that person is required for the purpose of the flight.

7. The cognizant FAA office must be notified and their response received in writing prior to flying this aircraft after incorporating a major change as defined by FAR section 21.93.

8. The operator of this aircraft shall notify the control tower of the experimental nature of this aircraft when operating into or out of airports with operating control towers.

APPENDIX 9. SAMPLE LIST OF OPERATING LIMITATIONS (CONT'D)

9. The pilot-in-command of this aircraft must, as applicable, hold an appropriate category/class rating, have an aircraft type rating, have a flight instructor's logbook endorsement or possess a "Letter of Authorization" issued by an FAA Flight Standards Operations Inspector.

10. This aircraft does not meet the requirements of the applicable, comprehensive, and detailed airworthiness code as provided by Annex 8 to the Convention on International Civil Aviation. This aircraft may not be operated over any other country without the permission of that country.

Phase II:

Following satisfactory completion of the required number of flight hours in the flight test area, the pilot shall certify in the logbook that the aircraft has been shown to comply with FAR section 91.42(b) (new FAR section 91.319). Compliance with FAR section 91.42(b) (new FAR section 91.319) shall be recorded in the aircraft logbook with the following or similarly worded statement:

"I certify that the prescribed flight test hours have been completed and the aircraft is controllable throughout its range of speeds and throughout all maneuvers to be executed, has no hazardous operating characteristics or design features, and is safe for operation."

The Following Limitations Apply Outside of Flight Test Area:

1. Limitations 1, 3, 7, 8, 9, and 10 from Phase I are applicable.

2. This aircraft is approved for day VFR only, unless equipped for night VFR and/or IFR in accordance with FAR section 91.33 (new FAR section 91.205).

3. This aircraft shall contain the placards, markings, etc., required by FAR section 91.31 (new FAR section 91.9).

4. This aircraft is prohibited from acrobatic flight, unless such flights were satisfactorily accomplished and recorded in the aircraft logbook during the flight test period.

APPENDIX 9. SAMPLE LIST OF OPERATING LIMITATIONS (CONT'D)

5. No person may operate this aircraft for carrying persons or property for compensation or hire.

6. The person operating this aircraft shall advise each person carried of the experimental nature of this aircraft.

7. This aircraft shall not be operated for glider towing or parachute jumping operations, unless so equipped and authorized.

8. No person shall operate this aircraft unless within the preceding 12 calendar months it has had a condition inspection performed in accordance with FAR Part 43, appendix D, and has been found to be in a condition for safe operation. In addition, this inspection shall be recorded in accordance with limitation 10 listed below.

9. The builder of this aircraft, if certificated as a repairman, FAA certified mechanic holding an Airframe and Powerplant rating and/or appropriately rated repair stations may perform condition inspections in accordance with FAR Part 43, appendix D.

10. Condition inspections shall be recorded in the aircraft maintenance records showing the following or a similarly worded statement:

"I certify that this aircraft has been inspected on (insert date) in accordance with the scope and detail of appendix D of Part 43 and found to be in a condition for safe operation."

The entry will include the aircraft total time-in-service, the name, signature, and certificate type and number of the person performing the inspection.

________________________ __________________
Aviation Safety Inspector — Date Issued

____
Office Designation

APPENDIX 10. SAMPLE - APPLICATION FOR REPAIRMAN AMATEUR-BUILDER

TYPE OR PRINT ALL ENTRIES IN INK

Form Approved OMB No. 2120-0022

US Department of Transportation
Federal Aviation Administration

AIRMAN CERTIFICATE AND/OR RATING APPLICATION

☐ MECHANIC ☐ AIRFRAME ☐ POWERPLANT

☒ REPAIRMAN Experimental Aircraft Builder (Specify Rating)

☐ PARACHUTE RIGGER ☐ SENIOR ☐ MASTER ☐ SEAT ☐ CHEST ☐ BACK ☐ LAP

APPLICATION FOR: ☐ ORIGINAL ISSUANCE ☐ ADDED RATING

I. APPLICANT INFORMATION

A. NAME (First, Middle, Last): Charles A. Mayer

K. PERMANENT MAILING ADDRESS: 1002 Cable Drive (NUMBER AND STREET, P.O. BOX, ETC.); Oakton (CITY); Virginia (STATE); 22022 (ZIP CODE)

B. SOCIAL SECURITY NO.: 134-90-5210
C. DOB (Mo.,Day Yr.): 3/15/43
D. HEIGHT: 70 IN
E. WEIGHT: 200
F. HAIR: blk
G. EYES: hazel
H. SEX: M
I. NATIONALITY (Citizenship): USA
J. PLACE OF BIRTH: Philadelphia, PA

L. HAVE YOU EVER HAD AN AIRMAN CERTIFICATE SUSPENDED OR REVOKED? ☒ NO ☐ YES (If "Yes," explain on an attached sheet keying to appropriate item number)

M. DO YOU NOW OR HAVE YOU EVER HELD AN FAA AIRMAN CERTIFICATE? ☐ NO ☒ YES
SPECIFY TYPE: Private Pilot

N. HAVE YOU EVER BEEN CONVICTED FOR VIOLATION OF ANY FEDERAL OR STATE STATUTES PERTAINING TO NARCOTIC DRUGS, MARIJUANA, AND DEPRESSANT OR STIMULANT DRUGS OR SUBSTANCES? ☒ NO ☐ YES → DATE OF FINAL CONVICTION

II. CERTIFICATE OR RATING APPLIED FOR ON BASIS OF —

☐ A. CIVIL EXPERIENCE ☐ B. MILITARY EXPERIENCE ☐ C. LETTER OF RECOMMENDATION FOR REPAIRMAN ((Attach copy)

☐ D. GRADUATE OF APPROVED COURSE — (1) NAME AND LOCATION OF SCHOOL; (2) SCHOOL NO.; (3) CURRICULUM FROM WHICH GRADUATED; (4) DATE

☐ E. STUDENT HAS MADE SATISFACTORY PROGRESS AND IS RECOMMENDED TO TAKE THE ORAL/PRACTICAL TEST (FAR 65.80) — (1) SCHOOL NAME; NO; (2) SCHOOL OFFICIAL'S SIGNATURE

☐ F. SPECIAL AUTHORIZATION TO TAKE MECHANIC'S ORAL/PRACTICAL TEST (FAR 65.80) — (1) DATE AUTH.; (2) DATE AUTH. EXPIRES; (3) FAA INSPECTOR SIGNATURE; (4) FAA DIST. OFC.

III. RECORD OF EXPERIENCE

A. MILITARY COMPETENCE OBTAINED IN → (1) SERVICE; (2) RANK OR PAY LEVEL; (3) MILITARY SPECIALTY CODE

B. APPLICANTS OTHER THAN FAA CERTIFICATED SCHOOL GRADUATES. LIST EXPERIENCE RELATING TO CERTIFICATE AND RATING APPLIED FOR (Continue on separate sheet, if more space is needed)

DATES—MONTH AND YEAR FROM	TO	EMPLOYER AND LOCATION	TYPE WORK PERFORMED
			Make - Mayer's Special
			Model - M-1
			Serial No. - 1
			Certification Date of
			Aircraft-
			(Date flt. test complete) xx-xx

C. PARACHUTE RIGGER APPLICANTS: INDICATE BY TYPE HOW MANY PARACHUTES PACKED → SEAT / CHEST / BACK / LAP — FOR MASTER RATING ONLY — PACKED AS A — ☐ SENIOR RIGGER ☐ MILITARY RIGGER

IV. APPLICANT'S CERTIFICATION

I CERTIFY THAT THE STATEMENTS BY ME ON THIS APPLICATION ARE TRUE
A. SIGNATURE
B. DATE: XX-XX-XX

V. I FIND THIS APPLICANT MEETS THE EXPERIENCE REQUIREMENTS OF FAR 65 AND IS ELIGIBLE TO TAKE THE REQUIRED TESTS. — DATE; INSPECTOR'S SIGNATURE; FAA DISTRICT OFFICE

FOR FAA USE ONLY

Emp.	reg.	D.O.	seal	con	iss	Act	lev	TR	s.h.	Srch	wrs	RATING (1)	RATING (2)	RATING (3)	RATING (4)

LIMITATIONS

FAA Form 8610-2 (2-85) SUPERSEDES PREVIOUS EDITION

Appendix 3

US Experimental Aircraft Association Technical Counselor Program: Policy Statement

GENERAL INFORMATION

Q. What is a Technical Counselor?

A. A volunteer aviation education counselor who, when asked to do so by an amateur aircraft builder, shares his knowledge, expertise and experience in order to assist the builder with the project.

Q. What are the qualifications for a Technical Counselor?

A. First, one must be a member of the National EAA. We have other qualifications, and they are listed below. Tony Bingelis puts it well when he says: 'Possibly one of the best qualifications for a Technical Counselor is his ability to listen.' This is very true, but a counselor must also:

a. Have built an amateur built aircraft or

b. Have restored an antique/classic aircraft or

c. Be an A&P, IA, DAR, DER or Aerospace Engineer (U.S. Ratings, other countries equivalents of these ratings are also acceptable) or

d. Have the qualifications for the above.

Q. How many Technical Counselors are A&P mechanics?

A. About 50% are A&P mechanics.

Q. My skill is in a special area, can I be a Technical Counselor?

A. An individual may have expertise in only one area such as woodworking or welding or covering. Passing on these talents would be beneficial to builders working on that part of the aircraft.

Q. Why does EAA have a Technical Counselor program?

A. To ensure that a well constructed, airworthy aircraft is presented to the FAA for final approval. To encourage the self-help nature of our organization, and to pass on aviation knowledge to promote aviation safety. We also are highly interested in maintaining the excellent reputation that the amateur built program has. The Technical Counselor program has been a very effective way of doing this.

TECHNICAL COUNSELOR ACTIVITIES

Q. Who is the typical Technical Counselor?

A. From a survey done, we know that the 'typical' Technical Counselor is 57 years old, the oldest being 80 and youngest 27. On the average, a Technical Counselor visits aircraft some 12-13 times per year, puts on an occasional technical program in his local chapter, and on occasion, sends technical information on to EAA Headquarters for consideration for publishing. 62% of the Technical Counselors are aircraft builders, having completed 1.9 aircraft each. 70% have completely restored an aircraft, and over 95% have either built an aircraft, completely restored an aircraft or hold A&P licenses.

Q. What activities must an EAA Technical Counselor perform to maintain his active Technical Counselor status?

A. Visit three aircraft per year, or provide three chapter programs per year, or send three articles to EAA for consideration for publication per year, or send in photographs from 3 different visits for publication, or any combination of three of the above. He may also work as a volunteer at the Oshkosh EAA Convention in a Technical Counselor capacity at the Homebuilder's Corner, workshops, etc. He must document this activity each year on a Revalidation form, which is sent out in November to all Technical Counselors. This form must be returned to EAA Headquarters to maintain his active status in the program.

PERMISSIBLE FUNCTIONS

Q. Does the Technical Counselor sign log books?

A. The Technical Counselor *must not* sign off any log book or document indicating an official inspection or judgement of airworthiness. To do so may abridge the authority of the Federal Aviation Administration.

Q. My FAA office wants my Technical Counselor to sign my builder's log book.

A. A Technical Counselor *must not* sign log books. If he is an A&P, IA, DAR, etc., he may sign log books in that capacity, but not in his official capacity as an EAA Technical Counselor. Advisory Circular 20-27C is explicit in that regard – the *builder* signs his own log.

Q. Can an EAA Technical Counselor approve design changes?

A. It is not the policy of the Experimental Aircraft Association and its Technical Counselors to design or redesign aircraft, components or parts thereof. This is outside the guidelines of the EAA Technical Counselor program. Any design changes or changes from the original drawings of the designer are outside the parameter of the program, and would be between the builder and the designer. A Technical Counselor should recommend good aeronautical practices.

Q. I want to modify an aircraft. Can the Technical Counselor help?

A. No, his function is to ensure compliance with the plans. Any modifications to plans must be by agreement between builder and designer only.

Q. Can a Technical Counselor work on or test fly an airplane that he visits?

A. If a Technical Counselor works on an aircraft that he visits or test flies the aircraft, either for free or for a fee, he is acting on his own behalf, and not in his capacity as an EAA Technical Counselor.

Q. Does a Technical Counselor charge for his services?

A. There shall be no fees charged for an EAA Technical Counselor's educational help in assisting a builder by visiting his project. Any renumeration for travel or lodging between an EAA Technical Counselor and a builder desiring his recommendations is between the builder and the Technical Counselor.

Q. Can a Technical Counselor combine his volunteer work as a Technical Counselor and his work for pay as an A&P?

A. No. The Technical Counselor is a non-paid volunteer, as described.

BENEFITS OF BEING A TECHNICAL COUNSELOR

Q. Are there any benefits to being an EAA Technical Counselor?

A. One of the benefits is receiving the Technical Counselor Newsletter, filled with technical tips and information, issued six times per year. However, the main benefit is derived from passing on knowledge on aircraft building and safety practices so that others can complete an airworthy project.

Q. Is the EAA Technical Counselor protected by insurance?

A. The Technical Counselor is insured for any legal liability presented against him while operating only within the policies of EAA and its efforts to ensure safety in aviation.

AN INVITATION TO BECOME A TECHNICAL COUNSELOR

Q. I want to be a Technical Counselor. How do I become one?

A. Write to the EAA Headquarters Technical Counselor Administrator for an application form.

Appendix 4

French Direction Générale de l'Aviation Civile: Certificat de Navigabilité Restreint d'Aéronef (CNRA)

Date *1er avril 1980*

à

Monsieur le Directeur Général
de l'Aviation Civile

Service de la Formation Aéronautique
et du Contrôle Technique

Bureau Certification

93, bd. du Montparnasse

75270 PARIS CEDEX 06

Objet : Demande de C.N.R.A.

P.J. : 3 dossiers techniques

Monsieur le Directeur Général,

J'ai l'honneur de vous transmettre ci-joint les pièces précitées dûment remplies en vue de l'obtention d'un Certificat de Navigabilité Restreint d'Aéronef (C.N.R.A.).

Je certifie exact les renseignements portés ci-dessous et sur les dossiers techniques.

Veuillez croire, Monsieur le Directeur Général, à l'expression de ma considération distinguée.

Signature du propriétaire :

NOM - Prénom : *DURAND Jean*

Profession : *employé de commerce*

Adresse complète : *13, avenue de Paris 14000 CAEN*

Téléphone :

Partie ci-dessous détachable à renseigner avec rigueur

AERONEF : *AVION* MARQUE : *JODEL* TYPE : *119* N° : *55*

Nombre de places *2* UTILISATION *privée*

Reproduction sur plans (1) ~~Prototype (1)~~ ~~Ancienne immatriculation (1)~~

PROPRIETAIRE

Nom - Prénom : *DURAND Jean*

Adresse complète : *13, avenue de Paris 14000 CAEN*

Téléphone :

CONSTRUCTEUR

Nom - Prénom : *DURAND Jean*

Adresse complète : *13, avenue de Paris 14000 CAEN*

VISITE TECHNIQUE : 1ère date proposée *5 mai 1980*

2ème date proposée *12 mai 1980*

LIEU : *Aérodrome de Caen-Carpiquet*

EPREUVES EN VOL : *Aérodrome de Caen-Carpiquet*

PILOTE PROPOSE : *DURAND Jean*

(1) Barrer les mentions inutiles ou sans objet.

MODELE DE DEMANDE DE CERTIFICAT D'IMMATRICULATION

Je vous prie de bien vouloir me délivrer le certificat d'immatriculation prévu par l'article D.121-2 du Code de l'Aviation Civile, pour l'aéronef désigné ci-après :

DESCRIPTION - (avion, ~~planeur~~, ~~hélicoptère~~)
- Type et Série : ..JODEL...119............
- N° dans la série : ...55....................
- Constructeur : ...DURAND..Jean........

CATEGORIE - (~~Normale~~ ou Restreinte)

PORT D'ATTACHE : ....CAEN-Carpiquet..................

CERTIFICAT DE NAVIGABILITE demandé le 1er avril 1980

PROPRIETAIRE : Nom et Prénoms ..DURAND..Jean........
Domicile 13, avenue de Paris 14000 CAEN

OU

Raison sociale ....
Siège social ....

Je déclare que cet appareil n'est pas immatriculé dans un autre Etat. (1)

A ...CAEN....., le.................

(indiquer la qualité du signataire si celui-ci agit au nom d'un groupement)

---

(1) s'il y a lieu joindre le certificat de radiation du registre d'immatriculation étranger où l'appareil était précédemment inscrit.

MINISTÈRE DES TRANSPORTS

DIRECTION GÉNÉRALE
DE
L'AVIATION CIVILE

Service de la Formation Aéronautique et du Contrôle Technique

Sous-Direction Technique
Bureau Certification

EXEMPLE

DOSSIER TECHNIQUE

de demande de Certificat de Navigabilité Restreint d'Aéronef

A remplir par le postulant

AÉRONEF :

Catégorie : Avion, ~~Planeur,~~ (1).

Nature de la construction : ~~Prototype~~, Reproduction sur plans (1).

Type ou appellation : JODEL D119

Numéro de série (2) : 55

Nombre de places : 2

CONSTRUCTEUR : Jean DURAND
13, avenue de Paris 14000 CAEN

Date de début de la construction : 15 juillet 1978

Date de la demande de C.N.R.A. : 1er avril 1980

(1) Rayer les mentions inutiles.

(2) Pour les avions reproduits sur plans, le numéro sera celui de la liasse.

IMMATRICULATION :

Numéro d'enregistrement par le Bureau du Matériel Volant :

Définition aérodynamique et géométrique de l'aéronef

PLAN TROIS VUES

Pour un aéronef qui diffère très notablement des schémas ci-dessous, coller sur cette demi-page un plan trois vues comportant les mensurations appropriées.

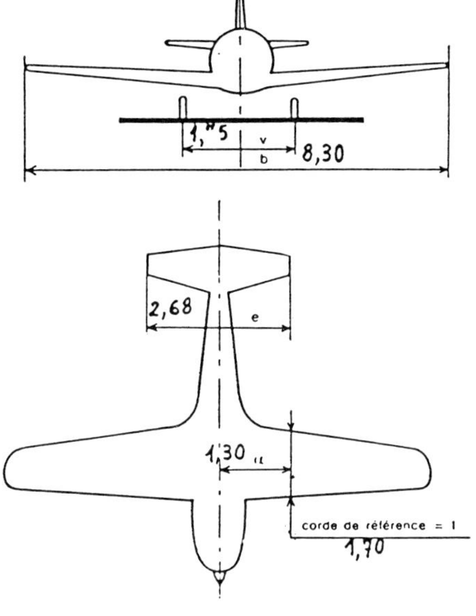

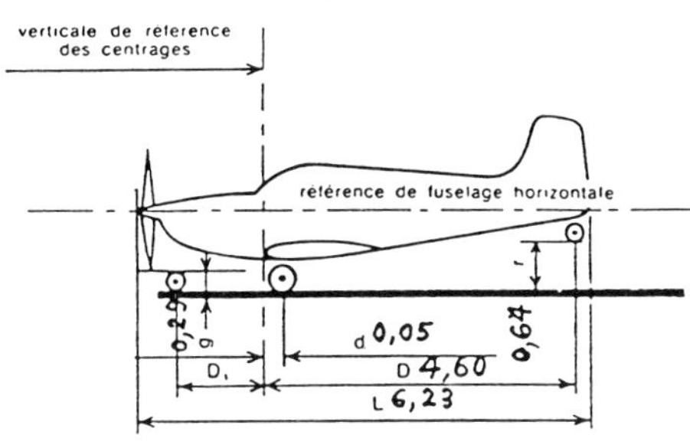

DÉFINITION DES RÉFÉRENCES DE CALAGES, INCIDENCES ET CENTRAGES
(par rapport auxquelles sont mesurées ces grandeurs)

— Référence de fuselage : *Longeron supérieur de fuselage mis à niveau*

— Distance de la corde de référence de voilure au plan vertical de symétrie de l'avion : *1,30 m*

— Verticale de référence des centrages (déterminée après mise à l'horizontale de la référence de fuselage) : *Bord d'attaque de l'aile à l'emplanture.*

VOILURE

Surface S : *12,75 m²*

Envergure b : *8,30 m*

Profondeur de la corde de référence l : *1,70 m*

Angle de calage de la corde de référence sur la référence de fuselage : *4°*

EMPENNAGE HORIZONTAL

Surface s' : *2,40 m²*

Envergure e : *2,68 m*

Angle de calage du plan fixe sur la référence de fuselage : *0°*

CENTRAGE

Distance entre la référence verticale des centrages et l'axe des roues principales d : *0,05 m*

Distance entre la référence verticale des centrages et l'axe de la roue d'atterrisseur auxiliaire D (ou D_1) : *4,60 m*

Centrages prévus en utilisation :

centrage limite avant : *0,29 m = 17%*

centrage limite arrière : *0,58 m = 34%*

VOIE DE L'ATTERRISSEUR PRINCIPAL : V : *1,75 m*

GARDE D'HÉLICE : g : *0,29 m*

HAUTEUR AU SOL DE LA ROULETTE D'ATTERRISSEUR AUXILIAIRE (la référence fuselage étant horizontale) :

r = *0,64 m*

Longueur de l'aéronef : 6,23 m

DÉBATTEMENT DES GOUVERNES (en degrés) :

Ailerons	G.	haut : *25°*	Profondeur	haut :	*30°*
		bas : *25°*		bas :	*25°*
	Dr.	haut : *25°*	Dérive	Dr. :	*30°*
		bas : *25°*		G. :	*30°*

DISPOSITIFS COMPENSATEURS :

Compensateur de profondeur.

Devis de masse et définition technologique

DEVIS DE MASSE ENVISAGÉ

Masse à vide :	330	kg
Combustible (1) :	85	kg
Lubrifiant (1) :	4	kg
~~Lest liquide (1)~~		kg
Charges mobiles	198	kg
Masse maximale totale en charge :	617	kg

INSTRUMENTS DE BORD (5)

Anémomètre (2)	☒
Niveau transversal (bille) (2)	☒
Altimètre (2)	☒
Tachymètre (3)	☒
Variomètre (4)	☒
Accéléromètre	☐
Manomètre huile	☒
Thermomètre huile	☒
Jauge carburant	☒

ATTERRISSEUR

~~Tricycle~~ - Classique (1).

Train principal :

Roues : 420 x 150

Freins : hydrauliques

Amortisseurs : rondelles caoutchouc

Train auxiliaire :

Roue : 155 x 50

Amortisseur. : lames acier

(1) Rayer la mention inutile ou sans objet.
(2) Obligatoire pour tous aéronefs.
(3) Obligatoire pour avions.
(4) Obligatoire pour planeurs.
(5) Mettre une croix dans le carré correspondant.

GROUPE MOTO-PROPULSEUR (1)

Hélice (1)

Constructeur : EVRA Type : D11 28 1B

Numéro : 2533 ST Diamètre : 1,76 m

Caractéristiques :

bois - ~~métal~~ (1),

pas fixe - ~~pas variable~~ (1).

Moteur (1)

Marque : Continental Type : C 90 12 F

Numéro : 1180 - 6 Cylindrée (1) : 3,29 dm³

~~Poussée~~ (1) : Puissance (1) : 91 cv

Régime nominal : 2475 t/min.

Températures d'huile :

mini : 30° C

maxi : 107° C

Pressions d'huile :

mini : 1 bar

maxi : 3 bar

Le présent moteur

— est d'un type homologué (1) ;

— ~~n'est pas d'un type homologué~~ (1) ;

— n'a pas été entretenu suivant les normes en vigueur (1).

ATTESTATION DU POSTULANT PROPRIÉTAIRE

« Je certifie sincères et véritables les renseignements portés sur le présent document. »

Nom, prénom : DURAND Jean

Lieu et date : Caen 1.4.1980

Signature : J. Durand

ANNEXE I

MOTEUR

(A remplir dans le cas où le moteur ne serait pas d'un type homologué entretenu suivant les normes en vigueur — porter les cotes essentielles des cylindres et pistons dans le tableau ci-dessous)

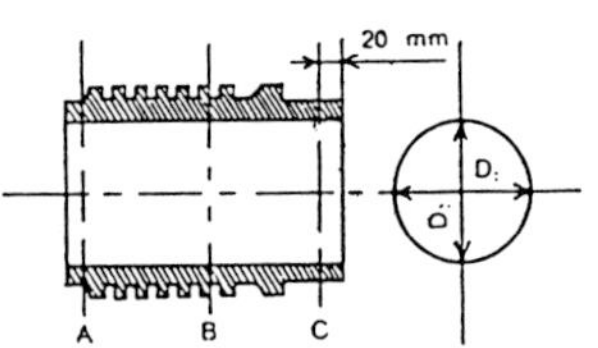

Cotes cylindres

	cylindre I		cylindre II		cylindre III		cylindre IV	
	D_1	D_2	D_1	D_2	D_1	D_2	D_1	D_2
section A	103,32	103,29	103,30	103,29	103,29	103,33	103,27	103,32
section B	103,32	103,31	103,29	103,30	103,31	103,32	103,27	103,33
section C	103,33	103,33	103,29	103,29	103,30	103,32	103,27	103,32
conicité	0,01		0,01		0,01		0,01	
faux rond	0,02		0,02		0,02		0,02	

Cotes pistons

	piston I		piston II		piston III		piston IV	
	D_1	D_2	D_1	D_2	D_1	D_2	D_1	D_2
section E	102,90	102,91	102,92	102,92	102,92	102,92	102,91	102,93
section F	102,85	102,84	102,84	102,85	102,86	102,84	102,85	102,87

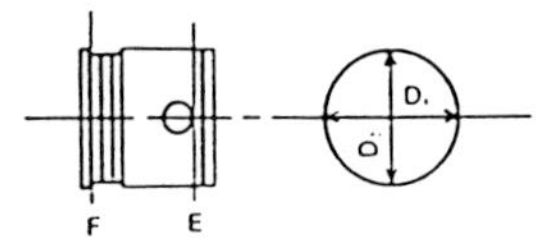

Remarques particulières : Sièges et soupapes pour essence 100 LL
Consigne de navigabilité 7647

C.N.R.A. — Attestation de Qualité des Matériaux

Formule A Prototypes - avions reproduits d'après des dossiers non homologués - avions reconstruits - avions extrapolés de dossiers connus.	Je soussigné ...... certifie que les matériaux et en particulier les bois utilisés par moi pour construire l'avion ...... pour lequel je postule le C.N.R.A. ont été choisis comme possédant la qualité et les caractéristiques nécessaires à la fonction qui leur a été dévolue.
Formule B Avions reproduits d'après une liasse de prototype CdN.	Je soussigné DURAND Jean ...... certifie que les matériaux et en particulier les bois utilisés par moi pour construire l'avion JODEL D.119 ...... reproduit d'après la liasse de plans n° 55 ...... ont été choisis, vérifiés et utilisés conformément aux stipulations de ladite liasse tant en ce qui concerne leur nature que leur qualité.
Formule C Avions destinés à des manœuvres acrobatiques.	Je soussigné ...... 1° déclare que les matériaux utilisés pour la construction du longeron ont été prélevés dans des lots de qualité aviation et qu'ils ont été soumis aux essais prévus pour les avions destinés à effectuer des manœuvres acrobatiques (ci-joint compte rendu d'essais et déclarations des fournisseurs). 2° certifie que tous les matériaux autres que ceux du longeron et en particulier les bois ont été choisis comme possédant la qualité et les caractéristiques nécessaires à la fonction qui leur est dévolue (1) ; ont été choisis et utilisés conformément aux stipulations de la liasse de plans de l'avion ...... n° ...... tant en ce qui concerne leur nature que leur qualité (1). (1) Rayer la mention inutile.

Ces matériaux sont les suivants : (liste des matériaux)

BOIS	Pin d'Orégon - Contreplaqué bouleau et okoumé Colle Aérodux 185
MÉTAUX	Acier XC18S et 25 CD4S . Alu 2024 T3 et 2017
TOILE	Polyester dacron 3000 kg.
ENDUITS	Enduits colle et tension, peinture polyuréthane Celomer
BOULONNERIE	Acier 80 kg/mm²

La présente déclaration est certifiée sincère et faite sous ma propre responsabilité, jointe au dossier technique de l'avion en vue du C.N.R.A.

Fait à CAEN ......, *le* 15.12.1980

Bon pour attestation de qualité des matériaux (mention à réécrire de la main du postulant).

Signature :

Bon pour attestation de qualité des matériaux

J. Durand

REMARQUE IMPORTANTE. — Cette attestation est à remplir par le postulant. Une seule des trois cases supérieures (A, B et C) correspond à la catégorie de son aéronef. Les deux autres cases seront rayées d'un trait diagonal.

Exemple : pour un avion prototype, rayer les cases « formule B » et « formule C », et remplir entièrement tout le reste de la formule.

Appendix 5

Organisations around the world: contact addresses

Argentina
EAA Argentina Chapter 722, c/o Ildefonso D. Durana (President), Valle 1362, 1406 Buenos Aires, Argentina
Tel: 432–1330

Australia
Sport Aircraft Association of Australia (SAAA), National Headquarters, PO Box 169, Clifton Hill, Victoria 3068, Australia
Tel: (03) 481 7912 Fax: (03) 481 3936

Austria
Igo Ettrich Club (Austrian Homebuilders), c/o Rudolf Holzmann, Stefan-Fadinger Strasse 18, A-4800 Attang-Puchheim, Austria
Tel: (07674) 2805

Belgium
Flemisch Amateur Aircraftbuilders (FAA), c/o Mr Georges Coussement (Secretary), Boomsesteenweg 57/59, B-2610 Wilrijk, Belgium
Tel: (0)3–827.0086 or (0)3–827.0087

Belgian Aircraft Homebuilders (BAH), c/o Mr Paul Verbruggen (President), Rue d'Irelande 26, B-1060 Bruxelles, Belgium
Tel: (0)2–538.7492

Réseau du Sport de l'Air de Belgique (RSAB), c/o Mr Alex Beghin (President) or Mr Francis Pourtois (Secretary), Rue Montoyer 1, Boite 65, B-1040 Bruxelles, Belgium
Tel: (0)2–720.2349 (Secretary)

Brazil
Aeroclube de Brazil, c/o Francisco Hublet, Base de Operacones, Aeroporto Jacarepagua, Av Alvorada 2541 – via 11, Rio de Janeiro, Brazil

Canada
Recreational Aircraft Association (RAA), 152 Harwood Ave S, Ajax, Ontario L1S 2H6, Canada
Tel: (416) 683–3517 Fax: (416) 428–2415

Czechoslovakia
Amateur Flying Association of Czechoslovakia (AFAC), c/o Petr Tucek, V Jezirkach 1544, 14900 Prague 4, Czechoslovakia

Denmark
KZ & Veteranfly Klubben (EAA Chapter 655), Secretary Kai S. Christensen, Vibevangen 1, DK-3700 Ronne, Denmark
Tel: (05395) 3890

Finland
Finlads Flygforbund (Experimental Section), Malmin Lentoasema 00700, Helsinki 70, Finland

France
Réseau du Sport de l'Air (RSA), 40 rue Sauffroy, 75017 Paris, France
Tel: 42.28.25.54

Germany
Oscar Ursinus Vereinigung (OUV), c/o Herr Ulrich Stiller, Friedrich Ebert Ring 54, 5400 Koblenz, Germany
Tel: 02613–7051

Great Britain
Popular Flying Association (PFA), Terminal Building, Shoreham Airport, Shoreham-by-Sea, Sussex BN43 5FF
Tel: (0273) 461616 Fax: (0273) 463390
British Microlight Aircraft Association (BMAA), Bullring, Deddington, Oxford OX5 4TT
Tel: (0869) 38888 Fax: (0869) 37116

Greece
Hellenic Experimental Aircraft Association (HEAA), c/o Pantelis Kalogerakos, 61 Vass, Sofia, Piraeus, Greece

Ireland
Society of Amateur Aircraft Constructors (SAAC), c/o David Ryan, 78 St Albans Park, Ballsbridge, Dublin 4, Eire
Tel: (0103531) 894212 (work); (0103531) 693101 (home)

Italy
Club Aviazione Popolare (CAP), Sig Alfredo Alemani, c/o CAP, 22 Via Roma, 21040 Venegono Superiore VA, Italy
Tel: (0331) 865204

Netherlands
Nederlandse Vereniging van Amateur Vliegtuigbouwers (NVAV), c/o Magda May, Beemsterlaan 13, 1718 AL Hoogwoud, Netherlands
Tel: (2263) 52639

New Caledonia
Réseau du Sport de l'Air du Nouvelle Caledonie, c/o Luciene Saucede, B P 25, Mont-Dore, New Caledonia

New Zealand
NZ Amateur Aircraft Constructors Association (AACA), National Office, PO Box 9711, Newmarket, Auckland, New Zealand
Tel: 09 520–4301 Fax: 09 524–9390

Norway
EAA Chapter 573 (Oslo-Norway), Grottenveinen 20, N-1177 Oslo II, Norway

South Africa
Experimental Aircraft Association of South Africa (EAASA), EAA Headquarters, PO Box 1993, Halfway House 1685, Transvaal, S Africa
Tel: (011) 318–1373

Spain
Asociacion de Aviacion Experimental (AAE), c/o M. Diego, Crehuet 34, 10004 Caceres, Spain
Tel: (02722) 9469

Sweden
EAA Chapter 222, Hägerstalund, 16476 Kista, Sweden
Tel: (08752) 7585 Fax: (08751) 9816

Switzerland
Réseau du Sport de l'Air Suisse (RSA-Suisse), President Bruno Vonlanthen, Fx Mullerstrasse 41, 3185 Schmitten, Switzerland
Tel: (037) 36.1352

United States of America
Experimental Aircraft Association (EAA), EAA Aviation Center, Wittman Airfield, Oshkosh, WI 54903-3086, USA
Tel: (414) 426–4800 Fax: (414) 426–4828

Note The addresses are believed to be correct at the time of publication, but will be subject to change thereafter.

Appendix 6

Directory of homebuilt and kitplane designs

A TOTAL OF 191 different basic homebuilt aircraft designs are included in the following tabulation. It includes both plans-built designs and kitplanes and is thought to contain the majority of significant designs available worldwide at the time of publication. Of necessity several lesser-known or less popular examples have been omitted, several two-seater derivatives of single-seat designs have only been briefly mentioned and, as with the general parameters of this book, it does not contain details of any rotorcraft.

The majority of the designs emanate from the USA, Canada, France and Great Britain, although one or two examples from Australia, Spain, Finland, Denmark and other less prolific countries can also be found. The inclusion of a design is not to be taken as a recommendation of the type's suitability for construction in any particular country, and a potential builder of a type is recommended first to approach the representative body for homebuilders in his particular country (see Appendix 5) before a final decision is made on construction of any particular type.

The variety of types included in this Directory is immense, ranging from the diminutive Volmer VJ.24W SunFun and MiniMax (both of which can be operated as microlights/ultralights) to the sophistication and speed of the Brockaw Bullett, and the Glasair III and Lancair IV kitplanes. Some designs, such as the Pietenpol Aircamper, from the very early days of homebuilding are included, as well as a few, such as the Ronnenburg Berkut, Tri-R KIS and Opus-3, that have only flown in prototype form at the time of publication. Where a significant proportion or all of a particular type is available in pre-manufactured kit form this is indicated by a 'K'—however, many plans retailers also produce significant substructures and components for a particular type to assist the homebuilder in the construction of his/her aircraft. Again, the availability of such components in, say, the USA does not necessarily mean that they will be approved for incorporation in a homebuilt in any other country.

The specifications are published here as a general guide. Dimensions between different homebuilt examples of the same type may vary and weights are particularly sensitive to the skill of a builder and the requirements of regulatory bodies in individual countries. Engine types are given as a guide and in most cases performance figures are quoted based on the hp rating also quoted. However, different engine types can be installed in many designs and engines of the same manufacturer but with different power outputs can also be used. Propellers of different pitches will determine performance in the climb and the cruise—the Rate of Climb and the Cruise Speed figures are therefore included only as a rough guide.

Addresses to contact for the purchase of plans and kits are correct at the time of publication—the inclusion of an address will not necessarily guarantee a response to any enquirer. A few French plans suppliers are known to be fickle and only to respond to requests actually written in French. Where a British agent is operating other than in the country of the plans/kits origin, two addresses are given.

The types included in this Directory are split in to Single-Seat, Two-Seat and Other (three, four and five-seat) designs. They are then subdivided within these seat-number categories into basic types of construction such as wood and fabric, steel tube/wood and fabric, metal, and composite—no particular design is exclusively in each category, but each has been included in the section covering a significant proportion of its construction. For example, a wood and fabric design will contain many metal fittings and could have a part steel-tube framework. Similarly, sheet metal designs may incorporate steel-tube or wood for certain parts. 'Composites' is an all-embracing word for the many different forms of foam, laminate, fibreglass, etc, structures that have developed in recent years.

Single-seat monoplanes—wood and fabric

Design name	Usual engine (hp)	Length ft/ins (m)	Span ft/ins (m)	Wing area (gross) ft² (m²)	Max weight lb (kg)	Empty weight lb (kg)	Rate of climb ft/min (m/min)	Cruise speed mph (km/h)	Contact address for more information
Alpha J-1B Don Quixote	VW (50)	16 0 (4.88)	23 7 (7.19)	76 (7.07)	690 (313)	390 (177)	785 (239)	112 (180)	Alpha Aviation Supply Co, PO Box 8641, Greenville, TX75401, USA
Bowers Fly Baby	Continental (65–100)	18 10 (5.75)	28 0 (8.54)	120 (11.15)	925 (420)	605 (274)	1100 (335)	109 (175)	Peter Bowers, 10458 16th Avenue S, Seattle, WA98168, USA
Brügger MB-2 Colibri	VW	15 9 (4.80)	19 8 (6.0)	89 (8.3)	727 (330)	474 (215)	590 (180)	99 (159)	Max Brügger, CH-1724 Zenauva, Switzerland
Butterfly Banty	Rotax 277 (28)	18 10 (5.74)	32 0 (9.76)	128 (11.90)	500 (227)	237 (108)	400 (122)	50 (81)	Butterfly Aero, 1333 Garrard Creek Rd, Oakville, WA98568, USA
Capena 01	Lycoming (200)	17 8 (5.39)	26.6 (8.08)	99 (9.20)	1212 (550)	970 (440)	3150 (960)	202 (325)	Louis Pena, Les Hts de Saubagnacq, 6 imp Grand Piton, 40100 Dax, France
Clutton FRED	VW (65)	16 0 (4.88)	22 6 (6.86)	110 (10.23)	800 (363)	550 (250)	400 (122)	70 (113)	Eric Clutton, 913 Cedar Lane, Tullahoma, TN37388, USA
Corby Starlet	VW (49)	14 10 (4.52)	18 6 (5.64)	68 (6.32)	750 (341)	450 (204)	850 (259)	130 (209)	CSN, 510 NW 46th Terrace, Plantation, FL33317, USA
Croses Ec-3 Pouploume	VW (10.5)	9 10 (3.00)	25 7 (7.80)	172 (16.0)	573 (260)	310 (140)	650 (198)	31 (50)	Emilien Croses, 63 route de Davayé (Aerodrome), 71000 Charnay-les-Macon, France
Druine D.31 Turbulent	VW	17 6 (5.34)	21 7 (6.58)	77 (7.16)	620 (281)	395 (179)	450 (137)	100 (161)	Rollasons Aircraft & Engines Ltd, Shoreham Airport, Shoreham-by-Sea, Sussex, England
Evans VP-1	VW (50)	18 0 (5.49)	24 0 (7.32)	100 (9.30)	750 (341)	440 (200)	400 (122)	75 (121)	Bud Evans, Box 744, La Jolla, CA92038, USA (Also from the PFA in England)
Fisher FP-202 Koala	Rotax 277 (28)	17 11 (5.47)	29 11 (9.13)	120 (11.16)	500 (227)	245 (111)	750 (229)	57 (92)	Fisher Flying Products Inc, PO Box 468, Edgeley, ND 58433, USA.
Isaacs Spitfire	Continental (100)	19 3 (5.87)	22 11 (6.99)	87 (8.09)	1100 (499)	805 (365)	1100 (336)	134 (214)	John Isaacs, 23 Linden Grove, Chandlers Ford, Hampshire SO5 1LE, England
Jodel D.9	VW	17 10 (5.44)	22 11 (6.99)	97 (9.02)	705 (320)	420 (191)	590 (180)	85 (137)	SA Avions Jodel, 37 Route de Seurre, 21200 Beaune, France
Jurca MJ.2 Tempete	Lycoming (110)	18 6 (5.64)	19 6 (5.95)	86 (8.00)	950 (431)	639 (290)	555 (169)	102 (164)	Marcel Jurca, 2 rue de Champs Phillipe, 92250 La Garenne-Colombes, France; also Ken Heit, 1733 Kansas, Flint, MI48506 USA
Jurca MJ.10 Spitfire	V.8 (200–300)	23 5 (7.14)	27 8 (8.44)	135 (12.56)	2860 (1298)	1450 (658)	1650 (503)	180 (290)	(See MJ2 Tempete)
Loehle Sport Parasol (K)	Rotax 503 (50)	18 5 (5.62)	25 6 (7.78)	114 (10.60)	548 (249)	252 (114)	750 (229)	65 (105)	Loehle Aviation Inc, Shipmans Creek Road, Wartrace, TN37183, USA
Loehle 5151 'Mustang' (P-40 also) (K)	Rotax 503 (50)	27 6 (8.39)	22 11 (6.99)	130 (12.09)	885 (402)	513 (233)	700 (214)	100 (161)	(As Sport Parasol above)
Luton LA-4 Minor	VW	20 9 (6.33)	25 0 (7.63)	125 (11.63)	750 (341)	390 (177)	300 (92)	69 (111)	PFA, Terminal Building, Shoreham Airport, Shoreham-by-Sea, Sussex BN43 5FF, England

Design name	Usual engine (hp)	Length ft/ins (m)	Span ft/ins (m)	Wing area (gross) ft^2 (m^2)	Max weight lb (kg)	Empty weight lb (kg)	Rate of climb ft/min (m/min)	Cruise speed mph (km/h)	Contact address for more information
Mini Max GB (K)	Arrow (34)	15 6 (4.73)	25 0 (7.63)	112 (10.46)	497 (226)	240 (109)	800 (244)	65 (105)	Ultra Light Flying Machines, 19 Kingshill Rd, Dursley, Glos GL11 4EU, England (also from TEAM, Rte 1, Box 338c, Bradyville, TN37026, USA)
Nicollier HN433 Ménestrel	VW (50)	17 4 (5.29)	23 0 (7.02)	88 (8.18)	727 (330)	443 (201)	845 (258)	112 (180)	Henri Nicollier, 13 rue de Verdun, 78130 Besancon, France
Piel CP.80 Zef	Continental (100)	20 10 (6.35)	23 8 (7.22)	67 (6.23)	770 (350)	495 (225)	1000 (305)	150 (242)	M. E. Littner, 140 Philippe Goulet, Repentigny, Quebec J5Y 3MI, Canada
Statoplan AG-02 Poussin	VW	14 10 (4.52)	21 0 (6.41)	66 (6.14)	617 (280)	375 (170)	435 (133)	89 (143)	Siravia, Aerodrome de Pons-Avy, 17800 Pons, France
Stern ST.80 Balade (St.87 Europlane 2-seater also)	VW	15 9 (4.80)	20 4 (6.20)	75 (6.98)	772 (350)	507 (230)	785 (240)	112 (180)	Rene Stern, 10 rue de Chateau, 57730 Folschviller, France
Taylor JT-2 Titch (also Monoplane)	Continental (85)	16 1 (4.90)	18 9 (5.72)	68 (6.32)	745 (338)	500 (227)	1100 (336)	154 (250)	Terry Taylor, 79 Springwater Road, Leigh-on-Sea, Essex SS9 5BW, England

Single-seat monoplanes—wood and composites

Design name	Usual engine (hp)	Length ft/ins (m)	Span ft/ins (m)	Wing area (gross) ft^2 (m^2)	Max weight lb (kg)	Empty weight lb (kg)	Rate of climb ft/min (m/min)	Cruise speed mph (km/h)	Contact address for more information
Hipps Super Sportster (metal tubing also) (K)	Rotax 447 (40)	16 4 (4.98)	28 0 (8.54)	112 (10.42)	550 (250)	260 (118)	800 (244)	70 (113)	Hipps Superbirds Inc, PO Box 266, Saluda, NC28773, USA
Jurca MJ-7 Gnatsum	V-8 (200)	21 6 (6.56)	24 8 (7.52)	118 (10.97)	1900 (863)	1465 (665)	1000 (305)	210 (338)	(See MJ 2 Tempete)
WAR Corsair replica (also FW-190/P.47/Sea Fury)	Continental (100)	16 6 (5.03)	20 0 (6.10)	79 (7.35)	1200 (545)	650 (295)	1400 (427)	145 (233)	New plans/components believed to be no longer available

Single-seat monoplanes—steel tube/wood/fabric

Design name	Usual engine (hp)	Length ft/ins (m)	Span ft/ins (m)	Wing area (gross) ft^2 (m^2)	Max weight lb (kg)	Empty weight lb (kg)	Rate of climb ft/min (m/min)	Cruise speed mph (km/h)	Contact address for more information
Aerolites Bearcat (K)	Rotax 447 (42)	17 6 (5.34)	30 8 (9.35)	160 (14.88)	750 (341)	300 (136)	700 (214)	63 (101)	Aerolites Inc, Route, Box 187, Welsh, LA70591, USA
Corben Baby Ace D	Continental (65)	17 8 (5.39)	26 5 (8.06)	112 (10.42)	900 (409)	575 (261)	1200 (366)	90 (145)	Ace Aircraft Co, 05-134th Street, Chesapeake, WV25315, USA
Cassutt Racer II	Continental (100)	16 0 (4.88)	15 0 (4.58)	66 (6.14)	900 (409)	550 (250)	2500 (763)	190 (306)	National Aeronautics & Mfg. Co, PO Box 1718, Independence, MO64055, USA
Kolb Firestar (K)	Rotax 447 (35)	21 3 (6.48)	27 6 (8.39)	148 (13.76)	550 (250)	254 (115)	1000 (305)	55 (89)	Kolb Company Inc, RD3, Box 38, Phoenixville, PA19460, USA
Light Miniature LM-1 (J-3 Cub replica) (also LM-2 LM-3) (K)	Rotax 377 (35)	17 8 (5.39)	28 0 (8.54)	120 (11.16)	600 (272)	345 (157)	450 (137)	55 (89)	Light Miniature Aircraft, Bldg 411, Opa Locka Airport, Opa Locka, FL33054, USA
Maxair ARV582 (K)	Rotax 582 (65)	19 0 (5.80)	23 0 (7.02)	117 (10.88)	570 (259)	315 (143)	1300 (397)	60 (97)	Maxair Aircraft Corp, 3855 Highway 27 North, Lake Wales, FL33853, USA

Design name		Usual engine (hp)	Length ft/ins (m)	Span ft/ins (m)	Wing area (gross) ft^2 (m^2)	Max weight lb (kg)	Empty weight lb (kg)	Rate of climb ft/min (m/min)	Cruise speed mph (km/h)	Contact address for more information
Monnett Sonerai I (2-seat version also)		VW (60)	19 0 (5.80)	16 8 (5.08)	75 (6.98)	700 (318)	440 (200)	1200 (366)	150 (242)	Great Plains Aircraft Supply Co Inc, PO Box 304 St Charles, IL 60174, USA
Pober Pixie		VW (55)	17 3 (5.26)	29 10 (9.10)	134 (12.46)	900 (409)	543 (247)	700 (214)	83 (134)	Acro Sport Inc, PO Box 462, Hales Corner, WI53130, USA
Preceptor N-3 Pup/ Super Pup	(K)	Mosler MM-CB (35)	16 6 (5.03)	26 0 (7.93)	95 (8.84)	600 (272)	300 (136)	500 (153)	80 (129)	Preceptor Aircraft, 1230 Shepherd St, Hendersonville, NC 28739, USA
Quicksilver MX Sport	(K)	Rotax 447 (40)	18 2 (5.54)	28 9 (8.77)	161 (14.97)	520 (236)	253 (115)	825 (252)	58 (93)	Quicksilver Enterprises, PO Box 1572, Temecula, CA92390, USA
RANS Coyote	(K)	Rotax 447 (42)	17 0 (5.19)	29 6 (9.00)	127 (11.81)	587 (266)	254 (115)	1200 (366)	60 (97)	Sportair UK Ltd, The Airfield, Felixkirk, Thirsk, N Yorks YO7 2DR, England (also at RANS Co, 1104 E Hiway 40 Bypass, Hays, KS67601, USA)
RANS S-9 Chaos	(K)	Rotax 503 (47)	15 8 (4.78)	22 0 (6.71)	92 (8.56)	670 (304)	360 (163)	1200 (366)	90 (145)	(As RANS Coyote above)
Stolp SA-500 Starlet		VW (65)	17 0 (5.19)	25 0 (7.63)	83 (7.72)	1000 (454)	650 (295)	1200 (366)	105 (169)	Stolp Starduster Corp, 4301 Twining St, Riverside, CA95209, USA
Tipsy Nipper		VW	15 0 (4.58)	19 8 (6.00)	81 (7.53)	750 (341)	465 (211)	650 (198)	92 (148)	Nipper Kits & Components Ltd, 'Foxley', Blackness Lane, Keston, Kent BR2 6HL, England
Volmer VJ.24W SunFun		Yamaha (15)	18 6 (5.64)	36 0 (10.98)	163 (15.16)	410 (186)	210 (95)	350 (107)	30 (48)	Volmer Aircraft, Box 5222, Glendale, CA91201, USA
Whittaker MW-6 Merlin (also MW-7)		Rotax 503 (47)	18 0 (5.49)	32 0 (9.76)	160 (14.88)	820 (372)	360 (163)	700 (214)	63 (101)	Mike Whittaker, Dawlish Cottage, Pincots Lane, Wickwar, Wootton-u-Edge, Gloucestershire, GL12 8NY, England
Flightworks Capella (also 2 seat version)	(K)	Rotax 503 (46)	17 4 (5.29)	27 6 (8.39)	110 (10.23)	625 (284)	340 (154)	830 (253)	92 (148)	Flightworks Corp, 4211-C Todd Ln, Austin, TX 78744, USA

Single-seat monoplanes—steel tube/composites

Design name		Usual engine (hp)	Length ft/ins (m)	Span ft/ins (m)	Wing area (gross) ft^2 (m^2)	Max weight lb (kg)	Empty weight lb (kg)	Rate of climb ft/min (m/min)	Cruise speed mph (km/h)	Contact address for more information
Advance Aviation Carrera (also Sierra sail plane)	(K)	Rotax 447 (40)	20 4 (6.20)	27 10 (8.49)	134 (12.46)	600 (272)	285 (129)	850 (259)	60 (97)	Advance Aviation Inc, 323 N. Ivey Lane, Orlando, FL32811, USA

Single-seat monoplanes—metal

Design name		Usual engine (hp)	Length ft/ins (m)	Span ft/ins (m)	Wing area (gross) ft^2 (m^2)	Max weight lb (kg)	Empty weight lb (kg)	Rate of climb ft/min (m/min)	Cruise speed mph (km/h)	Contact address for more information
Bushby Midget Mustang		Lycoming (150)	16 6 (5.03)	16 6 (5.03)	68 (6.32)	1000 (454)	620 (281)	2800 (854)	235 (378)	Bushby Aircraft Inc, 674 Rt. 52, Minooka, IL60447, USA
Colomban Cri-Cri		2×JPX (22 each)	12 10 (3.91)	16 1 (4.90)	33 (3.07)	375 (170)	176 (80)	1280 (390)	112 (180)	Michel Colomban, 37 bis Rue Lakanal, 92500 Rueil Malmaison, France
Davis D-5A		Continental (65)	15 9 (4.80)	15 8 (4.78)	62 (5.77)	775 (352)	460 (209)	900 (275)	140 (225)	D2 Inc, PO Box 524, LaPine, OR97739, USA

Design name	Usual engine (hp)	Length ft/ins (m)	Span ft/ins (m)	Wing area (gross) ft^2 (m^2)	Max weight lb (kg)	Empty weight lb (kg)	Rate of climb ft/min (m/min)	Cruise speed mph (km/h)	Contact address for more information
Hummel Bird	½ aVW (30)	13 4 (4.07)	21 0 (6.41)	63 (5.86)	520 (236)	268 (122)	675 (206)	105 (169)	Morry Hummel, 509 E. Butler, Bryan, OH43506-0880, USA
Pazmany PL-4A	VW (50)	16 6 (5.03)	26 9 (8.16)	89 (8.28)	850 (386)	578 (262)	650 (198)	97 (156)	Pazmany Aircraft Corp, PO Box 80051, San Diego, CA92138, USA
Pottier P.80S	VW (50)	16 9 (5.11)	19 0 (5.80)	80 (7.44)	640 (291)	397 (180)	985 (300)	102 (164)	Jean Pottier, 4 rue de Poissy, 78130 Les Mureaux, France
Teenie Two	VW (60)	12 10 (3.91)	18 0 (5.49)	59 (5.49)	585 (266)	320 (145)	1000 (305)	120 (193)	Teenie Co, Box 2092/Box 625, Harker Heights, TX76543, USA
Vans RV-3	Lycoming (150)	19 0 (5.80)	19 4 (5.90)	90 (8.37)	1100 (499)	750 (341)	2300 (702)	200 (322)	Vans Aircraft Inc, PO Box 160, North Plains, OR97133, USA

Single-seat monoplanes—metal/composites

Design name	Usual engine (hp)	Length ft/ins (m)	Span ft/ins (m)	Wing area (gross) ft^2 (m^2)	Max weight lb (kg)	Empty weight lb (kg)	Rate of climb ft/min (m/min)	Cruise speed mph (km/h)	Contact address for more information
Alturair Bede BD-5	Honda (90)	14 0 (4.27)	17 0 (5.19)	variable	1000 (454)	600 (272)	1900 (580)	200 (322)	Alturair, 1405 N Johnson Ave, El Cajon, CA92020 (also Bede Micro Avn Inc, 1484 Carmel Drive, San Jose, CA95125, USA
Taylor Mini-Imp	(50-100)	16 0 (4.88)	25 0 (7.63)		850 (386)	500 (227)	1000 (305)	150 (242)	Molt Taylor, PO Box 1171, Longview, WA98632, USA

Single-seat monoplanes—composites

Design name	Usual engine (hp)	Length ft/ins (m)	Span ft/ins (m)	Wing area (gross) ft^2 (m^2)	Max weight lb (kg)	Empty weight lb (kg)	Rate of climb ft/min (m/min)	Cruise speed mph (km/h)	Contact address for more information
Araco Windex 1200 (motor glider) (K)	Konig (24)	16 2 (4.93)	39 9 (12.12)	80 (7.44)	661 (300)	330 (150)	800 (244)	130 (209)	Araco, 1121 Lewes Ave, Sarasota, FL34237, USA (also at AB Radab, PO Box 92054, S-12006 Stockholm, Sweden)
Australite Ultrabat (K)	Rotax 583 (85)	16 3 (4.96)	21 0 (6.41)	52 (4.84)	650 (295)	350 (159)	1800 (549)	126 (203)	Australite, Inc, 1301 Tower Square, #3, Ventura, CA 93003, USA
Lightning Bug (K)	AMW 636 (90)	17 6 (5.34)	17 10 (5.44)	40 (3.72)	750 (341)	375 (170)	1200 (366)	225 (362)	Lightning Bug Aircraft Corp, PO Drawer 40, Sheldon, SC29941, USA
Lunds Tekniske Silhouette (K)	Rotax (50)	19 3 (5.87)	32 0 (9.75)	76 (7.06)	824 (374)	578 (262)	800 (244)	120 (193)	Lunds Tekniske, Vikaveien, 2, N-8600 Norway

Single-seat biplanes—wood and fabric

Design name	Usual engine (hp)	Length ft/ins (m)	Span ft/ins (m)	Wing area (gross) ft^2 (m^2)	Max weight lb (kg)	Empty weight lb (kg)	Rate of climb ft/min (m/min)	Cruise speed mph (km/h)	Contact address for more information
Currie Wot	Continental (65)	18 3 (5.57)	22 1 (6.73)	140 (13.02)	900 (409)	395 (179)	600 (183)	90 (145)	PFA, Terminal Building, Shoreham Airport, Shoreham-by-Sea, Sussex BN43 5FF, England
Falconar/Mignet HM. 293 (also HM. 360)	VW (60)	13 0 (3.97)	20 0 (6.10)	113 (10.51)	600 (272)	350 (159)	1400 (427)	90 (145)	Falconar Aviation Ltd, 19 Airport Rd, Edmonton, Alberta, T5E OW7, Canada

Design name	Usual engine (hp)	Length ft/ins (m)	Span ft/ins (m)	Wing area (gross) ft^2 (m^2)	Max weight lb (kg)	Empty weight lb (kg)	Rate of climb ft/min (m/min)	Cruise speed mph (km/h)	Contact address for more information
Fisher FP-404EXP (K)	Rotax 503 (52)	14 6 (4.42)	18 0 (5.49)	120 (11.16)	540 (245)	275 (125)	800 (244)	72 (116)	Anglian Vintage Aeroplanes, 127 Lifstan Road, Southend-on-Sea, Essex, SS1 2XG, England (also Fisher Flying Products Inc, PO Box 468, Edgeley, ND 58433, USA)
Guerpont Biplum	Konig (22)	16 9 (5.10)	21 4 (6.50)	137 (12.7)	419 (190)	210 (95)	394 (120)	57 (92)	Maurice Guerpont, 12 rue Vigée Lebrun, 75015 Paris, France
Isaacs Fury	Lycoming (125)	19 3 (5.87)	21 0 (6.41)	124 (11.53)	1000 454	710 (320)	1600 (488)	100 (161)	John Isaacs, 23 Linden Grove, Chandlers Ford, Hants, SO5 1LE, England
K & S Jungster 1	Lycoming (100)	16 0 (4.88)	16 11 (5.16)	80 (7.44)	1000 454	606 (275)	1000 (305)	102 (164)	Macfam, PO Box 788, Great Falls, MT59403-0788, USA
Replica Plans SE.5a	Continental (85)	18 2 (5.54)	22 10 (6.96)	140 (13.02)	1100 (499)	790 (359)	500 (153)	85 (137)	Replica Plans, PO Box 346, Yarrow, British Columbia, VOX 2AO, Canada
Skycraft/Staaker Z-1 Flitzer (K)	VW/JPX (55)	14 9 (4.50)	18 0 (5.49)	100 (9.30)			600 (183)	80 (129)	Skycraft, Whitehouse, Monkswood, USK, Gwent NP5 1QB, Great Britain
Wolf W-11 Boredom Fighter	Continental (65)	15 7 (4.75)	20 0 (6.10)	100 (9.30)	770 (350)	473 (215)	1200 (366)	110 (177)	Donald Wolf, 17 Chestnut St, Huntington, NY11743, USA

Single-seat biplanes—steel-tube/wood/fabric

Design name	Usual engine (hp)	Length ft/ins (m)	Span ft/ins (m)	Wing area (gross) ft^2 (m^2)	Max weight lb (kg)	Empty weight lb (kg)	Rate of climb ft/min (m/min)	Cruise speed mph (km/h)	Contact address for more information
EAA Acro Sport 1 (also 2-seat version)	Lycoming (180)	17 7 (5.36)	19 8 (6.00)	116 (10.79)	1178 (535)	739 (336)	3500 (1068)	130 (209)	Acro Sport Inc, PO Box 462, Hales Corner, WI53130, USA
Oldfield Baby Lakes (also 2-seat version)	Continental (85)	13 8 (4.17)	16 8 (5.08)	88 (8.18)	850 (386)	480 (218)	2000 (610)	118 (190)	Barney Oldfield Aircraft Co, PO Box 228, Needham, MA 02192, USA
Redfern Fokker Triplane Replica	Warner (145)	19 0 (5.80)	23 9 (7.24)	202 (18.79)	1456 (661)	1112 (505)	2000 (610)	100 (161)	W. W. Redfern, N.26009 Silverwood Lane, Athol, ID 83801, USA
Sorrell Hiperlight SNS-8 EXP (K)	Rotax 377 (36)	15 7 (4.75)	22 0 (6.71)	140 (13.02)	550 (250)	300 (136)	1000 (305)	70 (113)	Sorrell Aircraft Co Ltd, 16525 Tilley Rd S, Tenino, WA98589, USA
Stolp V-Star SA-900	Lycoming (65)	17 2 (5.24)	23 0 (7.02)	141 (13.11)	1000 (454)	700 (318)	600 (183)	75 (121)	Stolp Starduster Corp, 4301 Twining St, Riverside, CA95209, USA
Ultimate 10 Dash 100	Continental (100)	17 6 (5.33)	15 10 (4.83)	96 (8.92)	1350 (612)	790 (358)	1150 (350)	140 (225)	Ultimate Aircraft Corp, Guelph Airpark, Guelph, Ontario, N1H 6H8, Canada

Single-seat biplanes—metal

Design name	Usual engine (hp)	Length ft/ins (m)	Span ft/ins (m)	Wing area (gross) ft^2 (m^2)	Max weight lb (kg)	Empty weight lb (kg)	Rate of climb ft/min (m/min)	Cruise speed mph (km/h)	Contact address for more information
Aerosport Scamp	VW (1834cc)	14 0 (4.27)	17 6 (5.34)	105 (9.77)	800 (363)	520 (236)	750 (229)	90 (145)	Aerosport Ltd, Box 278, Airport, Holly Springs, NC 27540, USA
Andreasson BA-4B	Continental (100)	15 0 (4.60)	17 7 (5.34)	89 (8.30)	827 (375)		2000 (610)	120 (193)	Björn Andreasson, Collins Vag 22B, 23600 Höllviksnäs, Sweden

Design name	Usual engine (hp)	Length ft/ins (m)	Span ft/ins (m)	Wing area (gross) ft² (m²)	Max weight lb (kg)	Empty weight lb (kg)	Rate of climb ft/min (m/min)	Cruise speed mph (km/h)	Contact address for more information
Two-seat monoplanes—wood and fabric									
Anderson Kingfisher	Continental (115)	23 7 (7.19)	36 0 (10.98)	185 (17.21)	1600 (726)	1092 (496)	550 (168)	85 (137)	Warner Aviation, PO Box 187, Covington, LA70434, USA
Buethe (Jeffair) Barracuda (K)	Lycoming (250)	21 6 (6.56)	24 10 (7.57)	120 (11.16)	2300 (1044)	1500 (681)	2000 (610)	195 (314)	Buethe Enterprises, Inc, PO Box 486, Cathedral City, CA92234, USA
Bilouis 01	Lycoming (200)	21 2 (6.45)	27 6 (8.40)	123 (11.40)	1896 (860)	1279 (580)	2360 (719)	168 (270)	Louis Pena, Les Hts de Saubagnacq, 6 imp Grand Piton, 40100 Dax, France
CAP-10	Lycoming (180)	23 6 (7.16)	26 5 (8.06)	117 (10.85)	1829 (830)	1213 (550)	1575 (480)	155 (250)	Avions Mudry et Cie, Aerodrome de Bernay, BP214, 27300 Bernay, France
Coupe JC-3 (also JC-200)	VW (68)	21 0 (6.40)	27 5 (8.35)	126 (11.69)	1279 (580)	728 (330)		87 (140)	Jacques Coupé, La Trute, Azay-sur-Cher, 37270 Montlouis sur Loire, France
Cvjetkovic CA-65	Continental (115)	19 0 (5.80)	25 0 (7.63)	108 (10.04)	1500 (681)	900 (409)	1000 (305)	155 (250)	Anton Cvjetkovic, 5324W 121st Street, Hawthorne, CA90250, USA
Fisher Horizon 1 (K)	Limbach (80)	18 8 (5.69)	30 0 (9.15)	165 (15.35)	1050 (477)	570 (259)	900 (275)	85 (137)	Fisher Aero Visions, Portsmouth Regional Airport, Route 2, Sciotoville, OH45662, USA
Fisher Super Koala (also single-seat Koala) (K)	Rotax 503 (52)	18 2 (5.54)	31 0 (9.46)	140 (13.02)	740 (336)	330 (150)	800 (244)	70 (113)	Anglian Vintage Aeroplanes, 127 Lifstan Road, Southend on Sea, Essex SS1 2XG England (also at Fisher Flying Products, PO Box 468, Edgeley, N58433, USA)
Fournier (Aero Jaen) RF-5 'Serrania' (K)	Limbach (80)	25 7 (7.80)	45 0 (13.74)	163 (15.16)	1433 (650)	948 (430)	640 (195)	117 (190)	Aeronautica de Jaen SA, Aeródrome 'El Cornicabral', PO Box 40, 23280 Beas de Segura, Spain
Jodel D.11	Continental (65–100)	17 10 (5.44)	27 0 (8.24)	137 (12.74)	1240 (563)	595 (270)	550 (168)	99 (159)	S.A. Avions Jodel, 37 Rt de Seurre 21200 Beaune, France (also Falconar Aviation Ltd, Airport Rd, Edmonton, Alberta, T5E OW7, Canada)
Jodel D.150 Mascaret	(100–115)	20 8 (6.30)	26 8 (8.13)	141 (13.11)	1587 (720)	750 (341)	630 (192)	135 (217)	SA Avions Jodel (see above)
Jodel D.18 (also tri-gear D.19)	VW	18 8 (5.69)	24 7 (7.50)	106 (9.86)	1014 (460)	551 (250)	688 (210)	105 (169)	SA Avions Jodel (see above)
Jurca MJ.5 Sirocco	Lycoming (160)	21 0 (6.41)	21 6 (6.56)	108 (10.04)	1860 (844)	1260 (572)	1850 (564)	172 (277)	Marcel Jurca, 2 rue de Champs Philippe, 92250 La Garenne-Colombes, France (also at Ken Heit, 1733 Kansas, Flint, MI48506, USA)
K & S Cavalier	Continental (100)	21 7 (6.58)	27 6 (8.39)	118 (10.97)	1800 (817)	950 (431)	1200 (366)	138 (222)	Macfam, PO Box 788, Great Falls, MT59403-0788, USA
Nicollier HN700 Menestrel II	Limbach (80)	17 5 (5.30)	25 7 (7.80)	105 (9.80)	1102 (500)	622 (282)	1280 (390)	116 (187)	Avions H. Nicollier, 13 rue de Verdun, 25000 Besançon, France

Design name	Usual engine (hp)	Length ft/ins (m)	Span ft/ins (m)	Wing area (gross) ft^2 (m^2)	Max weight lb (kg)	Empty weight lb (kg)	Rate of climb ft/min (m/min)	Cruise speed mph (km/h)	Contact address for more information
Pereira GP.4	Lycoming (200)	21 0 (6.41)	24 7 (7.50)	104 (9.67)	2000 (908)	1240 (563)	2500 (763)	240 (386)	Osprey Aircraft, 3741 El Ricon Way, Sacramento, CA95825, USA
Piel CP328 Super Emeraude	Lycoming (100)	21 0 (6.41)	26 6 (8.08)	117 (10.88)	1500 (681)	850 (386)	700 (214)	125 (201)	E. (Gene) Litner, 140 Philippe Goulet, Repentigny, Quebec, J5Y 3M1, Canada
Pietenpol Aircamper	Ford model A (40)	17 10 (5.44)	29 6 (9.00)	140 (13.02)	1020 (463)	620 (281)	500 (153)	75 (121)	J. Wills, 1 Humber Rd, Blackheath, London SE3 7LT (also at Don Pietenpol, 1604 Meadow Circle SE, Rochester, MN55904-5251, USA)
Sequoia F.8L Falco (K)	Lycoming (150–180)	21 4 (6.51)	26 3 (8.01)	108 (10.04)	1880 (853)	1212 (550)	1140 (348)	190 (306)	Sequoia Aircraft Corp, 2000 Tomlynn St, PO Box 6861, Richmond, VA23230, USA
Turner T.40	Lycoming (150)	20 1 (6.12)	28 0 (8.53)	102 (9.48)	1650 (748)	828 (376)	1500 (457)	175 (282)	Turner Aircraft Inc, Route 4, Box 115AB3, Grandview, Texas 76050, USA
Volmer VJ-22 Sportsman	Continental (85)	24 0 (7.32)	36 6 (11.13)	180 (16.74)	1500 (681)	1000 (454)	550 (168)	80 (129)	Volmer Aircraft, Box 5222, Glendale, CA91201, USA

Two-seat monoplanes—wood/metal/composites

Design name	Usual engine (hp)	Length ft/ins (m)	Span ft/ins (m)	Wing area (gross) ft^2 (m^2)	Max weight lb (kg)	Empty weight lb (kg)	Rate of climb ft/min (m/min)	Cruise speed mph (km/h)	Contact address for more information
Taylor Coot	(150–225)	22 0 (6.71)	36 0 (10.98)	180 (16.74)	2150 (976)	1450 (658)	1200 (366)	120 (193)	Molt Taylor, PO Box 1171, Longview, WA98632, USA

Two-seat monoplanes—wood and composites

Design name	Usual engine (hp)	Length ft/ins (m)	Span ft/ins (m)	Wing area (gross) ft^2 (m^2)	Max weight lb (kg)	Empty weight lb (kg)	Rate of climb ft/min (m/min)	Cruise speed mph (km/h)	Contact address for more information
Brandli BX-2 Cherry	Continental (65)	17 2 (5.24)	23 0 (7.02)	90 (8.37)	1212 (550)	683 (310)	680 (207)	125 (201)	Max Brandli, BX Aviation, Höheweg 2, CH2553 Safnern, Switzerland
Junqua RJ03 Ibis	VW (47–65)	15 1 (4.60)	19 8 (6.00)		926 (420)	496 (225)	800 (244)	124 (200)	Jean-Claude Junqua, c/o S.C.A.M., 69 rue Garibaldi, 94100 St Maur, France
Martenko ATOL (K)	Rotax 582 (64)	20 5 (6.22)	31 6 (9.60)	155 (14.40)	992 (450)	472 (214)	500 (153)	87 (140)	Martenko, Nikkarinkuja 8, 96910 Rovaniemi, Finland
Mirage Celerity (K)	Lycoming (160)	22 8 (6.91)	25 0 (7.63)	100 (9.30)	1800 (817)	1169 (530)	1800 (549)	205 (330)	Mirage Aircraft Inc, 3936 Austin St, Klamath Falls, OR97603, USA
Pereira Osprey 2	Lycoming (150)	21 0 (6.41)	26 0 (7.93)	130 (12.09)	1570 (713)	960 (436)	1300 (397)	130 (209)	Osprey Aircraft, 3741 El Ricon Way, Sacramento, CA95825, USA
Rand KR-2	VW (2100cc)	14 6 (4.42)	20 8 (6.30)	80 (7.44)	1100 (499)	580 (263)	600 (183)	138 (222)	Rand-Robinson Engineering Inc, 15641 Product Lane, #A5, Huntington Beach, CA92649, USA

Two-seat monoplanes—steel-tube/wood and/or fabric

Design name	Usual engine (hp)	Length ft/ins (m)	Span ft/ins (m)	Wing area (gross) ft^2 (m^2)	Max weight lb (kg)	Empty weight lb (kg)	Rate of climb ft/min (m/min)	Cruise speed mph (km/h)	Contact address for more information
Aces High Cuby II (K)	Rotax 503 (52)	18 3 (5.57)	33 6 (10.22)	161 (14.97)	1058 (480)	413 (188)	700 (214)	80 (129)	Aces High Light Aircraft Ltd, RR#1, London, Ontario, N6A 4B5, Canada

Design name	Usual engine (hp)	Length ft/ins (m)	Span ft/ins (m)	Wing area (gross) ft^2 (m^2)	Max weight lb (kg)	Empty weight lb (kg)	Rate of climb ft/min (m/min)	Cruise speed mph (km/h)	Contact address for more information
Acey Deucy	Continental (65)	21 0 (6.41)	32 0 (9.76)	155 (14.42)	1275 (579)	750 (341)	500 (153)	87 (140)	Acey-Deucy Plans, 4 Donald Drive, Middletown, RI-02840-6226, USA
Advanced Aviation Buccaneer II (K)	Rotax 582 (65)	21 10 (6.66)	33 6 (10.22)	171 (15.90)	1025 (465)	520 (236)	500 (off water) (153)	60 (97)	Advance Aviation Inc, 323 N-Ivey Lane, Orlando, FL32811, USA
Anglin Spacewalker (K)	(65)	19 9 (6.02)	28 0 (8.54)	126 (11.72)	1250 (568)	730 (331)	1100 (336)	115 (185)	Anglin Engineering, Rt2, Box 281B, Rutherfordton, NC28139, USA
Arrow (K)	Rotax 532 (64)	19 6 (5.95)	33 0 (10.07)	158 (14.69)	850 (386)	430 (195)	1100 (336)	75 (121)	Arrow Aircraft Co, 14877 Buena Vista Ave, White Rock, BC, V4B 1X3, Canada
Avid Amphibian (K)	Rotax 582 (65)	19 5 (5.92)	36 0 (10.98)	150 (13.95)	1200 (545)	600 (272)	940 (287)	75 (121)	Martin Ott, The Elms, Cutlers Green, Thaxted, CM6 ZQA, England (also at Avid Aircraft Inc, PO Box 728, Caldwell, ID 83606, USA
Avid Flyer (also Avid Mk IV) (K)	Rotax 532 (64)	17 0 (5.19)	23 11 (7.30)	97 (9.02)	911 (414)	430 (195)	1200 (366)	110 (177)	(As for Avid Amphibian above)
Carlson Sparrow II (K)	Rotax 532 (65)	18 0 (5.49)	31 6 (9.61)	140 (13.02)	1050 (477)	515 (234)	1200 (366)	95 (153)	Carlson Aircraft Inc, 50643 S.R. 14, East Palestine, OH44413, USA
Classic Aircraft Replicas LM-5 (full scale Super Cub) (K)	Rotax 532 (65)	22 7 (6.89)	35 2 (10.73)	178 (16.55)	1050 (477)	625 (284)	650 (198)	80 (129)	Classic Aircraft Replicas, Bldg 411, Opa Locka Airport, Opa Locka, FL33054, USA
Denney Kitfox IV (K)	Rotax 582 (65)	17 8 (5.39)	32 0 (9.76)	131 (12.18)	1050 (477)	440 (200)	1600 (488)	100 (161)	Border Aviation Ltd, Unit 6, Tweedvale Mills, Walkerburn, EH43 6AJ, Scotland, UK (also Denney Aerocraft Co, 100 N Kings Rd, Nampa, ID83687 USA)
Elmwood Christavia Mk.1	Continental (65)	21 0 (6.41)	32 6 (9.91)	146 (13.58)	1500 (681)	720 (327)	900 (275)	105 (169)	Elmwood Aviation, RR#4, Elmwood Dr, Belleville, Ontario K8N 4Z4, Canada
Junior Ace E	Continental (85)	18 0 (5.49)	26 5 (8.06)	112 (10.42)	1300 (590)	782 (355)	500 (153)	90 (145)	Ace Aircraft Co, 05-134th Street, Chesapeake, WV25315, USA
Monnett Sonerai II	VW (70)	18 10 (5.74)	18 8 (5.69)	84 (7.81)	925 (420)	520 (236)	500 (153)	155 (250)	Great Plains Aircraft Supply Co Inc, PO Box 304, St Charles, IL60174, USA
Montana Coyote (K)	Lycoming or Honda (85–150)	23 0 (7.02)	39 0 (11.90)	166 (15.44)	1600 (726)	850 (386)	2000 (610)	90 (145)	Montana Coyote, 3302 Airport Road, Helena, MT59601, USA
Nesmith Cougar	Continental (85)	18 11 (5.77)	20 6 (6.25)	83 (7.72)	1250 (568)	624 (283)	1000 (305)	135 (217)	Acro Sport Inc, PO Box 462, Hales Corner, WI53130, USA
Piel CP.750 Beryl	(150)	22 11 (6.99)	26 6 (8.08)	117 (10.88)	1800 (817)	1000 (454)	1400 (427)	160 (258)	E. (Gene) Litner, 140 Philippe Goulet, Repentigny, Quebec J5Y 3MI, Canada
Preceptor N3-2 Pup (K)	Mosler MM-CB (35)	16 9 (5.11)	30 6 (9.30)		800 (363)	350 (159)	500 (153)	60 (97)	Preceptor Aircraft, 1230 Shepherd St, Hendersonville, NC 28739, USA
Protech Prostar PT-2B (K)	Lycoming (150)	17 6 (5.34)	32 0 (9.76)	137 (12.74)	1550 (704)	700 (318)	1000 (305)	110 (117)	ProTech Aircraft, 24215 FM1093, Richmond, TX77469, USA

Design name	Usual engine (hp)	Length ft/ins (m)	Span ft/ins (m)	Wing area (gross) ft^2 (m^2)	Max weight lb (kg)	Empty weight lb (kg)	Rate of climb ft/min (m/min)	Cruise speed mph (km/h)	Contact address for more information
Quad City Challenger II (K)	Rotax 447 (42)	19 0 (5.80)	31 0 (9.46)	175 (16.28)	800 (363)	310 (141)	1000 (305)	70 (113)	West Country Aviation, Motor Point, Fenney Bridges, Devon EX14 0BG, England (also Quad City Aircraft Corp, 3610 Coaltown Rd, Moline, IL61265, USA
Rans S-6 Coyote II (K)	Rotax 582 (65)	20 0 (6.10)	34 6 (10.52)	155 (14.42)	950 (431)	425 (193)	1000 (305)	95 (153)	Sportair UK Ltd, The Airfield, Felixkirk, Thirsk, N. Yorks YO7 2DR, England (also RANS Co, 1104E Hiway 40 Bypass, Hays, KS67601, USA)
Rans S-10 Sakota (K)	Rotax 582 (65)	17 10 (5.44)	23 0 (7.02)	95 (8.84)	875 (397)	400 (182)	1000 (305)	100 (161)	(As for Rans S-6 above)
Rans S-12 Airaile (K)	Rotax 503 (47)	19 9 (6.02)	31 0 (9.46)	132 (12.28)	900 (409)	348 (158)	500 (153)	60 (97)	(As for Rans S-6 above)
WagAero Sport Trainer	Continental (85)	22 4 (6.81)	35 3 (10.75)		1400 (636)	720 (327)	870 (265)	94 (151)	Wag-Aero Inc, 1216 North Rd, Box 181, Lyons, WI53148, USA
Wittman Tailwind	Continental (100)	19 4 (5.90)	22 6 (6.86)	90 (8.37)	1300 (590)	800 (363)	900 (275)	155 (250)	S. J. Wittman, Red Oak Ct, Box 2672-3811, Oshkosh, WI54903-1265, USA

Two-seat monoplanes—steel tube/wood and fabric/metal

Design name	Usual engine (hp)	Length ft/ins (m)	Span ft/ins (m)	Wing area (gross) ft^2 (m^2)	Max weight lb (kg)	Empty weight lb (kg)	Rate of climb ft/min (m/min)	Cruise speed mph (km/h)	Contact address for more information
Smyth Sidewinder S	Lycoming (125)	19 4 (5.90)	24 9 (7.55)	96 (8.93)	1450 (658)	867 (394)	900 (275)	160 (258)	Wicks Aircraft Supply, 410 Pine Street, Highland, IL62249, USA

Two-seat monoplanes—steel tube/wood and/or fabric/composites

Design name	Usual engine (hp)	Length ft/ins (m)	Span ft/ins (m)	Wing area (gross) ft^2 (m^2)	Max weight lb (kg)	Empty weight lb (kg)	Rate of climb ft/min (m/min)	Cruise speed mph (km/h)	Contact address for more information
Beaver RX-550 (K)	Rotax 582 (65)	20 7 (6.28)	35 0 (10.68)	163 (15.16)	900 (409)	395 (179)	950 (290)	70 (113)	Beaver RX Enterprises, #3 9351-192 Street, Surrey, BC, V3T 4W2, Canada
CFM Streak Shadow (K)	Rotax 582 (65)	21 0 (6.41)	28 0 (8.54)	140 (13.02)	512 (232)	388 (176)	1600 (488)	101 (163)	CFM Metal Fax Ltd, Unit 2D, Eastlands Ind. Est, Leiston, Suffolk IP16 4LL, England (also at Laron Aviation, Rt 1, Box 69B, Portales, NM88101, USA)
Ultravia Pelican GS (K)	Rotax 912 (80)	19 6 (5.95)	30 9 (9.38)	135 (12.56)	950 (431)	425 (193)	1000 (305)	110 (177)	Ultravia Aero Inc, 300-D Airport Rd, Mascoche, Quebec J7K 3C1, Canada

Two-seat monoplanes—metal

Design name	Usual engine (hp)	Length ft/ins (m)	Span ft/ins (m)	Wing area (gross) ft^2 (m^2)	Max weight lb (kg)	Empty weight lb (kg)	Rate of climb ft/min (m/min)	Cruise speed mph (km/h)	Contact address for more information
Andreasson MFI-9	(100)	19 2 (5.85)	24 4 (7.42)	94 (8.74)	1268 (575)	750 (341)	900 (275)	130 (209)	Björn Andreasson, Collins Vag 22b, S-23600 Hollviksnas, Sweden
Brokaw Bullett	Lycoming (380)	23 9 (7.24)	24 0 (7.32)	94 (8.74)	3539 (1607)	2345 (1065)	2000 (610)	286 (460)	Brokaw Aviation Inc, 30033 Johnson Pt Road, Leesburg, FL32748, USA
Bushby Mustang II	Lycoming (180)	19 6 (5.95)	24 6 (7.47)	97 (9.02)	1600 (726)	950 (431)	1600 (488)	210 (338)	Bushby Aircraft Inc, 674 Rt 52, Minooka, IL60447, USA

Design name	Usual engine (hp)	Length ft/ins (m)	Span ft/ins (m)	Wing area (gross) ft^2 (m^2)	Max weight lb (kg)	Empty weight lb (kg)	Rate of climb ft/min (m/min)	Cruise speed mph (km/h)	Contact address for more information
Davis DA-2A	Continental	17 10	19 3	88	1210	670	700	126	D2 Inc, PO Box 524, La Pine,
	(100)	(5.44)	(5.87)	(8.18)	(549)	(304)	(214)	(203)	OR 97739, USA
Lucas L-5	(115)	20 4	30 10	129	1631	1058	623	137	Emile Lucas, Corbonod, 01420
		(6.20)	(9.40)	(12.0)	(740)	(480)	(190)	(221)	Seyssel, France
Pazmany PL-2	Lycoming	19 4	27 9	116	1416	875	1200	119	Pazmany Aircraft Corp, PO Box 80051,
	(108)	(5.90)	(8.46)	(10.79)	(643)	(397)	(366)	(192)	San Diego, CA92138, USA
Pottier P.170/P.180S		17 6	20 4	84	970	529	550	102	Jean Pottier, 4 rue de Poissy,
(data)		(5.34)	(6.20)	(7.81)	(440)	(240)	(168)	(164)	78130 Les Mureaux, France
Powers/Bashforth Mini	2×Rotax	23 4	32 7	159	1800	1075	1550	130	Powers Bashforth Aircraft Corp, 4700 188th
Master (K)	(79 each)	(7.12)	(9.94)	(14.79)	(817)	(488)	(473)	(209)	St NE, SteG, Arlington WA 98223, USA
Prowler	Rodeck V8	21 0	25 0	104	2650	1450	3000	250	Prowler Aviation Inc, 3707 Meadowview Dr,
(K)	(350)	(6.41)	(7.63)	(9.67)	(1203)	(658)	(915)	(403)	Redding, CA96002, USA
Questair Venture	Continental	16 4	27 6	73	2000	1240	2500	276	Questair Inc, 7700 Airline Rd,
(also spirit) (K)	(280)	(4.98)	(8.39)	(6.79)	(908)	(563)	(763)	(444)	PO Box 18946, Greensboro, NC24719, USA
Stewart S-51D Replica	V-8	22 0	26 0	117	2620	2010	2380	235	Stewart 51 Inc, Vero Beach Airport,
	(350)	(6.71)	(7.93)	(10.88)	(1189)	(913)	(726)	(378)	PO Box 6070, Vero Beach, FL 32961, USA
Thorpe S-18	Lycoming	19 4	20 10	86	1600	923	1200	165	Sport Aircraft Inc, 44211 Yucca, Unit A,
	(150)	(5.90)	(6.35)	(8.00)	(726)	(419)	(366)	(266)	Lancaster, CA93535, USA
Vans RV-4/RV-6	Lycoming	20 5	23 0	110	1500	905	2050	194	Vans Aircraft Inc, PO Box 160,
(data for RV-4)	(160)	(6.23)	(7.02)	(10.23)	(681)	(411)	(625)	(312)	North Plains, OR97133, USA
Zenair CH.300	Lycoming	22 6	26 6	130	1850	1140	1400	153	L. Lewis, 30 Avon Rd, Redcar, Cleveland,
(also CH.250)	(180)	(6.86)	(8.08)	(12.08)	(840)	(518)	(427)	(246)	TS10 5NW, England (also at Zenair Ltd, Huronia
									Airport, Midland, Ontario, L4K 4K8, Canada)
Zenair Zodiac CH.601	Rotax 582	18 10	27 0	130	1058	550	1200	120	(As CH.300 above)
	(65)	(5.74)	(8.24)	(12.08)	(480)	(250)	(366)	(193)	
Zenair STOL CH.701	Rotax 912	20 0	27 0	122	960	460	1400	85	(As CH.300 above)
	(80)	(6.10)	(8.24)	(11.35)	(436)	(209)	(427)	(137)	

Two-seat monoplanes—composites

Design name	Usual engine (hp)	Length ft/ins (m)	Span ft/ins (m)	Wing area (gross) ft^2 (m^2)	Max weight lb (kg)	Empty weight lb (kg)	Rate of climb ft/min (m/min)	Cruise speed mph (km/h)	Contact address for more information
Aero Designs Pulsar	Rotax 582	19 6	25 0	80	900	450	1000	130	Aero Designs Inc, 635 Blakeley,
(also Pulsar XP) (K)	(66)	(5.95)	(7.63)	(7.44)	(409)	(204)	(305)	(209)	San Antonio, TX78209, USA
Cosy Classic	Lycoming	17 9	26 4	96	1750	960	1500	187	CO-Z Europe, Ahornstrasse 10,
(also 3-seater)	(160)	(5.26)	(8.03)	(8.93)	(795)	(436)	(458)	(301)	D-8901 Ried, Germany
Dragonfly	VW	20 0	22 0	102	1150	610	800	140	Preceptor Aircraft, 1230 Shepherd St,
		(6.10)	(6.71)	(9.49)	(522)	(277)	(244)	(225)	Hendersonville, NC28739, USA
Neico Lancair 320	Lycoming	20 6	23 6	76	1685	1075	2400	245	Neico Aviation Inc, 2244 Airport Rd,
(also Lancair 235) (K)	(180)	(6.25)	(7.17)	(7.07)	(765)	(488)	(732)	(394)	Redmond, OR97756, USA
Progress Discovery	Lycoming	17 10	30 0	102	1750	1100	1000	180	Progress Aero Inc, 813 Airport Rd,
(K)	(180)	(5.44)	(9.15)	(9.49)	(795)	(499)	(305)	(290)	Monterey, CA93940, USA

Design name	Usual engine (hp)	Length ft/ins (m)	Span ft/ins (m)	Wing area (gross) ft^2 (m^2)	Max weight lb (kg)	Empty weight lb (kg)	Rate of climb ft/min (m/min)	Cruise speed mph (km/h)	Contact address for more information
Ronnenburg Berkut (K)	Lycoming (205)				1700 (772)	1035 (470)	2000 (610)	235 (378)	Dave Ronneberg, Experimental Aviation 3021 Airport Ave, Hangar 109, Santa Monica, CA90405, USA
Stoddard-Hamilton Glasair II-S RG (K)	Lycoming (180)	20 3 (6.18)	23 4 (7.12)	81 (7.53)	2100 (953)	1325 (602)	2700 (824)	235 (378)	Stoddard-Hamilton Aircraft, 18701 58th Ave NE, Arlington, WA98223, USA
Stoddard-Hamilton Glasair III (K)	Lycoming (300)	21 4 (6.51)	23 4 (7.12)	81 (7.53)	2500 (1135)	1625 (738)	3750 (1143)	284 (457)	(As above for Glasair II-S RG)
Tri-R Kis (K)	Limbach (80)	22 0 (6.71)	23 0 (7.02)	88 (8.18)	1200 (545)	680 (309)	1000 (305)	135 (217)	Tri-R Technologies, 1114E 5th St, Oxnard, CA93030, USA

Two-seat biplanes—wood and fabric

Design name	Usual engine (hp)	Length ft/ins (m)	Span ft/ins (m)	Wing area (gross) ft^2 (m^2)	Max weight lb (kg)	Empty weight lb (kg)	Rate of climb ft/min (m/min)	Cruise speed mph (km/h)	Contact address for more information
Croses EC6 Criquet	Continental (90)	15 3 (4.65)	25 7 (7.80)	172 (16.02)	1213 (550)	639 (290)	1000 (305)	99 (160)	Emilien Croses, 63 route de Davayé (Aerodrome), 71000 Charnay-les-Macon, France
Falconar/Mignet HM380	Continental (90)	16 0 (4.88)	27 0 (8.24)	175 (16.28)	1100 (499)	580 (263)	1400 (427)	95 (153)	Falconar Aviation Ltd, 19 Airport Rd, Edmonton, Alberta, T5E 0W7, Canada
Fisher Celebrity (K)	Continental (75)	17 0 (5.19)	22 0 (6.71)	176 (16.37)	1000 (454)	525 (238)	700 (214)	85 (137)	Fisher Aero Visions, Route 2, Portsmouth Regional Airport, Sciotoville, OH45662, USA
Fisher Classic (K)	Rotax 532 (64)	16 9 (5.11)	22 0 (6.71)	154 (14.31)	850 (386)	400 (182)	900 (275)	85 (137)	Anglian Vintage Aeroplanes, 127 Lifstan Rd, Southend, Essex SS1 2XG, England (also Fisher Flying Products Inc, PO Box 468, Edgeley, ND58433, USA)

Two-seat biplanes—steel-tube/wood and/or fabric

Design name	Usual engine (hp)	Length ft/ins (m)	Span ft/ins (m)	Wing area (gross) ft^2 (m^2)	Max weight lb (kg)	Empty weight lb (kg)	Rate of climb ft/min (m/min)	Cruise speed mph (km/h)	Contact address for more information
Acro Sport II	Lycoming (180)	18 10 (5.74)	21 10 (6.66)	155 (14.41)	1520 (690)	875 (397)	1200 (366)	123 (198)	Acro Sport Inc, PO Box 462, Hales Corner, WI53130, USA
Aviat (Christen) Eagle II (K)	Lycoming (200)	18 6 (5.64)	19 11 (6.08)	125 (11.62)	1578 (716)	1125 (511)	2100 (641)	165 (266)	Aviat Inc, Airport, 50 Washington St, PO Box 1149, Afton, WY83110, USA
Hatz CB-1	Continental (100)	19 0 (5.80)	25 4 (7.73)	178 (16.54)	1400 (636)	850 (386)	750 (229)	85 (137)	Dudley R. Kelly, Rt 4, Box 194, Versailles, KY40383, USA
Kelly D	Lycoming (115)	19 3 (5.87)	26 4 (8.03)	230 (21.38)	1500 (681)	950 (431)	800 (244)	90 (145)	(As above for Hatz CB-1)
Marquart Charger	Lycoming (125)	20 0 (6.10)	24 0 (7.32)	170 (15.80)	1550 (704)	1000 (454)	1000 (305)	116 (187)	Ed Marquart, Box 3032, Riverside, CA92519-3032, USA
Murphy Renegade Spirit (K)	Rotax 532 (64)	18 6 (5.64)	21 4 (6.51)	153 (14.22)	850 (386)	390 (177)	1300 (397)	80 (129)	Meridian Ultralights Ltd, 51 Wold Rd, Pocklington, E Yorks YO4 2QG, England (also Murphy Aviation Ltd, 8880-C Young Rd S, Chilliwack, BC, V2P 4P5, Canada)

Design name		Usual engine (hp)	Length ft/ins (m)	Span ft/ins (m)	Wing area (gross) ft^2 (m^2)	Max weight lb (kg)	Empty weight lb (kg)	Rate of climb ft/min (m/min)	Cruise speed mph (km/h)	Contact address for more information
Sorrell Hiperbipe	(K)	Lycoming (180)	20 10 (6.35)	22 10 (6.96)	150 (13.94)	1911 (868)	1236 (561)	1500 (458)	160 (258)	Sorrell Aviation, 16525 Tilley Road S, Tenino, WA98589, USA
Steen Skybolt		Lycoming (260)	19 0 (5.80)	24 0 (7.32)	153 (14.22)	1800 (817)	1250 (568)	3500 (1068)	160 (258)	Steen Aero Lab, 1210 Airport Road, Marion, NC28752, USA
Stolp Acroduster Too (also Starduster Too)		(200)	18 6 (5.64)	21 5 (6.53)	130 (12.08)	1750 (795)	1050 (477)	2300 (702)	155 (250)	Stolp Starduster Corp, 4301 Twining St, Riverside, CA95209, USA

Two-seat biplanes—metal

Design name		Usual engine (hp)	Length ft/ins (m)	Span ft/ins (m)	Wing area (gross) ft^2 (m^2)	Max weight lb (kg)	Empty weight lb (kg)	Rate of climb ft/min (m/min)	Cruise speed mph (km/h)	Contact address for more information
Kestrel Kit Hawk	(K)	Rotax 582 (65)	23 10 (7.27)	24 6 (7.47)	172 (15.99)	830 (377)	395 (179)	800 (244)	85 (137)	Kestrel Sport Aviation, PO Box 1808, Brockville, Ontario, K6V 6K6, Canada

Two-seat biplanes—composites

Design name		Usual engine (hp)	Length ft/ins (m)	Span ft/ins (m)	Wing area (gross) ft^2 (m^2)	Max weight lb (kg)	Empty weight lb (kg)	Rate of climb ft/min (m/min)	Cruise speed mph (km/h)	Contact address for more information
Aero Composite Sea Hawker	(K)	Lycoming (150)	21 6 (6.56)	24 0 (7.32)	118 (10.97)	1600 (726)	850 (386)	1100 (336)	150 (242)	Aero Composite Technology, RD3, Somerset, PA15501, USA
Croses Airplum	(K)	Cuyuna (35)	17 1 (5.20)	25 11 (7.90)	205 (19.00)	714 (324)	383 (174)	985 (300)	62 (100)	Yves Croses, 35 avenue de Saxe, 69006 Lyon, France
SMAN Petrel (also Seabird Avn)	(K)	Rotax 532 (64)	19 4 (5.90)	29 3 (8.90)	186 (17.30)	882 (400)	430 (195)	985 (300)	93 (150)	SMAN, Anse de Mané Braz, St Philibert, 56470 La Trinite-sur-Mer, France (also Seabird Aviation, Terminal One, 4920 5th Ave, Columbus, OH43219, USA)

Larger types—all configurations/all materials

Design name	Seats	Usual engine (hp)	Length ft/ins (m)	Span ft/ins (m)	Wing area (gross) ft^2 (m^2)	Max weight lb (kg)	Empty weight lb (kg)	Rate of climb ft/min (m/min)	Cruise speed mph (km/h)	Contact address for more information
Piel CP.1302 Saphir (wood and fabric)	3	(150)	21 8 (6.60)	25 11 (7.90)	120 (11.15)	2072 (940)	1190 (540)	1220 (372)	161 (259)	E. (Gene) Litner, 140 Philippe Goulet, Repentigny, Quebec, J5Y 3MI, Canada
Dyke Delta JD.2 (steel-tube/ wood and fabric)	4	Lycoming (180)	19 0 (5.79)	22 3 (6.78)	178 (16.54)	1950 (884)	1060 (481)	2000 (610)	180 (290)	Dyke Aircraft, 2840 Old Yellow Springs Rd, Fairborn, OH45324, USA
NuWaco T-10 (steel-tube/ wood and fabric) (K)	3	Jacobs (275)	22 6 (6.86)	30 3 (9.22)	227 (21.09)	2600 (1179)	1886 (855)	1850 (564)	120 (193)	Aircraft Dynamics Corp, 2978 East Euclid Place, Littleton, Colorado 80121, USA
Spencer Air Car (steel-tube/ wood and fabric/composite)	4	Continental (300)	26 5 (8.05)	37 4 (11.38)	184 (17.10)	3200 (1451)	2150 (975)	1000 (305)	135 (217)	Spencer Aircraft Inc, PO Box 327, Kansas, IL61933, USA

Design name			Usual engine (hp)	Length ft/ins (m)	Span ft/ins (m)	Wing area (gross) ft^2 (m^2)	Max weight lb (kg)	Empty weight lb (kg)	Rate of climb ft/min (m/min)	Cruise speed mph (km/h)	Contact address for more information
Murphy Rebel		3	Lycoming	21 6	30 0	150	1250	675	1400	100	Murphy Aviation Ltd, 8880-C Young Rd South,
(metal)	(K)		(115)	(6.55)	(9.15)	(13.94)	(567)	(306)	(427)	(161)	Chilliwack, BC, V2P 4P5, Canada
Pottier P.230S Panda		3	Continental	20 10	26 7	108	1543	838	788	130	Jean Pottier, 4 rue de Poissy,
(metal)			(100)	(6.35)	(8.10)	(10.00)	(700)	(380)	(240)	(210)	78130 Les Mureaux, France
											Aerodis America Inc, 8319 Thora,
Aerodis Orion AA-200		4	Lycoming	22 1	29 11	137	2500	1400	885	185	C5 Hooks Airport, Spring, TX77379, USA
(composite)	(K)		(180)	(6.73)	(9.13)	(12.73)	(1135)	(636)	(270)	(298)	(also Aerodis SARL, Notaire, Allée de la Ronce,
											10340 Les Riceyes, France)
Cabrinha Free Spirit		3	Continental	20 7	28 0	82	1850	900	2000	220	Cabrinha Engineering, 7000 Merrill #41,
(composite)	(K)		(160)	(6.28)	(8.54)	(7.62)	(840)	(409)	(610)	(354)	Chino, CA91710, USA
Christensen Opus-3		3	Continental	15 10	24 7		1600	886		165	Kai S. Christensen, Vibevangen 1,
(composite)			(130)	(4.83)	(7.50)		(725)	(402)		(266)	DK-3700 Rønne, Denmark
Cirrus VK.30		4/5	Lycoming	26 0	39 6	124	3550	2350	1500	248	Cirrus Design Corporation, S3440 A Highway 12,
(composite)	(K)		(300)	(7.93)	(12.05)	(11.52)	(1612)	(1067)	(458)	(399)	Baraboo, WI53913, USA
Co-Z Devs Mark IV		4	Lycoming	16 11	28 2	102	2050	1050	1500	205	Co-Z Development Corp, 2046 No 63rd Place,
(composite)			(180)	(5.16)	(8.59)	(9.48)	(931)	(477)	(458)	(330)	Mesa, AZ85205, USA
Freedom Master Airshark		4	Lycoming	22 9	32 10	133	2800	1500	1850	190	Freedom Master Corp, 450 Hamlin Ave,
(composite)	(K)		(200)	(6.94)	(10.01)	(12.36)	(1271)	(681)	(564)	(306)	Satellite Beach, FL32939, USA
Neico Lancair IV		4	Continental	25 0	31 3	98	2900	1760	2600	341	Neico Aviation Inc, 2244 Airport Rd,
(composite)	(K)		(350)	(7.63)	(9.53)	(9.11)	(1317)	(799)	(793)	(549)	Redmond, OR97756, USA
Seawind 2000		4	(300)	27 0	35 0	160	3200	2100	1000	191	S.N.A. Inc, PO Box 607, Kimberton,
(composite)	(K)			(8.24)	(10.68)	(14.87)	(1453)	(953)	(305)	(308)	PA 19442, USA
Velocity		4	(180)	16 3	28 8	125	2250	1100	2000	205	Velocity Aircraft, 200 W Airport Drive,
(composite)	(K)			(4.96)	(8.74)	(11.62)	(1022)	(499)	(610)	(330)	Sebastian, FL32958, USA
Wheeler Express		4	Lycoming	25 0	31 0	130	2895	1600	1600	200	Wheeler Aircraft Company, Tacoma Narrows
(composite)	(K)		(200)	(7.63)	(9.46)	(12.08)	(1314)	(726)	(488)	(322)	Airport, Dept 8, Gig Harbor, WA98335, USA
White Lightning WLAC-1		4	Continental	23 4	27 8	89	2400	1400	1900	265	White Lightning Aircraft Corp, Walterboro Airport,
(composite)	(K)		(210)	(7.12)	(8.44)	(8.27)	(1090)	(636)	(580)	(427)	Box 497, Walterboro, SC29488 USA

NOTE It is stressed that the author, publisher and their associates accept no liability for either the inclusion (or non-inclusion) of any data or information included in this Directory, nor for the accuracy of that data and information.

Appendix 7

Specialist magazines and recommended further reading

Magazines and periodicals

Popular Flying House journal of the Popular Flying Association (PFA) in Great Britain. Published six times a year. Contact PFA, Terminal Building, Shoreham Airport, Shoreham-by-Sea, Sussex BN43 5FF.

Sport Aviation Published monthly by the Experimental Aircraft Association (EAA) in the United States for EAA members but with worldwide circulation. Available in Britain from Cord Ltd, 2(B) Cleveland Street, Kempston, Bedford MK42 8DN, or EAA, Wittman Airfield, Oshkosh, WI 54903-3086, USA.

Kitplanes Published monthly by Fancy Publications Inc. Contact Subscriptions Division, PO Box 487, Mt Morris, IL61054-0487, USA, or PO Box 6050, Mission Viejo, CA 92690, USA.

Les Cahiers du RSA Published six times a year by the Réseau du Sport de l'Air (RSA] in France and available from RSA, 46 Rue Sauffroy, 75017 Paris, France.

Experimental Published four times a year in French by Air Press, 14 Cité de l'Aneublement, 75011 Paris, France.

Flyer Monthly British magazine with regular homebuilt and kitplane content. Contact Insider Publications Ltd, 43 Queensferry Street Lane, Edinburgh EH2 4PF.

Pilot Monthly British magazine with frequent features on homebuilts and kitplanes. Contact Pilot Publishing Co Ltd, The Clock House, 28 Old Town, Clapham, London SW4 0LB.

Other recommended publications

Aircraft Spruce & Speciality Catalogue Available annually and one of the most comprehensive selections of homebuilders' supplies available. Contact PO Box 424, Fullerton, CA 92632, USA. Tel: (800) 824–1930, Fax (714) 871–7289.

Choosing your Homebuilt—The One You'll Finish and Fly by Ken Armstrong. Published by Butterfield Press, 990 Winery Canyon Rd, Templeton, CA93465, USA.

Kitplane Construction by Ron Wanttaja. Published by TAB Books, Blue Ridge Summit, PA 17294, USA.

Stress Without Tears by Tom Rhodes. Published by Jacobs Publishing Inc, 10585 N Meridian Street, Suite 220, Indianapolis, IN 46290, USA.

The Builder Book by Bill Welch. Published by Sand Hill Books, Hampton, Connecticut, USA, and distributed by Skycraft Corp, 85 N Main St, Yardley, PA 19067, USA.

1990 Worldwide Homebuilt Aircraft Directory by Philip Terpstra. Published by Spirit Publications, PO Box 23417, Tucson, AZ 85734, USA.

Pilot Handbook and Owners Manual for Experimental Aircraft by Tom Brown. Published and distributed by the Aviation Book Co, 1640 Victory Boulevard, Glendale, CA 91201, USA.

The Simple Guide to Propeller Making by Ken Fern. Published by Ken Fern and available from him at 311 Congleton Rd, Scholar Green, Stoke-on-Trent, Staffs ST7 3JQ, price £11.00.

PFA Homebuilt Aircraft Guide Available from the PFA (see *Popular Flying* for address), price £4.00 plus 50p p&p.

Jane's All The World's Aircraft Edited by Mark Lambert and published annually by Janes Information Group, Sentinel House, 163 Brighton Road, Coulsdon, Surrey CR5 2NH. 800 pages including over 100 extremely detailed pages with facts and figures on most of the world's commonly available kitplanes, homebuilts, microlights, etc.

Oshkosh by Colin Addison. Published by Osprey Aerospace.

Sun'n'Fun—Florida's Aviation Extravaganza by Geoff Jones. Published by Osprey Aerospace.

Henri Mignet and his Flying Fleas by Ken Ellis and Geoff Jones. Published by G. T. Foulis (Haynes Publishing Group).

Ultralights—The Early British Classics by Richard Riding. Published by Patrick Stephens Limited.

Aeroplane Affair—An Aeronautical Autobiography by John O. Isaacs. Published by Air Research Publications, 34 Elm Road, New Malden, Surrey KT3 3HD.

Voyager—The Flying Adventure of a Lifetime by Jeanna Yeager and Dick Rutan with Phil Patton. Published by Heinemann, 10 Upper Grosvenor Street, London W1X 9PA.

The following books are all available from the PFA Bookshop at Shoreham-by-Sea (see address):

Sportplane Builder by Tony Bingelis
Firewall Forward (Engine Installation Methods) by Tony Bingelis
Sportplane Construction Techniques (a Builders Handbook) by Tony Bingelis
Light Aircraft Design Example by Lloyd Jenkinson
Light Aircraft Design Handbook edited by F. Maccabee
Light Plane Design by L. Pazmany
Light Airplane Construction (Metal) by L. Pazmany
Landing Gear Design for Light Aircraft by L. Pazmany
Enjoy the Sky—the construction of an Evans VP-1 by Robert Lowe
The Design of the Aeroplane by Darrol Stinton
The Anatomy of the Aeroplane by Darrol Stinton

Index